NOLO *Your Legal Companion*

"In Nolo you can trust." —**THE NEW YORK TIMES**

Whether you have a simple question or a complex problem, turn to us at:

NOLO.COM

Your all-in-one legal resource

Need quick information about wills, patents, adoptions, starting a business—or anything else that's affected by the law? **Nolo.com** is packed with free articles, legal updates, resources and a complete catalog of our books and software.

NOLO NOW

Make your legal documents online

Creating a legal document has never been easier or more cost-effective! Featuring Nolo's Online Will, as well as online forms for LLC formation, incorporation, divorce, name change—and many more! Check it out at **http://nolonow.nolo.com**.

NOLO'S LAWYER DIRECTORY

Meet your new attorney

If you want advice from a qualified attorney, turn to Nolo's Lawyer Directory—the only directory that lets you see hundreds of in-depth attorney profiles so you can pick the one that's right for you. Find it at **http://lawyers.nolo.com**.

ALWAYS UP TO DATE

Sign up for NOLO'S LEGAL UPDATER

Old law is bad law. We'll email you when we publish an updated edition of this book—sign up for this free service at nolo.com/legalupdater.

Find the latest updates at NOLO.COM

Recognizing that the law can change even before you use this book, we post legal updates during the life of this edition at **nolo.com/updates**.

Is this edition the newest? ASK US!

To make sure that this is the most recent available, just give us a call at **800-728-3555**.

(Please note that we cannot offer legal advice.)

DATE DUE

~~8/22/11~~	
11-19-11	

Pleas

We believ ...)

you solve ... a

substitute ... :

If you wa ...

point out ... **NOLO**

consult a ...

DEMCO, INC. 38-2931

2nd edition

Effective
Fundraising
for Nonprofits

Real-World Strategies That Work

by Ilona Bray

SECOND EDITION	JANUARY 2008
Cover Design	SUSAN PUTNEY
Production	MARGARET LIVINGSTON
Proofreading	PAUL TYLER
Index	SONGBIRD INDEXING SERVICE
Printing	CONSOLIDATED PRINTERS, INC.

Bray, Ilona M., 1962-

 Effective fundraising for nonprofits : real-world strategies that work / by Ilona Bray.--2nd ed.

 p. cm.

 Includes bibliographical references and index.

 ISBN-13: 978-1-4133-0748-1 (pbk.)

 ISBN-10: 1-4133-0748-5 (pbk.)

1. Fund raising--United States. 2. Nonprofit organizations--United States--Finance. I. Title.

HG177.5.U6B73 2008

658.15'224--dc22

2007031796

Dedication

To my mother, who showed me how commitment to a cause can help you accomplish things you never thought possible; and my father, who knows how to greet each new day with entrepreneurial optimism.

Acknowledgments

This book was envisioned as a collaborative effort, in which the voices of many nonprofit staff and experienced fundraising experts would be heard. Still, I was overwhelmed by the generosity with which the people named below offered their time, knowledge, and stories of successes as well as frustrations. You'll see many of their names and stories within the book—others preferred to play a more behind-the-scenes role. My deepest thanks to all of them for their contributions, and for keeping me inspired during the many months of pulling this book together. In addition, I'd like to thank the various organizations whose sample letters and printed materials you'll see throughout the book (not listed below).

Bob Baldock, KPFA Radio

Randolph Belle, formerly of the East Bay Nonprofit Center

Lauren Brown Adams, nonprofit fundraising consultant

Sarah Clark

M. Eliza Dexter, formerly of Save The Bay (Oakland)

Grant Din, Asian Neighborhood Design

Laurie J. Earp, events planner

Lisa Ruth Elliott, Zen Hospice Project

Jan Etre, KPFA Radio

Judy Frankel, Project Open Hand

Susan Freundlich, The Women's Foundation (of San Francisco)

Lupe Gallegos-Diaz, Multicultural Student Development Office at UC Berkeley

Karen Garrison, Bernal Heights Neighborhood Center

Schuyler Gottwald, PTI Graphics

Leanne Grossman, Global Fund for Women

Christine Grumm, Women's Funding Network

Keven Guillory, KQED Radio

Don Kiser, formerly of the Human Rights Campaign

Pat Joseph, Sierra Club

Lynn Eve Komaromi, Berkeley Repertory Theatre

Greg Lassonde, San Francisco Symphony

Sophie Lei Aldrich, Boston University

Marisa Lianggamphai, formerly of the World Institute on Disability

Harry Lin

Jim Lynch, Compumentor

Sonja Mackenzie, WORLD

Kate McNulty, formerly of Sacred Heart Cathedral Preparatory

Susan Messina, professional grantwriter

Cathy Meyer, Children's Hospital & Research Center Foundation

Nick Parker, Communications Director, the California School Age Consortium

Angelina Ramsay, independent marketing consultant

Peggy Rose, San Francisco Mime Troupe

Ron Rowell, The San Francisco Foundation

Jim Schorr, Juma Ventures

Duane Silverstein, Seacology

Linda Solow-Jaffe

Elizabeth Stampe, Greenbelt Alliance

Anthony Tusler, World Institute on Disability

Amanda Vender, DAMAYAN

Mona Lisa Wallace, formerly of the East Bay Nonprofit Center

Anita Wetzel, Women's Studio Workshop

Lauren Williams, Mission of the Sacred Heart

J.R. Yeager, CompassPoint Nonprofit Services

Audrey Yee, Golden Gate National Parks Conservancy

Many of my colleagues at Nolo also helped this book in important ways: **Marcia Stewart**, with early conceptualization and advice; **Stan Jacobsen,** with research; **Jake Warner,** whose first-draft edits incorporated his own extensive nonprofit as well as business experience; final editor **Lisa Guerin,** who took the manuscript up a notch with her wit and practical instincts; **Wendy Copley,** with technical advice on blogging; and the production folks, with all-important design and graphics help, including **Margaret Livingston, Jaleh Doane, Emma Cofod, Susan Putney,** and **Toni Ihara**.

A final special "thank you" to **C.S.** and other friends, for ongoing support, and for apparently remembering my name even after these many months of self-imposed hermitage.

Table of Contents

7 Funds From the Great Beyond: Bequests and Planned Gifts 211

8 Special Events 239

9 Raising Money Through Business or Sales Activities 287

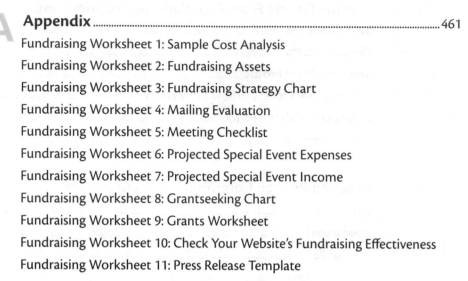

Your Fundraising Companion

"But I don't have time to read a book on fundraising!" If that phrase could have come from your lips, you're not alone. I've worked in some of the hardest-to-fund nonprofits around, and fully appreciate that you may be reading this while simultaneously gulping down lunch and photocopying a grant proposal. But you probably know in your heart that when a person is too harried to learn to do fundraising right, mistakes and inefficiency are the inevitable result.

With all this in mind, I'm going to skip the traditional lectures on personal philosophy and fundraising history, and get right to the heart of the matter: how this book will help you succeed as a fundraiser. It's an attempt to distill and assemble, in plain English, the most important things you need to know in order to do your fundraising job well (most likely as a development director or staffperson, executive director, or board member). I won't be expounding new theories of nonprofit philosophy, or giving you touchy-feely ways of using Jungian symbols to contemplate your mission. (I've sat through too many meetings and retreats that did just that, without giving me any new information on how to actually raise money.)

Instead, I'll discuss how fundraising is being done, at its best, today. Gone are the days when a nonprofit could charm people with its desperation and grassroots inefficiencies. You'll learn how current technology, business savvy, and public attitudes toward nonprofits are shaping the fundraising environment. You'll get right into the nuts and bolts of how to plan your fundraising strategy, assemble the right people, technology, and other tools you'll need in order to maximize your returns, attract supporters, ask for gifts from individuals, businesses, and foundations, and much more.

Though this book will teach you the basics, it will also help you to think creatively. By understanding how other nonprofits are raising funds, you'll be better able to think up ways to outdo them, or to see where bending the rules a bit may attract positive attention. Throughout the chapters, you'll find stories from experienced development professionals—many of them at small, struggling nonprofits whose constraints may be similar to yours—who've employed interesting strategies to gain fundraising success.

The next question is, how much of this book do you really need to read? Everyone should start with Chapter 2, which lays out all the tools you'll need for effective fundraising, including staffing, personal skills, and technology. Also take a look at Chapters 11, 12, and 13, which explain how to bring visibility to your organization—and therefore potentially higher donations from all possible sources—through printed materials, the media, and your website.

After these, you can decide which additional chapters to refer to based on the types of fundraising your organization plans to engage in; and you'll decide that after reading Chapter 3, where you'll find instructions and worksheets that will help you create a fundraising plan that strategically uses your organization's existing strengths and assets.

Other chapters cover fundraising methods. I'll preview those chapters here, especially for those readers who may be new to the fundraising field or whose organizations are considering branching into a new type of fundraising. Even if you don't use these methods now, many of the first-edition readers of this book report keeping it on their shelf for ongoing reference.

Chapter 4, Attracting Individual Supporters. The real, everyday people who believe in your organization should be its bread and butter. Their donations are a sign of community relevance and support, and (conveniently for your organization) come with very few strings attached. Yet many new fundraisers, as well as established organizations, come to over-rely on foundation grants, at the expense of paying attention to individual supporters. Read this chapter to learn how to reverse that trend and begin or expand your community support. It includes sample appeal letters.

Chapter 5, How to Keep the Givers Giving. Your new supporters probably won't give very large gifts, and they're statistically likely to leave in a couple of years unless you take active steps to increase their interest in, and connection to, your organization. Read this chapter to learn how to analyze your donor base and further engage donors through personal contacts, appeal/renewal letters or emails and other communications, and invitations to volunteer or attend other activities sponsored by your organization. Sample letters are included.

Chapter 6, Midscale and Major Donors. This chapter explains how to identify your most committed supporters and encourage them to give more. New fundraisers who have some anxiety about asking for major gifts will especially appreciate this chapter's gradual approach to building relationships between your organization and its potential major donors before popping the money question. It includes an extensive list of websites to help you do background research on prospective major donors.

Chapter 7, Funds From the Great Beyond: Bequests and Planned Gifts. This final chapter on working with individual donors focuses on offering them alternative ways to give, namely through wills and living trusts. This chapter isn't appropriate for organizations whose existence is temporary or tenuous, because it involves planning around events that may take place far in the future (usually, the donor's death). However, the chapter will show how smaller, grassroots organizations can start a program to attract inheritance gifts without worrying about the more financially complex arrangements that some larger organizations are able to offer (such as charitable annuities). The chapter also provides plain-English explanations of these more complex arrangements, so you can plan your transition toward offering them.

Chapter 8, Special Events. There's almost no organization that won't put on a special event at some point in its existence, both because it's fun and because the simpler events, such as bake sales and garage sales, offer a quick way to raise money without much advance planning or experience. However, the bigger the party, the greater the chance that it will be a flop, financially and otherwise. This chapter explains how to choose an event that's most likely to be a success for your organization, and how to maximize the fundraising potential of virtually every kind of special event, from auctions to walkathons. It includes budget worksheets that will help you make sure your event will bring in money.

Chapter 9, Raising Money Through Business or Sales Activities. If your bake sale went well, why not open a bakery? Thinking along these lines, many nonprofits have been exploring ways to make money through business activities, thereby reducing their reliance on foundations and the more limited donor—as opposed to consumer—pool. Unfortunately, enthusiasm has exceeded planning in many cases, and all too many nonprofit-run businesses have failed. Read this chapter to learn where others went wrong, how IRS requirements affect your business possibilities, and how to develop your own viable business idea, assess the competition and set appropriate prices, and launch your business in a gradual, low-risk way. Or, learn how to enter business at a less ambitious scale, such as through partnerships with existing businesses. This chapter includes a checklist that will help you identify a winning business idea.

Chapter 10, Seeking Grants From Foundations, Corporations, and Government. Nonprofits cannot live on grants alone, though many try. Nevertheless, grant funding, from foundations, corporations, and local or federal government sources, continues to have an important place in almost every nonprofit organization's budget. Such funding is especially good for jump-starting a new project or initiative. Even if you've written grant proposals before, you'll want to read this chapter for tips on how to excite a foundation's interest in your organization before you start writing; how to fully address every important component of a grant proposal; and how to write in a voice whose clarity and passion wake up the overburdened reader at the other end. It includes worksheets for breaking down and comparing different grant possibilities, and a sample query letter.

So, enough preliminaries. It's time to learn how you can raise more money for your group—and create the long-term relationships with your community, supporters, and foundations that lead to sustained fundraising success.

Fundraising Tools

Since the days when fairy tales were first told, people have been looking for a way to spin straw into gold. Unfortunately, this impulse remains alive in too many of today's nonprofits. With sources of new money hard to come by and old revenue streams threatening to dry up—not to mention staff members and volunteers overextending themselves to do the basic work of the organization—the fundraising office is often expected to perform feats of magic, sometimes with few more resources than the legendary pile of straw.

Don't allow your organization to be trapped into this kind of fairy-tale thinking. Until your group understands that its success will depend, in large part, on your fundraising efforts—and is willing to invest in the people, resources, and technology necessary to do the job right—you'll be spinning your wheels rather than spinning gold. And investing in fundraising should never mean investing only in activities that will produce immediate results: A successful fundraising program must also budget for the long term, with plans for such things as donor recruitment, cultivation, stewardship, and acknowledgment. These activities may not yield the immediate payback that writing a grant proposal would, but they will provide a solid foundation for the rest of your fundraising structure.

This chapter introduces the tools you'll need to create and execute a successful fundraising effort. The way you use these resources will depend on your group's size and experience, but most groups, no matter how large or small, use some combination of these basic tools to raise money.

This chapter covers:

- how the position of each person in your organization—including volunteers and paid staff—can play a role in fundraising

- personal skills that any development professional will need to have or develop, and

- equipment and technology for fundraising, including computer and Web tools.

RESOURCE

Need help with legal tasks like incorporating your nonprofit? This book assumes that your organization has already taken care of some legal and tax basics—namely forming a nonprofit corporation and successfully applying for

501(c)(3) tax-exempt status and any required state tax permits. In addition, most states require you to register with the attorney general before soliciting funds within that state, and many states also require you to report on your fundraising expenditures and revenues. For further information on these requirements, see the links provided on the Association of Fundraising Professionals' website at www.afpnet.org (click "Research & Statistics"). For step-by-step instructions on incorporating your nonprofit and applying for tax-exempt status, see *How to Form a Nonprofit Corporation* (National and California versions), by Anthony Mancuso (Nolo).

Fundraising People

In an ideal situation, your well-recognized and highly successful nonprofit would have a bustling staff of paid fundraising professionals, each with separate responsibilities and areas of expertise. Unfortunately, this level of organization and professionalism is far beyond the financial reach of most nonprofits. More often, you'll need to cobble together a mix of as many board members and other committed volunteers as you can recruit to the fundraising cause, hopefully with the assistance of one or more paid fundraising staffers. The roles and functions of various fundraising positions are covered below, including how to involve and motivate your fundraising team. Don't worry if your organization doesn't have all of these people in place. Especially during a nonprofit's early years, it's common for several people to wear two or more hats—your best fundraiser may also serve as your volunteer coordinator, your executive director, or even the president of your board of directors.

Those who might participate in your fundraising efforts include:

- the executive director
- the development director
- the board of directors
- an advisory council
- other paid development staff
- paid staff in nondevelopment roles
- other volunteers, and
- outside consultants.

> **TIP**
>
> **Track your own hours to find out your staffing needs.** If you have the chance to expand your development staff, you'll need to figure out what type of help will give you the most bang for your buck. The answer may be no farther away than your own workday. Try keeping track, on a separate pad of paper or your calendar, of where each hour goes. Even quickly scribbling entries such as "9:30 to 11:00 planning meeting, 11:00 to 12:30 research" can work. You'll discover that you spend hours in ways you wouldn't have guessed. If, for example, you find that most of your time is spent on events planning, it might be appropriate to contract with an outside events planner rather than put a new person on salary. Or, if most of your hours go toward clerical tasks, you might save some money by hiring a support staffer and freeing up more of your own time for development activities.

The Executive Director

Fundraising is, or should be, part of every executive director's ("E.D."'s) job description. This includes getting to know the organization's supporters, meeting individuals to solicit major gifts, interacting with staff at foundations, reviewing grant proposals, helping oversee special events, speaking at events, and more. Sounds like a lot of hours, doesn't it? And most E.D.s already have plenty of issues on their plates concerning the organization's mission, programs, and personnel. But any E.D. who doesn't somehow make the time for fundraising activities isn't fulfilling the job requirements, period.

> **TIP**
>
> **Former development directors are often poised to become great E.D.s.** According to J.R. Yeager, an affiliate consultant with CompassPoint (www .compasspoint.org) who specializes in executive transitions, "Many skilled, well-organized development directors are ready and well-positioned to step into the role of E.D., particularly with smaller nonprofits. Most smaller organizations truly need their E.D. to do much of the fundraising. As for the other parts of the E.D.'s job, these can be supported (for example, the board treasurer and outside auditor can help with budgeting and financial matters) and ultimately learned as the new E.D. grows into the job."

The smaller your organization's staff, the more time your E.D. will have to spend on fundraising. But if your organization can afford to hire a development director, the E.D. might be tempted to delegate as many activities as possible to that person. This can be a mistake. To the outside world, the E.D. is the face of your organization, the person who (rightly or wrongly) is seen as having the fullest sense of how your organization's need for money intersects with its mission, goals, and day-to-day work. It follows that whether you are pursuing a large grant or trying to coax a major donor to increase support, the E.D. is usually the best staffperson to close the deal. In this context, the E.D. is like the author of a famous book, while the development director is like the behind-the-scenes publicist who sets up the author's appearances. The publicist may do much or most of the nitty-gritty work of publicizing the book, but when it comes to doing a book signing or a key interview, everyone wants to talk to the author.

Fortunately, the E.D. won't be solely responsible for all or even most parts of the fundraising process. The E.D. should help solicit major gifts, for example, but need not be present for every gift request. Nor will the E.D. have to be involved in the day-to-day work of staying in close contact with major donors. Your board and staff members may also participate, depending on who is being approached. And when it comes to grant applications, the E.D.'s role should be limited to reviewing proposals, not writing them. If you can afford a development director, grant writing and other behind-the-scenes tasks will be done by that person. If not, your organization may use board members and other volunteers, as well as paid consultants and freelance contractors, to do this day-to-day work.

On the other side of the coin, an E.D. must be willing and able to share fundraising tasks with other board and staff members, especially the development director. An E.D. who can't bear to part with these tasks, or won't trust others with them, can spell trouble for the organization's long-term survival. Over and over, one hears stories of a charismatic, successful E.D. who successfully grows a small nonprofit—but then continues to attempt to single-handedly raise all the money and lead the organization. This one-man-band approach doesn't work over the long haul. Either the E.D. will burn out from overwork, neglect important tasks while trying to cope with too many others, or, in the worst possible scenario, move on to another job, leaving the nonprofit with a huge leadership and fundraising void. J.R. Yeager of CompassPoint notes that, "The wise organization (no matter its size) engages in 'Succession Planning.' This means having an internal structure in place where a formal and clear line of succession, cross-training, and information sharing is planned in advance, so that a 'void' will not happen—or will at least be minimized if an organization's E.D. departs."

The Development Director

Perhaps you are the development director at your nonprofit, or perhaps you are a board member or E.D. of a smaller organization that hasn't yet mustered up the funds to hire for this position. Although some small nonprofits that plan to stay small—let's say, Friends of the Hillsdale Rose Garden—find it practical to delegate fundraising to volunteers, most growing organizations will find it highly cost-effective to hire a part- or full-time development director. (According to *The NonProfit Times*, the mean salary that development directors could command in 2006 was $62,455.)

Ideally, a full-time development director's role is to oversee all aspects of the fundraising process, including planning the fundraising strategy, gathering input from the board and E.D., identifying potential funding sources, and ensuring smooth operation of fundraising activities. Typically, however, the development director's role also includes carrying out practically every other aspect of the fundraising program: writing the mail appeals and newsletters, writing grant proposals, meeting with donors to solicit gifts, writing acknowledgment and stewardship correspondence, and more.

Because this busywork can prevent the development director from concentrating on important fundraising tasks, it will be key to your long-term success to identify other people who can help take care of any discrete or routine tasks.

A successful development director brings certain skills and abilities to your organization. Among the most important of these skills is good communication—in writing as well in person. You need a "people person"—someone who not only can express him- or herself, but also genuinely enjoys interacting with others. Remember, asking for money is just a small part of the greater—and often more fulfilling—process of building the nonprofit's relationship with donors. Without a true interest in (and appreciation for) other people, your development director will have a hard time building these important relationships—and forging a close connection between your organization and its supporters.

Unfortunately, experienced and personable development directors are hard to find. There are more organizations seeking development directors than there are people up to the challenge, which means that the best development professionals can pick and choose where they work. Those with an ounce of savvy won't hitch their wagon to an organization that's teetering on the edge of financial collapse, dealing with internal dissension, or experiencing other serious problems. Less-established organizations often have to compromise by, for example, sharing a development director with another (noncompetitive) organization, hiring someone who isn't fully qualified for the job, or hiring a part-time or assistant development director. Groups that use these types of compromises usually give the E.D. primary responsibility for fundraising.

> **TIP**
>
> **A little recognition goes a long way.** Smart E.D.s and board leaders know that a dedicated and effective development director is a huge asset to the organization. Protect this precious resource by taking steps to prevent development director burnout. One way to do this is to make fundraising a high priority and encourage all key people to participate without whining. Another is to recognize the development director's hard work by thanking him or her, sincerely and in front of others, for jobs well done. Too often, recognition goes primarily to board members and volunteers, as if receiving a salary diminishes the value of the passion and energy the development director throws into a project. Don't make this mistake—a development director who feels overworked and underappreciated will quickly make tracks for a friendlier organization.

Board of Directors

By law, every nonprofit must have a board of directors (sometimes called a board of trustees, board of governors, or other similar term). This is usually a volunteer group of about 12 to 15 people, whose responsibilities include overseeing the organization and being accountable for its compliance with legal and other requirements. Board members are not mere figureheads—if they neglect their duties and your organization is sued or collapses as a result, they can be held financially accountable. (Many boards buy insurance to guard against this type of liability.)

As a practical matter, a good board not only sets the direction of your programs, but will also be critical to the success of your fundraising efforts, both by making fundraising an organizational priority and by participating personally. To this end, it's a big help to have someone on the board with a thorough understanding of nonprofit budgeting and finance. There's little point in working hard to raise money if the board can't make sure that the organization is meeting its financial obligations and spending wisely.

Find Board Members Who Are Willing—And Able—To Raise Money

Unfortunately, there's often a wide gap between what nonprofits hope board members will do for them and how prospective board members envision their roles. In my earlier life as a corporate law associate, for example, my law firm/employer encouraged me and my fellow associates to join a nonprofit board. The firm wanted us to get involved with the "community"—that is, with people whose incomes were high enough to hire lawyers—by any means necessary, and offered to help us get onto the board of just about any organization we wanted—the opera, the symphony, whatever. That sounded good to me: I envisioned myself sitting around a meeting table, mulling over a group's mission and giving sage advice. In short, like most novice board members, I was clueless. I not only had no idea about the depths of a board's responsibilities, I hadn't even considered that it might include plenty of time fundraising. Worse yet, I was only a few years out of law school, with little life experience beyond minimum wage summer jobs, so I was spectacularly ill-equipped for this role. (Luckily, I quit corporate law before inflicting myself on any boards.)

What lessons can be gleaned from my experience?

- Willing board members may be easier to find than you think, but
- you must be selective to find the ones with the knowledge and experience you need, and
- you need to be up front about your fundraising expectations.

Most board members serve terms of only three years, with one or more renewals allowed. Check your bylaws to be sure—and think about amending the bylaws if your board members can serve "life terms," and you've got a few who are running low on energy and ideas. (Or think about enforcing your bylaws if people are overstaying their prescribed welcome!) If your board members serve limited terms, you must build a process to incorporate new board members into the ongoing work of your organization.

If you are new to the nonprofit world, you may wonder why anyone would voluntarily commit many hours per month to a demanding position, usually on top of work, family, and other responsibilities. A few board members are truly selfless—they live to help others. Some are newly retired, with an adequate income and time on their hands. Most are hard-working people genuinely interested in the cause, who hope that they'll be able to fit board responsibilities into their already-stretched schedules. Unfortunately, too many busy people turn out to be unrealistic in their hopes, and end up unable to do much more than attend meetings (if that). Finally, there are the staff of corporate law and accounting firms and other companies that have a material interest in encouraging their employees to join a board. Even this category isn't all bad, especially if you can make use of their professional skills (but realize that nonprofit finance and law are specialty areas that your average accountant or lawyer will know nothing about).

No matter what people's motivations, many of them will have trouble making the kind of long-term commitment that active board membership entails. At the same time, organizations have a larger pool of potential volunteers who might be interested in more substantial work than the odd photocopying job. Recognizing this, some nonprofits are rethinking how their board is structured—perhaps paring it down to ten or fewer members, but asking these members to farm out work—including some fundraising—to committees. The committees may be composed of nonboard volunteers who can commit to the occasional sprint of activity—say, a donor campaign or a special event—but not the marathon of full board membership.

Recruiting board members is a topic well-covered in other places (see the resource list at the end of this section), so this book won't go into detail. To quickly summarize, your organization will want to look for people with a mix of skills and experience, including people who have personal connections with your nonprofit's community, deep knowledge of the field, and valuable, specialized knowledge (in the field of law or accounting, for example). You may also want to find influential representatives from the political, social, ethnic, or donor community in which you work. Although board members should be able to get along with one another, they shouldn't all be of the same "type"—far better to assemble a quilt of people with different backgrounds and strengths.

No matter what else they bring to the table, however, you must make sure that potential new board members have an interest in fundraising—and understand that this will be a substantial part of their role. Because there are so many ways to raise money, there's a role for any willing board member to play. You can help by preparing materials that excite potential board members' interest, such as a packet of items highlighting your organization's mission, fundraising activities, and accomplishments. You should assemble a more extensive selection of such materials for purposes of training new board members.

Board Donations

Some organizations now give prospective board members a very clear up-front understanding of their fundraising responsibilities, by asking them to commit to making a major financial contribution every year. You might require board members to contribute a set amount or base contributions on a sliding scale.

Asking board members for donations may seem odd—after all, they are already asked to give generously of their time, and now they're being told they have to pay dearly for the privilege. One of the reasons usually given for this practice is that board members will be much better at soliciting large gifts from others if they can say that they've given themselves. It demonstrates their commitment to the cause and their confidence that the donation will be well-spent. This reasoning has become almost self-fulfilling: As more and more people become aware of this board practice, potential donors—including individuals as well as foundations—have learned to ask, "How much have board members given?"

For example, one environmental organization I know of not only specifically requires each board member to make a $10,000 donation as a condition of service, but also makes clear that each member's primary role will be fundraising. When the organization needs advice concerning the technical parts of its mission or activities, it turns to a separate advisory board, made up of scientists and other experts. This organization believes that policymaking and fundraising are the major roles of the board. Their experienced staff and advisers, they feel, are in the best position to know how the organization should be run. While there's merit to this approach, it also has a downside: If key staff members leave, or the organization faces another crisis or turning point, the board will not be well-equipped to step in and provide continuity or plot a new course.

Of course, your organization will need to decide for itself—based on part on what kind of work you're doing and what community you serve—whether to solicit mostly affluent board members, or to ask for a particular monetary commitment. (For less well-off board members, an alternative to the up-front donation might be to ask them to bring in an equivalent amount of money from a new donor or business.) For many community-based organizations or small advocacy groups, creating a financial requirement for entry could be just plain misguided. You might be lucky to have even a few affluent members. And the last thing you want is for representatives of a low-income community or dedicated former clients to be shut out. However, that doesn't mean you can't still ask financially able board members to make a major gift.

Board Involvement in Fundraising Activities

There is virtually no limit to what your board members can do to help raise funds for your organization—other than each member's own interests and time constraints. Board members can help plan your fundraising program, spearhead or help carry out a special event, represent your organization in public, provide names of likely supporters, approach supporters for gifts, host house parties or other events, institute giving programs within their own workplaces, coordinate a new member drive, write personal letters, make phone calls thanking people for gifts, and much more. All of this will help take some weight off the shoulders of your in-house development staff. The wide variety of possible fundraising roles also allows board members who are reluctant to ask for major gifts to find a role behind the scenes.

A well-run nonprofit will ask a great deal of board members, at the same time being sensitive to cries of "enough!" Once board members become genuinely committed to your organization, they are more likely to stay interested and involved if you call on them for help on a regular basis. Performing minimal board activities—attending meetings and the occasional workshop, for example—can be less than soul-satisfying. Ideally, you want board members to see that raising the money your group absolutely needs to do its good work

What If the Board Just Won't Fundraise?

Coping with board members who won't take the fundraising ball and run with it is a common problem in the nonprofit world. The thought of raising money often drives board members to flee, busy themselves with other tasks, or simply say, "No way." If you're a development staffer, it shouldn't be your responsibility to talk balky board members into helping raise money—this is the job of the board president or the chair of the development committee. However, because you're being judged by how much money you raise, you may find yourself with a vested interest in getting board participation. Here are some potential ways to approach this problem:

- **Identify the board's strongest leaders.** Often all it takes is one committed person on the board to inspire the others to put their shoulders to the wheel. Instead of taking on the "No way" Charlies directly, it probably makes more sense to engage and motivate board leaders. For example, Grant Din, Executive Director of San Francisco–based Asian Neighborhood Design (www.andnet.org), says, "We have one board member who's a development director at another nonprofit, which is perfect, because he can emphasize the importance of fundraising—and not have others tune him out the way they might if a staff member said the same thing. We also have another board member who has really pushed for full participation by the board, and the two of them have created more of a giving and getting environment."

- **Make sure your board members really understand and care about your organization's mission.** Some board members feel distant from the organization they serve. They may have joined the board for personal or career reasons rather than commitment to your cause. While you may assume that attending board meetings will cure this, occasional meetings, which often consist of a superficial report by the E.D. and hours spent worrying about financial issues, are unlikely to get them excited (or reinvigorated) about your organization's mission and work. But you can jazz up board meetings—for example, by bringing staff members or charismatic clients to talk about what they're currently doing. Do some "show and tell"—sample projects, art works by clients, videos, testimonials by local activists, or anything else that might rev up the board and get them to do something more than just sitting back and voting.

- **Enlist an outside voice.** Consultants are available to address a board meeting, lead a board retreat, and more. (Ask colleagues at other nonprofits to recommend a good one.) Or, you might hold a screening of *Grassroots Fundraising: The Kim Klein Video Series*, available at www.grassrootsinstitute.org.

can be the most rewarding part of board membership. Properly orchestrated, fundraising gets people out from behind the meeting table and into the community, where they can share what excites them about your organization. It also gives them a chance to enjoy the company of their fellow board members on a less formal and more friendly basis, thus helping them form bonds that may endure for years.

Creating fundraising opportunities for your board will also help board members feel that they've achieved something to be proud of. After all, part of each person's motivation to serve on your board was undoubtedly to ensure your organization's success, and there is no more direct way to have an impact than by helping to raise the funds your group needs to fulfill its mission.

> **RESOURCE**
>
> **Need more information on putting together your board?** For more on recruiting, structuring, and developing a strong, dynamic board, see:
>
> • *Beyond Fundraising: New Strategies for Nonprofit Innovation and Investment,* by Kay Sprinkel Grace (John Wiley & Sons, Inc.)
>
> • *Mission-Based Management,* by Peter C. Brinckerhoff (John Wiley & Sons, Inc.)
>
> • **BoardSource,** a membership-based group that offers consulting, training, and various publications, at www.BoardSource.org
>
> • *Secrets of Successful Boards,* by Carol Weisman (F.E. Robbins & Sons Press).

Advisory Council

Nonprofits aren't required to have an advisory council, but there are many good reasons to establish one. An advisory council is a group of people whose responsibilities include little more than—as the name suggests—offering advice and input on what the nonprofit is or should be doing. The group may also be called an advisory board or advisory committee. Members' responsibilities usually include meeting a few times a year—or not at all, if you prefer to call upon them only when necessary.

Whom you solicit as members will depend on what types of advice your group might actually need: perhaps scientific or other professional information, community input, contacts with the rich, famous, or influential, or continuity with your organization's past. That means you might look for members who are experts in a certain field, represent a community you'd like information from, are well known (whether or not they're in a field related to your organization's work), or are past staff or board members whose experience you don't want to lose—but who aren't able to commit to board membership.

When it comes to the famous folk, your expectations of their actual participation should be minimal. You might be content for them to lend nothing more than their name, so that it appears anyplace that you list people associated with the organization—perhaps on your letterhead, website, newsletter, and in other publications. Assuming your organization does good work, this is an arrangement that makes everyone happy: Your cause gains credibility, and the person named enhances his or her reputation by appearing to be caring and compassionate. If such people actually show up for your meetings, it's a bonus—if not, no big deal.

For fundraising purposes, your advisory council can be a source of additional friends. At a minimum, members' names should be added to your mailing lists. Their quasi-ceremonial role makes them particularly well-suited to special events—you might call on them to buy seats, sell tickets to their friends, greet arriving guests, make speeches or presentations, and more. As the advisory council members develop an increased sense of connection to your organization, you may be able to solicit them for major gifts. And you should, of course, find out about their other experience and interests—they may be willing to put in some short-term volunteer time on fundraising activities.

Other Paid Development Staff

Although there's always pressure to run a lean development office (so as to minimize the percentage of the organization's money spent on fundraising), penny-pinching isn't always a good thing. If your potential donor pool is large enough, you may actually become more efficient at raising money by hiring more people.

If you are able to bring on help, you'll need to confront the pleasant problem of figuring how to divide development responsibilities among a small staff. Although how you do this will depend in part on your organization's structure and fundraising strategies, a first priority is usually to hire a development assistant: someone to handle the mail, enter names and other information on supporters into your database, check for any email correspondence, prepare and mail thank you letters, and handle other day-to-day tasks. Obviously, these chores could also be handled by a dedicated volunteer or another clerical person in your office (such as a receptionist), but the person will need sufficient oversight to make sure that the tasks get done on time and that the paperwork doesn't get jumbled with other matters unrelated to fundraising.

If you don't have someone who will handle these tasks promptly and well, then you'll inevitably discover, while you're busy racing toward a grant deadline or staging an event, that important details have fallen through the cracks. The hazards of letting these matters slide are dealt with in other chapters—for example, Chapter 5 discusses how quickly you can lose a supporter's loyalty if the thank-you letter is sent out late. Relying on volunteers or temporary workers is the next best thing to having a paid assistant, but you need to be extremely careful to avoid mistakes, workflow stalls, or miscommunications, especially when more than one part-time person is involved.

A midsize organization may be able to afford a three-person department, adding a "development associate" to the mix. This is typically someone at a junior professional level, who works side by side with the development director, handling similar but less critical tasks. The associate would also have less responsibility for fundraising planning and dealing with key donors, and would be presumed to be "in training" for a director role.

Larger organizations often split fundraising tasks into subject areas, assigning a development officer to each. For example, care and feeding of major donors might be assigned to one person, while another is responsible for writing grant proposals. A few nonprofits, such as universities, have development officers who spend much of their time just researching future funding prospects.

Paid Staff in Nondevelopment Roles

A truly successful fundraising office will always be in close communication with the rest of the organization, and can call on program staff as needed. For starters, you want program people to keep your office informed about what they're doing, including supplying you with interesting stories (with photos, if possible) illustrating the important work donors are funding.

As a development staffer, much of your job is to explain the importance and success of your organization's work to the outside world, as part of your effort to gather a large flock of supporters. But simply repeating your mission statement ad nauseam is not going to bring in the donations you need. To be truly effective, you need details—colorful, lively stories of difficult situations that your organization confronted and hopefully helped to overcome. That's obviously why, when newspapers write their holiday giving stories, they focus on real accounts of homeless families and down-on-their-luck seniors. Here are some examples of compelling stories from my own days as an immigration attorney at a nonprofit:

- a father who literally got off his deathbed to take the citizenship exam and thereby ensure faster immigration for his children

- a Somali youth who was beaten in intertribal violence and who was desperate to get through the immigration process fast enough to go search for his missing mother, and

- a Guatemalan who'd watched his entire village massacred by the army only to have an unsympathetic immigration judge deny his case because conditions had supposedly "improved" in Guatemala.

Because all of these stories so graphically illustrated the important work our group was doing, they were good material to communicate to potential donors— but not all of them saw the light of day. Unfortunately, because few nonprofits develop a smoothly operating system for communication between program and fundraising staff, program staff members don't recognize their crucial role in the fundraising process. They may even resent the implication that they should weigh down their schedules or dirty their hands with the business of fundraising. If this is your situation, try gentle persuasion rather than a frustrated lecture. Take a few key staff members to lunch, ask them about what they're doing, and find out what fascinates—or frustrates—them about their work. This information will give you a fuller sense of what your organization does beyond its mission statement, and what challenges it faces day to day. But don't finish dessert without taking a minute to explain how you communicate with key donors and funders, who are likely to give more if they understand why your group's current work is so important.

When you later use information a staffer gave you, be sure to show the staffer the appeal letter, or tell him or her about your successful meeting with a supporter or foundation officer. To this end, some development professionals distribute brief emails or memos to staff describing recent fundraising efforts and successes. Some organizations put up signs within the office—for instance, the classic thermometer—to show progress toward a fundraising goal. Though you can do most of this casually and quickly, it's got a name—internal marketing. And it's a valuable tool for getting people within your organization to see how, by working closely with you, they can benefit through increased funding and recognition for their work.

Your next step may be to request something more systematic from staff members. For example, you could ask program staff to write up a regular report on their activities, or to simply stop by and let you know whenever something interesting happens. Asking program staff members to take photographs of their work is also a great way to get them involved. A nonprofit can always use photos, to illustrate its newsletters, brochures, and annual reports. A program staffer who is doing fieldwork—for example, visiting a project in the Maldives or taking children on a hike to see native wildflowers—should always bring a camera. Even in-house program staff consulting with clients over a desk should be encouraged to snap a few shots (with the client's permission of course), in order to put a face to your work. (Alternative methods of illustrating your work—hiring a photographer or buying stock photos of your subject matter—can be expensive, and will never be as representative of the daily business of your nonprofit.)

If a staffer is willing to bring his or her own camera to the office—and better yet, has some experience with photography—you're in luck. But even if you don't have an office full of shutterbugs, you can distribute disposable cameras to anyone interested and willing. Even someone without photo experience is likely to come up with a few worthwhile images. Also be sure to distribute small notebooks, so the photographers can record each photo's date and subject, including the names of any plants, animals, or people in the picture.

> **CAUTION**
>
> **Go light on the disaster shots.** Although evocative photos of grieving family members and emaciated victims are undoubtedly moving, and can be of some use in fundraising, more upbeat pictures showing your successes are

usually even more effective. For example, a photo of the new buds of a nearly extinct flower that your group helped preserve will be far more powerful than a photo of the cracked cement that previously covered its habitat.

If your organization holds staff meetings, make sure all development staff attend. If you're a development staffperson, this will give you a chance not only to keep abreast of what's happening, but also to give a regular report on the fundraising office's activities. Such reports should include more than dry numbers, but also convey your hopes, challenges, and disappointments. Staff meetings can also provide a convenient forum for holding a general fundraising training. Such trainings can cover basic issues like the importance of developing an extensive list of supporters, how staff can help contribute names, how they and their clients can help represent the organization at special events or meetings with funders, and what your organization's strategic plans are for the future, fundraising plans included. Also encourage brainstorming about fundraising. A staffer may have the next great idea for bringing in support.

As program staff hopefully get more attuned to the symbiotic relationship between themselves and your fundraising staff, you'll want to encourage the more charismatic ones to help you with occasional, specific fundraising activities—for example, participating in an important presentation to a potential major supporter or a foundation, or writing or editing a portion of a grant. While you must make sure that this doesn't prevent staffers from fulfilling their primary responsibilities, such involvement can be highly effective. A staff member who works directly with clients or issues is often the most eloquent and credible person to explain your nonprofit's work to the outside world.

Other Volunteers

Many nonprofits begin their lives with an all-volunteer fundraising effort, often led—initially, at least—by a few dedicated board members. Even some established organizations rely heavily on volunteer participation, or have more volunteers than paid staff. And the development office is certainly one place where volunteers can be useful, whether for ongoing office support, or for labor-intensive, one-time projects such as mailings or telethons. Not only do volunteers allow you to shift a lot more sand than would otherwise be possible, but they can also substitute for paid staff, especially if you can find competent people willing to work for several months at a time.

In many programs, volunteers aren't terribly difficult to recruit. You can advertise volunteer opportunities in your written materials, work with local volunteer placement organizations, and check with local colleges and schools, some of which require students to perform community service as part of their curriculum. There are also numerous Web matching services, as detailed in "Get Help From Volunteer Matching Organizations," below.

What's far more difficult is keeping volunteers around for more than a day or two, and managing them effectively. If you're going to inspire volunteers to provide you with meaningful free service over the long term, you must keep certain cardinal rules in mind:

- understand and respect people's motive for volunteering
- train volunteers well and ask for a specific commitment
- make volunteering as convenient as possible
- find ways to allow volunteers to have fun, and
- show your appreciation early and often.

TIP

Big businesses may offer their paid staff as volunteers if they get a benefit from doing so. While they don't get a tax deduction for these contributions, businesses do get goodwill, an opportunity for employee bonding, and an investment in a more economically stable community. Your best bet is to approach businesses that are geographically very near to your organization, especially ones whose goods or services your staff or clients might later purchase. Be ready to point out how, through your newsletter or other means, you'll publicly recognize their business's contributions.

Cater to Volunteers' Motives

Most people who agree to volunteer for your organization will be drawn to your cause, intellectually or emotionally. They really care about fair housing, avoiding conflict through mediation, or giving inner city kids a chance to develop their intellects by playing chess. But sincere interest in your mission is not the only reason that volunteers show up on your doorstep. Of equal importance to many volunteers is the chance to meet new people, develop skills, and feel needed. If a volunteer shows up full of energy and enthusiasm, and you ask that volunteer to photocopy stacks of reply cards for hours, you may never see him or her again.

This can be a hard lesson to learn. After all, the photocopying is crying out to be done, and you don't have the time to create work that will keep every new, inexperienced volunteer happy. But many organizations rely too heavily on their volunteers for thankless tasks, only to find that their volunteers don't stick around for long. And, at a deeper level, being involved in a grassroots, community effort should allow you to make a little room for the community to participate meaningfully.

TIP

Retirees constitute a huge pool of potential volunteers. As more and more Americans stay healthy and active for decades after their retirement, there is a vast and growing pool of people with time and energy on their hands. Even better, many of these people are at a point in their lives when they want to make a positive contribution to their communities—and they may well have significant expertise to share. A number of studies have also found that some older volunteers are fighting the loneliness and sense of purposelessness that can come from no longer taking part in the workforce. Others are interested in learning new things and keeping mentally active. For example, here's what Emily, a retired volunteer I know, says about her reasons for volunteering. It echoes what I've heard from many others:

"First I thought about what subjects interest me the most, then I looked for organizations that could connect me to them. I started volunteering at the art museum because I can keep learning more about art that way. I'm always getting notes from the museum coordinator asking me to volunteer in the museum shop, but I tell her no, I'll do anything that involves the artwork, but I'm not interested in merchandising."

Get Help From Volunteer Matching Organizations

You should know about the various programs that match or recruit and place volunteers with nonprofits, many of them through the Internet. Such volunteers might be useful in your development office or to substitute for paid positions in other parts of your organization. Some national sites worth looking into include:

- **The Clearinghouse for Volunteer Accounting Services (CVAS), at http://cvas-ca.org.** This group matches accountants with nonprofits in need of their professional services.

- **Idealist and Action Without Borders, at www.idealist.org.** Nonprofits can enter their own profile and update it to mention events and volunteer opportunities.

- **Jesuit Volunteers, at www.jesuitvolunteers.org.** The Jesuit Volunteer Corps. Its long-term volunteers accept one-year placements where they can provide direct services to economically poor or socially marginalized people. (Your organization doesn't have to be Catholic or religious to use JVC volunteers.) The program pays travel costs and provides some other support, while your organization pays for food, a monthly stipend, daily transportation, housing, and medical insurance.

- **Make a Difference Day, at www.usaweekend.com/diffday.** This is an annual (October) event sponsored by *USA Weekend* Magazine, in partnership with the Points of Light Foundation. Volunteers seek out projects for one-time work. Nonprofits as well as individuals can register project ideas.

- **Network for Good, at www.networkforgood.org.** This is an independent, 501(c)(3) organization founded by various corporate and nonprofit foundations and associations. Volunteers can go to the website and specify where, when, and for how long they want to work. Participating organizations are given a Web page where they can describe their work and the types of volunteers they need (click "are you a nonprofit," then "Volunteers").

- **Servenet, at www.servenet.org.** This is an online matching service, which allows nonprofits to register, and then wait for volunteers to search them out based on criteria such as subject matter, location, and length of volunteer stint.

- **Taproot Foundation, at www.taprootfoundation.org.** This organization focuses on professional volunteers, with expertise in technology, marketing, fundraising, and human resources, and places them in nonprofits that have successfully gone through a service grant application process.

- **Volunteer Match, at www.volunteermatch.org.** This site presents some interesting focuses, such as getting companies involved in group volunteer efforts, and virtual volunteering for those who want to work online, from home.

RESOURCE

Want more information on older volunteers? For an interesting report on baby-boomers who are great prospects for volunteering and giving in other ways, see *Experience at Work: Volunteering and Giving Among Americans 50 and Over*, prepared by Independent Sector in partnership with AARP, and available free at www.independentsector.org. Also see the studies and publications on the website of Experience Corps, a group that coordinates volunteerism by older persons as tutors and mentors to children, at www.experiencecorps.org.

If you're a development staffer, some, much, or even all the work of recruiting volunteers may fall to you. This makes some sense—your mailings and publicity may ask for donations of time as well as money. As you begin to fully grasp what it takes to get a full corps of volunteers going, you'll doubtless realize that this is one of those tasks that can turn into a full-time job. That's why, if your organization really does plan to rely on volunteers in a big way, you might want to create the position of volunteer coordinator. Because foundations are always interested in leveraging their grant money into maximum results, you may be able to attract the financial support necessary to make this a paid position. Or, if you find a person with lots of energy, time, and savvy, you may find yourself in the happy position of having someone volunteer to be your volunteer coordinator.

Fortunately, there are a number of relatively simple ways to satisfy volunteers' needs and interests. Asking them at the outset what they'd like to get from their experience is a good way to start! But be prepared to talk with them individually (or to save time, in small groups) about what you can and can't involve them in. Emphasize that, just as Rome wasn't built in a day, volunteers are most likely to construct a useful, fulfilling role with the organization if they commit to sticking around long enough to allow you to help them find a good fit. Another great approach, if you have regular volunteers, is to try to schedule them so that they overlap and can talk with each other. Especially if your organization uses volunteers in nondevelopment roles, arrange for volunteers to split their time between the development office and other work, for variety's sake.

To help with development tasks, you might capitalize on the fact that some volunteers are primarily interested in learning high-level job skills, in writing or marketing for example, which means that they might be interested in interning with your office for an extended time period. Local business schools are likely sources for this kind of help. And don't think only about the classic development office tasks, such as proposal writing and mailings; also look at the tasks you might otherwise hire out, such as photography, illustration, or designing a newsletter or an annual report.

Volunteer Training and Commitment

A formal training process, in which you explain the work of the organization and the volunteer's place in it, will make the experience more satisfactory for all concerned. If the volunteer is willing to help in the development office, briefly go over the annual budget and the fundraising plan. Explain the importance of seemingly mundane tasks, such as writing thank-you letters or entering data. Discuss what you normally expect volunteers to do, and what more interesting tasks they might "graduate" to after proven good work. You might also want to create a volunteer manual, something like an employee manual, explaining:

- what you expect of volunteers in terms of hours, calling when they'll be late or absent, and the like
- your commitment to making the volunteer experience a positive opportunity for community involvement, and
- basic office policies such as personal use of the phones and photocopiers.

Unless you are recruiting the volunteer for a one-time effort, ask for a commitment to a certain number of hours per week or month. Be prepared to make this flexible, however. With changes in the U.S. economy and work environment, the number of people who work traditional 9 to 5 jobs is declining. Your best source of daytime volunteers may be freelancers who have spare time—but not always at the same time each week.

You should be ready to provide feedback on how your volunteers are doing. Just because volunteers work free, that doesn't mean they don't need meaningful feedback—including constructive criticism as well as positive reinforcement. Volunteers who are trying to develop job skills, or will eventually ask you to serve as a reference, need to know how they are really doing. Your feedback will be taken best if you tell the volunteer during the initial training that you'll periodically sit down for a performance review—and if you make clear that the volunteer will then have a chance to give you feedback on the volunteer experience and what would make it better.

Make Volunteering Convenient

There just aren't many people running around with time on their hands these days. If the very mechanics of volunteering for your office are difficult—for example, if the volunteer has to call someone on your staff who's hard to reach—it creates another reason for the volunteer to drop the obligation.

Let's look at how a school literacy program in Oakland developed a volunteer program that's convenient for all concerned. The program is in a public school, in an area with numerous senior care centers. Seniors and others are encouraged to spend one hour a week reading to schoolchildren. No experience is required. To participate, they simply call one of the volunteer coordinators and say they'll be there that week. The coordinators prefer it if the volunteers can make a long-term commitment, but it's not required. For weeks when the program is short on volunteers, it has a list of backup people to call. And, to make sure the program doesn't become too much of a burden for any of the volunteer coordinators, each of them is in charge of managing one day a week.

This literacy program has run smoothly—and succeeded in boosting the children's interest in reading. As you can see, it creates a system in which no one feels overwhelmed by the amount of work, and people with more or fewer hours to spend can commit accordingly. It also has the virtue that volunteers perform the same task every time, to reduce the amount of oversight needed. This won't always be possible in your office, but it's something to bear in mind.

TIP

Do they really need to come into your office? Online volunteering is on the rise, by people who have just enough time to sit down at their computer. Take advantage of this trend. See www.onlinevolunteer.org.

Make Volunteering Fun

Although the volunteers are there to help you—and you don't have time to make it a party for them—they won't come back unless they can share in some way in your organization's sense of purpose. One of the most common requests volunteers make is to work directly with the people (or plants, animals, or environment) being served. If they're working in the development office, that won't always be possible. However, there are other activities that will allow them to work with the public, including:

- canvassing
- asking local businesses for raffle donations
- calling donors to express thanks, and
- participating in telethons.

> **CAUTION**
>
> **Your volunteers are the face of your organization.** Be choosy about who you let interact with the public on behalf of your group. If the only human contact a supporter has with your organization is a grouchy high schooler doing mandatory volunteer service and not well versed in your program, you'll turn the supporter off. (Not that all high school kids are grouchy—some of them are developing interests in community service that will last a lifetime, so giving them interesting and appropriate volunteer tasks is a community service in itself.)

Outside of the development office, you may want to suggest ways that your organization's other programs can use volunteers, in order to get a more vital all-around volunteer program going. To get you thinking, here are some creative ways that organizations in the San Francisco Bay Area use volunteers:

- An organization helping low-income girls prepare for college invites student volunteers to give talks about the college experience, including how to apply for financial aid and write essays, and what to expect regarding daily life on campus.
- An immigrant services organization has college students help write grant proposals, translate for clients, and call clients to collect information about their cases.
- A nonprofit providing art instruction to people with developmental, psychiatric, or physical disabilities asks volunteers to assist teachers in demonstrating art projects and assisting the art students.
- A homeless shelter asks volunteers to serve as mentors, tutors, chefs, and activity assistants.
- An organization helping students build literacy skills has volunteers help students write true stories about their lives.

Once your organization starts thinking innovatively about what volunteers can do, you may find that your volunteers breathe new life into your programs—thereby attracting more attention from funders and supporters.

Show Appreciation

Every volunteer, even the purely altruistic one who isn't trying to advance a career or other personal agenda, wants to know that he or she is making a difference and advancing the cause. And it's your job to tell the volunteer that. Especially when working with highly effective volunteers, it's important to say thank you early and often. For example, I fondly remember volunteering for a school garden tour committee that hardly ever let me walk out empty-handed—I was given a school T-shirt, a pair of gardening gloves, a poster from last year's tour, tomato seeds, and more. I was momentarily embarrassed by their generosity, but I got the message—they appreciated the help. And, most important from the school's point of view, I kept going back to do more.

Individual thank-you gestures are important. But they are only one of the possible ways to say "thank you." Try also to plan some organized volunteer-appreciation activities, particularly if you have a large volunteer corps. An annual volunteer party, for example, is guaranteed to be well attended. Inviting volunteers to your nonprofit's other events, such as a holiday party, lecture, or annual dinner, is also an excellent way to show your thanks. And don't forget to take advantage of a well-attended occasion by giving a little speech about how much particular volunteers have done for your organization—which you can accompany with awards, certificates, or small plaques.

Outside Consultants and Contractors

To supplement your salaried development staff, it can be useful to hire consultants and contractors. Be warned, however—the hourly rates of well-established writers, designers, accountants, and others may dwarf your own salary. But independent contractors start to look more affordable when you realize that you don't pay for their health insurance or office space, and you don't have to find a way to pay their salaries year-round. You can assign them to a limited task, and tightly control the hours they spend on it. Consultants and contractors are probably available in your area for just about every task a development office does, from grant writing to direct mailings to individual solicitations to leading board seminars or retreats. Ask other nonprofits for recommendations, or go to www.idealist.org, where you can post requests for volunteer consultants, or search for and read profiles of consultants for hire.

While outside workers can provide valuable expertise and take the pressure off when numerous deadlines seem to be looming all at once, you'll want to avoid three common problems. First, start by making sure you remain the "boss" in this relationship, and don't end up unsuccessfully trying to manage an opinionated and balky consultant. Second, carefully define in advance exactly what the contractor will do on your behalf, when the job will be completed, and how much it will cost. Third, be sure that the services to be completed according to the contract are ethical, honest, and follow fundraising approaches with which you are comfortable.

You've probably heard of scandals where hired fundraisers go out and solicit money (by telephone, for example), then take a healthy chunk for their own salaries and "costs" before turning the remainder over to the nonprofit. Although the nonprofit isn't directly at fault for depriving donors of money that doesn't go where they thought it would, the nonprofit won't emerge unscathed from any resulting negative publicity. In addition, some state's laws address nonprofits' use of professional fundraisers, for example, by requiring them to disclose their status to the people being asked to donate. Whatever you do, don't hire outside contractors on a commission basis—that is widely viewed as unethical, and in some states is even illegal.

CAUTION

Don't inadvertently turn a contractor into an employee. If you treat contractors or consultants like employees (by requiring them to keep regular office hours and closely supervising them, for example), you're headed for legal trouble. The IRS, as well as state tax and employment authorities, may claim that you should have paid the same taxes and benefits as you would for ordinary employees. For easy to access, free information about the legal differences between employees and contractors, see the independent contractors materials on Nolo's website at www.nolo.com. For more detailed information, including a wide selection of sample contracts, see *Working With Independent Contractors,* by Stephen Fishman (Nolo).

Can You Pitch Your Nonprofit in the Space of an Elevator Ride?

As part of your personal skill building, it's important to be able to quickly engage others about what your organization does, and why it's important. According to Mona Lisa Wallace, an attorney and nonprofit expert, "It's amazing how even some established organizations can't describe what they do—I'll hear vague statements like, 'We're sort of a homeless organization.' But what people really want to hear is who and where your organization is, what you're all about, where you're heading, and how you plan to get there. So, for example, a good elevator pitch might be, 'Our homeless families support network provides temporary housing and support services to parents and children with no place to go. We help them get back on their feet, and find a stable, long-term home. We may never be able to eliminate homelessness altogether, but we're going to keep trying to reduce it, one family at a time.'"

Oakland housing activist Randolph Belle recommends taking out a stopwatch, and practicing saying what you need to in 30 seconds or less. He also suggests practicing succinct answers to follow-up questions, such as:

- "What would you do with $10,000?"
- "Tell me about the needs of your constituency."
- "Who are the other service providers in your field and what makes you special?"
- "Tell me about the composition of your board of directors."
- "What made you get into this field?"

Fundraising Skills

This section briefly covers the most important personal characteristics and skills a good fundraiser needs. Of course, there's no one perfect way to raise money—a variety of approaches and styles can work well, depending on your audience, personality, and so forth. Some of these skills may be hard to develop if you weren't born with them, so be patient with yourself, and concentrate on bringing out the things you do best. This section will also help you evaluate prospective new staff, volunteers, and/or board members. It covers:

- interpersonal skills
- writing abilities, and
- profiles of various people who have made a career of fundraising.

Interest in Other People

You've probably heard the saying that "people give to people, not to causes." While that may be a bit of an exaggeration, it contains an important message: A fundraiser's ability to relate positively to his or her fellow human beings is crucial to that person's long-term success. Unless your fundraising office has so many staffers that a few people can sit in the back room and write grants all day, every person there should enjoy the idea of interacting with people outside the organization, be they donors, foundation funders, board members, or others.

Look for people skills and a personable demeanor when you're deciding whom to hire. If you're interviewing a prospective new development staffer, and the consensus is, "We're not crazy about his personality, but he's smart, writes well, and knows our work," you should proceed with extreme caution. Hiring that person could be asking for trouble if your supporters and funders have the same tepid reaction.

Whoever is handling fundraising should not only be ready to handle phone calls and meetings with major donors and funders, but also be proactive and enthusiastic about building personal relationships with these and other members of the public. Networking with other fundraisers is also an important part of this job. It's worthwhile for development professionals to join national or local groups such as the Association of Fundraising Professionals (www.afpnet.org).

Writing Abilities

The ability to write effectively plays an important role in nearly every aspect of fundraising, whether it's drafting a press release, a thank-you letter, a mail appeal, or a grant proposal. If you've always thought of yourself as more of a people person, who would rather swallow frogs than devote a few days to a writing project, you'll probably be very effective at some aspects of development work. However, if you hope to run a development office, you'll need to learn some new skills.

TIP

There may be a movement afoot to make the language of philanthropy more readable. Here's what The California Wellness Foundation had to say about the matter: "We also try to avoid the 'philanthropy speak,' which has been a nasty habit for too long in our field. ... If you think about it, philanthropic communications should be painless, as enjoyable as reading a good book."

RESOURCE

More on the jargon of giving. For a humorous deciphering of some of the most prevalent jargon found in the philanthropic world—terms like "at-risk," "capacity building," "empowerment," and "leverage"—see Tony Proscio's essays, "In Other Words" and "Bad Words for Good." They're available as free downloads on the website of the Edna McConnell Clark Foundation, www.emcf.org (click "Publications," then "Jargon Files"). Proscio's essays will make you think twice about some of the words that may have been slipping off your tongue.

Top Five Tips for Effective Writing

1. **Write like you talk.** Or better yet, write like you're on the phone with your Aunt Millie, who's a little deaf and wishes you'd get to the point and stop racking up long-distance charges. Too many people think that using long words and convoluted sentences makes them sound professional and authoritative. They're wrong. See if you can turn your writing into a conversation with the reader. Reading your written work aloud is a good way to put it to the test. If the voice you hear doesn't sound friendly, straightforward, and passionate about the cause, try again.

2. **Find out what makes your own writing flow.** With all due respect to high school writing teachers, many of them propounded rules that can stilt your subconscious writer—like the one about creating an exhaustive outline before setting pen to paper. I know many excellent writers who simply can't write that way—people who instead begin by writing in bursts, only later weaving them together to discover a structure. In short, if you have your own style of getting your thoughts out, go with what works for you.

3. **Be your own editor.** No one I know can produce a finished writing job in fewer than three drafts, and important tasks often take far more. So when you are finished writing something, read it over with a critical eye. Look for issues like:
   - **over-long sentences.** Any sentence that runs on for more than two lines can probably be chopped.
   - **boring or extraneous words.** Eliminate every word that's not necessary to the sentence. For words that cannot be removed, see whether they can be replaced with a more expressive alternative. For example, instead of using "difficult" three times in a paragraph, try "thorny," "obstinate," or "tough." Give your thesaurus a workout.
   - **potentially misleading word order.** We all love to laugh at signs that say "Half Baked Chicken, $7.99!" and the like—but some of your supporters may be less than amused if you announce that "Volunteers help burn victim's family."
   - **passive voice.** The passive voice is well named; it sounds as if the writer wearied of the cause long ago. So just say "no" to phrases like "it is of concern that" and "a donation of $xx was received." Instead, use active statements that explain who did what, like "our counselors are worried that" and "the Family Foundation generously donated $xx."

Top Five Tips for Effective Writing (continued)

4. **Never, ever send anything out without a final readthrough.** Mistakes and typos can lurk in any document—even one that's been read a dozen times. Ask someone you trust to give your written work a careful going over. Also, if you can, put every document aside for a few hours or days before you finalize it. You'll be amazed at what pops out at you—or what new inspirations arise—with a fresh reading.

5. **Lose the lingo.** After you've written a few grant proposals and attended some United Way trainings, your head will be full of terms like "outcomes," "mission statement," and "service-driven." And your organization's own area of expertise is probably jargon laden, too. You'll have to learn what the funders' words mean, and use them when funders or others won't be happy hearing any other word—but don't let them take over your entire vocabulary. Even the funders fall asleep when they read too much jargony stuff.

Profiles of Fundraisers

There is much more that one could say about what makes a good fundraiser—charm, tenacity, creativity, and so on. However, the odds of all possible useful traits being found in one person are slim. Many people's strongest points are balanced by less useful ones—a super-gregarious person might not have the concentration to sit and write for long periods, for example. Also, some traits are simply inborn. No one is going to become charismatic one day just because a book says it's a good idea.

To help you recognize and draw upon your own strengths, I've asked some experienced fundraisers to talk about how they got into the field, and what they bring to—and get out of—their work. These people don't represent the whole panoply of fundraising personalities—just ones who have found a niche that fits and fulfills them.

Jim Lynch

Jim Lynch is currently Computer Recycling and Reuse Program Manager at CompuMentor, a San Francisco–based nonprofit providing technological consulting and support to other nonprofits. In that capacity, he is developing a large national program and does most of his own fundraising. He was CompuMentor's development director for three years. Jim says: "I got into fundraising late in my career, having been a social work and teacher type for many years. I worked with difficult inner city teenagers and welfare mothers. But I tend to be restless, always looking for meaningful work, especially work where I can build something new or solve a problem. At one point I was working at an adult school that happened to be located close to a homeless shelter. I began working at the shelter in the evenings, developing a computer learning lab for them—a surprisingly useful tool for homeless people. The only problem was, we had no budget. We couldn't even buy a paperclip, much less any computers.

"The first challenge was just to get the homeless folks off the streets and into the schools. I went to Taco Bell and asked if they'd be willing to donate 35 tacos to one week of the program. They said yes. I followed that with McDonald's, Burger King, Pizza Hut, etc.—a different fast food vendor for every class. That got people coming, and we made sure to give some publicity to the vendor. It also pulled me into the world of nonprofit fundraising. I moved from hustling up junk food to filling up four homeless computer education labs with donated computers and software, and on to getting small grants.

"My next step was to accept a job with CompuMentor, with the idea of working on bigger, more national digital divide projects. I first worked as a regular project person, building computer systems for nonprofits. However, because I liked writing grant proposals and cultivating foundations, and seemed to be pretty good at it, CompuMentor asked me to fill in as a development director. I stayed in that post for three years.

"As development director, I got a chance to work closely with Daniel Ben-Horin, CompuMentor's founder and a great nonprofit fundraiser. His approach is to talk informally as much as possible with funders, to discover their philanthropic objectives. This helps him identify which of his own projects closely match those objectives. In other words, he talks the deal out first, only then following it up with a formal written proposal. Because I love schmoozing and making personal contact, this was a good fund development style for me. I'm an extroverted type who likes to engage people on the bus or in the carpool, if for no other reason than to find out who they are. (I have also tried the opposite method, of blasting out query letters and proposals, and found it didn't work very well.)

"To be successful with Ben-Horin's style of fundraising, I had to do the usual homework at the Foundation Center, to identify the funders in my field and then chat up anyone who might give me a name or other information about the exact right foundation person to approach. Unfortunately, funders are mostly firewalled against this type of informal engagement. But I found that if I could leave a voicemail or email, particularly saying that someone they knew recommended I speak to them, I could often get a call returned, and proceed from there. I felt like a combination of social networker and investigative reporter.

"Once we've connected, my interest in the foundation staffer isn't merely mercenary. I want to find out what makes the person tick, as well as how he or she views the foundation's mission. This level of interest is important, because funders seem to have specially attuned antennae to insincerity, or the hard sell, or canned pitches. And sometimes I discovered that the foundation's mission didn't mesh with CompuMentor's needs, but I'd keep checking in, year after year, until the staffer might actually start looking for ways to fund us, or one of our missions had changed so as to bring us closer together.

"It helps that I was born with a certain amount of tenacity. Once I find an area of our work that a foundation person thinks might be worth funding, I become unabashed about following up. In fact, I'll keep trying until they clearly tell me 'no.' This tenacity tends to make up for the fact that I'm not a great recordkeeper. I'm a bit haphazard about putting things on my calendar—but it's in my blood, enough that I'll be in the shower in the morning, thinking, 'I have to call the X Foundation today.'

"Beyond this, I'd say the main thing that suits me for fundraising is that I'm really passionate about my work. I'm not a professional salesperson. My father tried to make me into an insurance agent and I failed miserably. On the other hand, I can't help getting teary-eyed when talking about how intensely important a particular program is and why it makes the world a better place. Then it's just a matter of capturing the attention of the funders, to help them feel the same passion and understand what makes a program both effective and special."

Lupe Gallegos-Diaz

Lupe Gallegos-Diaz is currently director of the Chicano/Latino Academic Student Development arm of the Multicultural Student Development Office at UC Berkeley. She is also one of the founders and advisory board members of the Multicultural Alliance of the Association of Fundraising Professionals' Golden Gate chapter. In addition, Lupe serves on a number of nonprofit boards and committees, and offers consultant services.

Lupe describes finding her niche in fundraising this way: "Ever since I was young, I saw the power of community involvement. When my family came to the United States from Mexico, one of my first role models was my aunt, Enriqueta G. Rincon. By the time my aunt came to the United States from Mexico in the 1940s, she had already been a nurse, an active union member, and a self-made businesswoman. In the United States, she met my uncle, Pedro G. Rincon, who had lived in California when it was still part of Mexico. My aunt and uncle opened a Mexican restaurant, and later expanded it to two restaurants.

"Starting at a very young age, my aunt would take me along to business or community meetings. I loved this, and saw how important it was for the community to be represented. By watching my aunt help the community at various levels, I learned that I should always help people who are less fortunate.

"My parents also instilled in me the values of hard work and education. They were happy that I had the opportunity to go to college. In my mom's day, the choices were to become a nun or get married. I chose to go into social work. Then, while I was working towards my Master's in Social Work at UC Berkeley, I got involved in Casa Joaquin Murrieta, a social justice Xicana/o theme house that operates as a nonprofit. I was hired at first to assist the Executive Director, then found myself helping out with other things—everything from ordering food to cleaning the bathrooms. At one point, they were short an E.D., so I filled in for a couple of months. Of course, that involved some fundraising activities. I think that's when I first started to realize that by learning fundraising skills, I had a more powerful tool to bring about community change.

"Around this time, the University of San Francisco began offering a one-year certificate program in development. I got a scholarship, and signed up. The program was not only a good learning experience, but it exposed me to other fundraising professionals and organizations. Before long, I was recruited onto the board of the local Association of Fundraising Professionals. Back then it wasn't very diverse—basically, I and Mary, a white lesbian woman, and Rochon, an African-American woman, were about it for diversity. But since then, I've made it my personal mission to help people of diverse backgrounds learn about and get into the fundraising profession.

"One of the first things I did with my degree was to turn around and start teaching a course on development at UC Berkeley. At first, I put 'fundraising' in the course title, but students weren't attracted by this, not realizing that it would prepare them to make real change in their communities. So, I changed the title to 'Leadership and Community Involvement.' Once I get the students in the class, they say things like, 'Wow, we didn't know fundraising was a profession, something you can use.' I try to show them that fundraising can be both a career that utilizes their academic degree and skills, as well as a way of serving their own community. I emphasize basic fundraising skills like writing, communication, and how to pitch a request. But I also tell them you need to be a real people person, and be humble. No matter how much education or income the person you're talking to has, you need to know how to really listen to them and understand them. Besides, someone who's doing manual labor now may save up and be able to make some large donations later—you've got to be in this for the long term. I also tell students that you need to go beyond your own community constituency, and think broadly about who your possible donors might be.

"The hands-on fundraising that I do now is mostly as a consultant and a board member for various nonprofits. As a board member, I am always thinking about what people's interests might be and whether these interests might be a good match for the organizations I represent. Sometimes I'll just be talking on the phone to someone I know for another reason—like a project we're working on, or just to stay in touch—and I'll say, for example, 'I was wondering if you'd be willing to commit $500 to the Chicana/Latina Alumni Club.' They know me already, and they know it's a good cause, so often the answer is yes. If I were calling from out of the blue, and didn't have something of a relationship with the person, it would be a lot harder.

"I can't believe it took me so long to find my niche. It's great to be able to tie my education with my community interests, to merge theory and praxis. But I don't think I've yet reached my peak. I've got a daughter now, and many of the causes I'm involved in concern family and child issues. I believe it's essential to pass our knowledge of money and fundraising to our young ones, so that they become conscious of their world and the choices they will make to change it. Through my fundraising work, as well as my academic research, I hope to leave behind something that will last—a legacy of social change."

Grant Din

"As a child, I never imagined that fundraising would be part of my career. I remember going door-to-door selling candy for Cub Scouts, and not liking it very much. And as the years went by, it seemed as likely that I would end up in something like engineering or environmental science. But the seed may have been planted right after my graduation from Oakland High, when I got a Marcus Foster scholarship to support my college studies at Yale. At the ceremony, we heard speeches from Clark Kerr (the then-head of UC Berkeley), as well as Marcus Foster's widow Abby and others. While encouraging us to make the most of our educations, they also stressed the importance of coming back to serve our communities.

"Even then, it's not as though I said 'Aha, I need to be fundraiser!' Like many fundraising professionals, I found my way into it via a circuitous route—in my case, almost backwards. I started out as a staffmember at a small foundation, giving out grants to help community development in Oakland's Asian-American community. (I got the job based on my writing experience and academic background in sociology and urban studies.) I certainly learned a lot about community needs in that job. In fact, the hardest thing for me was that we had only a limited amount of money to give out, and numerous worthy applicants. I hated having to say 'no' to them. At the same time, I was on the board of the Asian Law Caucus, and I helped out on their special events.

"When I decided to move on, I looked at some corporate communications jobs, but realized that just wasn't for me. I ended up taking a job as Director of Resource Development (fundraising) with Asian Neighborhood Design, where I've been for the last 14 years. (Asian Neighborhood Design is a 31-

year-old nonprofit that provides urban planning, neighborhood revitalization, architecture, construction management, and other assistance, and also provides low-income people with job training and placement, as well as assistance in transitioning out of poverty. See www.andnet.org.) Currently, I serve as Executive Director, where fundraising remains an important part of my job. I work primarily on developing and maintaining relationships with foundations, while our development director works mostly with major donors.

"At the beginning, my natural tendencies were to prefer the quieter, written-work parts of fundraising. Although I've always enjoyed being with other people, I'd never thought of myself as hugely outgoing. But one of the great things about fundraising for me has been that it has pushed me to further develop my social side, which has helped me grow as a person.

"For example, I attended one seminar that I really enjoyed, by Debra Fine, author of *The Fine Art of Small Talk*. What I picked up from her was that, when meeting new people, you have to take responsibility for their comfort. If you're talking about your organization, you need to make it a real conversation. If you can achieve this, you won't come off as a phony just plugging for money.

"By now, I've so internalized the relationship-building parts of my work that I joke that I'm always on the job. I'll be at a party, and someone will tell me, 'Do you know that the person over there works with X,' and I'll approach that person about our organization. As long as you're not overbearing, this seems to be okay—after all, people in one's social circle seem to have mutual interests, and so they're truly interested in making another meaningful connection.

"Now the personal parts of fundraising are the parts I enjoy the most. There's nothing more exciting for me than having a potential funder visit our organization. The visit might include watching our student trainees learn to use hammers or power saws or develop their math skills, a neighborhood walk to see some of our architecture projects, or a conversation with one of our recent graduates about what he or she is now doing. I'll see the funding officer's eyes light up, realizing the impact our work has.

"One of the most important things I've learned over the years is not to get too discouraged. It's really easy to feel let down after a rejection. But it may just mean that a foundation has used up its money for the year, and will put you at the top of its pile for next year. I cope with the down times by commiserating with my colleagues, and reminding myself that a number of groups are competing for a limited pool of funds. You have to put out a lot of tries before you meet with success."

Fundraising Equipment and Technology

Though good equipment can be pricey, the inefficiencies that result from trying to raise money with tools and technology from the horse-and-buggy era will cost far more. Of particular importance are:

- adequate office space and equipment
- effective telecommunications equipment
- computer technology, and
- credit card capabilities.

Office Space and Equipment

If you're a development director or other high-level development staffperson, it should go without saying that you need a private office, a desk, and a phone to do effective fundraising work. Unfortunately, many a fundraising professional has had to make do with a table in the corner of the reception area or the E.D.'s office, so this is apparently less obvious than it should be. In case anyone in your office needs reminding, explain that you'll be placing important and sensitive phone calls to supporters and funders, so you'll need some quiet and privacy. Preparing proposals and mailings are also tasks for which you need adequate space to collect and organize your documents. For example, if you ever have to prepare a grant proposal for the federal government, you may end up with a five-inch-high stack of forms, reports, statistics, and more. If you don't have enough room to sort and organize your paperwork, you might lose track of important documents or leave something out.

RESOURCE

Need more information on office space for fundraising? For an eloquent and detailed exposition of a development office's needs, see Kim Klein's *Fundraising for the Long Haul* (Chardon Press).

Effective Telecommunications Equipment

Although you may not have much say in the type and condition of your office's telephone system, you should emphasize the important role communications play in your work. People must be able to reach you easily. To accomplish this, you'll want a wired phone system with a direct line to your desk, and, if at all possible, a mobile phone you can use to stay in touch when you are out of the office. It's also good to have a voicemail system that allows you to access your messages remotely.

Perhaps the best way to think about your phone needs is to put yourself in the shoes of a major donor or foundation officer who is trying to reach you. Can the caller make his or her way through your reception or voicemail system quickly and easily? What if the caller doesn't know or can't remember your last name, or your direct line or extension number? If you have a "live" receptionist, he or she can easily handle these kinds of contingencies. This is why many experts will tell you not to replace your receptionist with a machine if at all possible; if necessary, you can even line up volunteers to answer the phone.

If a voicemail system picks up the phone some or all of the time, make sure it's designed to help callers get what they need, quickly and easily. Too many offices rely on voicemail systems that force callers to listen to dozens of menu options, none of which has anything to do with their question, before the "secret" of how to reach a live person is revealed. (At the very least, such a system should include a quick menu option for people interested in contributing or volunteering.) In other systems, you must know how to spell an employee's last name in order to get past the initial recording. If you've got a potential donor on the line who doesn't know your name, you could lose him or her right there. Make sure the person has another option.

Another issue to think about is how many phone lines are coming into the office. If you're planning on having volunteers come in to do telethons, you'll need several lines that can operate at one time.

Computers and Software

Computer technology becomes obsolete quickly, and it's probably inevitable that many budget-challenged nonprofits are using yesterday's equipment, complete with software that was state-of-the-art last decade. Hi-tech tools that employees in the for-profit sector have long taken for granted, such as internal office networks, high-speed or wireless Internet access, and more, are often unheard of in nonprofit work environments.

Unfortunately, because you have to communicate with people in the for-profit sector (and in foundation and government work), relying on seriously inadequate technology risks leaving you quite literally out of touch. A donor who sits down at his or her office and regularly hears the email on his desktop beeping "new message!" tends to forget that not everyone lives like that. This donor is not going to be amused if he or she sends you an email only to receive an answer a week later, because someone in your organization just got around to checking the sole email inbox.

The good news is that you're not alone. Because inadequate computer systems are so endemic in the nonprofit sector—and money for upgrades is so short—you'll find classes at your local nonprofit support center, written materials specifically directed at nonprofits, and foundations offering grants and consulting to help you bridge the technology gap. All of these can help you meet your basic needs, such as:

- a computer
- a donor and finance database
- a client-tracking database, and
- Internet and email access.

Computers

Because technology prices have fallen so much in recent years, decent equipment—including computers and printers—may well be within your reach. And, buying your own equipment allows you to avoid the common trap that many strapped nonprofits fall into: accepting used computers from a corporate office. (They unload these dinosaurs and get a tax deduction; more often than not, you get junk.) Assessing donated equipment and fixing problems or adjusting it to fit your office's needs is often more trouble than it's worth, unless you have a staffperson or volunteer who's adept at information technology. Or, you might ask the donor to send a tech person to get everything up and running. Still, with new equipment, the odds are better that you'll reach a helpful person when problems arise.

If you haven't yet invested in a donor and finance database, start researching this before making any computer purchases. You'll want to be sure that your computers are powerful enough to support the database you choose.

RESOURCE

Need technical assistance? For consulting on computer equipment and technology needs, talk to:

- **CompuMentor,** a San Francisco–based nonprofit specializing in technology planning, implementation, and support for community-based organizations and schools, at www.compumentor.org (also the home of TechSoup.org)

- **NPower,** a nationwide network of nonprofits that provides free or low-cost technology assistance, at www.npower.org.

Donor and Finance Database

A high-quality database that keeps track of individual donors' names, other information, and gifts can be one of the best investments your organization makes. If you're still working with a homemade database that only you know how to use, lose it now. New databases are getting progressively faster, cheaper, and easier to use. They offer wonderful opportunities to segment donors into categories for special attention, and produce reports showing patterns you might never have dreamed of. They can also save you huge amounts of time— a mailing list that might take you two weeks to put together by hand can be generated in 15 minutes or less using a database.

TIP

Get free advice or even funding for your investment in a database. For example, a funder may be willing to offer a grant toward this, or some organizations may help you locate free or discounted software. See, for example:

- **Idealware,** a space for candid reviews and information about nonprofit software, at www.idealware.org

- **TechSoup,** offering free and discounted software to nonprofits, at www.techsoup.org

- **Network for Good,** which supports free ebase software; see www.groundspring.org and www.ebase.org

- **Technology Grant News,** a subscription-based service that tracks technology funding opportunities, at www.technologygrantnews.com.

Get Your Donor Records in Order First

A database is only as good as the information that goes into it. Whether you are two days or two years away from getting a sleek new database, now is the time to make sure you won't be feeding it garbage. In her work as a database management consultant, Lauren Williams has seen it all in terms of donor record quality—including organizations whose records were in such poor shape that she had to reconstruct donor information from Christmas cards and bank accounts. Lauren offers the following tips for grassroots organizations still working their way towards a database:

- **Keep every last scrap of paper.** "If your office is still very low-tech, it's safest not to throw out anything relevant to your donors, because you never know what you'll need later."

- **Write a date on everything.** "For example, if you've got someone's business card, but no one remembers having received it, it doesn't do much good unless a written date shows you how recent it is."

- **Write down your sources for information.** "For example, if your files contain a scrap of paper saying 'Donor may be opening a new business—partnership possibilities?' but the scrap doesn't say who mentioned the possible new business, or who took the notes, it won't do your records much good a year or two later."

- **Write down the context in which you gathered information.** "For example, with a business card, don't just date it and sign it: Write down the circumstances in which you received the card, and a note about the conversation you had with the person. A collection of thousands of names and addresses, each without context, is useless."

There are literally dozens of software programs available to handle your supporter database (and other technology needs). Many can be downloaded via the Internet, making upgrades automatic and information accessible to all your office locations. If possible, team up with your accounting staff when investigating databases and setting up your website. Many packages include accounting functions (thereby ensuring that donor gifts are tracked smoothly from the mailbox to the bank) and can handle the credit card portion of your website.

Instead of driving yourself crazy with research, talk to your colleagues at other nonprofits. As M. Eliza Dexter, then–Development Director of Oakland, California–based Save The Bay, says, "The smartest thing we did when choosing a database was to call around, ask what others are using, and ask what they've been disappointed in." You might even visit other offices and watch how they use their database—see if you can intuitively understand how they move between screens, and whether the visual layout appeals to you. Also ask your colleagues how much they're actually taking advantage of the various bells and whistles—many software packages promise a world of reports, tracking features, and more, but users find the features too hard to use or irrelevant to the organization's needs.

Once you've got some recommendations, research the possibilities online or call the company's customer service representative. In choosing a database, here are some factors to consider:

- **Cost.** Prices for fundraising software packages can vary from zero (especially for introductory periods) to $250,000. Some companies charge a flat fee, others a monthly one as well. Some customize the software to the user's needs and charge accordingly, others assess a per-user (or per concurrent user) fee. Even if your nonprofit is as tiny as it is financially challenged, you're likely to find a product that meets your needs. The prevailing rule of thumb is to spend 0.25% to 0.50% of your annual budget on this.

- **What's included.** Depending on your office's needs, you'll want to see some combination of:
  - ✓ transferability of your existing data
  - ✓ interface with your website
  - ✓ office management, including task reminders
  - ✓ information-keeping capability, with extensive biographical and gift records, the ability to segment supporters based on various biographical or gift criteria, the ability to link files on couples or related donors, and a hopefully

unlimited ability to enter contact information on individual donors

✓ mail merge and production of labels

✓ automated reports (including graphics) that draw together the information in the database, such as multiyear support trends, tracking of grants (when they're received, how much is received, and when reports are due), successes of particular mailings or campaigns, and detailed information on donors (how and when they've given, groupings by gift amount, and other criteria)

✓ automated production of receipts, thank-you letters, pledge reminders, and renewal requests

✓ easy generation of personalized correspondence (by letter or email)

✓ specialized modules for planned giving, special events, and more, and

✓ ability to import and export data to Word and Excel programs.

- **Record capacity.** Unless your organization is small and has no plans to grow, you'll want to make sure the database can accommodate plenty of donor records. They all promise this, of course, but some don't deliver. For example, if the vendor's definition of a "record" is every single gift entered, your database will quickly fill to bursting. You want every record to represent one donor, with unlimited capacity to enter relevant information.

- **Training.** Find out how much (if any) training is necessary. Some software packages are advertised as being so easy to use that you don't need training. (Check out this claim with some current users.) If, as is common with more sophisticated programs, some training is needed (somewhere between three days and two weeks' worth), find out how much, if any, you'll receive for free, and where classes will take place. Some companies conduct trainings only at their headquarters, which may quickly put the software out of your price range if you have to fly a number of staffers across the country.

- **Ongoing technical support.** Installation and support costs can mount if you're not careful. Make sure that the number to call for help is toll-free, or that email is an option. Also see whether the support contract runs out after a time (usually a period of months) and if so, how much it will cost to receive support after that.

- **The company's future.** You don't want to buy a product from a company that's about to be sold, go bankrupt, or discontinue the product line you're interested in. Unfortunately, this happens frequently, with the result that loads of nonprofits end up with "orphaned" software that will not be supported or updated in the future. Asking the company about whether they will be there in a few years won't help (even the shakiest company will claim to have a rosy future), but doing a little outside research (for example, a simple Google search of the company's name) often turns up interesting information.

- **Ease of use.** Here is another reason to take M. Eliza Dexter's advice and ask your friends for recommendations. A program that looked easy to use when the salesperson demonstrated it may turn into a nightmare when you're alone staring at a mystery screen. Another excellent approach is to ask for a demonstration model before you purchase the product. Instead of just seeing whether you can perform a few simple tasks, challenge it and yourself to doing something difficult. Also, see how easy (or impossible) it is to recover if the program fails. Finally, think about how hard this system will be for an office volunteer to learn to use quickly.

- **Upgrade frequency.** Does the company periodically publish newer versions, and will you receive these for free, or at a price? If you must pay for them, how well will the company continue to support the old version?

> ⊙ **CAUTION**
> **Pay careful attention to the database's available security measures—and use them.** The accuracy of your data is critical—so protecting it from accidental deletions or alterations, perhaps by inexperienced users, should be a first priority. Most software provides some protective measures, such as a backup system, but you may need to take an active role in implementing these measures. Find out what kind of security measures various programs offer before you decide which one to buy.

In making your final choice, consider the advice of Lauren Williams, a Maryland-based professional nonprofit database consultant: "You absolutely want to shop around, and get the best database you can afford. Do not go second class if you can afford first class. The difference between first class and second class in these systems is astronomical, in terms of the power you gain. By power, I mean how many different kinds of donor relationships you can track, how intimately and intricately you can track them (how much information you can store), and how many other fine details the software incorporates. As an example of important details, I recently worked with a product whose programmers didn't have the savvy to include a field for middle names! You could have a 'Lauren Agnes Williams' who is a completely different person from 'Lauren Amy Williams.'"

Service-Tracking Database

In addition to the donor database described above, you'll also want to consider a database that collects information on your outcomes or provision of services. Why is this a fundraising issue? Because your organization will have to send detailed reports to foundations and others on how their money was spent. If you're a development director or other development professional, it will likely be your job to review these reports. And if they're not up to snuff, you're obviously going to have a tough time approaching the same funder for more support next year.

Unfortunately, advancements in data collection software tend to lag behind donor software. This is in large part because the developers who profit by creating standardized software find that service provision is anything but standard. Even among nonprofits providing the same type of service—for instance, shelters for the homeless—one shelter might be accustomed to measuring success based on the number of beds filled, while another might measure the number of hours spent housing or counseling each client. In fact, many software companies throw up their hands, leaving nonprofits to try to develop their own databases.

Although this may seem like a daunting task, it's important that you tackle it. Otherwise, you'll end up keeping track of essential information using handwritten notes on file folders, index cards, or at best a Word document. Especially as your nonprofit grows, these old-fashioned methods will prove to be inadequate. Foundations and other donors increasingly want access to up-to-the minute information—and many want to know how you're collecting it. Put bluntly, they're tired of seeing the ad hoc, often questionable data that many nonprofits throw together at reporting time. To set your nonprofit apart, find or develop a database that makes tracking and reporting simple and accurate. Once you've done that, loudly advertise that fact to every foundation or other funder with whom you're in contact.

If you can't find off-the-shelf software that meets your needs, go to www. techfinder.org, and click "Databases" to find a list of nonprofit database developers. Other potential sources of advice and referrals include CompuMentor, a nonprofit dedicated to providing technical support to other nonprofits (www.compumentor.org), and NPower, dedicated to putting technology know-how in the hands of nonprofits (www.npower.org).

RESOURCE

Want to read more about service-tracking databases? Check out www.techsoup.org, including the "database" articles in its Learning Center.

Internet and Email

The Internet is both more and less important to nonprofit fundraising than was first predicted. Time has proved wrong the optimist's predictions that people would troll the Web looking for places to give their money. It's too bad, but people don't seem to wake up and say "Gosh, I think I'll go online to make a charitable gift today" (or not nearly as often as they wake up with an urge to do online discount shopping). But it's also true that the Internet has become a more important development tool than anyone first imagined. Not only does a website enhance your organization's credibility, but it is also the first place many people go to learn more about your group and obtain key contact information.

Email has had a similar mixed history for nonprofits (and other businesses). Though there were high hopes that the speed and affordability of email would eliminate the need for "snail mail" marketing, these hopes have been significantly dampened by one thing—spam. The good guys aren't the only ones who have figured out how easy it is to send their message far and wide, and most of us have become lightning quick at deleting any message from an unrecognized sender. But, on the positive side of the ledger, email is an easy and affordable method of communicating with existing supporters who have demonstrated an interest in hearing from you.

You'll find more on creating a website that effectively supplements your fundraising goals in Chapter 12. Chapter 5 explains how email can fit into your overall fundraising strategy.

Credit Card Capabilities

One of the mantras of every fundraiser should be, "Make it easy for supporters to give." To this end, allowing people to donate by credit card can be crucial. A person who doesn't feel like writing a check—or even thinking about his or her account balance—may be happy to give you his or her credit card number, whether on a reply card or online. Because there are costs associated with accepting credit cards, however, many nonprofits have been slow to take advantage of this, figuring that it's better to bank every penny of a donation. But a critical mass of nonprofits now accept credit cards, so you stand to lose far more by holding out.

To set up a credit card system, talk to a few banks. You'll be asking to open a "merchant banking account." The bank where you open your account will serve as the intermediary between you and the credit card companies. You'll have to pay a startup fee (usually no more than $100), a monthly or annual fee (usually no more than $15 per month or $150 per year; avoid banks that charge both), and a charge per transaction (usually either 1.5% to 5% of the amount of the transaction, or a flat fee of 10 cents to 75 cents, or a combination of the two). Transactional fees are usually higher in cases where you aren't given the actual card to swipe, as with a telephone or Internet donation.

You can see why it's important to shop around for a bank that charges low fees, and whose overall fee structure isn't so complicated that you find yourself paying high fees without knowing what you did "wrong." It's possible to find banks that waive some of the fees, or return a portion of the percentage normally charged, in recognition of your nonprofit status.

Developing Your Fundraising Plan

Every worthwhile endeavor starts with a plan, and your annual fundraising efforts should be no exception. If I could just give you a simple formula, such as "spend x% of your time proposal writing, x% on donors, and the rest on special events and planned giving," I certainly would. But, because every nonprofit has its own strengths and unique position within the community it serves, no such generic fundraising plan exists. It's up to you to create your plan, based on the work you need to accomplish and the financial support you can reasonably hope to attract.

No matter what size your group is or how long it has been in existence, you can gain something through the planning process. It doesn't matter if you've been operating for a while without one—it often makes sense for a new group to focus on the cause first and the funds second. Still, no matter how busy you are now, it's absolutely crucial to your long-term viability that you take some time to develop a coherent fundraising plan. And don't worry that coming up with a plan will be all drudgery and paper pushing: Developing a fundraising plan can be an exciting chance to reaffirm what works and rethink what doesn't, set goals, and make a commitment to keeping an eye on the big picture.

Take care, however, to fit your fundraising planning into the other types of planning that your nonprofit (hopefully) engages in—strategic planning, program planning, and budgeting, in particular. Every organization needs to make time to plan—and dream—without always viewing things through the lens of, "But how are we going to pay for this tomorrow?"

The Broader World of Strategic Planning

To keep your priorities in order, your organization should look at broad planning issues before focusing on fundraising. Because most nonprofits grow up around a particular issue or cause, this planning is often done on an informal basis, perhaps over coffee in one of the founders' or leaders' living rooms. But done right, the strategic planning process should also include researching, collecting community input, and coming to decisions about:

- the current concerns—and needs—of the community you serve
- whether your organization's original mission is still relevant and appropriate or needs to be modified
- whether your programs or policies still represent the best ways to go forward
- whether the community is sufficiently aware of your organization's existence, and, if so, whether it supports—or continues to support—your mission and goals
- whether your organization is paying enough attention to its own infrastructure, future viability, and the needs of its employees
- the risks and benefits of contracting or expanding your programs, and
- putting this all together, where your organization should focus its energy and fundraising resources in the coming year or years.

Various resources are available to help your nonprofit organization engage in overall planning, whether you're just starting up or well underway. See, for example, www.allianceonline.org (click "Frequently Asked Questions," then "Strategic Planning").

Here are the key tasks you'll have to tackle to create your fundraising plan for the next one to five years:

- determine a reasonable dollar goal to work toward
- evaluate your organization's greatest fundraising assets
- create a strategy that uses these assets to most effectively reach potential funding sources, and
- write down your strategy in a short, easy-to-understand document, to keep everyone on plan.

Getting Started: Set Your Fundraising Goal

Every nonprofit should produce an annual budget. When you first begin, this may be done informally, with the founding members chipping in a few dollars as needed. But certainly by your second year, the process of creating an annual budget should be institutionalized. Ideally, it should be a collaborative process, overseen by the executive director with input from the board, the accounting staff, and any relevant program managers or other staffers. The resulting budget will reflect all of the income that the organization brings in and all of the expenses it foresees paying out.

> **TIP**
>
> **Try to create a small reserve fund.** Too many nonprofits create a budget in which the total income exactly equals the total expenses. Given the shoestring on which most nonprofits operate, this isn't surprising—but it's still risky. If unavoidable extra expenses arise, the nonprofit may be pushed into the red. To forestall this problem, create a small reserve fund. Setting aside even a small amount each year—preferably out of donor funds or fees for services—can significantly enhance your organization's stability and limit the chances of a time-wasting midyear financial emergency. Depending on the size of your organization and how quickly it's expanding, it makes sense to create a cash reserve that will keep your organization going for a full 90 to 180 days.

Of course, it would be nice if someone could just tell you how much money you'll need to raise each year. But in the real world, arriving at your total income figure is—and should be—a complex process, in which planners typically look at:

- how much money would be needed in an ideal world to develop programs and infrastructure
- how much money was raised last year (probably a lot less)
- how much more can reasonably be raised this year
- how much the organization's programs and infrastructure can *really* get by on, with appropriate penny-pinching
- whether the reduced figure looks more realistic in terms of fundraising,
- and so on.

Without us examining the entire budget process, we'll look in this section at the particular and limited role that a development director and other development staff can and should play in developing a budget. This role may include:

- creating the development department's budget

- helping to arrive at accurate and reasonable income projections

- monitoring the percentage of the overall budget that is going to administrative overhead, that is, to nonprogram staff and activities

- identifying places where the group may be able to raise more by better marketing its services, and

- considering whether expensive equipment or services can be obtained via donations, rather than by paying for them.

> **CAUTION**
>
> **Don't arrive at your fundraising goal by simply ratcheting up last year's income.** Some nonprofits come up with their fundraising targets by simply increasing the previous year's number by a set percentage or amount—for example, by deciding that a fundraising effort that raised $100,000 last year can raise $120,00 this year, or something equally simplistic. But fundraising involves too many variables for this kind of approach to be accurate. And if some major grants aren't renewed, or other known income sources drop out of the picture, an ambitious goal like this could end up crippling the organization, as expenses keep mounting. You need to look at every revenue source and make a reasonable projection as to how much you're likely to receive this year to arrive at an informed total.

Create a Budget for Development Activities

At some point in the growth of your organization, the development staff may be asked to draft a separate subbudget for their own activities. If you're new to the organization, or to budgets in general, you might be daunted by this prospect. How on earth, you might wonder, can you estimate how much money you will spend on photocopying or travel for an entire year? You aren't even sure what events you will have, whether many of your donors will suddenly prefer a full lunch over coffee, or whether the economy will hit a period of inflation.

At the beginning, you'll have to rely largely on your instincts and your careful review of past years' budgets or records of expenditures. To help hone your instincts, try some simple budgeting exercises. Go through an entire day or week, noticing what supplies you use, how many photocopies you make, how many faxes or letters you send out, how many long-distance phone calls you make, and so forth. Then estimate the costs of these items and add up what they'd cost for a month, then a year. Also think about the things you're pretty sure you'll do over the course of the year—send out a certain number of mailings, hold an annual event, and the like—and add up their costs. Though unscientific, these exercises can be revealing, showing that some costs add up faster than you'd think and others are less significant.

Next, look at any budgets or fundraising-expense records from past years. The first thing you'll probably notice is that your biggest expenses are not for incidental items, but for employee salaries and overhead (taxes and benefits, plus the costs of the office space and utilities). That gives a certain predictability to any budget, year to year (though it also explains why, in tough times, all the cost-cutting in the world can't necessarily forestall the need for layoffs). Also look at what fundraising activities your organization undertook in past years, how much they cost, and whether these activities will likely be reduced, repeated, or expanded. Of course, this kind of analysis creates a chicken-and-egg problem—you can't know for sure whether you'll be doing more mailings and fewer grant proposals, or vice versa, until you've developed your fundraising plan. But you can at least get a sense of your operating constraints and, with experience, learn to balance the budget and planning possibilities more naturally.

If you've already been involved with the organization for a year or more, think about what will (or should) change this year. Was there enough money last year to order appropriate stationery and office supplies? Did you have a large one-time expense, such as the cost of renting a hall for a special fundraising event that won't be repeated?

After going through these various exercises and reviewing past budgets, you should be able to fill out the sample cost analysis below. There's a column for "notes," where you might write down the costs you're uncertain about, what might affect them, and the like. For example, if salaries are changing, you'll need to talk to your accounting department about how much the associated employment taxes and benefits will be.

Fundraising Worksheet 1: Sample Cost Analysis

Item	Cost per year	Notes
Salaries and benefits	$	
Fees to independent contractors and consultants	$	
Travel (trainings, donor visits)	$	
Office supplies	$	
Graphic design/printing	$	
Dues and publications	$	
Staff trainings and networking events	$	
Web, database, and other technical support	$	
Telephone	$	
Postage	$	
Food (such as coffee or meals with donors)	$	
Special event costs	$	
Other special program costs	$	
Total	$	

Obviously, no budget will reflect future expenditures with 100% accuracy. That's why, over the course of each fiscal year, it's important to keep an eye on what your development department or staff actually spends, to get a sense of what is normal and reasonable and to figure out where your estimates could use a little fine-tuning. Your accounting staff—or at least the volunteer who keeps the books—can help here, by putting together regular reports on actual versus budgeted expenditures. If this isn't practical in your organization, it will be up to you to make sure that you either stay within budget or receive permission from the powers that be to deviate from it.

RESOURCE

Need help with predicting actual expenses? For a good overview of likely costs associated with different parts of your fundraising program, see "Creating a Budget for Fundraising," by Octavia Morgan, *Grassroots Fundraising Journal*, May/June 2003, Volume 22, No. 3.

Check Your Income Projections

The income side of your organization's proposed annual budget should include known or projected income from reliable sources such as ongoing grants, annual member renewals, and income that your fundraising efforts will almost surely bring in. For example, if a particular fundraising event has raised between $22,000 and $26,000 for three years running, it's probably safe to assume that it will raise at least $20,000 this year. You may even want to use a slightly higher number.

Your most important budgeting task is to make sure that the known income figures are accurate. Check to make sure that all of the grants will continue as the budget says they will, and that they don't run out in the middle of next year. Your treasurer or paid accounting staff should be tracking this too, but mistakes can be made.

CAUTION

Be particularly careful when your fiscal year and a grant year are different. If, for example, half of the grant will be received in one fiscal year, and the other half in the next, you'll need to be sure that you allocate income and expenses accordingly.

Also look at the estimated amount of member donations. Most budget planners estimate this figure based on recent years' results, with adjustments for any known or likely changes. In your review, you will need to consider whether these estimates and adjustments are appropriate. Obviously you don't have a crystal ball. But, if you have a regular base of members who are encouraged to renew annually, and you can review this history of renewals, you've got a good starting point for your predictions. You can also estimate how many interim mailings or appeals you'll send out to existing members or supporters, and make a realistic assessment of how much these will bring in.

Be sure to consider any unusual circumstances that affected recent years' giving patterns. If you know, for example, that individual donations hit a spike last year because of a particular hot issue or disaster, you'll need to make sure that this figure is revised downward. By the same token, if your development office was unusually short-staffed and sent out only one appeal letter last year, you can assume that individual donations will be at least a little higher this year (allowing for those lost donors who were turned off by the lack of communication). A planned hike in your membership dues will also affect your likely income.

The income projections probably will, and should, have a separate line for the amount of major donations you're likely to solicit. If your group is typical, at least a few people will contribute more—sometimes far more—than any annual dues. You can put any existing estimates through the tests described above—what will be different this year? Was there anything unusual about last year or recent years, like a lapse in stewardship of major donors, a huge one time gift, or a change in the tax laws, that affected your major donations?

Another thing to consider is how certain the various anticipated income items are. Identify the areas of greatest vulnerability—where would your organization be hurt the most if money you've included in the budget doesn't come through? Your organization might want to develop a "worst-case scenario" budget, so you can think ahead about how you would adjust your fundraising plan accordingly.

EXAMPLE: Save the Banana Slugs (SBS), an Oregon-based nonprofit, has always received half its budget—$25,000 out of its annual $50,000—from a local timber company trying to better its reputation. The company has indicated a willingness to renew that support. However, SBS has heard rumors that the company will be sold to a multinational conglomerate whose motto is "Cut the trees down and get out of town." SBS therefore creates two budgets—one including the projected $25,000 in corporate support, and another that omits the $25,000 (and cuts certain staff and programs to make up the difference).

Administrative Overhead

Your public relations needs can have a major impact on your budget planning. Every nonprofit needs to pay careful attention to how much it spends on actual services and programs, versus how much goes to administrative costs—the salaries, equipment, and supplies for people and activities behind the scenes, such as management, accounting, and fundraising. Your grant makers and individual supporters will be keeping an eye on the ratio between these two amounts, and will cast a wary eye whenever more than 35%–50% of your total budget is spent on administration.

This doesn't mean that your organization absolutely cannot spend more than 50% on administrative costs. Not only is there no law against it, but for some organizations it might even be appropriate. A new nonprofit, for example, might sensibly spend large portions of its budget on administration while building the very programs, and reaching the very size, at which maximum effectiveness and efficiency become possible. The percentage of the budget allocated to administrative costs will then drop quickly. But you'll have to recognize—and make sure your group's leaders understand—that high administrative costs will make your job as a fundraiser harder. Not only do some foundations and corporate funders limit the amount of their grant that can be spent on administration, but they may also simply refuse to support any group that spends too much on administrative overhead in general. When you submit a proposed budget with a grant proposal to one of these funders, you'll have to allot an artificially small figure to administrative overhead in order to get the grant.

If you have a shortfall like this, the pressure will be on the development staff to make up the difference elsewhere—probably from individual supporters, but you'll also have to explain to them why such a high percentage of their dollars is going right back into fundraising and other nonprogram functions. If you're stuck in this situation, at least make sure that your departmental budget allows for sufficient staff and other resources with which to ramp up an individual donor program.

TIP

Grow your nonprofit slowly. Most nonprofits begin with volunteers doing much or all of the work, including fundraising, which all but ensures that administrative overhead and fundraising costs are a tiny percentage of the budget. To avoid tipping the balance, grow your paid staff slowly, only as you really need and can justify it. Resist trying to jump-start growth by engaging in expensive fundraising campaigns.

Look for Places Where Your Organization Sells Itself Short

Nonprofits obviously exist to help others, not to profit from doing so. That means any fees that you charge for services to clients or others should be fair. But many nonprofits have taken "fairness" too far, with the result that they significantly undercharge for their services and end up exploiting their own underpaid staffers. This is a losing strategy—especially when you consider that to succeed in the long run, you'll have to count on those same staffers to stick around and help build your organization.

Client fees have been studied and agonized over in all sorts of contexts, but one conclusion comes through loud and clear: Except when you are dealing with the truly indigent, it's better to charge fees for services than to give them away. For one thing, clients tend to think more highly of services they've paid for. Things gotten for free are seen as throwaways—as evidenced by the phrase I and others heard while providing immigration law advice at a free clinic, "Thanks, but do you think I need a *real* lawyer now?" Later, I learned another valuable lesson: Clients who have paid even a modest fee are more likely to keep their appointments and actively participate in problem solving.

So again, I firmly believe that both your organization's mission and budget will benefit if you charge reasonably for your services. If you've never charged fees before, you'll want to start by understanding how much each service really costs you to provide, then survey your client population to consider how much they can reasonably pay. Often, you'll find that people's incomes are spread across a wider range than you at first imagined, which means that a sliding fee schedule may be a good approach. Finally, you'll have to let your clients know why you're imposing fees (especially if you have provided free services in the past) and what you are doing with the money.

You should also take a close look at other areas where your organization might be able to charge a reasonable fee for services or other benefits it's currently giving away:

- Are you letting a local group use your space at no charge?

- Are you taking members of the public on educational tours or outings that also happen to be fun or much sought after? Full rosters or waiting lists are a sign that it might be time to start charging.

- Are you giving lectures at other organizations' events (for-profit or nonprofit) where the attendees are being charged money? Charging for some or all such things won't turn your organization into the nonprofit equivalent of a Scrooge.

- Are you providing services to private businesses that could afford to pay for them? For example, if you are picking up surplus food from local restaurants to feed the homeless and prominently listing the restaurants as program sponsors, you may actually be providing them with economic benefits (a lower garbage bill and free promotion). If you explain these benefits to the restaurants, they may agree to chip in for the salary of the person who does the food pickup and delivery.

Noncash Contributions

Before rushing out to raise every dollar that your organization needs, consider whether you can supplement your fundraising with:

- in-kind donations of goods, or

- donations of professional services.

You've no doubt seen "wish lists" that other organizations place in their newsletters, event programs, and the like. They're usually for major items of equipment, such as a typewriter, a used car, or a costume for an event. These lists work. Though you can't count on receiving every item on your list, you'll get some of them—and quite possibly from supporters who wouldn't have given money. Some supporters may be more willing to part with a used object than with their hard-earned cash, particularly if it was just sitting in their garage gathering dust.

Berkeley Repertory Theatre's Wish List

Few organizations have as wide and varied material needs as a theatre, and the Berkeley Repertory Theatre, in Berkeley, California, is no exception. As an award-winning, professional company that stages everything from modern world premieres to ancient Greek drama, their props alone fill a warehouse. In addition to paying a good-sized staff, the theater has all sorts of additional expenses, such as apartments for visiting actors and directors, which need furniture, cooking equipment, and more. So, Berkeley Rep posts a wish list in its programs and on its website (www. berkeleyrep.org). You might spot such items on their list as a touch-tone phone, tumbling mats, a forklift, and low-cost physician's services, to name but a few.

I asked Lynn Eve Komaromi, Berkeley Rep's Director of Development for the Annual Fund, how well the wish list has worked: "It's been very successful—sometimes too successful! We occasionally have to refuse gifts, such as clothing. But we've been helped a lot by gifts of washers and dryers, as well as computers. The most common gift we receive is furniture, which we use for the artists' apartments. Someone also once donated a Volvo, so that became the car that our visiting directors used—much better than the old beater we could offer them before.

"We make sure to give donors receipts for their contributions. We also list the names of those who gave high-value gifts within the donor list in our theatre programs, with an asterisk indicating that they're 'in-kind' contributors.

"Although we name specific items on our list, I try to be open to whatever comes along. The most interesting unsolicited gift we got was a live, miniature horse. Not exactly something we could put in our prop warehouse until the right play came along! Fortunately, we had an auction coming up at one of our special events, and someone bought the little horse. We heard later that the buyer had been a bit swept up in the moment, and the next morning had some doubts about what he'd do with his new acquisition. But he had a good friend with a farm, who was delighted to receive the horse, so things worked out happily all around."

An alternative to the wish list is to ask local businesses for equipment or supplies, either new or used (but still serviceable). Nonprofits routinely receive donations of everything from computers and desks to flowers for their front entrance by following this approach. The key is usually to contact the owner of the business directly, and be ready to provide the owner with written materials—and, if needed, references—establishing your credibility. Also be sure to highlight any place that the business will be publicly thanked, such as in your newsletter, website, or event program. If your organization or its key members are regular customers of that business, be sure to mention that, too.

RESOURCE

Need to know more about corporate giving? For more information on the tax and financial aspects of seeking corporate donations, see *Financial & Strategic Management for Nonprofits,* by Herrington J. Bryce (Jossey-Bass). Also see Chapter 10 of this book.

Soliciting in-kind donations is an excellent task for board members and other volunteers, especially for those who find asking for objects easier than asking for money. It's best if you can muster up a good-sized group with an effective volunteer coordinator. Otherwise, you risk diverting board or staff energy from the core of your development efforts. I've fallen into this trap—spending days before an October silent auction running around picking up donated pumpkins from the local grocery store and the like, when I should have been back at the office.

Your organization should always be looking for ways to get volunteers involved, as covered in more depth in Chapter 2. As you look at the budget, see whether any discrete new possibilities emerge, particularly for professional services. If a new program is being created, ask whether the planners considered ways to involve volunteers—including whether any needed positions could be filled by a quasi-volunteer who receives a stipend from another program, such as a Jesuit volunteer (see Chapter 2).

Professionals customarily donate all kinds of services—everything from consulting to proposal writing to graphic or Web design to legal and accounting services. Considering that their hourly rates may look staggering next to your nonprofit's budget, soliciting such donations can be useful and necessary.

As long as the quality of work is good and you can count on the provider to perform as promised, this can be a great arrangement all around. Be aware, however, there are a couple of downsides to accepting such donated services: Your volunteers may not maintain their commitment over time or may not have the time and energy to meet deadlines. Unlike a donated pumpkin, which you can pop into your back seat and take away, donated services usually involve a series of commitments by the donor—meetings, initial proposals, drafts, and final results. These commitments may be hard for donors to keep, depending on their initial motive for volunteering. For example, some service providers use volunteering as a way to launch their business or establish their reputation. If their paying customers start filling their time, you may find your project pushed to the back burner.

Also be careful about accepting free services that the provider wants to leverage into a paid relationship. Unless you're clear at the outset about how much you'll pay and for what services, you could find yourself drawn into an overly expensive or otherwise problematic arrangement. To guard against this, it's wise to lay out your agreement and mutual expectations with any volunteer of professional services in a written letter at the start of the relationship.

Evaluate Your Nonprofit's Fundraising Assets

Every nonprofit's mission, property, program, and history are different, which helps explain why there's no one-size-fits-all fundraising plan. Beyond this, however, different organizations also have different fundraising strengths, both tangible and intangible. This section explains how to evaluate your existing assets, with an eye toward strategically deploying them as part of your overall fundraising plan.

Identify Your Assets

An organization's assets come in all shapes and sizes. The reputation you build by running an effective and well-known program is an asset, as is a building or a truck. Skills, people, and experience can also be assets. Some of your assets would hardly be noticed by outsiders looking at your organization—for example, low employee turnover. With such hidden assets, it becomes even more important for you to identify them and, if and when appropriate, use them to attract supporters or funders.

As you'll quickly realize, many of your organization's assets may not be suited to every type of fundraising. That's okay. In fact, you can expand your fundraising reach by thinking creatively about what types of assets would best attract your different audiences, among them foundations, corporations, and individual donors. Take, for example, CompuMentor, a San Francisco nonprofit that provides technical support for other nonprofits' computing needs. As much as CompuMentor might like to recruit a long list of individual contributors, they've had to realize that attracting them may not be possible in a world where baby seals, hungry children, and disaster victims are the first to capture donors' hearts. For CompuMentor, a far more realistic strategy has been to focus energy on foundation grants. This allows them to play to their real strengths, such as providing a hugely needed service to literally hundreds of other organizations that might otherwise grind to a halt.

Your organization might be in the opposite situation. If you have a program that individual donors can readily understand—such as advocating for urban bike paths or supporting the arts in area schools—but your program doesn't happen to fit neatly into any foundation's niche, you'll want to concentrate on individual and perhaps small business donors.

Some organizations have unusual assets or fundraising advantages. A community radio station, for example, has the airwaves—and can request donations from anyone willing to listen during their pledge drives. The International Institute of Buffalo, New York, resides in a classic 19th-century mansion, the gift of a long-ago donor—which it rents out for meetings and parties. The Berkeley Repertory Theatre, after its annual clean-out of its props and costume warehouse, holds a sale of all the items it doesn't think it will need for a future production. Lynn Eve Komaromi explains, "We get lots of folks who like to shop for Burning Man—they find costumes and bits and pieces for their art displays. It's a win-win."

The people within your organization—your staff, board, and volunteers—may well be its most important assets. Consider people's skills and personalities without being either overly judgmental or overly optimistic. Thinking to yourself, "I'm sure Sarita will finally make time for fundraising this year," or "If I can just talk Jay out of his shyness, he'd be great with major donors," is not likely to make the cash register ring. Instead, identify specific and proven strengths, such as:

- personal connections with particular communities (for example, ethnic, political, or interest-based groups) or potential major donors
- personal connections with foundation staff members or potential corporate donors
- good people skills
- reputation—or even fame
- writing or marketing skills
- artistic skills
- event-coordinating skills
- Internet or computer skills
- ownership of or access to a nice home, club, boat, or other facility
- eagerness to participate in a certain type of fundraising (for example, someone who hates to phone potential donors may delight in running an annual silent auction), and
- any other special skills and interests.

Face—And Embrace—Your Organization's Weaknesses

In the course of considering what makes your organization and its people great, you'll have to also consider what you lack—gaps or weaknesses, personal or organizational, that might undermine the use of a particular fundraising strategy. If, for example, you've got a great writer on your team, foundation support might be an obvious fundraising choice—but if you know that you've already tapped every possible foundation for all your programs and they've all indicated that they aren't interested in funding you for now, you'll probably have to find some other uses for your writer's talents. Or, let's say there's a famous person on your board who could be the keynote speaker at a fundraising event—but that person is controversial or, even worse, disliked by a significant number of your supporters. It will be of little long-term benefit to run a successful event that alienates a significant part of your constituency.

Fortunately, recognizing your organization's weaknesses can help you figure out strategies to minimize them. Rather than writing off the people or fundraising methods you had in mind, consider how to turn supposed negatives into positives. Such creative thinking has been a central theme in the fundraising work of Lupe Gallegos-Diaz, who at one point worked with a national Chicano studies organization. The group had a large membership, but one composed mostly—about 80%—of financially challenged undergraduates, with the remaining 20% mostly underpaid faculty members. Because this population was not ripe for major gifts, the group instituted a campaign asking members for donations of at least $1. In addition, they educated every donor about the importance of giving even a little. Although they didn't bring in big dollars the first year, they got people into the habit of giving, thus laying the groundwork for continued—and larger—gifts in the future.

Another example Lupe cites is of a group whose members were mostly stay-at-home mothers. Because they were neither socially prominent nor affluent, they didn't feel ready to reach out to rich and powerful donors. But they did know plenty of people in their own community who would enjoy a good meal. To start their fundraising, they held a series of in-house dinners, hosted by their own members, with everyone helping prepare food and sell tickets. Later, they used the goodwill they'd developed through these small events to put on a bigger, more elaborate dinner event—by which time the prospective guests knew each other and were eager to attend. The group raised significant funds, and educated many people in the community about their excellent work.

List Your Assets

As soon as you're ready, take a piece of paper and write, in a column, all the relevant assets—whether people, property, or abstract qualities—that you can identify within your organization. When it comes to people, you might want to mention individuals by name, and give each a separate line. Next to each asset or strength, list the types of fundraising it could support.

The chart below will help you create your list of your nonprofit's assets and their possible fundraising applications:

Fundraising Worksheet 2: Fundraising Assets

Asset Type	Asset Description	Possible Fundraising Use
Organization's mission		
Organization's programs		
Organization's reputation or history among certain foundations or individuals		
Organization's access to certain members of community		
Organization's physical facilities or resources		
Physical facilities or resources owned or accessible by board, staff, or volunteers		
Executive director		
Development director		
Development assistant		
Other development staff		
Board members		
Board fundraising committee		
Particularly active individual volunteers		
Volunteer program generally		
Other friends of your organization		

Don't just fill out this chart on your own and put it in a drawer. Take a blank version of the chart and meet with staff, board members, and other stakeholders. Ask them to brainstorm and record their ideas on the chart. Remind them about the various tasks and activities involved in fundraising, and ask them to think specifically about what and whose skills and advantages might be helpful. Explain the reasons behind some of the items on the list—for example, under physical facilities, a boat could be used for a special event, or a weekend at someone's lakeside vacation home could be offered up during a silent auction. Your brainstormers may come up with something you didn't think of—or didn't even know about. For example, a board member might say, "You know, my brother's wife is part of a famous band that sings about social justice issues—I bet they'd do a benefit concert for us!"

After you've collected input from others, create a master chart of your organization's assets and their fundraising applications (using the same format as before). You'll use this to develop your fundraising strategy, as described next. You'll also probably want to refer to this chart again during next year's planning process.

> **CAUTION**
>
> **Special events aren't always so special.** When you get volunteers together to think "fundraising," you'll often see most of the excitement and ideas generated around proposals for special events. "Hey, we could do a carnival, with a dunking booth, and I'll bake 1,000 cookies … it'll be great!" In part, this tendency is natural: Most people have more experience with events, from bake sales and raffles to silent auctions and wine tastings, than with any other kind of fundraising. And who wouldn't rather plan a party than write a grant proposal or call ten major donors? Too bad that when you figure all the time and energy that goes into them, special events are, on average, the least profitable form of fundraising (though they have their other benefits; see Chapter 8 for more information). Try to keep your brainstormers focused on the overall goal, the full breadth of fundraising methods needed to meet it, and the assets that might support those methods.

Develop Your Fundraising Strategy

Now that you know how much income you'll need for the coming year's activities and you know your organization's fundraising strengths and weaknesses, it's time to figure out how you'll get the money. Start by calculating how much money you'll have to raise. From the total amount you'll need for the coming year, subtract the amount of money that you can count on receiving, such as committed grants and fees for services you're fairly sure to provide. The number that's left is the amount you'll actually need to raise. You're now ready to decide on a fundraising strategy—that is, to identify which of the fundraising techniques or sources described in this book can be tapped for maximum advantage. You'll have to consider some general tactical issues, such as what your core assets are and how much you'll need to diversify your funding sources. Then consider how your assets match up with the possible range of fundraising methods. Finally, make sure the board and key staffers are enthusiastically behind the final plan.

Tactical Considerations

Your fundraising strategy should depend, in part, on your organization's purpose and goals. Make sure you stick with those fundraising activities that are time-tested or core to your organization's identity; stay within the boundaries of your organization's strategic plan and mission; and otherwise try to diversify your funding sources and activities.

Although you should engage in an open-ended planning process, that doesn't mean that your whole fundraising strategy has to change. If certain fundraising activities have worked well for your organization in the past, you'll probably want to continue to use them—they are proven assets, and may contribute positively to your group's public image. There's no point in junking a well-run individual member program (ever), or a much-loved annual event (unless it's truly draining other resources or you feel you've gotten into a rut). In fact, donors appreciate a certain degree of consistency. Just as with fast food restaurants, there's a certain value in letting people know what to expect in terms of offerings and quality. Some supporters may even mentally plan around your traditional fundraisers, thinking "I'll buy my greeting cards from X organization again this year, and take my friend Cynthia to its annual auction." If you bounce between an auction one year, a holiday tree sale the next, and a walkathon the year after, you may confuse and frustrate your most loyal supporters.

Fundraising isn't tangential to an organization's work; indeed, to be truly effective, fundraising must be an expression of a group's philosophy and identity. For example, the Mayflower Historical Society would probably not do too well with a rock concert, and the West Flatbush Neighborhood Improvement Association might concentrate on getting new individual members who live in and care about the neighborhood, not on soliciting large corporate donations.

> **TIP**
>
> **Focus on individual donors.** No matter how else you plan to raise money, virtually every nonprofit should be trying to increase the number of people who support it each year and the amount of money each of these individual donors gives. Not only does increasing member support send an important signal about your organization's vitality to larger donors; it's also an important hedge against economic hard times.

You should also try for a certain level of diversity among funding streams—we all know the risks of putting all your eggs in one basket. It's sad to watch all the work and energy that goes into building or developing a program go down the drain because the funding faucet gets turned off. And sometimes the staff who get laid off are the lucky ones—the remainder have to pick up the workloads they left behind, because of promises made to the remaining funders.

At the same time, you'll want to diversify thoughtfully. Having numerous baskets each holding one egg can be problematic, too. If you have too many separate sources of funds, each with its own time, staffing, and reporting requirements, you'll be pulled in too many directions to be effective. Maybe that's why a study of the nation's largest nonprofits—with revenues over $50 million—came to the surprising conclusion that concentrating on just a few funding sources helped their success. The National Wild Turkey Federation, for example, has found hunters to be its biggest and best funding source. (See "How Nonprofits Get Really Big," by William Foster and Gail Fine, *Stanford Social Innovation Review,* Spring 2007.)

EXAMPLE: Nonprofit X had built a successful track record at providing overnight shelter and job training to the city's homeless population. The city and county government knew that the agency's work directly improved conditions in their area, so they were all willing to pony up a few thousand dollars when asked. There was just one problem. Nonprofit X had never built up much of an individual donor base. Meanwhile, the city and county money was restricted to program activities—little or none of it was allowed to go toward administrative overhead costs. That meant it was always a scramble to pay the E.D. and accounting staff's salaries, and hiring a development director was out of the question. Less and less time was devoted to soliciting individual—and unrestricted—donations, and the financial picture got progressively worse. Everyone knew that the loss of any one of the main funders could bring down the entire agency.

Instead of trying to diversify the funding, the E.D. kept applying for more grants from local governments, hoping to pool enough overhead funding from the contracts to make up the shortfall. Unfortunately, with every grant came new requirements—to provide more beds and more trainings, which required more staff time.

The funding situation finally hit a crisis point—when the overworked staff members (those who didn't quit) were ready to mutiny. The board, which had been reluctant to acknowledge how critical the situation was, finally couldn't stand idly by. A new fundraising plan was developed, which focused on outreach to individual donors and foundations. A new E.D. was also brought in—with a firm mandate to implement the new plan and end the agency's overreliance on restricted funds.

The ideal is to have a manageably sized mix of stable sources providing the bulk of your budget, with some additional sources to provide balance, create future potential, and fill in the fundraising gaps. Author and expert Kim Klein recommends that no more than 20% of your total funding come from any one person or source. (See *Fundraising in Times of Crisis,* a Chardon Press Series book from Jossey-Bass.) She also recommends that no more than 20%–30% of your total budget come from foundation or government sources, because foundation money tends to dry up after a year or two, and government funding is notoriously affected by recessions and elections.

CROSS REFERENCE
Information on developing donor diversity. Diversity among the race, ethnicity, and lifestyles of your donors is also worth striving for. Refer to Chapter 4 for information on developing such diversity.

Spread Out Fundraising Responsibilities Among Your Staff

The goal of diversifying applies not only to your fundraising sources—where the money is coming from—but also to the people who go after it. If you've ever worked in an organization where the E.D. or development director quit, and all development efforts went stagnant for a few months because no one else had any idea what was planned or underway, you know all too well what this principle means. There are similar dangers in having one person who reigns over development efforts and guards his or her territory from other's input and participation like a jealous Gollum in *Lord of the Rings*.

If you are unable to hire a large development staff, it's even more important that various members of your board, as well as other volunteers, are committed to your fundraising program. There may even be times when you want to build activities into your fundraising program specifically to keep certain board members enthusiastic and involved—sort of like writing the script to fit the actors.

Your First Draft Plan

Now it's time to make some important decisions about your future fundraising activities. This is not a task to handle alone; instead, bring in some combination of the E.D., development staff, and key board members (depending on your organization's size and number of paid staff). Pick up the chart that was created of organizational assets and possible fundraising applications. You'll use it to create another chart, shown below, in which you choose the best fundraising activities for your organization and make sure that these activities will help you reach your goal without draining your budget. Plan on creating several copies of the chart below, for drafting purposes.

Fundraising Worksheet 3: Fundraising Strategy Chart

Activity or Funding Source	Amount It Should Raise	New or Unusual Expenses	Total Amount (column 2 minus column 3)
	$	$	$
	$	$	$
	$	$	$
	$	$	$
	$	$	$
	$	$	$
	$	$	$
	$	$	**Grand Total:** $

Using this chart, play around with various scenarios. Start by choosing a promising fundraising activity, such as "proposals to foundations," in column 1. Estimate how much you'll be able to raise through that activity in column 2. Then estimate any new or unusual costs the fundraising activity will require in column 3 (which is there to make sure you don't render your departmental budget irrelevant). Particularly if you're shifting course toward a strategy that requires a high up-front investment, such as a new direct mail program or special event, you'll need to estimate the added costs carefully and make sure that they aren't going to break the bank. Subtract the amount entered in column 3 from the amount in column 2, and enter the result in the fourth and final column.

As you go, keep a running total of the amounts entered in column 4, until the "Grand Total" equals (or preferably exceeds!) the amount you need to fundraise for that year. (To get even more scientific about this, you might go back to your department budget to see if there are any costs you won't be incurring because you've shifted strategy away from the activities with which those costs were associated.)

Let's say, for example, that your organization is a clinic. Its greatest asset may be satisfied ex-patients and their family members, who already support a successful major donor program. The major donor program is no doubt worth continuing—or better yet, increasing at a realistic rate. Enter the likely fundraising proceeds in column 2 (and, if you're expanding, any new costs in column 3).

However, even an expanded major donor program probably doesn't cover all of your monetary needs. Moving on down your assets chart, you may see that you have a volunteer who is willing and able to take patients' artwork and turn it into greeting cards, and another volunteer willing and able to market the cards. This may, however, require some up-front investment (unless the cardstock and printing are donated). Enter the amount this strategy could realistically raise in column 2, being sure to estimate the new expenses in column 3.

Check your running total from column 4 to see how much that leaves to be raised from other funding sources. Grant proposals to foundations, corporations, or government are a likely prospect for most nonprofits. In the clinic's case, submitting proposals would be particularly appropriate if the organization's assets include a good reputation, any history of foundation support, current board or staff members with inside contacts, and someone who can write up a compelling proposal.

Keep matching up your organization's greatest strengths and their corresponding fundraising uses, being sure not to assign more tasks to any one person than he or she can handle.

Also remember that your department will have to take on responsibilities that don't raise money directly. You'll need to decide what tasks the development office will carry out that won't have an immediate payback, such as preparing an annual report, setting up a new database, or planning appreciation events for major donors. Make sure you've left time for someone to take care of these activities, too. Play around until you've found a way to raise all the needed money.

Finding a balance that seems to work is incredibly satisfying—but it's no cause for complacency. In fundraising, as in everything else in life, things can and will go wrong. Pick up that chart one last time, and ask, "What if?" For example, what if several major donors don't contribute this year? What if your board member with the party yacht takes it on a year-long trip to New Zealand? What if donations to your silent auction aren't as generous as in past years? Focus only on the greatest, foreseeable risks—there's no point in obsessing over plagues, floods, or pestilence. But now that you're scared a little, modify your plan so that you have an adequate financial cushion if things go wrong.

Strategize With—And Seek Buy-In From—A Larger Group

Creating a fundraising plan involves estimating how much help, and what type of help, you'll get from the people involved in your organization. Before chiseling your plan in concrete, it's wise to make sure that all these folks will happily support it. You should have already enlisted their voices at the brainstorming stage—now it's time to go back to them at the commitment stage. Draft your preliminary fundraising plan and present it to staff and board members, at the same or at separate meetings. If there are key volunteers outside the board, meet with them separately.

You have three principal objectives in holding these meetings. First, you want to give people a clear idea of what it will take to raise a particular amount of money. Second, you want to give them an opportunity to be heard, so that you can, if necessary, adjust the plan based on their ideas. Third, you want to be sure that they buy into the plan and will commit to doing the necessary work.

To facilitate this process, create a final version of your fundraising strategy chart. Distribute copies, labeled "Draft," to everyone in attendance. Go through each intended fundraising activity one by one, explaining whose help will be needed, how much work will be asked of them, how much up-front investment the organization will be adding, and the risks of failure. If there are any alternate plans you considered and rejected, or are still considering, describe these as well.

Then it's time to sit back and listen as open-mindedly as possible. There is no need to be defensive—if your ideas are excellent, others will come to see that. One effective strategy for doing this is to start by writing down everyone's ideas on a whiteboard or easel-mounted pad. It's best to use just a few words for each, saving discussion for later. Once this is done, come back to those ideas, one by one, to consider them as a group. Be clear, however, about who will make the final decision on the fundraising plan.

If you are hearing major resistance to a particular element of the plan— especially if it's from the very people on whom you're relying to carry it out—it may be time to rethink. Try to gauge the level of resistance. If you're hearing embarrassed laughter about the prospect of soliciting in-person donations, then a pep talk or training may be all that's needed to tip the balance. If, however, you've got a room full of stone-faced board members who think that starting a car donation program is the worst idea they've ever heard of, it's time to reconsider—unless you want a parking lot full of used cars and no one to service them but yourself.

If, at the end of this planning process, you realize you don't have enough staff or volunteers to raise the needed funds, talk with the leaders of your organization. You may need to invest time and resources in finding this help before setting your budgetary or fundraising goals. In the worst-case scenario, your organization may have to scale down its programs or ambitions, or look into merging with another organization. These can be painful decisions, but ones that will be better in the long run than hobbling along without sufficient staff or funding.

Create the Final Plan

You'll want to write your fundraising plan down, so that you and others can remember what you decided and refer to it later. But this isn't like school, where more pages get you a higher grade. A document that's padded with lofty expositions of your goals, spreadsheets, and long-winded analyses will intimidate everyone and undermine its very purpose. Keep it simple and usable.

You'll need to choose a format for your fundraising plan, because you'll need to develop one that works for you and your staff—one that everyone will intuitively understand and want to look at. It can be as long or as short as you want it to be. Some helpful components to include in your plan are:

- **An indication of the time duration of the plan.** One year is the standard, but it can also be helpful to include less detailed projections for the next few years.

- **A narrative description of your various goals.** For example, if the plan is to continue on your current course, say so—or if it's to reduce the amount of donor mailings by a certain number in favor of spending time on special events, describe that. And again, include goals that support fundraising indirectly, such as staff training, projects involving your database and website, and the like.

- **A calendar showing what you'll work on month by month.** This should including mailings, grant proposals, events, and whatever else you've decided on.

- **A breakdown of responsibilities.** Describe who will lead each task, who else will be involved, and if appropriate, approximately how much time the person will devote to this task. For staff persons, this can be expressed as a percentage of overall time.

- **How you'll measure interim success over the year or years.** (Plan on revisiting your plan at least quarterly, to see how reality is measuring up to your projections.)

- **Descriptions of backup plans if particularly risky strategies don't pan out as hoped.** The picture is sure to change over the course of the year, and having a "Plan B" is a great way to minimize any shock or need for new planning meetings.

Once you've written the plan down, make copies for the appropriate people and slip these into colorful folders. Also post the plan on your internal server if your computers are networked, and do whatever else it takes to make sure that everyone can find it. Emphasize your commitment to making this a living document by bringing it to board or management meetings, reporting back on progress toward its various goals, and asking for feedback on what's working and what isn't.

And don't forget to draw up a new plan when the old one runs out. Preparing a detailed fundraising plan once a year is a good idea. This doesn't mean reinventing the wheel or overturning your strategy every year—it will get easier each time. Part of your organization's goal should be to develop an annual cycle of fundraising, in which you develop years-long relationships with donors and funders. The more systematic you get about this, the easier it will become.

Fundraising Pros Start With a Plan

With 30-plus years of development experience, Christine Grumm of the Women's Funding Network has come to appreciate the importance of planning ahead. "People go wrong by not having a plan—they start out assuming that they should simply write a grant or ask for money. But they've forgotten to do the up-front work of understanding the various possibilities. It's a very systematic process. You can't just look at a grid of fundraising techniques and say, 'I'll do some of this and some of that.' Unless there's a connect between the financial need and the assets that you have to support that need—such as a Board contact, or interest on the part of foundations—it's not going to happen.

Attracting Individual Supporters

The day-to-day work of a nonprofit can feel isolated. Your staff may be toiling away on research projects, meeting one-on-one with low-income clients that society seems to have forgotten, or worrying about an indigenous population a continent away. However, you have a nearby constituency and a support network you may never see: your donors and dues-paying members. I'll call them "supporters" or "donors." Some people also use the term "investors."

Think about organizations that you have given money to—didn't you feel that you personally were helping to clean up a waterway, save a dog or cat from being euthanized, or release a political prisoner? Until every member of your staff realizes that these unseen supporters are a vital part of your work, and learns to communicate with and actively solicit more of them, your organization will be heading towards stagnation.

Why Not Call Them "Members"?

In some states, the word "member" has a specific legal meaning in the nonprofit setting—it indicates a person with legal rights to participate in and sometimes vote on important organizational decisions such as appointments to the board of directors, amendments to the articles and bylaws, the sale of certain assets, or mergers with other nonprofits. Most organizations don't want this many people involved in such decisions. Therefore, they go without a formal membership structure (stating this in their articles and bylaws), and avoid using the term. For more information, including state-by-state summaries of membership rules, see Anthony Mancuso's *How to Form a Nonprofit Corporation* (Nolo).

From a practical standpoint, recruiting individual supporters is particularly worthwhile, because their donations come with very few strings attached. While a grant from a foundation or the government may yield your organization a lump sum of tens or even hundreds of thousands of dollars, such grants can come with enough restrictions to significantly hamper your work—and paperwork requirements that gobble up precious staff time. Many foundations insist, for example, that an unreasonably low figure be allotted to the costs of managing your organization, or pressure you to prove immediate success in settings where it can't be realistically measured. New or smaller nonprofits may have difficulty attracting grant money in the first place. Also, a grant may be here one year and gone the next.

When fundraising professionals are asked about their strategy during economic downturns, they almost inevitably say, "We're looking to our individual donors." As an unusual example, Habitat for Humanity, when interviewed by the *New York Times* about how it was responding to economic tough times, said it had hired nine additional fundraising staffpersons to solicit major gifts from individuals. (See "Finding a Way to Keep It All Going," by Stephanie Strom, *The New York Times*, Monday, November 18, 2002, page E1.) No matter how bad the economy gets, goodhearted people will part with a small amount of cash—and a little bit from here and there can add up quickly. In fact, individual donors typically account for over 75% of all funds raised by nonprofits. And even better, you can generally use this money as you wish, to fund programs, compensate your staff, or simply pay the rent.

The question for most nonprofits is not whether to solicit funds from individuals, but how to go about doing it. This chapter will address both subtle and more direct approaches to attracting new supporters, including:

- demonstrating that your organization can meet individual supporters' increasingly high expectations

- understanding why people give—and what will encourage them to give to your organization, and

- using direct mail, email, and other techniques to solicit new supporters.

Make Your Organization Look Support-Worthy

Some articles and books on raising money focus on how to bring in the largest amount in the shortest time. Over the long term—and even over the not-so-long term—this can be a huge mistake. Even if you are lucky enough to hit on a magic message that brings in lots of quick cash, your success will not be sustainable unless your organization is worthy of that support—and can demonstrate that to its supporters and the public at large.

Individual supporters don't normally attach conditions to their donations, but that doesn't mean they don't have expectations. Just the opposite—a number of forces are driving individual supporters to expect more and more from nonprofits in terms of efficiency, results, and reporting—and to be suspicious if they don't get this information. Of course, your supporters don't have the time or energy to poke around behind the scenes to see whether your nonprofit is really what it claims to be. They'll have to rely on more external indicators, such as your publications and media coverage. This doesn't let you off the hook—the true quality of an organization's work and people becomes known in the community one way or another, and its reputation eventually affects its ability to attract financial support.

Although there are a number of metrics by which nonprofit performance can be evaluated, most everyone has their eyes on one ratio: the proportion of funds being recycled into administration and fundraising instead of fueling the core work of your organization. A ratio of more than 50% of your funds going to administrative costs is generally considered too high. And the Better Business Bureau (BBB)'s Wise Giving Alliance (which many look to as a leader in this area) recommends that no more than 35% of total funds raised be churned back into fundraising—and that 65% of a nonprofit's budget be spent on program activities.

RESOURCE

More information on the Wise Giving Alliance's recommendations. The BBB Wise Giving Alliance has published detailed standards to guide nonprofits in developing fair solicitation practices and measures of accountability. These are intended to foster public confidence in, and support of, charitable organizations. You can access their latest standards at www.give.org.

You probably realize how widespread the public's concern over nonprofits' misuse of funds has become. Studies show that the average donor now considers the nonprofit's costs of fundraising and administration in making his or her decision about whether to send a gift. And tellingly, one study of wealthy individuals found that 56% said they would give "a great deal more" to charity if they knew that the organizations were effectively managed. So, while financial accountability and organizational efficiency aren't components of fundraising, they are the cornerstone upon which your fundraising hopes and plans must be built.

Of course, taking the time to build a support-worthy organization is easier said than done. I know firsthand the frustration of having outsiders fussing about your so-called "efficiency" when you're putting in long hours with bare-bones staffing, antiquated equipment, and the world's least ergonomic chairs. And while there is much truth in the prevailing wisdom that the majority of organizational resources should be spent on direct services or programs, it's also true that no organization can succeed over the long term without adequately supporting an appropriate managerial staff. People who can carry out fundraising and other managerial activities are absolutely necessary to keep an organization running—at a minimum, someone has to be there to comply with the various demands for reports and other accountability measures!

What has led to this current fashion for intense nonprofit scrutiny? In large part, it stems from the media's age-old interest in scandal, and its investigative reports on the United Way, the Red Cross, and many far more culpable groups. Hardly a month seems to go by without another nonprofit becoming the subject of a media "exposé" or even a Congressional inquiry.

Another contributing factor is the increasing entrepreneurial savvy among financially successful donors, particularly those who made their own money through high-tech, biotech, or other start-up efforts. Many of them believe (sometimes naively) that the principles that made their businesses successful should be applied in the nonprofit sector as well—though perhaps forgetting that you can't reach optimal levels of efficiency without a certain size and level of infrastructure.

In addition, many foundations have adopted and loudly advertise their own efficiency and accountability demands on the nonprofits that they fund. When you put it all together, you may start to feel like you are working in a Petri dish, under maximum magnification.

The bottom line is that your organization should try to meet or exceed generally accepted guidelines measuring nonprofit efficiency. Even if your organization is a start-up with few resources, you'll need to do your best to keep the administrative side of your operations lean and channel as many funds as possible to the program/services side. This may require you to have volunteers perform some administrative functions longer than you would like, but there is nevertheless a significant bright side to this lean and hungry approach. As your organization grows, careful attention to financial procedures and reporting should help you guard against sloppiness, self-dealing, or worse, embezzlement by a bad apple on your own staff. For example, developing good financial tracking systems will quickly alert you to instances where you're spending more money than is appropriate. And knowing that you can back up your assertions about well-spent donations will make you and your volunteers more confident when it's time to raise funds.

Once you have taken steps to ensure that you are spending donated money responsibly and well, how can you make that apparent to your supporters? This section discusses four ways to demonstrate your financial bona fides:

- deliver accurate, up-to-date reports to foundations, the IRS, and other watchdogs
- open your books and be willing to share financial information with individual supporters
- be courteous and efficient in your dealings with supporters, and
- set realistic but visible benchmarks for success.

Responsible Reporting to Foundations and Government

Running a nonprofit means dealing with a mountain of paperwork. At a minimum, you'll be required to submit reports to your grantors, to the federal government (the IRS), and possibly to your state and local government throughout the year.

Whenever you get a grant, whether from a foundation or the government, you'll likely be asked to write a report, in a very specific format, detailing how you spent the money. These reports may be due once a month, once a year, or somewhere in between. Some funders even require you to provide a financial report before they write a check. While some of the material you provide in the report will be general and narrative, you'll also have to supply an up-to-date accounting of actual costs and expenditures.

For the IRS, your organization will probably need to fill out a Form 990 annually (an informational form, used to assess your compliance with the tax laws; organizations with receipts normally less than $25,000, faith-based organizations, and some others need not file, except that starting in 2008, they must e-file a short form called a 990-N). On your Form 990, you'll need to supply information about where your revenues came from and where they were spent. The Form 990 then becomes a public record. You're obligated to give a copy to anyone who asks for it, or to post it on the Web.

> **TIP**
> **Fill out your Form 990 with an eye to marketing.** Most nonprofits enter minimal information on their Form 990s, just enough to satisfy the IRS and no more. However, the form—in particular, Part III—offers an opportunity to toot your own horn. Part III asks how your nonprofit has used the gifts it received. Why not add some colorful description of your programs, activities, and successes? Though space is tight, there's nothing to stop you from adding a supplementary schedule, telling the story as you want the world to hear it. Some potential supporters will review this information when deciding whether to give.

Some state governments also monitor nonprofit finances. Most states now require nonprofits that solicit money from individuals to register with the state. In addition, a few states also require financial reports in connection with nonprofits' regular re-registration. All of these reports may become public information. Most states now publish the nonprofits' reports in some form— including on the Internet. For more information, see Anthony Mancuso's *How to Form a Nonprofit Corporation* (Nolo).

Apart from these registration requirements, many states also require registered nonprofits to submit reports (annually or in connection with each fundraising campaign) detailing how much they spent on fundraising activities in order to bring in a certain amount of donations. These states also tend to require that, along with any request for support, the fundraising organization disclose to prospective supporters the percentage of their donation that will be used for fundraising purposes.

Will your individual donors ever see these various reports? Probably not, unless they're savvy enough to look up your Form 990. But that doesn't mean the information won't come to them by other means. For example, investigative reporters have become dogged about checking out Form 990s, always looking for the latest, hottest nonprofit ripoff. And a number of groups now evaluate and compile data on nonprofits, using the Form 990s and other reports. Potential donors can view the results on the Internet, on websites such as:

- **www.charitywatch.org,** by the American Institute of Philanthropy. Provides grades on selected nonprofits based on their financial practices.

- **www.charitynavigator.org.** Rates nonprofits on a four-star system based on their short-term spending and long-term sustainability, with a detailed financial analysis of each group reviewed.

- **www.give.org,** by the Better Business Bureau Wise Giving Alliance. Provides reports and information on nonprofits, reviews them against a list of 20 standards, and posts complaints about nonprofits in the United States.

- **www.guidestar.org,** by Philanthropic Research, Inc. Posts the Form 990s of virtually every nonprofit in the United States, and allows nonprofits to register and post information about themselves.

I highly recommend that you have a look at these websites. Search for a few organizations that you know, and see how well—or poorly—they appear onscreen. Ask yourself whether you would continue to support an organization whose expenses appear disproportionately high. Also notice how half-hearted it looks when a nonprofit has an opportunity to register on a site (which usually involves merely filling in a few blanks) but doesn't—and vow never to make the same mistake.

In a world in which people are more and more demanding of information, and increasingly adept at Web research, the message is clear: Recording high quality, transparent financial and other information is crucial to your success at attracting not only institutional support, but individual donors as well.

Share Financial Information With Supporters

Your organization has to compile financial reports and statistics for funders and the government, and there's no reason not to make this information available to individual supporters. You'll enhance your credibility—and convey that your organization is committed to good planning, wise spending, and rigorous oversight practices—by presenting the information up front. (In many instances, this may require your fundraising staff to keep in regular contact with your accounting staff—always a good idea.)

There's no need to overwhelm your supporters with facts and figures. Instead, concentrate on clearly and concisely providing the key financial metrics that will allow them to judge whether you are meeting your goals in a cost-efficient way. The data they are most likely to want are the spending ratios described above, as well as your budgets for particular projects. It's also helpful to your donors—and very effective for fundraising—to break down expenses on a "per unit" basis, such as "every $4 allows us to feed one hungry person for a day."

Your website is an excellent place to post this sort of information. More and more potential supporters, upon hearing about an organization, reach first for their mouse to check it out online, writing a check only if they like what they see. Because these folks will be very interested in your finances, you should make that information easy to find.

For an example of well-presented financial information, check out the website of the Global Fund for Women (at www.globalfundforwomen.org). In late 2007, if you clicked on "About GFW," then on "Financial Highlights," you would have quickly found the following information for their most recent fiscal year:

The Global Fund for Women recorded approximately $11.6 million in revenue and support in fiscal year 2005–2006…On the expense side, the Global Fund for Women ended the fiscal year 2% under budget. Of total expenses, 79% was allocated for Program Services and 21% for Fundraising and General Administration.

That paragraph provides most of the information readers will want, in a manner that's clear, straightforward, and easy to find.

You should also include financial information in any newsletter you regularly send to supporters, perhaps in an article entitled "Where Your Money Goes" or "How Your Gifts Support Our Services." Important tidbits of financial information can also be incorporated into articles on other topics. For example, if you're discussing a particular program, you might discuss the challenges of raising funds when "bus rentals to transport the children cost $250 alone." Specific dollar figures catch people's eyes and make them better understand why you're tackling an ambitious financial goal.

If you don't have a newsletter or website (and many new or struggling organizations don't), you might consider preparing an annual statement of your finances. You can send your statement along with a mailing, or simply make it available to interested supporters. You should also include financial and budgetary information in any written material you present in individual meetings with potential major supporters, as discussed in Chapter 6.

Be Professional in All Contacts With Supporters

Supporters will see every interaction with your organization as a reflection of how well you actually deliver services or fulfill your mission. A donor who gets a thank-you letter from your marine mammal protection organization three months after contributing probably won't think, "Oh, they must have been too busy saving the whales to get to my letter"; instead, he or she will probably wonder, "Hmm, if this place can't get its act together to answer one little letter, how are they going to save a whole whale?"

Of course, thanking supporters promptly is just one of the ways your organization can demonstrate its good management and interest in donors. Other ways include good writing and careful editing of letters, newsletters, and website content; returning phone calls courteously and promptly; handling supporters' checks and credit card pledges responsibly; and demonstrating an obvious desire to treat supporters as both friends and, at some level, customers.

Knowing that you're under this kind of scrutiny can raise your stress levels—but it can also give you a sense of purpose as you engage in the tedious tasks of printing out supporter acknowledgments, checking your supporter database for mistakes and duplications, entering new data quickly, and so on. Make sure your staff and volunteers understand the importance of such tasks—and be sure to thank them profusely when they do them well.

TIP

Respond to donors' questions quickly. When a donor or prospective donor asks anyone in your organization a question, you are being offered a golden opportunity to engage that person in a subject that already interests him or her. Don't pass it up. Promptly pick up the phone, fire up your email, or even better, arrange to meet for coffee.

Focus on Your Successes

If you can focus the public's perception on the great work that you're doing, you'll defuse the concern over ratios. Who's going to quibble about how much you're spending on services if it's clear that you're getting a giant bang for your buck? To convey this enormously positive and effective message, fundraisers need to sit down with program staff and look hard at what you're really achieving. Try to break things down—look not only at your long-term goals, but at the step-by-step or indirect successes that you achieve along the way.

> **EXAMPLE:** A youth project runs an after-school program that gives kids who might otherwise join gangs an opportunity to build friendships and leadership skills, and to learn about their ethnic heritage. One of their funders has asked them to prove that they've measurably changed society and reduced teen violence. Because it's hard to prove this kind of major impact, the group is understandably nervous. However, when they sit down to consider successes they can share with the funder, they come up with the following:
>
> - the number of students who voluntarily join their program each year
> - the percentage of students who regularly attend the program
> - the number of students who have voluntarily met with counselors on a long-term basis
> - the improvement in their students' grades relative to the rest of the students in their school, and
> - the community service projects that the students have successfully completed.
>
> All of these are legitimate successes. If their program wasn't really providing a valuable service, the kids wouldn't be coming, improving their grades, and giving something back to their community.

Part of your job as a fundraiser is to identify these successes and communicate them effectively to your supporters and the public.

Understand What Motivates Your Supporters

If fundraising scientists could definitively locate the "giving bone," bankrupt or struggling nonprofits might become a thing of the past. The question of what motivates donors has been examined in excruciating detail by fundraising professionals, but at some level, this discipline will probably always be in its infancy. After all, understanding givers' motivations doesn't directly lead to knowledge of which fundraising techniques will tap into those motivations. Almost as soon as a particular technique achieves outsize returns, it becomes overused, which in turn causes donors to pull back. An example is the heart-wrenching direct mail appeals that became popular in the '80s (they worked brilliantly for a few years, until everyone's mailbox became full of pictures of clubbed baby seals).

Still, it helps to have some understanding about what leads people to give, and especially to give to one type of cause over another. This section looks first at the more abstract, altruistic reasons for giving, then at the more tangible benefits you might offer donors in return for their support.

Why People Give

Despite what some cynics maintain, evidence is mounting that humankind possesses a sense of altruism, and gives to charity accordingly. Some sociologists even claim that an instinct to help others is hardwired into the human race, as a way of ensuring group survival. The statistics certainly look good: Though the U.S. economy has its ups and downs, Americans tend to be generous in their giving: an average of 70% of households give some money to some causes. And total giving climbed to an all-time high of nearly $223 billion in 2006.

With numbers like that, you may already be realizing that it's not just the rich who give—in fact, studies consistently find that the typical donor is middle or lower income. So you should feel comfortable approaching people with the sense that their hearts and minds may be generally open to giving. It's just a matter of finding the supporters who will give to your organization.

But there are clearly limits on everyone's altruism. If a belief in supporting the needy were universal, there would be a lot more giving and a lot less need. Clearly, then, some other motivators are at work.

Why Altruistic People Choose One Cause Over Another

People's motivations for giving become clearer when you look at how people choose how much to give, and choose between the various good causes seeking their support. People seem to give when they feel they will get something in return—something that satisfies them at a deeply personal level. Although the giveaway baseball cap or coffee mug might tip the balance for a few, most are looking for something loftier, but no less tangible. These rewards might include, for example:

- feeling good about themselves
- returning a favor, if they or their family has been helped by a particular organization
- getting a tax deduction
- helping solve a social, environmental, political, or medical problem that they find personally important or that has affected their friends or family
- sending a message about their beliefs
- receiving quality information about a topic that interests them
- aligning themselves with friends, peers, or a community, or
- bringing about justice, or even vengeance, in an area where they or their loved ones have been hurt.

If the length of this list surprises you, remember that people are complex and often have more than one reason for giving. For example, you might give to your college alumni association because giving makes you feel good, because you get a tax deduction, because you feel that supporting quality education will help society, and on top of this because your alumni friends asked you to give! But, by the same token, if you get a letter from an organization within which you have no prior friends or contacts, which supports a cause that has never touched you or your family personally (say, the restoration of a landmark in a city you've never visited), about which you have no interest in reading a newsletter, and whose message you might agree with in the abstract but don't feel strongly about, you're unlikely to support it. (Simply feeling good and getting a tax deduction don't seem to be enough to persuade someone to give to an organization.)

The more links you can draw between a person's motivations and what your organization offers, the more likely that person is to give. Understanding this much about your supporters' motivations can help you devise ways to interact with them. You're looking for a way to hook into each supporter's personal interests—to make him or her realize that your organization has been competently and effectively working on issues close to his or her heart all this time, and is a natural match for his or her support.

Of course, it's always a good idea to look first for readily identifiable people who are closely affected by the issue you are trying to address. For example, if you're working on a campaign to block the construction of a shopping mall, you could rush out and buy mailing lists of people who are against shopping malls in general, but a better bet is to start by simply contacting people who live in nearby neighborhoods.

Although some people's links to an organization will be obvious—for example, because they are former patients of your clinic—others can only be accounted for by the vagaries of personal taste. Just as some people like chocolate ice cream better than vanilla, some people will be drawn toward environmental causes, not human rights issues. There's not much you can do to convert people on such fundamental matters (those who prefer chocolate can be pretty adamant about it). But you can learn more about the general characteristics of the type of supporter your own organization will attract.

CROSS REFERENCE

Why people choose one group. Particularly in major cities, you'll often find a number of groups addressing the same cause or issue. In such cases, people may choose the group with the best reputation, or the one in which they know people, or simply the one that got to them first. Virtually all of the advice in this book is intended to help you distinguish yourself from the competition.

Don't Expect Everyone to Give

You'll save yourself some grief by realizing that people whose interests don't line up with your organization's mission aren't going to donate, no matter how strong your message. Finding supporters isn't like winning an argument—you'll rarely convince someone to part with some cash against his or her early inclinations. Even if a person uninterested in your cause was willing to debate with you, you probably wouldn't get a check after you won. The bottom line is that no one has an obligation to support you, no matter how great the work your organization is doing.

If you're nodding your head, or saying "I knew that already," reflect on how easy it is for an organization to give the wrong impression. You've probably seen newsletters whose stridency implied that everyone should support them now, or feel bad if they didn't. I've even heard nonprofit staff shrilly proclaim that all wealthy people should feel guilty about their relative comfort, and therefore give money to their causes. The unfortunate truth is that most affluent people either don't realize how good they've got it, aren't listening, or are already major nonprofit donors. In none of these instances will a guilt-based pitch help—and it might end up breeding resentment.

Find Out Why Your Supporters Give

Within the big picture of why people give in general, or give to particular causes, you'll want to focus on why people choose to give to your organization. Although you probably have a pretty good idea already, further exploration should lead to both useful information and surprises—all of which will help you predict where you might find additional supporters.

As an obvious example, your research might show that most of the people who support your battered women's shelter are women—no surprise there. But you might additionally find that a number of your supporters are the fathers of women who have been abused by their spouses or partners. Or, if your organization works on an age-related illness such as Alzheimer's or macular degeneration, you might not be surprised to find that most of your supporters are in the over-55 age range—but your research might also unexpectedly reveal that a significant number of your supporters are in the medical profession.

Your first step in this exploration is to develop a "donor profile." Developing a profile is not much different from the market research that any business does to learn how and where to sell its product. The object is to find out as much relevant information about your donors as possible, focusing, of course, on aspects of their background or lifestyle that might explain why they feel an affinity to your organization. For example, you might gather the following information about your donors:

- household income
- educational level
- job or profession
- neighborhood of residence
- family status (for example, whether they have children or are caretakers for elderly parents)
- experience with social or medical issues that your organization addresses, and
- recreational activities and hobbies.

Once you decide what you want to know, there are a number of ways to gather the information. The simplest is to survey your existing donors. You can collect information from them along with their pledges of support; call them to say thanks after you receive a contribution and chat a bit about who they are and why they're interested; or send out survey forms along with your other mailings. Negative information can also be useful—you may occasionally wish to send out surveys to lapsed donors, asking for their honest input on how they felt about your organization's performance and why they elected to end their support.

At a more personal level, some organizations set up focus groups, in which a selected group of supporters gather to talk for an hour or two about why they care enough about your organization to support it financially. This kind of research can serve a double purpose—not only does it help your efforts to fundraise from individuals, but the information you gather about community needs and concerns can help you update your mission, design your programs, and approach foundations and corporate funders for support (covered in Chapter 10). If you have a website with a tracking system, this too can provide useful information. You can follow which pages viewers visit the most, and whether these viewers go on to become donors.

RESOURCE

Want more information on surveys? For more information about conducting surveys that will get you the kind of information you need, see:

- *Designing and Conducting Survey Research: A Comprehensive Guide,* by Louis M. Rea and Richard A. Parker (Jossey-Bass), and

- *Mail and Internet Surveys: The Tailored Design Method,* by Don A. Dillman (John Wiley & Sons).

For Web-based surveys, check out these sites:

- **www.inetsurvey.com**

- **www.sparklit.com**

- **www.quask.com**

- **http://intercom.virginia.edu/SurveySuite** (free for the first 14 days, but survey limited to 200 users), and

- **www.zoomerang.com.**

If your organization is already busy (and whose isn't?) and can afford it, you can hire outside experts to do your donor profiling. Plenty of consultants make a profession out of analyzing organizations' existing donor pools, as well as their goals and subject areas, and matching these with a description of its potential new supporters. This matching will become particularly important if you embark on a program of finding donors through the mail, as discussed later in this chapter.

Once you develop a feel for why people give to your organization, it will help inform many aspects of your fundraising efforts, including your personal interactions with donors, the information you choose to convey via newsletters or written appeals, and the steps you take to more actively involve them in your work. For example, an organization that carries out a number of simultaneous projects—such as a greenbelt group that works in a large metropolitan area— might be able to identify one project that really gets its supporters inspired, such as a campaign to stop a housing development on the area's signature mountain. The group should then make sure to highlight this campaign in its mailings and literature.

What Donors Gain Materially

Although receiving tax deductions and freebies aren't the main reasons that people give, they're on the list. This section will help you work these considerations into your fundraising strategies.

Tax Deductions

As a nonprofit corporation organized under Section 501(c)(3) of the Internal Revenue Code, you are eligible to offer tax deductions to those who give you cash or certain other gifts. Many nonprofits throw the word "tax deductible" around when asking for gifts, but not all of them have a clear idea of what this means for the supporter. And even those that do often speak in generalities instead of providing specific information. Here is some basic information that will help you make the issues clear to your donors.

Not every donor can make use of the tax deduction for charitable contributions—only those who itemize their deductions using Schedule A. This means that their itemized deductions must be higher than the standard deduction available to all taxpayers. This benefit isn't lost on potential donors, especially the affluent ones: A 2003 study by the Independent Sector found that itemizing households give 37% more than nonitemizing households. (See *Deducting Generosity: The Effect of Charitable Tax Incentives on Giving,* available through www.independentsector.org.) However, because people who contribute to nonprofits aren't necessarily the wealthiest in our society, you cannot assume that all your supporters will itemize their deductions. Those who don't itemize have no use for a tax deduction, and get no tax benefit from donating to your group.

For those who can use the tax deduction, however, the benefits can be substantial. Taxpayers are allowed to deduct the full amount of their charitable contributions, up to 50% of their adjusted gross income. This helps explain why charitable giving goes up so much in December. People aren't just possessed by holiday goodwill: they also realize that it's their last chance to top up their deductions for the year.

Exactly how much a particular donation will be worth in tax deductions depends first on what type of tax return the donor will file (single, married, etc.) and then on which tax bracket the donor falls into. (The tax bracket is the percentage of income a taxpayer must pay in tax; those who earn more fall into a higher bracket, and therefore must pay a higher percentage of each dollar they earn in income tax.) For every dollar contributed to a charitable group, the donor will save what he or she would have had to pay in tax on that dollar—and because wealthier taxpayers pay more tax on the dollar, they also save more tax by taking tax deductions.

> **EXAMPLE:** Maria, a single woman, earns $29,000 a year in taxable income. That puts her into the 15% tax bracket (at 2007 tax rates). If Maria donates $100 to charity, she will actually be out only 85 cents for every dollar, (one dollar minus 15 cents), because she'll pay less at tax time. Her total expenditure will come out to $85. In other words, she'll be able to reduce her taxes by 15% of the $100, or $15.
>
> If Maria's taxable income were to rise to $32,000, she'd be in the 25% tax bracket. Now, every dollar she donates would cost her only 75 cents (one dollar minus 25 cents). That means her out-of-pocket costs are only $75 for a $100 contribution.
>
> Should Maria's fortunes improve even more in the next few years, and her taxable income rise to $65,000, she'd be in the 28% tax bracket. Every dollar she contributes will cost her only 72 cents, and her $100 contribution will cost her only $72.

Donors in even higher tax brackets than used in the example above benefit as well, but the calculations become more complex, and are beyond the scope of this book.

CAUTION

Donors who take a lot of deductions may have to pay the alternative minimum tax (AMT). The AMT was intended to prevent wealthy taxpayers from avoiding taxes, but has turned into a monster that penalizes middle-class earners with painfully high tax rates. The AMT also happens to be highly complex, so you should advise your donors to consult their accountants for further information.

Donations of property. Donors may deduct gifts of both cash and property (land or personal property). However, special rules apply to setting a value on property—for details, see IRS Publication 561, *Determining the Value of Donated Property* (this is surprisingly readable, and will tell you how to value anything from used clothing to Old Master paintings). If you're planning a vehicle donation program, also be sure to see Publication 4302, *A Charity's Guide to Car Donations*.

Supporters have a particular incentive to donate property that has gone up in value since they bought it, such as stock. If they sold the property for cash, they might have to pay capital gains tax, thereby reducing the amount of cash they had available to give to charity. By donating the property directly to charity, however, they can deduct the full, current fair market value of the donated item, without worrying about the capital gains tax.

> **EXAMPLE:** Arif bought stock 12 years ago for $100. The stock is now worth $2,000. By donating the stock directly to the charity of his choice, Arif can take a $2,000 tax deduction. If he sold it instead, he would owe tax on his $1,900 profit.

Quid pro quo contributions. The value of a gift of cash or property must be reduced, for tax purposes, by the market value of anything substantial the supporter receives in return. (And, if the gift was worth $75 or more, you must send the donor a written statement with your good faith estimate of how much he or she can deduct, after subtracting the fair market value of the item— though there's an exception for cars, boats, and planes worth over $500.) For example, if a supporter sends you a $80 check that entitles her to a calendar with a fair market value (the amount it normally sells for) of $15, her contribution is valued at $65. It doesn't matter whether your organization paid anything at all for the item—the donor must subtract the value of what he or she receives.

> **EXAMPLE:** A soup kitchen holds a silent auction to raise money. One of its board members donates a weekend at her cabin. Roger and Allison put in the winning bid, at $60. They're excited, because this is a bargain—weekends at cabins in this area usually go for at least $150. However, if they were also hoping for a tax deduction, they're going to be disappointed. Because they didn't pay anything over and above the fair market value of what they received in return, they cannot claim a charitable donation.

Token or insubstantial items, like stickers or bookmarks, need not be subtracted from the donation. (For 2007, their fair market value could be no more than either $89 or 2% of the amount of the donor's payment, whichever is less.) But the cost of raffle, bingo, or lottery tickets is never tax deductible (perhaps because every buyer is hoping for the grand prize). For more information, see IRS Publication 557, *Tax-Exempt Status for Your Organization,* and IRS Publication 1771, *Charitable Contributions: Substantiation and Disclosure Requirements.*

RESOURCE

Need more information on tax rules? IRS publications are available at any local IRS office, or can be easily downloaded at www.irs.gov. If you have further questions, the IRS provides an information line for tax-exempt organizations, at 877-829-5500. Also see *J.K. Lasser's Your Income Tax* (updated annually), by J.K. Lasser (John Wiley & Sons).

Volunteer work. Separate tax rules apply to people who volunteer their services. The market value of the services themselves is not tax deductible. So, for example, if a licensed massage therapist donates services at your health clinic, or a lawyer gives your organization a free consultation, neither can claim a tax deduction. They can, however, deduct the costs of their unreimbursed expenses, including the use of their cars on behalf of your organization (gas, oil, parking, and tolls), and travel expenses if they're away from home (transportation, meals, and lodging).

You're required to send donors a receipt for any gift valued at $250 or more, for them to keep in their tax files in case they're audited. But as a matter of good donor stewardship, you should send thank-you letters that also serve as receipts for all gifts. The receipt can simply be a letter, or even an email, but should always specify the value of the gift. (See Chapter 5 for more about thanking and providing receipts to donors.) For more information, see IRS Publication 526, *Charitable Contributions.*

Freebies

People don't give to good causes solely because of the promotional items they commonly get in return—but they might act faster or more decisively because of them. For example, if you were planning to give to your favorite public radio station anyway, but by pledging within the next hour you'll get a Bulgarian music CD that you can't get anywhere else, you might just get out of your chair and pick up the phone. And, because so many of us procrastinate, this might make the difference between the station receiving your gift right now and the station waiting forever for you to finally take action.

Many organizations offer promotional items in return for donations, particularly when they're asking for an annual renewal of support. The lowest level of donation usually receives a token item (such as a poster) or nothing at all, but each higher level of donation comes with a gift of higher value. It's customary to list the gift premiums on the reply card right next to the suggested dollar amounts. Make sure to include a box to check if the person doesn't want the gift (perhaps because they want to maximize the amount of their donation going toward services or they want the full tax deduction).

From your standpoint, the best promotions are the ones that don't cost anything to produce. For example, those radio station gifts are usually solicited in advance from publishers, stores, and restaurants, who realize that they'll get free advertising in return for giving the station some free or reduced-price products. Some organizations create their own low-cost gifts—for example, artworks or greeting cards with images drawn or photographed by their clients.

> **CAUTION**
>
> **Be prepared to market any homegrown items separately.** The costs of producing items like bumper stickers, mugs, or T-shirts usually mean that you're best off creating a large number at once. However, these could end up in a stack on your floor if not enough supporters respond to your appeal. See Chapter 9 for more on marketing and selling goods for your organization.

Bring in New Supporters

In the early days of your organization's life, finding supporters will usually be a grassroots effort—friends, fellow activists, fellow community members outraged by the prospect of a new local supermall or the like, relatives, and people you meet on the street while getting petition signatures are among those who might be inspired to help. These early supporters might, in fact, be some of your most loyal ones, because they will feel a stake in an organization they helped found and a deep personal connection to your issue or cause.

As your organization grows, however, donations from the cookie jars of your founders' mothers and neighbors won't be enough to pay the rent. You'll need to look toward building a broader base of support, among people with whom much of your communication may be by mail. And you'll need to realize that this is an ongoing task—there should never come a day when you arrive at your office, open your database of supporters, take a count, and say, "That's enough, we have all the supporters we need to keep us going."

The sad truth of the matter is that most of your rank and file supporters probably won't stick around for more than two to three years. That may have nothing to do with the quality of your nonprofit; it's just an average based on other nonprofits' experience of people's giving patterns. In part, it's because many people who give to charity actually prefer to spread their giving around, and will deliberately withdraw their support when they think it's someone else's turn.

Your goal should always be to turn every casual supporter into someone who will stick with you over the long haul (see Chapters 5 and 6 for more on them). Because a fair percentage of your core supporters will come out of your rank and file, you should treat every supporter as a potential major donor in the making.

But it's also important to be realistic. As your organization grows and your relationship with supporters becomes more distant, so does their level of loyalty. Even in a healthy organization, the majority of your supporters will be of the "here today, gone tomorrow" variety. Yet their support remains critical to your organization just the same.

Where do you find the new supporters who will replace those who move, die, or just have a short attention span? Here are some possibilities:

- individuals contacted personally by your board members, volunteers, and staff
- overlooked ethnic, racial, and other diverse communities
- the people your organization serves, or their caregivers or others in close contact with them

- people you meet in face-to-face solicitations
- people who hear about your organization through the media
- people you bring in through special events, and
- people you locate through direct mail solicitations.

> **TIP**
>
> **Don't limit yourself to these techniques.** Converting new donors to your cause is an area where tapping your own creativity is key. And your entire staff, not only your fundraisers, should be encouraged to speak out positively about the work of your organization, and to collect the names, addresses, and other contact information of people who might want to help.

Your Circle of Friends

The most likely people to take an interest in your organization are those you already know, who may be living in the same community, dealing with or personally interested in the same social, political, health, environmental, or other concerns, or perhaps just moved by hearing you talk about your cause. And don't forget people who were once part of your community, but have moved on. Alumni of a school, class, or performance arts group are the most obvious example. Less obvious examples are people who have moved away in search of better opportunities, perhaps from a low-income or rural community. Such people may still feel the tug of their roots, and be willing to help—and their local friends and family are the ones likely to know how to reach them. Even if the leaders of your organization tapped into their own friends early on, remember that as your nonprofit continues and grows, there will be additions and rotations among staff and board members.

It should be a regular policy of your office to ask for names and contact information of potential prospects. If this sounds like a lot of work for a few names, remember that the most effective way to raise money is through personal contacts. For an example of how one organization put this theory into practice, see "Zen Hospice Project Mobilizes Volunteers," below.

The name-givers shouldn't have to worry that you'll hassle their buddies. You can approach potential new prospects with anything from a simple letter to an in-person meeting, depending on what seems appropriate. For further information on personal meetings with potential major donors, see Chapter 6.

Zen Hospice Project Mobilizes Volunteers

The Zen Hospice Project, a San Francisco organization whose collaborative services include residential hospice care, volunteer programs, and educational efforts to foster wisdom and compassion in service, was facing a common challenge: The economy was down, individual donors were feeling exhausted by desperate appeals, and every nonprofit in town was trying to drum up new support. Lisa Ruth Elliott, then–Development Manager, described how Zen Hospice conducted one of its most successful campaigns ever:

"Mailing is generally a good strategy for us, since our organization touches people in a very personal way. However, we decided to take this approach one step further. We really engaged our volunteer caregiver corps—about 150 of them. These are people who ordinarily spend their time in the residential care part of our hospice, interacting on a weekly basis with terminally ill patients. Now, we asked them for their help in taking their stories to their communities, meditation groups, families, and friends, and obtain their support. We put together fundraising packets for them that included talking points, newsletters, brochures, a sample fundraising letter, and a reply envelope. Some of the volunteer caregivers crafted letters based on their own experience—these were particularly effective.

"There was a bit of resistance at first. Some volunteer caregivers said things like, 'This is not something we should have to do,' or 'I'm scared, I can't fundraise.' However, we gave them a lot of support and the opportunity to ask questions as the campaign went along. Once they started to see the generosity of their communities, they got excited about the process. The results were impressive—the volunteer caregivers raised over $35,000 and contributed about $18,000 among themselves."

Your circle of contacts also includes anyone who volunteers for your organization—even if it's just a one-shot deal. If, for example, a local company sends a crew of its employees to paint your building, staff a telethon, or provide other services, don't just say "thanks" and "goodbye"—get names and contact information from each and every person who arrives, then put them on your mailing list. Your first mailing should start with individual thank-you letters, then add brochures and other information on how they can become further involved.

New Friends in Diverse Communities

Some people think that you can raise substantial amounts of money only from society's traditional string-of-pearls elites. It isn't necessarily so: Diversifying one's donor base makes ample sense in a country where minorities are soon to be the majority (and an increasingly affluent majority, to boot). Today, achieving real representative community involvement means we can't all go chasing after the same old donor groups until final bequest do us part.

There's been much study lately on how to increase donor diversity—not only ethnic and racial diversity, but also diversity of lifestyle, age, gender, and physical ability. What the emerging findings show is that you may have to throw some of your old fundraising practices out the window in order to succeed with diverse donor groups.

When it comes to certain ethnic minorities, for example, research shows that their altruism is traditionally directed at groups other than mainstream nonprofits, often staying closer to home with family, church, and community groups. And contributions are often made in forms that fly under the traditional fundraising radar, such as collecting clothing or food for distribution to recent immigrants, or making small cash contributions directly to friends or community groups. Some of the supposedly tried and true methods of attracting new members, such as the direct mail approach we'll describe below, may seem distant and cold—and therefore, may not be effective.

Where and how you focus your diversification efforts obviously depends on the community in which you're located as well as the clients or constituencies you're serving. If this is a new outreach effort for your organization, you have a lot of learning to do and shouldn't expect overnight success. You'll need to think carefully about who your most likely allies are, and incorporate a long-term strategy to attract them into your fundraising plan. As part of this effort, you'll need to identify ways to increase the relevant community's trust in your organization, such as visibly participating in ethnic and community festivals and celebrations, advertising your job openings or special events in ethnic or group-based media, and recruiting diverse staff and board members. In other words, you need to get out and make friends before you can start turning people into donors.

A nonprofit whose own staff and board aren't representative of those from whom they seek support may have a tough time establishing credibility within a new group. Without a history of working together, you may encounter understandable suspicion that you're not "one of them" and are hoping only for a quick new cash source. The most natural way to break through this perception is by strengthening preexisting, natural relationships among your staff, board, and community members. This too will have to involve long-term planning—you can't just fire and replace your trusted staff and board members.

> **RESOURCE**
>
> **Need information on donor diversity?** In addition to the various books on this topic, you can find some solid information online, such as The Association of Fundraising Professionals' discussions of diversity, found via its home page at www.afpnet.org. Also check out the "Youth in Philanthropy" link.

People Your Organization Serves

You may already be overlooking some of your most obvious supporters. Here's a typical scenario:

> **EXAMPLE:** An agency that helps immigrants and refugees opens its phone lines once a week for questions from the public. A woman calls, identifies herself as Kathy, and expresses concern that her children's nanny, who is from El Salvador, has been waiting years to hear whether she'll be granted political asylum. The nanny has a work permit, but nothing more. The staff lawyer explains that this is a normal delay, and describes how to send the immigration authorities an inquiry just in case. Kathy is relieved, says, "Thank

you, I couldn't seem to find this information anywhere else," and they politely end the call.

You can probably guess what went wrong in this example. The lawyer completely missed an opportunity to make Kathy, an already concerned citizen, an active supporter of the organization. It's an understandable mistake—the lawyer is focused on providing direct services to the public, the next caller is already waiting, and the lawyer probably thinks fundraising is "not her department." But it would have been quite simple for the lawyer to get Kathy's full name and address, explain that thousands of people are in her nanny's position, and ask whether she could send Kathy some more information about the organization. That's one more name on the database and at least one more potential check in the mail.

Look at your own organization's procedures and contacts with the public—are there people with whom you're missing a chance to connect? Not just your own clients, but people who call or visit your organization for information, buy a craft article at a fair, or even bring their kids trick-or-treating at your front office can all be given information and an opportunity to become supporters. Also think broadly about your beneficiaries—for example, if you provide child care training services, the parents who hire your graduates are also benefiting from your organization, and should be given an opportunity to support your work. You're not twisting their arms; they can always say no.

What if your organization provides direct services to low-income clients who you believe can't possibly support you now, either by paying fees or making donations? Don't underestimate their value as supporters. For example, if you provide great services for homeless people, who knows better than they the value of your organization? They may even enjoy seeing the endeavor as a team effort in which they have a role to play. In fact, some organizations have found that, until they got better at telling their clients about their fundraising needs, the clients just assumed the money flowed from the government or other source on high—and may have wondered why their service providers often seem frazzled and overbooked.

Even if they are truly penniless, your existing clients may provide help as volunteers, particularly on one-time projects such as painting your facilities or participating in a special event. Longer-term, it's possible that their economic

> ## Looking Beyond Your Client Base
>
> Fundraising guru Tony Poderis tells the following story, which aptly illustrates how a little creative thinking can turn up potential supporters based on their existing links to your organization. (Check out his website at www.raise-funds.com.)
>
> "One of the first organizations I ever worked with was Big Brothers of Greater Cleveland. At the time it served more than 500 boys who did not have fathers at home. The boys' mothers weren't able to give much, but we did a little research and discovered that more than 10% of the women were employees of a local utility. Our funding request to the utility pointed this out and came complete with endorsements from many of those employees. The gift we got was far larger than the utility's usual contribution."

and life circumstances may improve. (That may well be part of your goal in helping them.) Though keeping in touch after the immediate crisis is over can be difficult, try your best.

There's no need to send current clients every fundraising solicitation, but an occasional newsletter may increase their sense of pride in the work that you did together—and result in real contributions down the road. In an immigrants' services organization with which I worked, one of the staunchest supporters was a man from the Sudan whom the organization had helped gain political asylum. He happened to be a highly educated professional; once he got on his feet, he become a board member and tireless advocate.

What if your organization doesn't provide direct services at all, and so doesn't have a client base to mobilize? There may still be ways in which you benefit a sector of the public that doesn't even realize it. Your job is to find those people while they're getting the benefit at issue. An organization in Utah, for example, was working to save an unprotected canyonland from mining and other development. While it relied on some of the traditional techniques for garnering interest and members—such as publicity and mailings—it realized that loads of potential supporters would probably never hear about its existence. To help reach them, the organization took the simple but brilliant step of posting volunteers outside the entrance to one of the area's existing parks. The volunteers briefly explained to people coming to enjoy the park what the future might hold, and asked for financial and other support. In this way, they reached visitors from far and wide, who might never have seen or responded to their local efforts—but who were concerned enough to support the cause.

Grassroots Methods of Reaching Out to Supporters

With recent fits and starts in the economy, the question on everyone's mind is whether some great new technique can be found for raising badly needed funds. Ironically enough, what's "new" on the block is a rediscovery of some of the most traditional, grassroots fundraising methods out there. The value of person-to-person contact is being hailed anew—and rightfully so, especially as potential donors become tired of the barrage of indistinguishable direct mail letters and intrusions by professional telemarketers. In this climate, meeting an enthusiastic volunteer outside a grocery store or coffee shop can seem like a breath of fresh air. An environmental organization in my area has made good use of this strategy, and for a two-month period, one could hardly visit Berkeley's more popular shopping areas without being approached by a friendly young volunteer offering pamphlets and information about California's air and water issues, and signing up members. (I've been talked into giving twice!)

> **TIP**
>
> **Grassroots efforts aren't just for nonprofits anymore.** Even the for-profit sector is discovering the value of personal communication. For example, *The New York Times* reported in early 2004 that a Broadway musical, in order to boost its flagging ticket sales, sent actors out onto the street to sell tickets. Their main pitch was a completely personal one, encouraging people to come see them in a play that night.

Another grassroots technique that shouldn't be forgotten is leafleting. A simple one-page explanation of the issue at hand, what your organization is doing about it, and how people can get involved may be all you need—particularly for urgent or local issues, such as a pending development, a movement to restore a local landmark, or a need to support a local team or school. Don't forget to distribute your leaflets to local business owners, particularly if it's an issue in which they have a vested interest, such as neighborhood aesthetics.

If sending volunteers to wander outdoors seems a bit random, try more targeted presentations. Ask your board and staff whether their church, service organization, or other club would be open to a presentation from your organization. Make your presentation colorful and fun, then tell people how they can join in your exciting efforts through volunteering or donating. People's workplaces are also potential venues for such presentations, particularly if there's a thematic tie-in. For example, I was first introduced to immigration law while sitting around a conference table in a corporate law firm, listening to nonprofit lawyers whose time was spent helping people who'd fled persecution present their political asylum cases to a judge. Like many corporate law firms, mine then allowed me to spend numerous hours helping these clients for no fee.

Supporters From Media Outreach

Getting your name into the public's eye can have both direct and indirect fundraising benefits. Hopefully, at least a few of the people who hear or read a news story about your work will be moved to contact you afterwards and offer financial support or volunteer help. At an indirect level, the more exposure people have to your organization's good name, the more credibility they'll attach to it if and when you solicit them individually. Because media outreach is an important tool for reaching many types of funding sources (not just individual supporters), it's addressed separately, in Chapter 13.

Supporters Through Special Events

Any event that you hold or participate in—whether it be an arts or entertainment event, lecture, crafts fair, walkathon, petition drive, or annual dinner—is an opportunity for you to inspire and bring in new donors. Because special events are an important fundraising tool of their own, and not merely useful for bringing in new supporters, they're covered in detail in Chapter 8. But now is a good time to remind yourself that every special event provides a great opportunity to collect the names and contact information of potential new supporters.

There are various ways to collect this information without seeming intrusive. For example, I once attended a concert given by a nonprofit musical society, at which attendees were invited to enter their names and addresses into a raffle for free tickets to a future concert. Not too surprisingly, I've been receiving newsletters and fundraising appeals from them ever since. (An alternative raffle prize might be items donated by local businesses.) I fell for a similar technique at a theater event recently, in which audience members were invited to "vote" on the outcome of the plot. The ballots asked for our name and address, and also offered a raffle prize. And yes, I'm on yet another mailing list.

Also remember that personal checks you receive from ticket buyers and others have addresses on them. Don't cash them without first making a photocopy, so that you can enter the information into your database.

Be sure to make people aware of your organization's name at any event. I've attended a number of benefit concerts where the charitable organization never made it clear who they were and what they planned to do with the money raised. Perhaps they just weren't very efficient, they assumed that most attendees were long-time supporters, or they were shy about intruding on people's "pure" enjoyment of the event. But in fact, many audience members' enjoyment is enhanced by hearing that they are helping a good cause.

If there's an intermission, the opening of the second half is a good time to have a representative of your organization speak briefly but directly about its work and how donations help. Also make clear where people can pick up brochures or learn more, and put out a clipboard so people can, if they so desire, sign up to be on your mailing list. A collection basket by the ticket desk doesn't hurt, either. And, of course, the event program should mention your organization's name, website, and other contact information, and give a brief blurb on the activities the benefit is helping fund. Many people bring these programs home!

Donors Through Direct Mail

Even if you, your staff, and your board members have used all the techniques described in the earlier sections to attract supporters—personal contacts, media publicity, and special events—you still may not have the numbers of supporters you need or want. And because your budget probably doesn't allow you to buy commercial air time during the Super Bowl, you are eventually almost sure to consider a direct mail campaign.

Soliciting new supporters by mail is a small subset of all the types of mail your organization will send out. It doesn't include brochures, newsletters, or even fundraising letters you send your existing supporters. A direct mail, new supporter solicitation is one in which you beg, borrow, trade, or buy a mailing list that comes from another organization or a marketing specialist. You then send letters to all the names on the list, or to a test sample (usually 1,000 to 10,000 names) from that list, explaining the work of your organization and asking for support.

In theory, you could do the same thing via email, rather than U.S. mail—and of course, do it for much cheaper. However, because of the backlash against spam and everything that could be interpreted as spam, I neither recommend nor cover email solicitation. Today, unless your nonprofit has a highly reputable name that everyone will recognize on the sender line, it will likely be impossible for recipients to separate your message from the hundreds that offer cures for baldness, bad debts, impotence, and supposedly undersized body parts.

Because Internet rules and courtesies are still developing, however, keep your eyes on the nonprofit journals, and keep talking to your colleagues—eventually a way may be found to use email for new donor solicitation. Also remember that this chapter addresses only finding new donors. When it comes to communicating with your existing supporters, email can be a fantastic and timesaving resource, as discussed in Chapter 5. And, as explained in that chapter, you can use your emails to existing supporters to encourage them to get their friends involved in your cause—by forwarding your email to others who might be interested.

> **CAUTION**
>
> **Don't misuse membership rosters.** Many professional, social, and alumni groups publish lists of their members, with contact information—and it can be awfully tempting to borrow a friend's roster and put the members of this select group on your mailing list. However, read the fine print: Many such rosters specifically warn the members that letting the list be used without permission will be frowned upon, or worse. And even if they don't, you are implicitly invading people's privacy—something that is sooner or later (probably sooner) going to anger key supporters.

Most everyone has mixed feelings about direct mail fundraising. We all receive too much of it—whole forests' worth, it sometimes seems. And we're increasingly hip to all the tricks—the "urgent" stamps on the outside, the seemingly handwritten envelopes, the promises of free gifts inside, the little see-through windows trying to fool us into thinking it's a check. It's all starting to look like it was produced by the same band of consultants. In point of fact, even if the letters your organization sends out are understated and honest, the majority will be thrown in the trash. You'll be lucky to break even on your first mailing, and you will probably have to invest a few years in trying out various lists and refining your methods before you see a return in immediate and long-term support.

Worse news still, because of its overuse, direct mail is a method whose effectiveness peaked a few years back, and is now clearly on a downslope. Back when receiving a letter containing shocking facts and asking for urgent help was a novelty, recipients often welcomed and responded to the appeal. Now it's getting harder and harder to even get them to open the envelope.

Despite this trend, however, direct mail can still be a cost-effective way to reach donors who might not hear of your organization by any other means. If you've designed your letters well and sent them to the appropriate recipients, a certain percentage of them will be opened and read. One percent is considered a respectable number, and 0.8% is more normal. While these immediate returns may seem negligible, look at the longer term. Small-time supporters whom you initially find via direct mail may turn into your long-time contributors and major donors—and all for the initial cost of some staff time, some paper, and a stamp.

> **CAUTION**
>
> **Don't start a direct mail campaign until you're ready for major donors.** This discussion assumes that you're in a position to handle donor stewardship and major donor solicitation. If you're not, be wary about investing heavily in direct mail now. If you back out halfway, those initial letter and stamp costs will have been wasted—and they add up fast.

Direct mail solicitation involves much more than simply sending out a bunch of letters. You'll have to choose the right mailing lists, design and write an attractive appeal, have it printed and packaged, and deal with arcane postal regulations if you send the letters bulk mail. Then comes opening the return letters, cashing the checks or running the credit card donations, entering the results into a database, sending out thank-you letters—and just when you think you're ready for a rest, starting all over with another list.

RESOURCE

Want more information on direct mail? This section covers the basics of a direct mail campaign, but you might want to consult some additional resources, like these:

- **The website and products of consultant Mal Warwick** (the self-created guru of direct mail fundraising), such as *Testing, Testing, 1, 2, 3: Raise More Money with Direct Mail Tests* (Jossey-Bass) at www. malwarwick.com.
- *Fundraising for Social Change,* by Kim Klein (Chardon Press Series/Jossey-Bass). Kim Klein's entire book is a must-read, being eminently practical. The book is available at www.chardonpress.com.

Choose a Mailing List

One of your first preparatory steps is to find a mailing list and decide how many people to solicit. In some situations, you can create your own list. For example, if you've just held a special event and you have the names of the ticket buyers, they should go on your list. Similarly, names collected from board members and other volunteers can be added to a mailing list. You can also cull your organization's old records for the names of donors who haven't given for a few years, and have thus been dropped from recent mailings.

Your next best bet is to trade lists with another nonprofit organization. Though that may sound entirely counterintuitive—like everyone trying to take bites out of the same cookie—studies have shown that many supporters give to more than one organization anyway. There's usually no direct harm in revealing the names of your supporters to others, or vice versa. That said, you may sensibly conclude that you want to avoid direct competition with a very similar group. Your best bet is to look for an organization whose work is complementary to yours in a way that reflects underlying affinities between your donors. For example, an ethnic arts organization and an immigrants' rights organization might be logical trades, or a women's musical group and a women's political group.

After a little testing, you can expand your list trading to groups whose members have less obvious affinities to your members. The concept of affinity is both psychologically simple and ultimately unpredictable. Your goal is no more and no less than to locate lists of people who are most like your typical donors—whose hearts are not only in the right place (because they give to charity) but are in similar places when it comes to choosing a charity. With enough testing, you're likely to find affinities you wouldn't have expected. For example, Project Open Hand, a Bay Area organization that provides home-delivered, hot, nutritious meals to homebound people with critical illnesses, has found that donor lists from arts and environmental organizations yield particularly good results for them.

> **CAUTION**
>
> **Watch out for duplicates.** If you're combining lists to get to the number you want, some names may appear more than once. You may want to run what's called a merge/purge to identify and delete the duplicates.

If you've already run through these options, your primary remaining avenue is to rent a mailing list. Sometimes this is loosely referred to as "buying" a mailing list. However, mailing lists are valuable property—you probably couldn't afford to buy the whole thing for keeps. But many are made available for a one-time rental, from sources including other nonprofits, magazines, businesses, museums, schools, and many more. Again, you should be looking for lists of people with likely affinities to your group, but who are preferably not already donors of organizations nearly identical to yours.

Mailing lists vary widely in price, because they vary in quality. The closer the list is to what you need, the more you're likely to pay for it! Before agreeing to rent any list, ask questions to assure yourself of its quality, such as when it was last updated, and whether qualified professionals do the data entry.

To prevent you from copying the list, you will probably never actually get your hands on it—the list will be handled by a go-between. Even if you are given direct access to it, however, most organizations plant a couple of "seed" names into their list, addressed to their own staff or board members, so that they catch anyone who tries to use the entire list a second time. When your organization gets around to trading or renting your list, you should implement the same security measures.

> ⓘ **CAUTION**
>
> **Your own list is a commodity, too.** As your own list of supporters develops, you'll naturally feel very protective of it. You should be—never just give your list away for free. But also consider this: You've got a commodity that can bring in rental fees, and such a source of revenue shouldn't be ignored. You definitely don't want to rent the list out too frequently—both because you'll anger your supporters, and because a less-frequently rented list has a higher value. But with some careful thought, and screening of the list renters to assure that they are appropriate and not too competitive with your own organization, the occasional rental can work for everyone concerned. For the sake of your supporters, be sure to honor any of their requests that you not include their names on any shared mailing lists.

The result of the one-time use practice is that you've got only one chance to turn the names on any one list into supporters. But once a mail recipient responds to your mailing, you're free to continue the relationship. You can see why direct mail solicitation is an ongoing process—you'll need to keep trying out various lists, homing in on the categories of recipients that seem to produce good results, and culling names from there.

Finding a mailing list to rent is a less mysterious process than you might think (although, because of the costs and level of effort, it's probably not appropriate for newer, low-budget organizations). In fact, a whole profession has grown up around matching nonprofits and other businesses with mailing lists, known as "list brokers." Ask your colleagues at other nonprofits for recommendations of good brokers who specialize in working with nonprofits, or look for ads in the *Nonprofit Times* and *Chronicle of Philanthropy*. The great thing is, you don't usually pay the broker directly for his or her services (though you'll pay for the rental of the lists themselves). The broker is ordinarily paid by arrangement with the organization that rents you the list. For more details on this process (when you're ready for it), see "Working With a List Broker," below.

Working With a List Broker

In the typical scenario, you never meet the actual list owner—your broker acts as the intermediary from start to finish. It's best to start by providing the broker with some written materials, including a sample of the mailing you intend to send (it can be a mock-up or an idea, not the completed version) and a summary of what you're hoping for. This summary should include your:

- **Target audience.** This can be as broad as "people who like animals" or as narrow as "biology teachers at private schools along the Eastern seaboard."
- **Rental budget.** Until you get a feel for this you'll probably want to consult with the broker before putting down a figure. There's certainly no upper limit on what you can spend—prices vary depending on who's selling the list and how narrowly you've defined your target audience.
- **Timing.** Explain how soon you need a list and how soon you expect to send out your mailing.
- **Desired results.** State how many names you're hoping to rent.

The broker will then shop around and get you some list options. These may be described on a "data card," telling you each list's rental fee, the date the list was last updated, the spending power of the list members as a whole, and your selection options within that list. Some lists will be too expensive—remember that you're competing for these lists with big for-profit businesses who are willing to spend more than you are. You'll review the rest of the data cards and pick any that look like good prospects. If none seem right, you can reformulate your proposal, perhaps broadening or narrowing the target audience. After a bit of back and forth, you and the broker will arrive at your final choice or choices.

But the broker's role isn't over yet. Once you've arranged the list rental, the broker also helps you access the list—without ever actually letting you lay hands on it. If, for example, you use a printer or a mail house to send out the final piece, the broker would send the mail house the list—and the mail house or printer would be duty-bound to destroy the information or send the list back to the broker when you're done with it.

How large a list should you start out with? That depends mostly on the size of your organization and how much you're willing to invest in initial test mailings. However, the prevailing wisdom is that an initial mailing should include no fewer than 2,000 names and as many as 500,000.

Prepare the Letter and Remainder of the Mailing

Now you have to come up with something to send to this select group. The central item should be a letter, on your organization's stationery, between one and four pages long. With people's attention spans steadily declining—and because too many other groups send out long, heavily underlined pitch letters—I recommend you keep it to one or two pages. If you're going to go for a four-pager, it had better be a real page turner (or start out so strong that only a few people will feel the need to keep reading before donating). Even if you're getting help from a direct mail professional, it's best to keep control of the process, by writing the initial draft of the letter yourself or suggesting detailed material for it.

Before you even get to the text, you've got to figure out who your letter will be addressed to. In fact, you might get hung up on the "Dear So and So." If you've got the technology, it's best to use the person's name rather than "Dear Friend." Here's the first reason why it's important to use a quality mailing list, however. People whose names are misspelled may toss the letter right then and there. ("Dear Friend" sounds far better than "Dear Mr. Carolyn Reeeed.")

A number of nonprofits don't even wait for the "Dear" line to launch into their story. They've found it easier to capture people's attention by starting with a "teaser" paragraph, usually in a different font, in the upper right area of the letter. See, for example, the below sample from the ASPCA, with a photo of a starved dog and an account of his treatment and rescue. The letter then picks up the story from there.

With or without a teaser paragraph, the opening paragraph of your letter can be the hardest to write. Nonprofits have tried every catchy opening in the book. However, the type that seems to draw people in the most effectively is a personal story. This isn't just a quirk among people who donate to charity—human nature makes us all particularly interested in other humans (or animals). If your organization doesn't work directly with living creatures, don't worry—there's always a way to connect it to something alive. For example, one of your volunteers could describe why she has devoted every Saturday afternoon for the

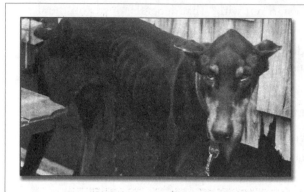

His belly was empty. So empty it hurt. The back door would open and shut, and Astro would hope for food. But his abuser never brought any. In fact, he didn't even look at Astro as he came and went.

Astro drank out of a puddle near the stake he was chained to. The dirty water kept him alive, but then the puddle dried up. Astro had only a few days to live.

last several years to your cause. Personal quotes, either from clients or others participating in your work, are also a powerful way to remind people that you're not just making this stuff up.

TIP

Make the letter from "me" to "you." This is a personal letter, not a college essay or academic paper—so make liberal use of personal pronouns! The letter should address the reader as "you," and be written in the voice of the "I" who will sign it. That helps emphasize the personal connection between the two of you. Any other personal links you can mention—even simple statements like, "I know you share our concern for urban creek protection," will also help to draw the reader in.

In the rest of the letter, you'll want to build on the opening story, so that the reader comes to appreciate:

- the scope of the problem
- why your organization is well placed to help solve that problem
- why this should capture the reader's heart or mind, and
- how the reader can help, primarily financially, but possibly with volunteer and other opportunities as well.

In a way, your letter is like a mininovel. There's a conflict, or perhaps a person in distress. (That someone should be your clients or the cause you serve, not your own organization—potential failure doesn't sell well.) Then there's a duo of heroes—your organization and the person you're reaching out to. The plot you are constructing should also point to the prospect of a happy resolution. This is particularly important, because people's usual reasons for giving often include a healthy dose of self-interest—they want their voices to be heard, and to help create a world that's more in tune with their values and dreams.

Unlike a novel, however, your letter's reader is not going to be curled up in a chair with a cup of hot cocoa. More likely, he or she will be ripping open the envelope while shedding coat, bag, and groceries after a long day's work. This means that your main points need to stand out strong and stand out fast. Some helpful tools for this are old-fashioned underlining and bullet points. You can underline important words or phrases, such as "<u>While our theatre productions are ever more popular, ticket sales only cover 60% of our annual expenses.</u>" If an important list of items is buried in a long string or separated by many commas, think about using bullets to highlight them. For example:

"Instead of having nothing to do after school, youth in our program can:

- participate in our basketball team
- volunteer in community activities, or
- receive one-on-one support from trained counselors."

TIP

If your letter is good enough, you may be able to use it more than once. There's no need to rewrite your letter every time. Once you hit on a content and presentation that works to inspire donations, keep using the letter—or its basic structure, with some freshening up of content—for as long as it's effective.

At the end of the letter, there's no need to be subtle. The reader probably already guessed you were going to ask for money. Come straight out and say something like, "We hope you'll help us with your contribution," or "Now we are asking you to make a tax-deductible donation," or "Every $xx you give will put a meal onto the table of a housebound senior."

In the past, there was much brow-knitting on the subject of who should sign these solicitation letters, with nonprofits frantically looking for a famous person to lend his or her name. However, the consensus that has developed is that your executive director or a board member is the most natural signer, and will get as good a response as anyone else. The exception is if a famous person is intimately involved with your organization and eager to speak out about it and back this up with future involvement.

P.S.: Most organizations end their letters with a postscript. They do it for a reason: It adds a sense of up-to-the-minute urgency that the rest of the letter doesn't have. And because of that, it often gets read first. For example, your P.S. might say "Every gift that we receive before xx date will be matched by a gift from the xx Foundation," or "Eighty percent of every dollar you give goes straight to helping people in need." Or, you can simply reemphasize your message. For example, here's a "P.S." from a letter I received with Richard Gere's signature, for the International Campaign for Tibet: *You, more than most, understand the importance of religious freedom. And even though the atrocities and abuse thousands of miles away from your home does not affect you directly or physically, it is something we can all help to stop.*

Even better is to organize your volunteers to come in and handwrite personal notes as P.S.s—though this will preclude you from using bulk mail, because all the letters will no longer be identical. The personal touch may be worth a first class stamp, however.

At the end of this chapter, you'll find samples of well-written, persuasive first-time donor solicitation letters, from organizations including Project Open Hand and the Julia Morgan Center for the Arts. Though you'll notice stylistic differences among these letters, what they have in common is that each is rich with facts and stories about their organizations, leaves out unnecessary flowery speech, and moves the reader quickly through brief paragraphs and accessible text. The Project Open Hand letter was written by Diane Benjamin, and the Julia Morgan Center for the Arts letter was written by organization staff in collaboration with Robin Woodland, of Laura McCrea & Associates.

> **CAUTION**
> **You may have to run your letter past a local government body.** Check with your lawyer, board members, or other organizations for more information.

The rest of the package should look good (but not too glossy or expensive) and make the giving easy. You should include a reply card, in which the person indicates how much they're giving and by what means (check, credit card, by monthly installments, or whatever you're prepared to offer). You've seen a thousand of these reply cards before—by now, the format is fairly standard, though the card should be attractive and self-contained—some people toss the letter, but keep the reply card around in case they decide to donate.

The biggest decision you'll make is simply what gift amounts to suggest (for example, "$25 ___, $50 ___, $100 ___, Other ___"). Starting out with too low an amount may encourage people to take advantage of that option. On the other hand, I know of an organization that suggested $1, simply as a way of building their membership, in accordance with a strategy of approaching foundations with a strong showing of community support. You'll need to choose suggested donation levels based on your sense of your potential supporters' giving capacities and your ability to credibly ask for high amounts.

Some organizations like to attach names to the various giving levels, such as "bronze, silver, and gold." This helps inspire people toward higher gifts and allows you to group donors' names in publications such as your annual report. Naming the giving levels can, however, be tricky. Each giving level needs to sound appropriately recognized, with no one falling into a category like "tin" or "aluminum alloy." The Aurora Theatre in Berkeley, for example, in its printed program, ranks its $50 to $199 donors as "stars," then advances donors up the stratosphere, from "novas," "constellations," "supernovas," "nebulae," "quasars," "pulsars," and "cosmos" to—what else?—"the big bang" (at $100,000 and up). It's probably safe to say that most donors wouldn't be offended at being called a pulsar rather than a nebula.

Some groups get around the ranking problem by assigning value-neutral names. Bryn Mawr College, for example, names its "donor societies" after historic college buildings, such as Cloisters, Pembroke Arch, and Goodhart. Yet another alternative is to give a quick summation of what each gift level will fund: as in "___$500 (funds one student fellowship for four weeks)."

If people will receive something in return for different gift levels (a fleece vest or baseball cap, for example), your suggested amounts should of course bear some proportional relation to the value of this return gift. If you have a website, be sure to list its URL on the reply card and indicate whether supporters can donate online.

The reply card should fit neatly into a reply envelope (which has to be small enough to fit into your cover envelope). Your address should, of course, be printed on the front of the envelope. But should you provide return postage or not? Fortunately, most people willing to donate to your organization are also willing to put their own stamp on the letter. You'll add a lot to your costs if you put first class stamps on the envelopes. Organizations with higher budgets and more experience at direct mail may wish to send preprinted, Business Reply Envelopes (with those postal seals that say "No Postage Necessary If Mailed in the United States"). But believe it or not, the postage on these is actually higher than a first class stamp, though your overall costs should be lower because you only pay for those envelopes that donors actually mail back to you.

There are also optional items you can include in your direct mail package—a post-it note with an urgent or "late-breaking" message, a relevant news clipping, or a "freebie" such as return address stamps or a bumper sticker. All of these will, of course, add to the costs of your package. If you're new to direct mail, you might as well go without them—particularly the freebies, which are getting so common that people feel less and less obligated to give anything in return. You can always add such extras to your package later, after you've gained experience, a sense of your audience, and sufficient funds to invest in these.

Eventually, however, you may find that certain types of extras are very effective. For example, Project Open Hand, a Bay Area nonprofit that provides nourishing meals to people living with AIDS and other serious illnesses, consistently gets the best response to mailings that contain a copy of a little handwritten shopping list, showing how much food it takes to feed their clients each week—no less than 2,490 lbs. of chicken, 450 lbs. of rice, 400 lbs. of hard cheeses and tofu, and more. According to Andrew Arnold, the project's Director of Annual Fund, the shopping list insert increases each mailing's printing and other costs by about 1%, but the returns are markedly higher, easily justifying the extra cost.

Mailing Insert From Project Open Hand

Project Open Hand Kitchen

This Week's Shopping List

2,490 lbs Chicken
1,700 lbs Beef
1,900 lbs Other meats such as Turkey
$4,000 Fresh Vegetables, Fruits, Herbs
360 lbs Beans
450 lbs Rice
400 lbs Pasta
200 ½ Gallons of Milk
400 lbs Hard Cheeses & Tofu
750 Dozen Eggs
$2,500 Various Groceries

Clients can request regular meals,
vegetarian meals, or special client meals.

Reprinted with permission

CAUTION

Don't add extras to some letters and not others. If you're planning to mail via bulk mail, the U.S. Post Office demands that each of your letters be of the same weight.

Can you prepare a mailing without a professional designer or printer? If you're on a low budget, sure. Simply print a bunch of letters on your organization's letterhead, go to a local copy store to have reply cards printed and cut, and send it all out using first class stamps. The letter should be single-spaced, but with short paragraphs and wide margins so that the pages have plenty of white space. (If your budget is extremely low, however, remember that investing in direct mail solicitation may not be the right thing for you at this time, given that its payoff may take a few years.)

I know people who've given to organizations in part because the solicitation letter was so obviously homespun. When all the rest of the fundraising letters start to look suspiciously similar and even slick, a grassroots production can set you apart. As long as your content is intelligent and carefully considered—in other words, your letter doesn't seem hysterical or slapdash—your readers will be pleased to hear a "true" voice. (But homespun letters are not a strategy you can use forever—people may start wondering why you can't seem to get your operation off the ground.)

With new technology and in-house publishing programs, however, assembling professional-looking packages on your own is getting easier. A staff or board member who has photographic or artistic abilities (not just amateur) may come in handy to add visuals to the package. A compelling picture can be worth pages of explanations. Many fundraising pros ruefully joke that they could bring in much more money if they worked for an organization that protects baby seals—one good baby seal picture brings in supporters' dollars like nothing else in fundraising history.

If you'll be using a professional printer or mail house, get recommendations from other nonprofits. Some printers specialize in working with nonprofits, and will help you figure out ways to keep down costs and produce something in line with your own values. For example, an environmental organization might want to use obviously recycled paper—but still have the mailing package look classy and be affordable.

Whether you'll be using a professional or printing in-house, make sure to proofread everything several times. You'd be amazed at the mistakes that crop up. Professional printing is not like photocopying; a word that you typed perfectly in your version can suddenly transmute into something else through the "miracles" of scanning or program conversions. And don't forget to be alert for sins of omission—for example, the one board member whose name was left off, or a photo without explanatory text.

The Mechanics of Mailing

Getting a mailing out creates a busy time at a nonprofit, whether you're handling it in-house or through a printer and/or mail house. No matter which, you'll want to give everything one last looking over—or two. Then have everyone—including volunteers and possibly staff members who don't normally participate in development activities—ready to kick into high gear.

If someone at your organization or from your board is going to sign the letter, make sure he or she won't be on vacation that week. You'll need to have an hour or two set aside, unless you use a stamp that reproduces the signature. (This may be worthwhile or necessary for larger mailings.) On the other hand, it makes the letter one step less personal, because readers have learned to recognize these stamps.

If you're doing the mailing in-house, several boxes of paper will arrive from the printer, and you'll need to have staff and volunteers lined up to deal with them. Depending on what services you ordered from the printer, you may need to have volunteers fold the letters and combine them with the reply cards and envelopes before placing them in the mailing envelope. Give your workers a clean space and make sure that any coffee or snacks are miles away from the letters. Carefully train everyone in the assembly process. Letters should be neatly folded and placed in the envelope so that the greeting is the first thing the reader sees upon opening it, with the other inserts behind.

As a nonprofit, you can take advantage of the U.S. Post Office's bulk mail rates if you're sending 200 or more identical pieces of standard mail (same size and weight, up to 15.999 ounces). You'll need to plan for this in advance, first by getting a permit, using Post Office Form 3624, *Application to Mail at Nonprofit Standard Mail Rates*. (As of 2003, your permit will lapse if you don't use it at least every two years, and you'll need to reapply.) The exact rates you will pay will vary, depending on the size of your letter and the rate for which you qualify. Be warned, however, that the bulk mail regulations are tricky. In fact, people usually attend trainings just to find out how to organize and prepare mail in a way that meets the Postal Service's requirements. And you can't just go to any post office once you're done—you'll have to work through one of the special Bulk Mail Centers. (They're listed online at www.usps.com/bulkmailcenters. Click "BMC Office Information" for a list of almost 30 centers nationwide.)

Various software programs (either within your fundraising database program or separate) can make preparing your bulk mailing—in particular, the envelopes and labels—easier. Nevertheless, mail houses are the choice of many nonprofits. Though using a mail house adds to the costs, it also significantly reduces frustration and lost time. As Lisa Ruth Elliott (formerly of Zen Hospice) points out, "With a mail house, there's less chance of the process dragging on. You can ask them to have it done within a certain length of time. If you do the mailing in-house, the paper can build up and consume your office. At least make sure to have a number of experienced volunteers on hand if you go this route."

After assessing and comparing the time and costs of a mail house and of learning and handling bulk mail yourself, you may discover that first class stamps are actually your most cost-effective option. This isn't a cop-out—many organizations decide the same thing (take a look in your mailbox and see). First class mail can also be forwarded if the addressee has moved; bulk mail doesn't offer this advantage.

RESOURCE

Want more detailed information on bulk mailing? Take a look at these resources:

- **The U.S. Postal Service's website at www.usps.com.** Be careful, however—many of the links lead you to for-profit business bulk mail rules, which are different. Look for Publication 417, *Nonprofit Standard Mail Eligibility,* by clicking "All Products and Services," then "Publications." (The application form is also available on this page.)

- **The website of the Alliance of Nonprofit Mailers, at www.nonprofitmailers.org.**

Follow Up

After your mailing goes out, you can collapse for a few days and see what else has been piling up in your inbox. Plan on no more than a ten-day collapse, however, because with any luck at all, the replies will be rolling in steadily by then.

I don't need to tell you to rip open those first envelopes quickly—you'll be eager to know what's inside. But you'll have to keep up a steady pace, carrying out critical follow-up tasks including:

1. photocopying the checks and forwarding these and all credit card information to your accounting department

2. entering the supporter information and gift amounts in your database, and

3. sending thank-you letters.

Each of these should be done within 24 hours to two days of receiving the replies (the sooner the better). For one thing, many people don't balance their checkbooks, and will keep drawing out money until it's gone, unless you get there first. For another, developing an up-to-date system of data entry is crucial at every stage of your organization's activities—once you start getting behind on this, you may never catch up. And third, supporters who aren't thanked immediately can take it personally.

To illustrate, I recently heard a radio show debate over whether a charity-based bicycle event had become too corporate. One person called in for the sole purpose of announcing that she'd stopped her support because it took the event organizers two months to send her a thank-you letter. Thinking back through my nonprofit career, it's easy to understand how this might have happened. The event itself takes up staff time, the data entry person quits and is replaced by a part-time temp, and the reply cards pile up in a corner with the most recent cards tossed on the top of the pile as the bottom ones molder. But the supporter doesn't know about all this, nor should she. She simply views the thank-you letter as an indication of how much you need and appreciate her support.

The lesson is clear—if you want continued support, try for a turnaround of one to two days, not two months. And if you don't think you can handle this type of follow-up, either hire a professional, or delay soliciting supporters by direct mail until your organization is better prepared for the aftermath. If you've got an efficient system, you can inspire even greater donor loyalty by combining a thank-you phone call with the letter.

Most supporters will send their replies within about the first month after you sent the mailing. Wait until your replies have fallen to a mere trickle, then evaluate the success of your mailing. Fill out the form below.

For **item B,** include not only the costs of printing, postage, and materials, but also any special staff or professionals hired to help. You don't, however, need to include the hours put in by development staff who would be working

Fundraising Worksheet 4: Mailing Evaluation

For mailing sent [*date*], consisting of:

Describe appeal and any special enclosures:

A. Number of letters sent out		
B. Total expenses of mailing		$
C. Number of new supporters		
D. Total amount of donations		$
E. Usual donation amount		$
F. Percentage of response	(C divided by A)	%
G. Net profit	(D minus B)	$
H. Cost of acquiring each new supporter	(B divided by C)	$

Comments

anyway. For **item F,** don't be surprised at a low percentage—a 1% response rate is considered successful. Hopefully **item G** will be a positive number, indicating that the mailing at least broke even. But if it isn't, focus your (and your board's) attention on the number of new supporters. With proper cultivation and renewal efforts, one of them could turn into your next $10,000 donor.

Julia Morgan Center for the Arts

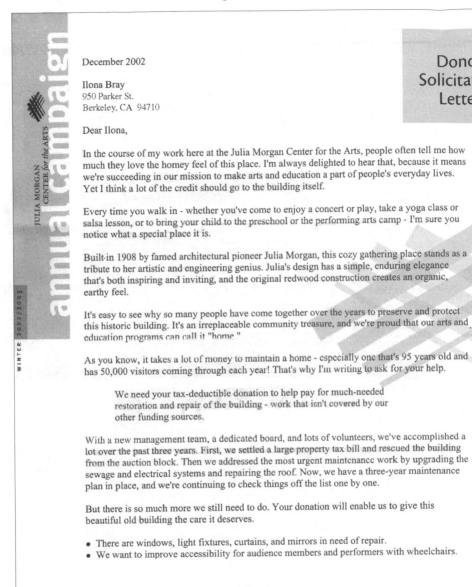

December 2002

Ilona Bray
950 Parker St.
Berkeley, CA 94710

**Donor
Solicitation
Letter**

SAMPLE

Dear Ilona,

In the course of my work here at the Julia Morgan Center for the Arts, people often tell me how much they love the homey feel of this place. I'm always delighted to hear that, because it means we're succeeding in our mission to make arts and education a part of people's everyday lives. Yet I think a lot of the credit should go to the building itself.

Every time you walk in - whether you've come to enjoy a concert or play, take a yoga class or salsa lesson, or to bring your child to the preschool or the performing arts camp - I'm sure you notice what a special place it is.

Built in 1908 by famed architectural pioneer Julia Morgan, this cozy gathering place stands as a tribute to her artistic and engineering genius. Julia's design has a simple, enduring elegance that's both inspiring and inviting, and the original redwood construction creates an organic, earthy feel.

It's easy to see why so many people have come together over the years to preserve and protect this historic building. It's an irreplaceable community treasure, and we're proud that our arts and education programs can call it "home."

As you know, it takes a lot of money to maintain a home - especially one that's 95 years old and has 50,000 visitors coming through each year! That's why I'm writing to ask for your help.

> We need your tax-deductible donation to help pay for much-needed restoration and repair of the building - work that isn't covered by our other funding sources.

With a new management team, a dedicated board, and lots of volunteers, we've accomplished a lot over the past three years. First, we settled a large property tax bill and rescued the building from the auction block. Then we addressed the most urgent maintenance work by upgrading the sewage and electrical systems and repairing the roof. Now, we have a three-year maintenance plan in place, and we're continuing to check things off the list one by one.

But there is so much more we still need to do. Your donation will enable us to give this beautiful old building the care it deserves.

- There are windows, light fixtures, curtains, and mirrors in need of repair.
- We want to improve accessibility for audience members and performers with wheelchairs.

2640 COLLEGE AVENUE, BERKELEY CA 94704
510.845.8542
WWW.JULIAMORGAN.ORG

WINTER 2002/2003
JULIA MORGAN CENTER for the ARTS
annual campaign

- We need a new stage floor for our dance, theater, and children's programs.
- And if you've ever been to a performance in the theater during the winter, you know we need a new heater! That alone will cost about $10,000.

We've never asked before, but now we really need your support. Your tax-deductible gift of $50, $100, $500 or more will immediately be put to work. All donations will be acknowledged in our newsletter and website. If you can give $100 or more, look for your name on "Julia's Wall" in our lobby later in 2003.

The cost of protecting and preserving this historic building increases if we delay, so please give as generously as you can – as soon as you can.

Thank you so much for your help.

With best wishes for the holiday season,

Sabrina Klein
Executive Director

P.S. Please know that *any* amount you can give will truly make a difference! Help us preserve this wonderful home for the arts by making your donation today.

Project Open Hand

Project Open Hand
meals with love

"A young neighbor of mine died last week.
But during the last, and what must have been the most
poignant part of his life, you fed him.
Such a simple act. Such a humbling lesson."

Dear Friend:

There are few things more basic than feeding someone who's hungry and ill.

Project Open Hand has been feeding people who are sick and in need every day for over twenty years. And every day we learn the same, humbling lesson: a hand extended to someone in need never comes back empty.

I'm writing to ask your help in our mission -- meals with love -- because we truly cannot accomplish it without generous gifts from people like you.

My name is Julie Wasem. Here at Project Open Hand I am responsible for the team of volunteers and cooks that prepares and cooks the nourishing meals we serve to thousands of people each day ... meals for every day of the week, 52 weeks a year.

I am Director of Programs at Project Open Hand, and have worked here for over seven years now. I started working here because I was impressed with the commitment to providing only the freshest and healthiest food for people battling serious illness. Working at Project Open Hand is rewarding, seeing firsthand how the amazing dedication of the volunteers and staff working together makes a difference in the lives of so many people sick and often alone. At Project Open Hand, our saying is: "We're cookin' up love" -- and it's so true.

You may already be familiar with the story of Project Open Hand's beginnings -- how Ruth Brinker, a retired grandmother, started it all

730 Polk Street, San Francisco, California 94109 • (415) 447-2419 • www.openhand.org

in 1985, by delivering meals she cooked herself to seven people sick with AIDS.

Back then, no one could have foreseen how devastating the AIDS epidemic would become, or how many other people would join those first seven clients. Today, Project Open Hand feeds over 3,200 people with AIDS each year, and has extended its much-needed services to include weekly groceries as well as home-delivered meals.

In all the years of feeding people we've never had to turn down a request for help from a person living with HIV. That, I think you will agree, is nothing short of miraculous. <u>And it's because of the caring and commitment of people from all over the Bay Area that we've been able to do it</u>.

Every evening, volunteers arrive at our kitchens in San Francisco and Oakland to pick up hot, freshly prepared dinners, helping to deliver health-enhancing nourishment to over a thousand people who otherwise might not eat. Other volunteers await the nearly 300 people who visit our Grocery Centers each day -- loading grocery bags filled with nutritious food that will help combat malnutrition and weight loss associated with AIDS.

Almost daily we get notes from people like Richard, who wrote to say,

> "Your meals have meant the difference! The difference between eating and not eating. When you started bringing meals to me, I had lost over 30 pounds. I had just come home from the hospital and was in no shape to cook. In the last month, thanks to your 'open hearts' (the meals too), I can now get around and have started to put on weight."

We've grown and changed in many ways since the AIDS epidemic began, but again and again we've seen that people reaching out to others in loving compassion -- whether by chopping vegetables ... packaging groceries ... delivering hot meals ... or donating resources -- bring healing as surely as the nourishing food does.

Now, in addition to serving people with HIV/AIDS, we are also sharing that compassion and healing with people who are homebound and living with any serious illness as well as with seniors in our community lunch program.

Reprinted with permission

They may be people who are alone, without family or other support in the area. They may have just been released from the hospital or are homebound, suffering from a long-term, critical illness or even an acute, temporary crisis.

For people like Kristine, Project Open Hand is a lifesaver. Kristine lives alone and has a degenerative condition that is crippling her. Some days she can walk with the help of canes, but her disease has gotten so bad that she is unable to shop or stand up in the kitchen to prepare meals for herself. Before a social worker put her in touch with Project Open Hand, she actually went several days without eating because she couldn't get any help.

Doctors say she will soon be in a wheelchair, but Kristine is determined to keep her independence. She thinks she'll be able to do that with Project Open Hand's home-delivered meals. She says that "someone stopping by to check in on me with a hot, delicious meal and a smile is a wonderful thing."

Richard and Kristine are only two of the people who receive daily nourishment from Project Open Hand because of the generosity of caring individuals like yourself. <u>To someone who is alone and frightened, this caring and love are sometimes as healing as the nutritious food we provide.</u> With your help, we'll be able to provide meals with love to even more who are in need and alone.

Many times over the years it seemed like there just would not be enough food to go around. But we've found that whenever we've asked for help, compassionate and caring people have always stepped forward to lend a hand.

I'm urging you to do just that. Will you help feed those who need the proper nourishment to fight their illness, keep up their spirits and better tolerate often drastic medical treatments?

Fortunately, because of the volunteer efforts of so many, the donations of food and time, and the efficiency of everyone involved with Project Open Hand, <u>we can still serve a person in need a nourishing meal for just about $5 a day</u>.

A donation of $25 will feed a person living with a serious illness a daily, nourishing meal prepared with love for five days. A gift of $140 will feed someone for a month. Please use one of the enclosed meal certificates as you make your gift. The certificate you return will give a message of life -- life-giving nourishment to someone who is sick and in need.

Please know that whatever you can give will go a long way -- and it will be very special because you cared to give it.

With your help, we can fulfill our promise that every day of the year, rain or shine, the men and women who face so many uncertainties will know one thing for sure: Project Open Hand will always be there with a smile, a word of encouragement, and a hot, nutritious meal.

Thank you,

Julie Wasem

Julie Wasem
Project Open Hand

P.S. Please consider what your gift can mean to a person who is homebound and depends on us each day for nourishing food. Send the most generous gift you can today in the enclosed reply envelope. Or if you prefer to give online, go to **www.openhand.org/cm308**

How to Keep the Givers Giving

A first-time donation is an opportunity, not a fait accompli. Typically, it means that the person was momentarily persuaded to contribute, by one or another of your organization's fundraising efforts. Unfortunately, without your creative intervention, the donor's impulse may well turn out to be fleeting. In fact, studies of lapsed supporters have found that a significant number couldn't remember having supported the particular organization in the first place! Given the high cost of finding a first-time supporter, this is not what you want from your own supporters. Retaining a supporter costs only one-fifth of what you'll spend to attract him or her in the first place, which makes donor retention a relatively low-cost source of untapped potential for many organizations.

This chapter will help you figure out how to keep your donors giving. To do that, you'll have to keep your organization's name, and the important work that it does, in the hearts and minds of your supporters. From the moment your supporters first contact your organization, you need to give them a sense of personal identification with your group and its mission. Over time, this initial rapport can turn into a sense of true belonging, encouraging your supporters not only to continue their donations and involvement, but to increase their support over the years. Some people refer to this progressive process as moving supporters up a giving ladder, or bringing them closer and closer within concentric circles of engagement. Eventually, your most committed supporters should see that your organization is the most effective instrument by which they can carry out their hopes to improve at least a little corner of the world. Currying this relationship with donors is known as "stewardship."

To inspire this type of commitment, you'll have to carry out the core work of your organization well. But no one is going to know about the great things your organization does unless someone tells them. That's why the most effective strategies for keeping supporters, and drawing them into an increased sense of engagement with your organization, include:

- thanking them for gifts, immediately and appropriately
- keeping them informed and (hopefully) inspired about the great things you do
- offering them other ways to contribute to your work
- periodically analyzing your donor base to look for trends, groupings, and weaknesses

- communicating with donors frequently, through regular mailings, news-letters and annual reports (covered in Chapter 11), and media outreach (covered in Chapter 13), and

- calling supporters on the telephone.

Thank Your Supporters

You probably first heard about the importance of thank-you letters from Mom and Dad, soon after you had mastered the alphabet. Just as the letters worked to keep your grandparents enthusiastic about giving to you when you were a child, they work to keep donor gifts coming to your organization. As a rule, anyone who makes more than a token pledge or gift to your organization should receive a prompt, ideally handwritten thank-you letter. The letter should go out no later than within 24 hours or a few days.

For smaller gifts—say, $15 or under—an email or postcard is sufficient or even preferable to a formal letter; you don't want the donor to feel like you spent his or her entire gift on return postage. For example, see the postcard sent by the San Francisco Mime Troupe, (a theater group that performs political satire in the parks of the Bay Area and beyond), reproduced here. According to Peggy Rose, General Manager of the San Francisco Mime Troupe, "We think it's important to thank people, but we don't want to waste the resources they've just provided us with.

Reprinted with permission

People want to see that you're using their resources in the best way you can. Plus, the postcards are colorful and fun."

Your thank-you letter serves two important functions:

- it lets the supporter know the gift was important to you, and
- it gives them written proof of their gift in case an IRS auditor ever pays them a visit (especially important if they gave cash).

The letter should be personal in style—it need not look like a receipt or follow any special format. In fact, you're encouraged to make your thank-you letters interesting, for example by using handmade cards crafted by your clients. Treat the letter as an opportunity to reiterate how the gift is helping your organization do its work. It's also compelling if you can tell the donors something they haven't heard before—like how many other donors have joined in on this recent effort, what progress is already underway on the project to which they gave, or what upcoming projects and events you have planned.

No matter what else you say in your letter, however, include the following information in order to meet the IRS's requirements:

- your organization's name
- the amount of the donation
- whether the donor received anything in return for his or her gift of $75 or more; if not, it's good to say "No goods or services were exchanged for your donation"
- you needn't mention token items of insubstantial value (such as a membership sticker, pen, or refrigerator magnet) or a membership privilege worth less than $75 a year (such as event tickets or free parking at events), and
- in cases where the giver received something substantial in return ("substantial" meaning it has a fair market value of $89 or more, or exceeded 2% of the amount of the donation, whichever is less), a good faith estimate of its value and notification that the donor will need to reduce his or her tax deduction by the value of what was received.

If the gift was very large, you'll want to take extra steps to thank and otherwise recognize the donor, as discussed in Chapter 6.

Below is a sample thank-you letter from a fictional organization:

Sand Dune Restoration Project
5432 Beachside Way
Oceanside, LA 12345
123-555-1212
www.ladunes.org

Thank-you
Letter

SAMPLE

Mary Doane-Orr
2345 First St.
Oceanside, LA 12345

Dear Mary Doane-Orr:

We were delighted to open today's mail and find your generous gift of $80. Your support will help our staff and volunteers bring native plant life back to Oceanside's sand dunes for the enjoyment of present and future generations. Community support for this phase of the restoration project has been very encouraging—already we've received gifts from 120 people.

And, there's exciting news to report: Just yesterday one of our volunteers spotted some new shoots of one of the native flowers that once dominated these dunes—but have recently been threatened with extinction due to development and other problems. Our staff and volunteers will continue their efforts to weed out non-native species and put protective cages around the new, native growth.

Please save this letter, which will serve as your receipt for tax purposes. [*Alternatively, depending on circumstances:*]

To comply with Internal Revenue Service regulations, this letter also confirms that you are receiving no goods or services in return for your contribution.

[*or*]

We'll be sending you the sand sculpture that you requested as a recognition gift, by separate mail. For tax purposes, your contribution must be reduced by $10.00, the value of this sculpture.

Again, thank you. We hope you'll come see the difference your gift has made, at our celebratory evening ceremony this June 25th—on the beach, of course! Look for more details in an upcoming mailing, or on our website at www.ladunes.org.

Very truly yours,

Rocky Beech

Rocky Beech
Executive Director
Sand Dune Restoration Project

Communicate Your Essential Message

To retain your donors, you'll need to convince them of one basic thing: that your organization is still doing great work on a worthy cause. In an age when we're being barraged by information, you'll have to send powerful, directed communications to get your message across—hopefully without joining the ranks of the barragers. A number of different methods are available to convey these important messages. Some of these methods are discussed in other chapters of this book, including newsletters and annual reports, covered in Chapter 11, and media outreach, covered in Chapter 13. This section covers one of the best tools that nonprofits have for keeping up with donors: the mail, both traditional "snail mail" and email.

This section will help you develop a strategy for mailing communications to existing donors over the course of your funding year. The most important considerations include:

- how often to send mailings
- crafting your annual appeal
- designing special appeals
- what to say—and what not to say—in an appeal letter
- special considerations for sending email, and
- when to stop mailing to unresponsive donors.

How Often to Mail

There's much professional disagreement about how often your supporters should hear from you—especially because you will often be asking for money. A number of direct mail devotees recommend coming up with a reason to solicit funds every two to three months—and suggest that if you hold back, other organizations' more frequent mailings will get all the attention. I disagree. When donors are asked for money too often, they are likely to feel as though the organization forgot the fact that they just gave, or is wasting paper and postage with repeated solicitations. And many donors—especially the most generous ones, whose names are likely to appear on a number of mailing lists—are getting legitimately irritated with the flood of fundraising letters swamping their mailboxes.

TIP

Give the donor control. Some groups find that it's a good idea to ask donors their preferences about how often they'll receive mailings. For example, you might tell donors at the outset that you'll typically contact them once a year to renew their annual membership, and twice more for targeted solicitations— then give them a chance to elect to hear from you less often.

A Peeved Donor Story

Trisha had been a dues-paying member of a national nonprofit for several years. The mailings went to her parents' house in Portland, continuing on while she was away at college. The solicitations came so frequently that she'd find a pile of them waiting for her when she came home on break. Not only did she start feeling confused about how often she was expected to "renew" in order to get her newsletter, but given the huge pile, she wondered if she would actually save the organization money by ceasing to send her $25 per year. After college, she moved to California, did some volunteer work at the organization's local office, and signed up for a membership from there. She kept getting renewal letters at her parents' Portland address, but figured these would drop off eventually. They didn't. Then she let her California membership lapse. The organization called her, and she agreed to renew her membership—on the condition that they remove her Portland address from their database. "Sure, no problem," Trisha was told. She made the renewal gift.

The next time Trisha was home in Portland, she found an even larger pile of renewal letters and solicitations. She hasn't donated to this organization since.

While drawing on and respecting the fundraising style and history of your organization, you may also want to experiment a bit in order to develop the most effective possible mailing calendar. Retaining supporters has been shown to depend in large part on their sense that you've remained accountable and told them how your organization spent their gift—and the results you've achieved through their continued support. This means you'll have to balance your need to keep in touch against the danger of wearing out your supporters' goodwill.

PROTECTING OPEN SPACE AND PROMOTING LIVABLE COMMUNITIES

November 26, 2003

Please don't leave the greenbelt unprotected!
Renew your membership with Greenbelt Alliance today!

Ralph Warner
950 Parker St.
Berkeley, CA 94710

Dear Ralph,

<u>Your membership with Greenbelt Alliance is about to expire.</u> Don't let that happen — don't give up your chance to make a difference for the Bay Area's future!

Here's just one example of how your membership dollars made a difference last year:

> With your support, we secured protection for the rolling hills and open vistas of Solano County, the Bay Area's fastest-growing county. Just this month, with the help of concerned citizens in Fairfield and Benecia, Greenbelt Alliance beat back the efforts of big-spending developers and locked in protection for 74,000 acres of Solano County's orchards, farmlands, and wildlands!

> Now we plan to build on our successes by working to create Parks Districts in Solano and Napa Counties, the two remaining Bay Area counties without open space districts. These districts would purchase and manage parklands, ensuring permanent protection for scenic places that are now severely threatened by sprawl development.

With your help, we can continue our work to protect Solano County's threatened lands, as well as farmlands and wildlands all around the Bay Area. And as we work to promote smart growth within our existing cities and towns, we're not just stopping sprawl, we're offering intelligent alternatives.

As a Greenbelt Alliance member, you'll be helping to realize the vision of a Bay Area with clean air, walkable neighborhoods, fresh local produce, accessible parks, and affordable housing. You'll stay up to date on our progress toward that vision with our newsletter, *Greenbelt Action*. If you like, you'll also receive email action alerts and special invitations to events and outings.

Thank you for your support over the past year. I hope you'll continue to help shape the Bay Area's future by renewing today. **Have no doubt – your membership really does make a difference.**

Sincerely,

Tom Steinbach
Executive Director

P.S. If you've already sent in your renewal, thank you and please forgive this reminder.

Renewal Letter

S A M P L E

MAIN OFFICE ◆ 631 Howard Street, Suite 510, San Francisco, CA 94105 ◆ (415) 543-6771 ◆ Fax (415) 543-6781
SOLANO/NAPA OFFICE ◆ 725 Texas Street, Fairfield, CA 94533 ◆ (707) 427-2308 ◆ Fax (707) 427-2315
SOUTH BAY OFFICE ◆ 1922 The Alameda, Suite 213, San Jose, CA 95126 ◆ (408) 983-0856 ◆ Fax (408) 983-1001
EAST BAY OFFICE ◆ 1601 North Main Street, Suite 105, Walnut Creek, CA 94596 ◆ (925) 932-7776 ◆ Fax (925) 932-1970
SONOMA/MARIN OFFICE ◆ 50 Santa Rosa Avenue, Suite 307, Santa Rosa, CA 95404 ◆ (707) 575-3661 ◆ Fax (707) 575-4275
info@greenbelt.org ◆ www.greenbelt.org

Annual Renewal Letters

Of course, you'll want to send at least one letter per year asking for a "renewal" of support. This is a good time to remind donors of their long-term commitment to your organization, and about the vital work that you continue to do. Whether or not you have a formal membership program, try to style your appeal as a renewal of their alliance with your group—and of any membership benefits they receive. Remind them that their newsletter subscription and any other benefits will expire on a certain date, and let them know what other benefits would come with an increased gift.

Be prepared to send some follow-up letters, as well. It can take four or five letters before a past supporter is moved or remembers to renew. And don't feel that you have to stop with five letters—some supporters don't get around to renewing until they've seen a pile of mail from you. It rarely pays to send more than eight or ten renewal letters; better to put these donors in the "lapsed" section of your database and wait a decent interval before trying them again. But if your lapsed supporter received a newsletter or other benefit as part of his or her membership, make sure to cut it off when you said you would.

For a sample of a persuasive, upbeat, and to-the-point renewal letter, see the above letter from the Greenbelt Alliance.

TIP

Keep renewals separate. Some nonprofits send out so many fundraising appeals every year that donors have no idea when they're due for an actual renewal. Try to protect the integrity of the renewal cycle by clearly labeling other solicitations as special purpose appeals. Also, it's a great idea to tell donors if their last gift was made more than a year before; studies show that most donors mistakenly believe that they gave more recently than they actually did.

Special Communications and Appeal Letters

One good way to avoid overwhelming your donors is to vary the tone of your communications. A supporter who gets a letter every two months that says, in effect, "The situation is critical! Send money!" will almost surely tire of your tone of perpetual desperation. However, the same donor may be interested in reading a newsletter or an emailed notice discussing late-breaking news. (Emails are particularly good for quick updates, and helped many organizations advise donors of what they were doing in the aftermath of Hurricane Katrina, and raise funds accordingly.) For example, if your group is raising money to protect a particular estuary, supporters may be fascinated to know about a new study of the area's previously underappreciated biodiversity. And this, in turn, may be a powerful trigger for future gifts. Meanwhile, when a true emergency comes along, your supporters will be more open to hearing about it and responding.

It's also wise to encourage two-way communication within your mailings. For example, you might solicit readers' opinions on an issue via email or suggest ways in which interested readers can help with a particular task—including the development of your organization's policy. (The estuary group, for example, might ask for volunteers with a bioscience background to discuss the biodiversity study and come up with an appropriate organizational strategy.)

Tailoring your communications to different segments of donors, and to different donor interests, is another good way to make sure your mail is read with interest. For starters, your mail to major or midscale donors might take a more personal tone and refer specifically to their past gifts. But if your database technology can handle it, send out customized letters to donors grouped according to criteria other than gift levels. For example, you could customize letters to supporters of your women's center by sending an appeal just to donors who are most interested in the needs of low-income moms. If you don't have fancy technology, you can tailor letters to different donors by asking board members to write personal notes on the letters.

Many organizations send an informational newsletter two to four times a year and an annual report near the end of the year. (Newsletters and annual reports are discussed in Chapter 11.) Be sure to keep the newsletter and annual report schedule in mind as you plan your other mailings. It's usually counterproductive for people to receive these items just days before or after an appeal by letter— build in a break of at least four weeks.

TIP

Create a gift donation program. More and more families are substituting heartfelt gifts to nonprofits for yet another round of holiday gifts. And it's becoming popular to ask guests at weddings and other celebratory events to make a gift to a designated charity instead of to the people being honored. (This is especially true for second marriages, when the allure of all those new toasters may have worn off.) Appreciating the strength of this trend, savvy nonprofits let their supporters know that they are happy to establish special-occasion gift programs, complete with thank-you cards to the people being honored.

Appeal Letters

The standard device for communicating with supporters is the appeal letter. In drafting an appeal letter, some of the tools you used for your initial solicitation letter (described in Chapter 4) will be helpful. However, you shouldn't speak to the reader as if he or she has never heard of your organization. Opening with a reference back to your organization's recent history and the important role of your supporters is one way to set an appropriate tone: for example, "As we enter our second theater season, we know that you're as excited as we are by these rave reviews . . ." or "It has truly been a time for celebration, as support from you and many others has allowed us to move into our new space."

The most important elements to include in your letter are:

- **A defined project or event.** This is your reason for writing. For example, a holiday gift drive, in which you collect and wrap gifts for low-income children, would both make for a good story and provide an understandable reason for sending this separate letter. Even if you're asking for help to fund ongoing activities, find some new, seasonal, or otherwise special concern to highlight.

- **A personal story or hook.** Personal stories that illustrate how your group makes a difference are always good for drawing people in. For example, if your group is collecting and organizing lightly used sports uniforms and equipment in the U.S., and then transporting and distributing them to children in South American villages, you might feature accounts, quotes, and even before-and-after pictures of a particular low-income Peruvian team.

- **The financial challenge you're facing.** Be clear about the costs associated with the project, and how people's donations can make a difference.

- **A reminder of your organization's overall mission and how your current appeal fits into it.** Make sure to tie your appeal to your group's purpose and goals. When you ask for a contribution at the end of the letter, it will be in the spirit of asking the donor to reaffirm his or her support for your underlying mission.

- **A request for a donation (as well as for volunteer help, if appropriate).** Always be direct in telling people what they can do to make this project or event happen. Depending on your organization's technological capacities, you may want to refer specifically to the amount of the supporter's last gift, and ask him or her to increase it by a certain amount. Don't make the mistake that one San Francisco organization did, however, and simply ask all supporters to give the difference between their previous donation and a predetermined amount (in this case, $1,000). Someone who'd donated a mere $25 to the organization got a letter saying, "Won't you increase your donation by $975?" She thought it was a good joke, but the letter clearly didn't add to her sense of personal connection with the organization.

For a sample of how all these strands can be woven into a complete—and not overly long—letter, see below.

> **TIP**
>
> **Year-round holidays are good times to send appeal letters.** At the end of the year, people really do seem to experience a spirit of giving. However, this needn't be the only seasonal event to which you tie your appeals—especially given that every other nonprofit in town is also sending end-of-year letters. Check the calendar for other holidays whose theme is linked to your nonprofit's work; for example, a gay marriage project might send out a June letter discussing this month of weddings, an African-American studies group might send a letter around Martin Luther King Day, or a comedy troupe might have fun with an April Fool's Day letter.

After every mailing, tally up your returns and compare them with past mailings of the same type. Also keep track of any comments you get from recipients, to help you assess how well you did with the content and presentation of each mailing. Of course, events beyond your control may play a role in your returns—a month of bad weather or a disaster such as an earthquake, war, or terrorist attack can focus people's giving sympathies elsewhere.

Appeal
Letter

TVNewsMonitor
1234 Fifth St. NW
Washington, D.C. 20000
www.tvnewsmonitor.org
(212) 555-1212

Dear Friend:

Were you as outraged as we were about the television news' recent coverage of our state election? Once again, issues were ignored in favor of gossip, and voters were left with little to go on except the candidates' misleading attack ads.

With your support, however, we at TVNewsMonitor were able to turn our collective outrage into positive action. In keeping with our mission of increasing viewer awareness and applying pressure to the television media, we:

- sponsored well-attended voter forums for presentation and discussion of the issues in nine cities

- mobilized nearly 2,000 viewers to send critical letters to television news outlets

- disseminated critiques of dozens of news shows with suggestions on how to do better, and

- prepared a list of ten important overlooked news stories and overlooked resource suggestions and sent them to producers at 31 alternative media outlets.

Now, we are at a critical juncture. Our research has shown that in order to get our media reform message to a broad cross-section of people, we will need to buy advertising space on a cable television channel—at a cost of several thousand dollars per airing.

Will you give us the support to take this exciting next step? Already, one of our longtime members has pledged $25,000 in seed money. We know we can raise the remaining $100,000 with the help of supporters like you, who realize that the longer we wait, the less accountable our media will become—at an incalculable cost to our free society. Every $50 tax-deductible gift will allow us to buy two seconds of airtime. It may not sound like much, but working together we can make those seconds add up to a powerful pro-democracy message.

Thank you, and be sure to check our website for the latest news critiques and reports on TVNewsMonitor's activities.

With best regards,

Warfield Watcher

Warfield Watcher
Executive Director

P.S. As a special thank you, all donors who increase their past gifts by $35 or more will receive free passes to our next showing of Collected Worst News Clips; and all who donate $75 or more will receive a video of this hilarious and horrifying collection.

Special Considerations When Sending Email

Email messages are an increasingly important way for organizations to communicate meaningfully with their supporters. (MoveOn.org is a prime example.) But because of email's unique features, it is best used for discrete purposes only. Email is cheap, it's speedy, and it tends to be informal—which means it can too easily be overused. It's also not well suited to the standard, two-plus page appeal letter. However, email is good for:

- **quick updates,** such as news that all of the eagle chicks whose rescue was the subject of your previous appeal letter survived and were released

- **messages directing people to portions of your website**—for example, to a link with photos and a blog from staff members at a children's arts camp

- **member surveys**—for example, requesting input on whether to shift toward providing mental health services to only the most complex psychiatric cases, which would necessitate serving fewer people, or to continue to provide more services to less critical cases

- **newsletters** (usually as attachments or via a Web link) discussing recent projects and achievements

- **alerts on issues requiring member action,** such as an upcoming vigil or demonstration, and

- **requests and reminders for volunteer help, upcoming special events, and more.**

One good way to keep up with the range of email's possible uses is to observe what other nonprofits are doing. This is easy enough—just sign up for their email services. Often their websites will tell you how to do this.

Most of the types of email described above don't directly ask for money. However, they do bring in potential donors and involve them in your work—which, as you already know, is critical to bringing them up the giving ladder. And, there's no harm in adding a "how you can help" link within the message, taking readers back to your website's donation page.

Here are a few guidelines to remember when sending messages via email:

- **Confine your mailings to existing supporters who have either expressed an interest in receiving email communications ("opted in") or who are given a chance, in every message, to opt out.** (And make sure to process opt-out requests immediately.) As you collect email addresses from supporters, let them know your policy on sharing that address with others. The policy most likely to please your supporters is to never rent out your email lists unless you've gotten people's advance permission.

- **Make your subject line catchy, yet specific and clear.** Even existing supporters have to be convinced to open the message. A bland heading like "News from Our Nonprofit" can turn off the many people who've had enough doses of reality for one day. An overly general title like "What's New" may sound like spam. Create interest or excitement with something like "Otter Born in Captivity," or "Invitation to KidsOrg's 10th Anniversary."

- **Don't get caught in a spam filter.** First, be careful about subject line words or phrases that might trigger content filters. These are set to prescreen the spammers' latest favorite words or tricks. Though these are ever changing, sure-fire trouble words are any that sound remotely sexual (watch out for double entendres), strings of capital letters or punctuation marks, and mentions of debt, baldness, or popular health remedies. Second, try to avoid volume filters—that is, filters that interpret all messages sent to large numbers of people as spam. Talk to your email provider to make sure it has negotiated an exemption for your organization with major ISPs such as AOL, Yahoo, and Hotmail.

- **If a particular message is likely to resonate with a wide audience** (for example, a development that impacts a popular national park), encourage the recipients to forward the email to their friends. But be sure to date the message, and to tell people about any deadlines for action. You don't want your email to bounce around the Web for years.

- **Include enough information within the body of the message that someone who has never heard of your organization will see who you are and understand what you do.** Remember, your email may be forwarded beyond your immediate supporters. And it never hurts to remind donors exactly what their contributions are funding.

- **Informality doesn't mean sloppiness.** Typos look just as bad in an email as in a letter. And, IMHO (in my humble opinion), there's no need to use smiley faces or mindless abbreviations like TIA (thanks in advance) or, even worse, TTFN (ta ta for now).

- **Keep messages short and readable.** A few paragraphs, with lots of bullet points, is plenty. If you have the capacity to put the message in html format, great. If not, make sure to use a large font, put spaces between paragraphs, and review the text from the viewpoint of someone who will open it and give it a few seconds' quick scanning.

- **Be ready for two-way communication.** Your readers are only a click away from the "reply" button. They may have questions or concerns, or wish to respond to your requests for information or help. Whatever their motive, the speed of email creates an expectation that someone at the other end will answer right away. Make sure you've got someone lined up—if not with a full answer, then at least with a note saying "Thank you for your [comments, concerns, or offer]. I'll look into this, and get back to you within the week."

- **Encourage readers to click through to your website.** While your email message should be interesting on its own, it can also legitimately act as a "teaser" if it provides a compelling reason for people to go to your website to learn more.

- **Don't send emails encouraging donations unless your website is equipped to handle credit card transactions.** (And remember that only existing supporters who have indicated a willingness to be contacted via email should receive this type of solicitation.) If you have to add to potential donors' workloads by asking them to write a check and put it in the mail, you'll irritate the very ones who are most accustomed to doing things at the speed of email.

Another way to use email to your benefit is to send messages to segmented groups from your mailing list. For example, if you'll be posting a press release on your website that you know will appeal to a particular subset of supporters, alert them by email and provide a link to this Web page. Or, you might share a quick success story with donors or volunteers who recently helped with a project. This won't prevent you from fleshing out the full story in a letter, newsletter, or other communication later.

When to Give Up on a Donor

As you continue corresponding with supporters, you'll notice that very few of them respond to every single mailing with a gift. Some will inevitably start to drop off. After a year has gone by without any response, you may start to wonder whether it's worth keeping them on your list at all.

At what point do you give up? If you encourage supporters to think of themselves as members, then their lack of interest will become clear after your intense efforts at renewal fail. For those not on a renewal schedule, the dividing lines aren't so bright. Unless the supporter has died or joined an ascetic monastic order, you could choose to keep him or her on your list until you receive a request to remove his or her name. (Don't do this without analyzing your annual cost of mailing to lapsed donors, however.) The general rule is to continue regular correspondence until a year and a half has gone by, then stop wasting your postage for a while.

> **CAUTION**
>
> **Be vigilant in removing deceased donors from your database.** Remember, someone still gets the letters, even if the former donor isn't around to read them. A friend of mine who was responsible for tying up her deceased aunt's affairs wrote letters—for 20 years!—asking a charitable organization to take her aunt off its mailing list. The organization's appeal letters kept on coming. The bad news for the organization is that my friend had formerly been a donor too—but, as she said, "Even if they're a good organization otherwise, how can I support them when they're wasting so much money sending letters to dead people?"

As with all general rules, however, there are times when this one should be broken. With some case-by-case analysis, you're sure to find supporters who shouldn't yet be relegated to the "lapsed" file. In particular, look for supporters who have:

- **Made large gifts.** If the donor has made gifts of hundreds of dollars or more, he or she felt strongly about your organization's work at some point. Perhaps more mailings aren't the best strategy—try a phone call or an invitation to a lunch, meeting, or small event.

- **Given for a long time.** If the donor has given to your organization for five years or more—regardless of the amount given—don't give up hastily. The donor may be a little worn out, but not necessarily uninterested. You could reduce the number of appeal letters, but continue sending event-related mail, the annual report, and other pieces to reignite interest.

- **A personal tie to your organization.** Some people should be kept on your mailing list whether they give frequently or not. It's up to your organization, but these might include former staffmembers, clients, or alumni. Again, you can tailor the type of communications to the person or group.

CAUTION

Never call someone a "lapsed" donor. Sounds like some sort of failure, doesn't it? Few people who haven't made a donation for a year or two would describe themselves as "lapsed"—especially those who don't subscribe to your belief that they should give early and often. Your correspondence can forever simply refer to its recipients as "members," "supporters," or whatever term you customarily use.

CROSS REFERENCE

Some supporters clearly have the interest or ability to give frequent or larger gifts. These will require more than the occasional letter, as described in Chapter 6.

Invite Supporters to Get More Involved

Money may not be all that your supporters have to give, nor all that you want from them. In your various communications with supporters—thank-you letters, phone calls, emails, newsletters, and the like—be sure to describe other ways to support your organization's work. These could include volunteering, either on a regular basis or at a special event; participating in a campaign of writing letters or emailing congressional representatives; receiving email updates or news items relating to the work of your organization; attending lectures and events that you sponsor; and more. Author Kay Sprinkel Grace recommends contacting supporters twice with an invitation to get involved—perhaps to attend a lecture, tour, or reception—for every one time that you contact them for money. (See her book *Beyond Fundraising*, published by John Wiley & Sons, for further suggestions on donor stewardship.)

Whether or not your supporters' participation in these activities helps your organization directly is not the point. It develops a relationship, and makes them part of your inner circle. The more a supporter gets involved in your issue, with heart, mind, and body, the more the supporter will feel he or she "owns" it—and continue or increase support for your organization as a result. (See Chapter 2 for more on volunteer involvement and Chapter 8 for more on special events.)

Analyze Your Donor Base

As your base of support grows, you'll want to analyze your supporters' giving patterns and categorize them into groups. The purpose is to tailor your appeals and stewardship to these separate groups. Most nonprofit organizations sort their supporters by financial levels. Some also create groupings based on particular interests or connections with the organization.

Grouping by Giving Level

Traditionally, grassroots nonprofits divide their donors into three financial categories:

- **regular donors,** who give less than $100, or who give less frequently than once every two years
- **midscale donors,** who give between $100 and $500, or who give once or twice a year, and
- **major donors,** who give more than the high end of your midscale donor category ($500), or who give several times a year. This category would also include people who have made your organization a beneficiary of their estate.

You don't have to create three tiers of donors, or divide them along the dollar amounts suggested above—your groupings should depend on the giving levels among your organization's own supporters. You could also create a fourth category, perhaps of "top donors" whose gifts run to the thousands of dollars.

> ### CAUTION
>
> **Never call someone a "minor donor"!** The terms by which you segment donors are for internal purposes only. To your ears, they may not sound like value judgments; you know that all donors give from the heart, and may be giving all they can. But someone who is referred to as a "minor donor" or some other term that connotes an insignificant donation may understandably feel that you don't really appreciate his or her gift.

In creating these dividing lines, consider how your donors view their gifts. Research has shown that people see themselves as having made a major gift if they donate $500 to $1,000. If you're lucky enough to have so many high-dollar donors that you've stopped thinking about the $500 givers as "major," you may need to think again. These donors deserve more than a pat on the head while you carry on stewarding the "real" major donors.

Furthermore, this year's $500 to $1,000 supporters are your most likely source of next year's larger gifts—but only if you've treated them with due respect along the way. Very few supporters leap directly from gifts of a few hundred to several thousand dollars. Donors usually inch their way toward the large gifts. To truly cultivate your donor base for next year's growth, and to keep your pool of givers full (as protection against slumps in the economy) keep a sharp eye on supporters who seem to be positioning themselves to become major donors.

Where you draw the dividing lines between supporters may depend on how much time you and your staff and volunteers can devote to communicating with them. Include as many people as you can handle within the midscale and major donor categories—even if their gifts were fairly modest—and then lavish attention on them to encourage their continued or increased support. You'll find information on how to do this in Chapter 6.

> ### CAUTION
>
> **Are too many of your donors stuck at a certain giving level?** If your donors seem to be in a giving rut—particularly if it's at a low level of giving—you may need to look again at the message you're sending through your publications, marketing, and suggested gift levels. Make sure your communications encourage giving at higher levels—and explain exactly what these larger gifts will fund.

Other Donor Groupings

Giving levels are not the only possible distinctions you might draw among your donors. Equally important to your fundraising concerns are their special subject matter interests. At an immigrant rights organization, for example, donors may be clustered into different ethnic groupings. At a musical or arts organization, you might distinguish between audience members and present or past students or participants. At a health-related organization, patients and their families might form a separate and important grouping. While these groups will no doubt share many interests, paying attention to their personal reasons for identifying with your organization can also increase your fundraising effectiveness. For an example of how one fundraiser identified and cultivated a nonobvious subgroup, see "Reunion of the Founders," below.

> **TIP**
>
> **Identifiable subgroups may be part of the problem.** If your donor subgroups have vastly disparate interests, the real puzzle may lie in moving them to support your organization as a whole. This is the situation often faced by Greenbelt Alliance, which works to protect and create park districts in threatened lands, farmlands, and wildlands around the San Francisco Bay Area. According to Elizabeth Stampe, Greenbelt Alliance's Communications Director, "It can be a challenge explaining to donors why an issue in a distant part of the Bay region affects them, when they may have more local environmental concerns on their minds—so we try to focus on broader issues, such as how urban sprawl into a new area is precedent setting, and how air pollution and traffic don't respect city lines." By paying attention to the core values driving your donors, your organization can make use of a similar communication strategy.

Also keep an eye on trends within your donor base. Where are your new donors coming from? Is there a group that seems to be unmoved by your appeals? Such observations can help you tailor your publications and solicitations. They may teach you what's on the mind of the gift-giving public or alert you to weaknesses in your fundraising efforts. For example, if you find that most of those who support your rainforest protection group are eager to donate to campaigns to save butterflies but seem to feel that treefrogs can fend for themselves, that could mean that you should focus further campaigns on butterflies, figure out a way to demonstrate that treefrogs need support too, or both.

Reunion of the Founders

M. Eliza Dexter, then–Development Director at Save The Bay, relates the following: "We'd always known that an unusual number of our members had been around for 30 or 40 years, but we hadn't fully focused on what this meant. The more I got to know Save The Bay's donors, the more I realized that this group of early members was something special. They had been true environmental leaders in the '60s, when the movement was still in its fledgling stage. They were out there monitoring things, calling each other to say, 'Did you hear what they're going to do to this watershed?' or 'Let's organize something around that.'

"So, we decided to hold an event just for these 'founding members,' as we now call them. It was a tea party at the Berkeley Yacht Club, and included a speech by a former UC Berkeley Chancellor who had himself been a founding member of Save The Bay.

"I'll never forget watching people arrive—you would have thought it was a high school reunion. People were hugging each other. They were so excited to catch up and reflect on how far they and the organization had come together. Needless to say, we're going to make this a regular event."

CROSS REFERENCE

Information on major donors. For more on working with midscale and major donors, see Chapter 6.

When to Call Your Supporters

Many nonprofits try to incorporate the telephone into their donor communication efforts—but most make a hash of it. We all know how irritating unwanted calls can be. So the simple advice about telephone fundraising campaigns can be summed up in one word—don't.

But there are a few exceptions to this rule—ways you may be able to use the phone as an effective and nonoffensive way to raise funds, including:

- to thank donors for a gift
- in combination with a letter, and
- to follow up on an appeal.

FTC Efforts to Stop Telemarketing

In 2003, the Federal Trade Commission finally took steps to protect Americans from constant calls by telemarketers. It created a national "Do Not Call" list, for which people could register online or by phone (at www. donotcall.gov or 800-382-1222). The website and phone lines were swamped as soon as they opened—about 370,000 people registered within the first 12 hours.

What does this mean for nonprofits? The good news is that charities are not prohibited from calling people on the Do Not Call list. The bad news is that the public is clearly fed up with solicitors who intrude on their private life and space. The lesson is to use the phone judiciously—and hope that the FTC's actions will eventually create a world in which people no longer shrink from a ringing phone.

Thanking Donors by Phone

As discussed earlier, everyone who gives more than a token contribution should receive a written thank-you letter. In addition, for larger gifts, a phone call can be a nice added personal touch. Chances are, the donor will remember your call long after the form letter is buried in his or her files.

If you can muster up the volunteer resources, calling everyone who sent in a reasonable-sized gift will yield results in terms of donor loyalty and potentially larger gifts later. However, a "big-name" person—such as the E.D., development director, or a board officer—should always be the one to call the major donors.

TIP

Voicemail can be your friend. Chances are, you won't catch the person you're calling at home—in fact, he or she may be screening calls through a message machine. This isn't necessarily a bad thing. If you're calling with a thank you or other simple message, leaving it on the machine is all that's necessary. Give the supporter a way to contact you, but make clear that calling back is entirely at his or her option. If your message requires a return call, at least you'll know that the donor will be calling at a time that's convenient for him or her.

Fundraising Calls Introduced by Letters

A highly effective strategy to use with midscale donors (or donors not quite major enough to warrant a personal visit) is to send a brief letter explaining that you'll call to talk about how the donor can support an upcoming plan or project. This is known as a "lead letter." Studies have shown that this combo yields greater returns than either mail or telephone used alone.

Your letter should tell the donor approximately when to expect your call (in a few days or a week, most likely). The key, of course, is not to get too busy, because you must follow through on that promise to call!

This combination can also be done in reverse, by making phone calls alerting donors to expect a letter. This is slightly more sensitive, of course, because they aren't expecting the call. It's best to have a script that also includes a thank you for past gifts, and a quick word on what's new and interesting at your organization. You might also try calling when you know the person is unlikely to be at home, with the intention of leaving a message!

Calls to Follow Up on Other Appeals

If you've mailed or emailed an appeal letter, or sent a renewal letter without results, it makes sense to follow up with a phone call. This is another good time to mobilize your volunteers, so you can reach as many people on your list as possible. Train them on the contents of your appeal. They should be ready to summarize the issue for the callers, and be willing and able to answer questions about it—or know who's available to handle any difficult questions or concerns.

It's best if your callers identify themselves (truthfully) as unpaid volunteers. This distinguishes them from the masses of telemarketers, and makes the person on the other end more likely to stay on the line.

To give supporters an additional reason to donate when called, volunteers should remind them of what an early gift will mean—an immediate and needed boost for the project, and for the caller, freedom from future mailings on this issue! If you have a premium you can offer to the first several donors, all the better.

RESOURCE

Want to know more about fundraising by phone? For information on more specialized ways to use the phone in fundraising, see:

- **Mal Warwick's website,** in particular an article entitled "12 ways to combine direct mail and telephone fundraising," by Joseph White, Jr., at www .malwarwick.com (click "Learning Resources," then peruse "Articles").
- **"Revisiting the Phone-a-thon,"** by Kim Klein, *Grassroots Fundraising Journal*, April 1999; Volume 18, Number 2; you can purchase an archive of this journal online at www.grassrootsfundraising.org. ●

Midscale and Major Donors

Chapters 4 and 5 discuss how best to appeal to a broad base of individual supporters, most of whom you hope will donate between $15 and $250. To be sure, these donations add up. But the total probably won't be enough to support your growing organization. For most nonprofits, larger gifts—those in the range of $500 and up—are important pieces of their fundraising pie. So, where do you find someone who will give your organization thousands of dollars? Probably not from your regular appeal letters and other general outreach. Though you might dream of sending out a newsletter and getting a $10,000 check in next week's mail, that dream seems to come true only for the nonprofit across town.

To get donors to write big checks, you'll have to approach them individually. Most often, you'll be approaching existing supporters, asking them to upgrade their giving levels. In other cases, you may persuade people who haven't supported your organization in the past to give a large donation. Either way, to inspire gifts at this level, you will need to enter into a close personal relationship with each supporter. Fortunately, this won't require you to assume the role of a beggar. As any successful development professional will tell you, the donor-donee relationship that works most effectively can best be described as one of collaboration. You and the supporter work together, with shared excitement, toward the same goal: that of making a difference in the world. Your organization serves as simply a pass-through entity, through which the donor's generosity is transformed into social, educational, environmental, or other worthy change.

Still, you'll need to convince a good-sized group of major supporters that your organization is the best pass-through entity to achieve their goals. As discussed later in this chapter, an important part of doing this is showing the donor just how important his or her funding is to your results.

Even if this sounds frightening, or like hard work, it can also be a lot of fun. You probably didn't get involved in fundraising because you like counting money, but because you care about furthering a cause. Sharing your conviction and interest with other, like-minded people who can afford to help that cause can be a joy, not a chore. In fact, you generally shouldn't ask anyone for a major donation unless and until:

- the person is not a stranger, but a friend or someone with a demonstrated interest in your organization or the type of work it does

- the amount you request will be in line with the person's financial capacity or past giving history

- you've laid enough groundwork so that the person won't be surprised, shocked, or offended by your request, and

- you can convincingly explain exactly why the money is needed, how it will be spent, and what you hope to achieve.

The items on this list don't have to be accomplished in a day, week, or even a month. It's not unusual to spend two or three years cultivating a potential major donor until all of these conditions are in place.

So, if major donor fundraising is about building relationships, where do you begin? This chapter starts with the most comfortable and low-pressure parts of relationship building and works up to the more challenging. This gradual approach isn't for your comfort alone—studies of major donors have shown that when they feel rushed to give without having first gotten to know the organization well, they're more likely to say no. This chapter covers:

- doing background research on supporters

- getting to know your midscale and major supporters

- asking supporters for annual renewals

- designing special events for major supporters

- meeting with supporters one on one, and

- organizing a campaign in which you and your volunteers schedule numerous meetings with supporters.

Background Research

You've just walked into a nonprofit as a new development staffer. If you're lucky, you'll have a database of supporters, which you can use to print out a few reports. (If you don't have a database, look into getting one—see Chapter 2 for suggestions.) The most useful reports will tell you who the most generous and most frequent donors are. But the names may still be meaningless to you. Perhaps one of them sounds like an acquaintance from high school, and another has the same last name as a half-forgotten 18th century author, but that's about it. Although these facts may be useful as conversational icebreakers, you're going to need more information to figure out how best to approach the supporter in the future.

For example, learning more about the supporter will help you find common interests and shared history between that person and your staff and board members, which in turn should help you decide who in your organization the supporter should meet and which projects are most likely to interest him or her. In addition, doing background research will help you decide what size and type of gift to request, when the time comes.

Start your research in your own building, by talking to staff members. Ask them to name any supporters with whom they've had personal contact and to tell you their knowledge and impressions. Also check your development office and E.D.'s records for notes on previous meetings with supporters, personal correspondence, and lists of people who participated significantly in special events or projects. Compile these notes for your database and files. Then put together a list of the hottest prospects, for further research and cultivation.

Now do the same thing with key board members (past as well as present, if possible), especially those who have been connected to your organization or the community it serves for a number of years. Board members probably haven't kept systematic records, but their friendships with major donors may be deeper. In fact, board members may have been responsible for bringing certain supporters into contact with your organization in the first place.

Even after tapping into your organization's knowledge base, your database reports may contain mystery names, or supporters about whom you know little more than their name, address, and giving history. Also, you may receive names of new prospects, from board members, for example. This is the time to do some independent research. To accomplish this, nonprofit fundraisers once had to spend many hours in the library or turn to outside consultants to compile biographies on supporters (and hiring consultants is still an option). However, the Internet has also made it possible to obtain surprising amounts of information on someone at little or no expense other than your time. (This might also be an excellent task to turn over to a board member who's not good at or interested in the face-to-face parts of fundraising.)

For free, do-it-yourself research, see "Websites for Prospect Research," below, which contains a list provided by Lauren Brown Adams (a fundraising consultant with over 20 years' experience in working with major donors), to which I've added some commentary and a few more sites. Lauren describes this list as a "beginning," noting that you can delve much deeper using the Internet (including paid sites) and other sources. The entries on this list will help you figure out everything from your prospect's business affiliations to his or her birthday, and help you estimate how much the person earns and paid for his or her house or boat, so it may be sufficiently comprehensive for your needs.

Although some of the sites on Lauren's list may seem unlikely to be of help—how often, for example, are you likely to be curious about a supporter's royalties from a hit record?—Lauren has, over the years, used all of them in surprising and valuable ways. Once, for example, while working on a private school's fundraising campaign, she noticed that the bills for one child's tuition were being sent to her father, who had the same last name as a famous Hollywood producer. By looking on www.imdb.com, a database of actors, directors, technicians, and producers, she was able to confirm that the student's father was in fact the famous producer's son. Such clues help fill out the picture of a potential donor's life and background.

> **CAUTION**
>
> **Don't be a snoop.** While research on a donor's background is legitimate, invading his or her privacy clearly is not. For thoughts on where this sometimes wavering line should be drawn, see the Association of Professional Researchers for Advancement's Statement of Ethics, available at www.aprahome.org (see the Site Map). One of their key guidelines suggests seeking only information that is relevant to your fundraising effort. They also suggest never pretending to be someone else when seeking information, and checking carefully to make sure that your sources and the information you glean from them are reliable.

Websites for Prospect Research

Here are Lauren Brown Adams's favorite starting points for research:

General Information and News:

- **www.google.com.** You probably are aware of Google, but you may not know all the things it can do. For example, if you type in a phone number, you can find out the name and address of the person or establishment it belongs to. This can be particularly useful if you have a work number and want to know where your prospect is employed. Or, if you enter the person's name and click on the "News" tab, you can pull up articles in which the person's name has appeared, from approximately 4,500 news sources.

- **www.hotbot.com.** This is another favorite search engine for research on prominent or newsworthy people. Because every search engine has its own formula for sifting through the massive amounts of information in cyberspace, you'll get different results from different services.

- **www.ibiblio.org.** Ibiblio is a "library of libraries," containing a somewhat overwhelming array of Web links. However, by clicking "Collection Index," then (under the "Reference" heading) "Journalism," then "Newspaper Archives on the Web," you'll be brought to an archive of U.S. print news, some free and some available at a charge for articles or use. You can link to newspapers' websites, and search for the name of the person or his or her company.

- **www.internet-prospector.org.** This site, tailored to the nonprofit community, offers prospect research suggestions and pulls together links to a number of research sites. It even offers a free monthly email newsletter with new site tips.

Business Information (for after you've discovered where a prospect works):

- **http://finance.yahoo.com.** This site will tell you most of what you might want to know about a publicly traded company, including who is on its board.

- **www.forbes.com.** Forbes keeps some irresistible lists, such as the 400 richest Americans and the highest paid executives. Though local nonprofits are unlikely to gain much useful information from these lists, you might have better luck by subscribing to a function called "People Tracker" (within its "business" section), where Forbes will advise you of moves by company executives and other rich and famous folk on its lists.

Websites for Prospect Research (continued)

- **www.reportgallery.com.** This offers a readily searchable database of the annual reports published by U.S. and international companies.
- **www.money.cnn.com/magazines/fortune.** Another business magazine site, with lists and a free search function of articles appearing in the print publication.

Profession-Specific Information:

- **www.martindale.com.** This site compiles information on all practicing attorneys in the United States. By entering the name in its "Lawyer Locator" function, you can find out where someone works, and whether he or she is an associate (usually a lawyer in the first six years of practice who earns a set salary) or a partner (someone entitled to a share of the firm's profits). To find out what salaries the firm pays associates, try http://infirmation.com/shared/insider/payscale.tcl (in the "Greedy Associates" section of FindLaw's website at www.findlaw.com, though this is most likely to yield results only for medium to large-size law firms). To find out what partners earn, try www.law.com and look for its survey of the profits earned per partner for 100 U.S. law firms.
- **www.ama-assn.org.** Click the "Patients" link to use the nationwide "Doctor Finder" function, which will tell you where a physician works and what type of medicine he or she practices. Then go to physicianssearch.com/physician/salary2.html to learn the low, average, and high reported incomes for various medical specialties.
- **www.imdb.com.** The entertainment industry is the focus of this site. Using the search function, you can choose "bios" from the pull-down menu, then enter a name and get detailed biographical information—sometimes including earnings information.
- **www.amazon.com.** If your prospect is an author, search his or her name to get a list of book titles—then look at the rankings to see how well the books are selling. While these rankings aren't scientific, any number under 1,000 means a book is selling very well, and the author is probably pulling in decent royalties.

Salaries and Income:

In addition to the profession-specific salary information noted above, the following sites will help you figure out how much your prospect earns:

- **www.salaryexpert.com.** Provides general salary information for various positions in different regions of the country.

Websites for Prospect Research (continued)

- **www.sec.gov/edgar.shtml.** Here, you can check companies' proxy statements (Form DEF 14A) to find out the executive compensation of officers and directors of publicly traded companies.
- **www.ascap.com/musicbiz/money-intro.html.** Contains information about prospective music business profits.

Real Estate and Other Property:

- **www.domania.com.** If your prospect has purchased a home since 1987, and you know its address, this site will give you its purchase price. Obviously, the closer the purchase was to your search date, the more current this information.
- **www.boattraderonline.com.** Check out comparative prices of boats for sale here.
- **www.controller.com.** A prospect who owns an airplane is probably living well above the poverty line. But you might also like to know how much the plane costs. As long as you know the make and model, the answer is here.
- **www.askart.com.** If you noticed a Warhol or other work by a prominent American artist on your prospect's wall, find out its likely value here.

Political Contributions:

- **www.opensecrets.org.** This well-titled website helps you discover how much a person has contributed to political campaigns or causes. The home page has a handy box with which to search by donors' names.

Birth and Death Records:

- **www.ancestry.com.** By clicking "Search Records" and entering a name, you can find birth and death dates in someone's family. This might tell you when it's appropriate to leave someone alone—or, depending on circumstances, when you might approach the family about a memorial gift.
- **www.anybirthday.com.** This site links you to sites reporting the birthdates of adult Americans. (Searches for "Ilona Bray" came up blank, but you may have better luck with your prospective donor.) Sending out-of-the-blue birthday cards to donors might make them feel stalked, but if a donor has mentioned a birthday to you and you want to acknowledge it, try this site for the exact date.

Websites for Prospect Research (continued)

Fundraising Reference Lists:

- **www.indorgs.virginia.edu/portico.** If you haven't found a website to suit your search fancy on the list above, you may find it on this list of links to websites containing biographic, occupation, salary, and other relevant information.

- **www.specialissues.com/lol.** This site features a "list of lists," especially lists about top-ranked people and businesses. For example, if you choose "Arts, Entertainment and Recreation," the first thing to pop up is a list of the top 200 art collectors.

RESOURCE

Subscriptions are available. If you'd rather pay someone to do the research for you, several Web-based services offer subscription packages—sometimes with free trial demonstrations using actual names from your database! For example, you might check out:

- **Target America,** at www.tgtam.com, or
- **P!N,** at www.prospectinfo.com.

You may also want to research your donor's cultural background. Development pros are increasingly realizing that fundraising techniques that have been developed to reach upper-class persons of European descent don't work as well in a multicultural world. Particularly if your nonprofit is closely connected to an immigrant or minority community, you will need to understand the relevant norms and social codes. Because these can be quite different even from one generation to the next, a potential donor's age may also directly impact your fundraising efforts.

Various books exist that purport to help bridge these cultural divides. However, because most of these were written for people going to do business abroad, they are mainly helpful in avoiding major gaffes (like showing up at a Lithuanian person's house bearing an even number of flowers, which would connote a funeral arrangement, or giving the thumbs-up sign to someone in one of the many cultures that interprets this as equivalent to raising one's middle finger). Beyond that, you'll get furthest by finding a friend who's savvy about the culture of the donors you'll be cultivating, and who is willing to offer frank advice.

RESOURCE

Want more information on working with donors of different cultures? Try these resources:

- **New Directions for Philanthropic Fundraising No. 37, Fall 2002,** a special issue devoted to "Fundraising in Diverse Cultural and Giving Environments."

- The **"Diversity Essays"** section of the Association of Fundraising Professionals' website at www.afpnet.org (look under "Resource Center").

Get to Know Your Existing Supporters

In a perfect world, you'd have time to meet and get to know all of your supporters, even those who send you only $10 carefully saved from their pension checks. Of course, that's probably not possible, particularly in growing organizations. The most practical alternative is to focus your personal attention on supporters who have given donations in the major and possibly midscale range.

To put your relationship with these supporters on a solid footing, and to identify personality matches between them and your board or staff members, look for meaningful ways to establish personal contact. In your early interactions, these contacts should not involve a request for cash. Remember, you're trying to build a long-term relationship with a person whom you hope will contribute a tidy sum over many years, so it doesn't hurt to be patient at the start. Three good ways to foster your relationship are:

- conveying your appreciation for a supporter's recent gift

- inviting supporters to get an inside peek at your organization, and

- creating forums where supporters can come together to share thoughts and ideas about your work.

Express Appreciation for Recent Gifts

What better time to get to know a midscale or major supporter than when he or she has just made a gift? You know that your organization is already on the supporter's mind, and you don't need to do anything more elaborate than show your thanks. Make sure your database and office procedures are set up to let you know when an unsolicited midscale or major gift arrives.

Midscale gifts in particular may arrive without personal contact, perhaps through a mailed appeal or an event, or as a result of positive publicity. But you can make the contact personal by simply picking up the phone—preferably on the very day when you receive the gift. Thank the donor graciously, then follow up with a few friendly questions, such as, "What got you interested in our organization?"; "Is there a particular branch of our work that interests you more than others?"; and "What type of work would you like to see us do more of?"

> **TIP**
>
> **Read your file before you reach for the phone.** Although it may sound obvious, make sure you've studied all the information you already have on the donor before you call. And don't forget to review the reply card that came with the donation. It could tip you off to an important fact—for example, that the donor recently moved and changed her last name (as would be common for a woman after a divorce). In the words of development professional M. Eliza Dexter, "I read through everything I've got on a donor before I pick up the phone, even for a simple thank-you call. It's common for them to ask questions, or to refer to something, like 'I remember that great coastal walk with David [the E.D.].' The last thing I want is to sound surprised!"

Asking the supporter for his or her thoughts may bring inspired suggestions (remember, you and the supporter are in this together). But even if you don't learn anything earthshaking, it will give you valuable insights into the supporter's personality and motivation for supporting your organization. And depending on how the conversation goes, you might slip in some relevant personal questions, such as "Are you an artist yourself?" or "Do you spend time hiking in our state parks?"

At the end of the call, you'll probably want to suggest further involvement with your organization, again without asking for money. For example: "I'm sure you'll enjoy the information in our next newsletter, coming out in two weeks—if you'd like to help with any of the volunteer activities, give me a call and I'll connect you to the coordinator."

If you receive a solicited gift after a personal meeting or other direct contact, then your phone call obviously need not dwell on these preliminaries. You can simply pick up where your last conversation left off, perhaps with an update on the project you sought funding for. For starters, however, the person who solicited the gift should absolutely follow up with a personal thank you (in writing or by phone) when the gift arrives. For example, if your E.D. inspired the gift after making a talk at a local service club, she, not you, should give thanks.

What if, as is common, your organization is still so new or low-budget that you don't yet receive midlevel gifts? You'll simply have to scale your efforts down to call people who contribute $50 or even $25. This is not a waste of time; if a $50 gift is a large one for your organization, then it's very much worth a follow-up! You may find that the person has given all he or she can spare. Everyone appreciates being thanked—and your personal contact may inspire the donor to give more when his or her fortunes have improved, or perhaps to speak well of your group to other potential donors.

Especially if your organization receives many donations, you may, if you're a development staffperson, want to handle the follow-up on only the most promising donors yourself, delegating the task of thanking others to a board member or savvy volunteer. Be sure to use volunteers who have a pleasant manner and good interpersonal skills. This may be the first human contact some supporters have with your organization, and you'll want to make a good impression.

TIP

Train your volunteers first. They might need a word or two on proper phone manners. For example, remind them to ask, "Do you have a moment to talk?" before launching into the conversation. Also tell volunteers what issues or recent achievements the supporter might want to hear about. If the gift was made in response to a mailed appeal, for example, you should expect questions about how you're progressing on the issues described in the appeal letter.

When the conversation is concluded, make sure the volunteer enters detailed notes on the donor's interests and background into your database or the donor's file. And don't forget to record the name of the person who made the call.

Other Special Ways to Thank Supporters

Any time that you can reach out and show appreciation to a supporter, you increase his or her sense of connection to your organization. For example, if the supporter has mentioned his or her birthday to you, a card can be a nice gesture. If you're on a business trip or vacation in another city, check your database to see whether any major supporters live there. I don't recommend completely giving over your personal time to your work, but you might enjoy squeezing in one lunch with a major donor. (Use it as an excuse to take a long lunch with a friend when you're back at work.)

The December holiday season is also a good time for general supporter appreciation. For example, the Allerton Estate in Illinois (a historical home and park) celebrated the end of one year by sending select donors jars of honey made by local bees, together with a handwritten note from the group's development director. Many organizations send selected supporters cards or nicely printed one-page letters recapping the highlights of the past year. If you send a card, make sure the cover image represents a universal theme, such as snow, candlelight, or family togetherness, not a holiday image associated with a particular religion (which your supporter may not share).

Invite Donors to Watch Your Organization at Work

Once you've made your thank-you call, the next step is to broaden and deepen this personal contact. (This is also appropriate even if you've had no opportunity to place a call.)

Fundraisers often rack their brains for the perfect way to excite donors about their organization, when the answer is right under their noses: Invite the donor to watch what your organization does. Makes sense, doesn't it? If you were a donor, would you rather see glossy marketing materials and a staged event, or the real people or places that the organization is working to help? One of the best examples I've heard of is Save The Bay, which invites major donors (and foundation staff members) to get into canoes and see the watersheds they're working to preserve. (For more on that, see "Giving Donors a Canoe's-Eye View," below.) But you don't need a boat or a view of the Golden Gate Bridge to interest people: Activities involving children, nature, or animals tend to be popular for such donor invitations. If your group teaches foster parents how to raise good kids, the graduation ceremony from one of your courses is likely to be a similarly inspiring moment.

Of course, if you work with a think tank where people sit at computers all day, or at a hospice or shelter where visitors aren't allowed, this strategy may be harder to implement. But keep it in mind just the same. If, for example, your researchers receive an award and you'll be filling a table at the ceremony, see if you can make room for a supporter or two.

Inviting potential major donors to an event requires some forethought to make the day successful. For example, if you're planning a trip or outing, don't invite more than a few new supporters along. The focus should be on keeping things real, and reasonably intimate. Also, you don't want the supporter to feel out of place, or like she has interrupted something. Be sure that staff members and others in attendance know who your guests are and behave appropriately.

Because most real events—whether it be a morning at a clinic, listening in on a course, or helping at a shelter—won't offer you and the potential major donor much opportunity for one-on-one conversation, it's not the best time to ask for specific support. If the donor is asking financial questions, however, by all means give the answers, and tell the donor what a difference financial help could make. Being too nonchalant may give the impression that financing is the last thing on your mind.

Giving Donors a Canoe's-Eye View

Save The Bay works to restore and protect the San Francisco Bay and Sacramento/San Joaquin Delta Estuary. Founded in 1961, the organization has spent more than 40 years fighting to stop unnecessary fill, unwise construction, toxic chemical dumping, and invasive plant and animal life. To further that mission, Save The Bay has acquired a fleet of canoes, which it uses to create "outdoor classrooms." Adults take tours, children learn to take water samples, and teachers attend institutes where they get ideas for bringing water ecology concepts into the formal classroom.

All of this offers a prime opportunity to get supporters interested. Save The Bay arranges to bring donors, as well as foundation staff members, along on its educational tours. Or, sometimes it will create special outings just for donors—including short coastal walks for those who don't feel up to canoeing. M. Eliza Dexter, former Development Director at Save The Bay, remembers one donor who took a canoe tour, and shortly afterward gave a higher donation than ever before—but said, "I'm not giving this just because you took me on a canoe trip!" The way Eliza figures it, the canoe trip probably helped the donor "get" why Save The Bay's work was important, and increased her sense of connectedness to the organization—even if she didn't realize it!

Create Donor Forums

In addition to inviting potential donors to see the good work your group does, you may want to involve them more systematically, by creating small study or discussion groups. This approach was pioneered by women's foundations, particularly those that make grants. The foundations saw that they could raise donor enthusiasm by giving donors a more active, meaningful role in allocating funds. For example, The Women's Foundation in San Francisco, which raises funds in order to make grants that help women and girls, invites donors to "think with us." It has created a donor circle—a small group focused on grant-making in the area of race, gender, and human rights. Each member of the circle makes a commitment of both time and money. Circle members educate themselves about the chosen topic and decide what they'd like to support with their pooled contributions.

The Women's Funding Network, an international partnership of foundations committed to social justice for women and girls, has a similar program. It has initiated "Social Change Conversations," in which donors are brought together to discuss questions such as, "How is social change different now than it was ten years ago?" "What do you hear from friends about these issues?" The participants talk, take notes, and may eventually inform the way the Women's Funding Network and its coalition agencies do their work. As described by Christine Grumm, the network's CEO and President, "It's a wonderful way to bring donors to the table in a setting that's not contrived."

Although your organization probably doesn't make grants, there's no reason not to adapt this model to your own purposes. You might, for example, create a donor group around a particular project, such as a community outreach effort or an arts event. The important thing is to give the group members the freedom to make some real choices—in other words, don't just tell them to round up money for a health awareness campaign, but ask them to research and discuss what type of campaign they would be willing to support.

> **TIP**
>
> **Know the names of your top supporters.** You (and others who interact with the public) need to be ready for spontaneous calls or visits. Imagine your embarrassment if someone who's steadily given substantial gifts to your organization calls or stops by, and hears, "Sorry, what exactly can we help you with? Could you repeat your name? How do you spell that?" Far better to say "Wonderful to hear from you, Mrs. So-and-So. Your support is helping the kids already." Make up a list of these top supporters and put copies where you, your receptionist, and other people in regular contact with the public can access them when they pick up the phone (but keep them out of public view). Of course, you should also be friendly to anyone who calls, but time probably won't allow you to memorize all of their names.

Annual Renewals of Support

Your organization may or may not have formal "memberships," in which supporters receive annual benefits—such as a newsletter or gift—for certain levels of support. Whether you've created such memberships or not, the one-year anniversary of a gift is usually an excellent time to ask for a renewal of support. When it comes to midlevel and major donors, you'll obviously be talking to people who have already demonstrated a willingness to make substantial contributions—and an entire year may have passed since their last contribution.

A good database will tell you when supporters will reach their one-year anniversary. Even with a more basic database, you should be able to keep track of the month in which a supporter makes a substantial gift; at the beginning of every month, you can search that field for the same month from the previous year to come up with a list.

Once you've figured out who to ask for support renewal, you'll have to decide how to ask. A good computer-generated letter is okay for rank-and-file supporters, but for your midscale and major supporters, you should be able to issue a more personalized request.

The midscale supporters should receive, at a minimum, a personalized letter, signed by the executive director and mentioning relevant personal details such as, "We'd love to hear more about your trip to Kenya," or "The summer program that you helped sponsor is attracting record numbers of participants." At the end of the letter, ask for continued support, and suggest that, if possible, the person raise his or her donation amount. One good technique is to suggest an appropriate percentage increase above the last gift. But do the math, and tell the supporter what the new amount would be (rounding the number to the nearest sensible amount). Include a reply envelope just as you would with an ordinary mailing. If you don't hear from the supporter, a personal phone call is typically in order.

For major supporters, send a similar letter, but also suggest a personal meeting —perhaps over lunch—to discuss the supporter's renewal. Say that you'll call in a week, and then be sure to do so. The supporter may well renew before the lunch date or meeting. But if he or she instead schedules a meeting with you, it's still a good sign; it shows the supporter's potential interest and gives you an opportunity to reignite that interest and increase the supporter's involvement with your organization. For tips on conducting such a meeting, see "One-on-One Meetings," below.

> **CAUTION**
>
> **Beware the holiday rush.** You may find that a number of your supporters' giving anniversaries fall towards the end of the year. This makes sense; many people decide to make their first gifts around the holiday season, moved by seasonal goodwill, visions of sizable tax deductions, or both. Between contacting your midlevel and major supporters for renewals and thanking donors appropriately for their gifts, you may find yourself pressed for time. Try your best to plan ahead, and don't schedule many other fundraising activities during that time. With this flurry of activity, it is also especially important that gift information is entered into your database immediately. The last thing you want is to telephone a supporter asking for a renewal when the check has already arrived.

Lectures, Small Events, and Parties for Major Supporters

If you don't have many ready-made opportunities for donors to see what you do, then why not arrange one? Some organizations sponsor supporter appreciation events, such as a complimentary "major supporters only" dinner preceding a publicly open fundraising lecture or performance. You could also take a donor or small group of donors to lunch, invite them to a reception with your actors, artists, researchers or others, or do something else that resonates with your organization's mission or shows off its work. Note that we're now transitioning into occasions at which it can be appropriate to issue a general request for financial gifts.

For example, an immigrants' rights organization with which I worked invited about 20 major donors and board members to an informal luncheon at the organization's own office. The group selected well-spoken clients to join the group, including a Guatemalan who had survived a massacre and was receiving help to apply for political asylum, and a Laotian student participating in an after-school program that offered a positive alternative to gang membership. Both spoke briefly about their personal circumstances and how they'd been helped by the organization. There was also time during the meal for chatting and getting to know one another personally. When the executive director stood up at the end, thanked everyone for participating, and asked for financial support, one impressed donor wrote a $10,000 check on the spot.

TIP

Lunches don't have to drain the budget. There's no need to pay big bucks for catering or even restaurant take-out. The prevalence of partly prepared gourmet food has made it easy to serve a classy meal without breaking the bank. For example, if you have access to a kitchen, frozen tortellini or other pasta with a nice sauce, prewashed salad greens with dressing, some good bread, and a dessert may be all you need.

Lectures or talks by prominent people associated with your organization can be another effective technique to build support. These can be of any size, from an intimate discussion with a small group of supporters to an event at a larger venue, perhaps even open to the public. Because you will be inviting people who already contribute to your organization, it's usually best to keep these events free or donation-based. Look upon lectures as a vehicle for educating people about a specific topic and how your organization plays a critical role in it. If you do this graciously and well, your guests will find plenty of ways to support you in the future. For example, the San Francisco Girls' Chorus, prior to staging "It Is the Silence," based on the diary of Anne Frank, invited major donors to a lecture by the work's composer, Linda Tutas Haugen. (For more about large lectures as special events, see Chapter 8.)

Another popular type of event is what's known in the fundraising trade as a **house party**. These are usually held at the home of a board member, preferably one who has a fair amount of space and is comfortable playing host. Between ten and 40 midscale to major supporters are invited. However, there are many terrific variations on this theme, including holding the event at a gallery or private venue that would otherwise be closed to the public. Nevertheless, as Morrie Warshawski points out in his helpful and compact book *The Fundraising Houseparty*, "There is significance and symbolic power to crossing the portal into someone's private home."

Commonly, many of the invitees are midlevel donors suggested by your development staff. But it can also be effective to invite friends of the host or of key board members whom you hope to recruit as significant donors. A few representatives of your organization should also attend—some combination of E.D., board, and staff members. The object is to create a mostly social evening, in which supporters get to know one another and learn more about the organization. Food (usually hors d'oeuvres or dessert rather than a full meal) and drinks are served. The event should feature remarks by your E.D. and/or board president about your current programs and why you need more financial support.

> **CAUTION**
>
> **The invitation should make the purpose of the event clear.** Your guests will resent it if you play a "bait and switch" game, pretending that the party is an ordinary social event when it's actually part fundraiser. Also, you want to make sure that your guests bring their checkbooks or credit cards.

A house party can also include a prominent guest speaker, short video presentation, or similar "extra," but it's not really necessary. Believe it or not, people will be pleased to simply meet the people who run your organization and do its day-to-day work. And because they already care about your cause, it shouldn't be difficult to further inspire them with your enthusiasm, dedication, and stories of struggles and successes. Still, if someone in your organization has a contact with a famous artist, author, or other prominent person whom people would be eager to meet in an intimate setting, don't hesitate to build a house party around this person.

Depending on how much the host will be involved in the food preparation and how experienced he or she is with staging a house party, you may want to do some menu consultation. (Many hosts will pay for and arrange all the food themselves; others will want your organization's help or reimbursement.) Food is a powerful symbol. On the one hand, it offers opportunities for your organization to show its personality—whether formal or easygoing, regionally focused, vegetarian, or otherwise. If your organization has an ethnic link, then food prepared in appropriate style is all but essential. On the other hand, the party planners should make sure the menu doesn't contradict any of the organization's principles. An obvious example would be that a dolphin protection organization probably shouldn't serve tuna, unless it was caught using dolphin-friendly methods.

Plan in advance exactly who will address the group and when this will occur. After the party has gained momentum, but before anyone is thinking of leaving, the host should ask for everyone's attention. If some people are standing, it's often best to ask them to sit in prearranged chairs.

After welcoming everyone and acknowledging the people who helped plan the event, the host should introduce the board chair or E.D., who can provide a brief overview of the organization's current plans, upcoming projects, and recent successes. Then someone (usually not the host) whom the partygoers respect and think of as a peer should claim the floor to talk about money. One effective technique is to mention a specific dollar figure the organization needs to fund the projects the E.D. discussed. For example, "To buy cages and medicines for the rescued birds we'll need to raise $45,000." If you've already raised some seed money (no pun intended), let people know. This gives them a sense that others have confidence in the project.

Another effective technique is for the person making the ask to state how much they have already given to the project. For example, I recently attended an alumni event at which a classmate of mine was handed the microphone and said, "My husband and I have been steadily giving to various charities over the years, but this year we've agreed to make the biggest gift we've ever given, period, to the college." You can bet that caused some audience members' eyes to widen. I, for one, was thinking, "Gee, if she can do it, ..."

Finally, the speaker should make a polite but very direct request, such as, "I'm hoping everyone here can help us with $1,000." It's particularly powerful if the host can say that he or she has already written a check.

After making the request, you may want to pass a hat. But it's probably more appropriate to carry on with the party, making it clear where checks and pledges will be collected. Putting a couple of attractive boxes or jars in obvious places in the room works, or you could have certain people designated to receive checks or pledge cards. Those people should wear obvious hats or flowers on their lapels, and avoid standing behind any large potted plants. If you'll be accepting credit cards and have a machine that swipes the cards, the money-taker should be seated at a table—preferably near the front door.

TIP

A pledge is better than a promise. Some guests will tell you they'll send in a check soon. This is fine, but to help underline the seriousness of this promise, ask them to fill out a pledge card for your records. Also, be sure to give the donor an envelope in which to send their check.

Creating Donor Recognition Opportunities

Though a few donors wish to remain anonymous, they tend to be in the minority. At the other end of the spectrum are a few donors for whom heightening their reputation as a philanthropist, impressing their peers, or being part of a "club" of high-level supporters is a major motivation for giving.

At a minimum, use your annual report to list the names of all major donors, and as many other donors as space will allow. Newsletters or event programs are also good places to thank groups of donors by name, or perhaps to focus on a particular gift and what it helped to fund. Beyond this, you should talk to individual donors to come up with a way to publicly recognize their contributions (while realizing that not every gift merits a building with the donor's name on it).

Your organization should develop options that allow you to recognize substantial numbers of donors without having to come up with a fresh and creative approach for each one. A wall of tiles or walkway of bricks at your front entrance, each bearing the name of a donor, is one simple yet effective method. Donors don't seem to tire of having their names inscribed in this way—just look around you, at places like the Pike Place Market in Seattle or the beach boardwalk outside Asilomar State Park in California. If a gift went toward a particular use, such as a new piece of playground equipment, a small metal plaque saying "Gift of So-and-So, 20xx" can be affixed to it. For especially large gifts, media coverage may also be a possibility (see Chapter 13).

One-on-One Meetings

Once you've gained experience with midscale and major supporters and gotten to know some of them personally, you'll be ready to take the next step: asking for a large gift. And you'll also be ready to request gifts from people who haven't previously supported your organization.

Because the techniques for approaching existing and new midlevel and major supporters are quite similar, they're discussed together in this section, which covers:

- deciding who to ask
- arranging the meeting
- preparing for the meeting
- assembling materials for the meeting
- the psychology of making a request
- holding the meeting, and
- following up with the donor.

Who to Ask

For your existing donors, the question of who to ask will be partly answered by their personalities and giving histories. A major donor who gave last year should be asked again, and probably asked for more. An enthusiastic midscale donor who has been giving regular gifts—say, of $100 or $200—should be personally asked to take a step up in giving.

There is no reason to be shy about asking people who already support you. Very few contributors start out as major donors—instead, they work their way up from smaller gifts. Signs that they are ready to make a bigger commitment included repeated gifts of a good size and progressively larger gifts. Another good sign that someone is ready and able to give more is that they're making large gifts to other organizations. You can find this out by keeping an eye on other organizations' annual reports and other publications, or by doing background research on your midscale donors.

CAUTION

There is no "average supporter." Even when this book cites a general rule—for example, that most donors work their way up to large gifts—there are plenty of people who don't fit this mold. Think of the news stories you hear about people who save their pennies for years and then give a million to their alma mater—or to a poetry magazine—in their will. People have different thresholds at which they feel financially secure, and react to suggestions that they increase their support in different ways. If your donor avoids or resists your efforts to coax him or her to write a bigger check, back off on asking for money, but keep doing appropriate things to build the relationship. You never know—the big check you hope for may show up just when you've given up hope.

Finding potential major donors who aren't current supporters of your organization will require a little more research. If you haven't done so already, start by asking every one of your board and staff members for likely prospects. Issuing a general request may not yield many results, so some organizations make name collection part of a board meeting agenda—or even a contest. Board members are asked to bring their address books and be ready to supply contact information for everyone they know who might be interested in your organization, whether the person is financially well-off or not. The less-likely prospects can be added to the mailing list for written appeals, while those who are more affluent can be cultivated personally, preferably following at least some of the stages described in this chapter.

TIP

Your board members may be major-gift prospects. Though not all board members can necessarily volunteer a big chunk of money on top of their time, you should be asking them to increase their contributions. In the words of Tony Poderis, development consultant and author, ". . . a board that does not have members of sufficient wealth or influence to deliver major gifts is not a well-balanced board." The board president should be the one who approaches other board members for major gifts.

The best prospective supporters are people who have a known interest in your cause or a similar one, a financial ability to give, and a history of giving to other organizations. Prospects who match only one of these criteria might not be worth a personal visit, but should certainly be added to your database for a mail appeal. Prospects who match two or three of these criteria are probably worth pursuing in person.

Keep your eyes and ears open to find out who the generous members of your community are. One easy place to find their names is at the back of programs from the theatre, symphony, and special events held by other organizations. You can even read the inscribed bricks on other organizations' walls. (It may feel like spying, but everyone does it.) Though you may not know the person, someone on your board or staff may have a link with them, because they are alumni of the same college or members of the same church or other group, for example.

EXAMPLE: Alan, the development director of a school for autistic children, notices that Tedward Goldstein is listed as a major donor by both a local children's hospital and a homeless shelter that focuses on helping families. After research indicates that this individual is a retired family court judge with a long history of personal involvement with children's issues, Alan gets on the Internet and finds out Judge Goldstein's college, temple, and other affiliations. After some asking around, he discovers that one of the school's board members belongs to the same temple. That weekend, the board member casually approaches Judge Goldstein, describes the school's activities, and asks whether he's interested in more information. The judge is intrigued, they invite him to a lecture event, and through careful cultivation, he eventually becomes a major donor.

Focus your research on people with a history of giving. Though you might dream of finding that quiet rich person who, by some miracle, hasn't been approached by any other group, such dreams rarely come true. For one thing, being rich isn't enough by itself—the wealthy widow who spends half her year shopping and the other half traveling to trendy resorts probably is not going to engage in her first act of generosity as a result of your phone call. Remember, statistics show that it's not the upper strata of U.S. society who give the most; members of the middle class—especially those who have become borderline affluent in middle age—are probably your best bets, even for major gifts.

No matter who you ask, find out whether he or she is part of a couple. If you arrange to meet with someone who doesn't make decisions without his or her other half, then you won't get a decision on the day you meet—and may have to either schedule a second meeting or risk having the partner veto a gift without hearing what you have to say. Be ready to meet on an evening or weekend if that's the only time that works for both.

Arranging the Meeting

Once you've identified a likely prospect, it's time to call him, her, or them and suggest a meeting. (You might also send a letter in advance of your phone call, particularly if you're cultivating someone who doesn't know the organization well.) This shouldn't be a stealth mission—simply tell the person that you'd like to discuss the work of your organization and how he or she might support it. Exactly how you phrase this will depend on how well you know the person and how sophisticated he or she is about philanthropy. For the experienced giver, it's enough to say, "We have a project we'd like to share with you, and we could use your help." For someone who's new to charitable giving (and might think you're just going to ask for an opinion or a batch of brownies for your bake sale), try something more specific, like, "We're trying to fund scholarships for our kids, and I'd like to talk to you about supporting this effort."

You might think that such an initial phone call would cause any sane person to laugh or hang up, but you'd be wrong. Don't let your discomfort about asking for money cloud your perceptions. First, almost no one is offended by the request to meet and discuss how they can support a cause—you're paying the person a compliment, implying that you believe he or she has a good heart and is successful enough to be able to share. Second, you've given the person enough information to allow him or her to say no—you've been clear and straightforward, which means no one needs to feel uncomfortable.

In fact, many (if not most) people you call will probably decline this meeting, giving you all sorts of reasons, from the need to travel to Antarctica to sick grandkids. But just because your target is an artful dodger, don't assume the relationship is over. Six months or a year from now, the person may be receptive to your call—or may even call you. Third, and perhaps most importantly, you're calling someone whom you've already identified as inclined to give money to a good cause. (Some of the truly wealthy philanthropists say that they'd like to give more money away if only they could find causes good enough!) The upshot is that a surprising number of people will say yes to your request to meet. With that simple, short phone call, you've taken a huge step forward.

If you're calling someone who has no previous connection with your organization, the initial phone call will have to be slightly longer. Be ready to tell the person where you got his or her name (particularly if it was through a friend) and why you think your organization might be of particular interest. You should be able to sum up what your organization stands for and what it does in a few sentences. (Even if you sent an advance letter, it may now reside in the circular file.) It's particularly effective if you have a specific need in mind, something urgent enough to justify meeting soon (and without cultivating the donor more gradually). Here's a sample script:

"Hello Mr. Scarry, this is Ima Edie from the Society for Train Depot Restoration. We're working to restore the beautiful historic train depots in our community. We believe that, because of your interest in train history and in community improvement, you might be interested in supporting these efforts—particularly because the depot in your neighborhood is scheduled for demolition this summer. Could we meet at your convenience to talk this over?"

At this point, the prospective supporter will no doubt have questions, which you should take the time to answer in full. There's no harm in giving information that you will later repeat at a meeting (unless you tell the exact same "amusing anecdote" in the exact same words—it pays to have a good memory for these things when fundraising). If the person agrees to meet, be ready to suggest a location, such as the donor's home or office, your organization's office, or a restaurant. If the person doesn't want to meet one-on-one but is willing to talk the matter over at further length by phone, go ahead and agree to this. In either case, plan on a minimum one-half-hour's meeting time.

After the phone call, quickly send out a confirmation letter (or email, depending on the person's preferences), mentioning:

- the purpose of the meeting
- the meeting time and location, and
- who will be at the meeting.

And to cover all your bases, call the prospect a day or two before the meeting to confirm.

To Lunch or Not to Lunch?

Professional fundraisers are of mixed minds about whether to meet with major supporters over lunch. On the plus side, it makes the event seem more social, and gives you and the prospect a better chance to get to know each other through small talk before getting to the matter at hand. Also, assuming you make clear that you're hosting the lunch, it allows you to act magnanimous before asking the supporter to do the same—a sort of thanks for past support or thanks in advance for future support.

On the minus side, meeting at a restaurant guarantees not only that you'll use up more of your and the supporter's time, but also that the mechanics of ordering and paying will use up a good portion of that time. And you're leaving more up to chance—what if the food that day is terrible, the people at the next table have a screaming match, and the waiter spills the soup on your prepared materials? All of this helps explain why many fundraisers prefer meetings where food doesn't get in the way—such as your organization's offices or the donor's home or office.

If you invite a potential donor to a restaurant, don't pick the fanciest place in town. A pricey restaurant is likely to give the supporter some wrongheaded ideas about where his or her money will be going. This is especially likely to be true if the donor earned his or her own money rather than inheriting it—most wealthy people became wealthy by learning habits of frugality early in life.

Preparing for the Meeting

To prepare for your meeting, start by filling in any gaps in your research about the prospect. You'll also want to decide who will attend the meeting. If the supporter has a friend in your organization, that person should attend. Most development professionals prefer to bring a team of two, including some combination of the E.D., development director or other gift officer, and any board members, staff, or volunteers who know the prospect or have mutual interests or backgrounds. Not only are two heads better than one, but if one of you leaves the organization, the personal relationship with that supporter won't be broken. Also keep in mind that the E.D. or someone on the policy side of the organization may be better able than the development director to speak with conviction about your programs and activities.

Use the results of your background research, along with other considerations such as the scope of the project and who else will be asked to contribute, to decide how much and what to request. You'll want to suggest a specific sum (or item, if you're looking for property)—open-ended requests make donors uncomfortable, and lead to lowball offers. Obviously, you'll want to ask for an amount the person can afford. But no matter how much the person is worth, look into the person's giving history—to your organization and others—to figure out what gift level will feel right for them. Don't get fixated on your goals for this year or campaign—also realize that the donor might be more comfortable with a phased gift, or one made via a will.

Also, notice whether the donor has typically made gifts of something other than cash, such as property or stock. And consider the larger social context for the gift. If the donor has friends in your organization, how much do they give? In her instructive and often amusing book, *Fundraising for the Long Haul*, Kim Klein tells stories of donors who have, after discovering that they gave less than their friends or community peers, expressed annoyance that they were not asked for a higher sum.

Try to choose an amount that challenges the person to give a substantial percentage more than they've given before, but isn't off their personal scale. For example, if a donor has given $1,000 for the last couple of years, you might ask for $1,500 or $2,000 more for a special project.

TIP

Give the donor payment options. Even when you're anticipating a cash gift, you don't have to ask that it be made all at once, in one lump sum. Many people think of their finances in monthly terms, in which case a monthly pledge might suit them. Or, if your prospective supporter has an entrepreneurial streak, suggest a "staged" gift—one that is given piece by piece, conditioned on your organization's success along the way. If you're starting a new program that looks like an uncertain proposition, this can also allay the supporter's fears of pouring money into a sinkhole. The supporter might be excited at the idea of tracking how the program is going and of pledging further gifts if it rises to the challenge.

True, it's not a guaranteed income source for you—but if it leads to a larger overall gift, and a higher level of supporter interest in and contact with your organization, it will have been worth it.

Make sure that everyone who attends the meeting is clear on his or her role. In particular, figure out who is going to make the actual request for money. You can guess the probable result if you leave this vague—or worse yet, if both of you assume that "the ask" is the other person's job.

> **TIP**
> **Supporters may ask whether (and how much) your board members have given.** Wealthy people like to know that your board members believe in your efforts—and have backed up this conviction with financial contributions. Be ready with the most up-to-date, positive answer you can muster.

Assembling Materials for the Meeting

Depending on the nature of your relationship with the supporter, you may want to assemble or prepare some relevant written materials. This isn't always necessary, however. If the supporter has been involved in your organization for years, invites you to her house for tea, and prefers to think of the relationship as primarily social, showing up with a stack of brochures and budgets could ruin the atmosphere. For other supporters, however, written information may be welcome and necessary to help clarify your request. In general, the more unusual or specific your request for support—for example, if it's around a new project or a capital campaign—the more appropriate it will be to bring written materials.

Make sure you have your organization's brochure and annual report on hand. Even if you've already sent the supporter an annual report, you might bring another copy along. The person may not have read it carefully (or at all). If the person isn't very familiar with your organization, include some historical information and a detailed explanation of your mission in your written materials. If you're talking to an existing supporter, perhaps one renewing support, you can just focus on "what's new" since you last met, and what's special about your current request for funds.

If you plan to ask for support for a particular big-deal purpose—a new transmitter for a public radio station, a new building for a school, or a new outreach program—it's a good idea to prepare a "case statement": a two- to five-page document outlining your request. Again, depending on your history with the supporter, this document might also describe your organization's history, mission, clientele and their needs, current goals, money needed to meet those goals, and ability to use the donor's gift effectively. The statement can be tailored to the donor's prospective giving level, explaining how gifts of particular amounts will meet specified needs—for example, "Every gift of $x can fund x days of research into curing a medical condition," or "It will cost $1,200,000 to build a study annex onto our school's library. To start our campaign, we are seeking 20 founders' gifts of $25,000."

If your organization already has written materials discussing recognition opportunities for particular major gift levels, bring those along; it's often easier to motivate donors to make large gifts if a brick, tile, or plaque will commemorate their contribution. And if your organization is lucky enough to have been the subject of any press coverage (positive, of course), bring copies of the articles or transcripts. These are great for adding credibility to your own materials.

Always bring a copy of your organization's budget, a specific project budget, and information about how much of every dollar you collect supports your organization's work. (See Chapter 4 for information about the importance of showing that contributions support your cause, not just further fundraising.) Not everyone will read a budget, although your supporter may take a keen interest in it if he or she has a background in business or finance. For those who don't enjoy interpreting balance sheets, however, be ready to explain the budget in plain English. In particular, note what parts of the budget represent growth or shifts in program focus. And be sure to point out how much of your budget is made up of individual (as opposed to foundation or corporate) donations. Even if the percentage sounds less than impressive, you can put it in more realistic terms by saying, for example, that, "Without individual donations, we'd have to gut the entire educational portion of our program."

Some or all of your prepared materials should be assembled into a packet that you can leave with the donor after the meeting is over. Put it all together in a glossy folder. The packet shouldn't be overwhelming—the materials should all look professional and factual, and be easy to read and understand.

Fundraising Worksheet 5: Meeting Checklist

Here's a summary of things to consider bringing to your donor meeting:

❑ Brochure

❑ Annual report

❑ Historical information

❑ Mission description

❑ Case statement

❑ Budget

❑ Plans for the future

❑ Publicity materials

❑ Copies of any recent newspaper articles

❑ Premiums and recognition opportunities

❑ Pledge card

❑ Receipt book

TIP

Don't forget your calculator. Unless you're a math genius, a calculator may come in handy. For example, it will help if a donor says "I want to give scholarships to ten children with cancer to attend your camp each year for the next ten years. How much will that be if I make a firm pledge now but write you a check on the first day of each year, allowing for 3% annual inflation?"

The Psychology of Asking

To get yourself into a frame of mind that will allow you to survive—and even enjoy—the asking process, remember these simple rules:

- be yourself
- be direct
- focus on the cause
- don't beg, and
- be ready to adjust to opinionated donors.

Be Yourself

Parts of this chapter suggest actual words to use and to avoid when requesting major gifts, so that you won't lie awake at night wondering what the "right" thing to say is. However, no canned script can give you the words to describe what excites you about your organization's work. Although your rehearsed lines may do a good job framing your message, ultimately you'll want to put them aside and speak from the heart. In short, you need to have a "real" conversation with a real person. How you express things may be completely different from how another development person would. That's good—this is an area where, depending on the individual you are talking to and your own personality, there can be lots of right ways to do things.

Be Direct

You'll go a long way toward making yourself and your supporters comfortable by simply being direct. No matter how much you've done to ease into this relationship, there will come a time when you simply have to look the person in the eye and say, "A gift of $50,000 would provide a crucially important launch for this program." You can't back into it and you can't say it in code. But the wonderful thing is that once the words are out, the air becomes clear. Because you've shown that you're comfortable asking the supporter for a specific dollar amount, that person has the opportunity to respond with equal directness.

> **CAUTION**
>
> **A direct approach may not be appropriate in all cultures.** No advice is always correct. If you are working with people whose ethnic or cultural background requires or celebrates a more subtle approach, you'll obviously need to adjust your style. In some communities, the potential donor—not you—should mention money first, so as to allow that person to maintain "face" or "honor" if now is not a good time to give.

Focus on the Cause

You'll be more persuasive (and more comfortable) if you can mentally remove yourself from the giver/recipient picture. You're not begging for money for yourself—you're asking the supporter to partner with your organization to achieve a mutually desirable result. Remember, this person has a history of giving either to your organization or others. People don't dip their toes into the major giving waters unless they really do understand that their giving can make a difference in the world.

It will also help if you remember that whether a person writes a big check or doesn't, this isn't about you, your career, or your sinking feeling that you should have signed up for more training seminars. You're simply the intermediary who guides the supporter toward the best path to make a difference. If you are able to paint a compelling picture of the job that needs to be done—the impoverished people who need AIDS medicine, the inner-city child who can grow via your music program, or the sea turtles endangered by a proposed oil refinery—you've done your job.

> **TIP**
>
> **Ever made a major gift yourself?** Then you can mentally picture yourself on the same side of the table as the donor—and if the gift was made to your organization, assure him or her that you've made the same commitment that you're asking for. Also remember what doubts or concerns you had before making the gift, and how you overcame them.

Don't Beg

Even with your eye on the cause, it's easy to slip into phrases like, "Could you help us with," "We'd be so grateful if," and "I hope it's not asking too much if . . . ." People who humbly importune a potential donor to make a gift are more likely to get stepped on than they are to get a big check. That's because begging is almost always a sure turnoff. The supporter may wonder whether you lack other community support, or are in such dire straits that the money may just plug a leaking hole and nothing more. The supporter may also buy into your own accidental message and think he or she is being asked to support your organization's need as opposed to a greater good.

Be Ready to Adjust to the Donor's Interests

Plenty of major donors are just plain opinionated. They may have worked hard for their money, and they sometimes want to decide exactly how it will be spent. You may hear things like, "No, I won't give one penny to your group to provide extra funding for area public schools—the whole system is a mess—but I might fund a totally different approach, such as a small school demonstration project, focused on parental involvement." At times like these, you'll have to be quick on your feet. If the donor's suggestion is closer to your proposal than the donor at first realizes, then it may be worth steering his or her attention back to the proposal on the table. If it's not, however, then it is usually best to express sincere interest in the donor's ideas, explain that you will present them to the decision makers in your organization, and get back to the donor afterward.

Holding the Meeting

Now, all you have to do is meet! Some people wonder at first how they'll have enough to say to fill a whole meeting's worth of conversation. But filling the time is rarely a problem, especially if two people from your organization attend the meeting. And remember, you've got two fascinating subjects to keep you busy: the supporter (practically everyone likes to yak about their background, interests, opinions, and current activities) and your organization.

If it helps you to think about the meeting sequentially, here's the usual play-by-play: You and your teammate should meet a few minutes in advance to share any last-minute information and, if necessary, discuss what you'll talk about as an icebreaker. Once you have all assembled, start with introductions. Remind the supporter that you're there to talk about a specific need or new program your organization is embarking upon, the critical importance of financial support, and how long you expect to spend in this meeting. Work in a little fun small talk, with the idea of engaging the supporter. The best fundraisers say that if possible, they like to spend the majority—say, around 75%—of any meeting just listening to the supporter. This isn't idle or phony listening. You'll not only be learning more about the supporter's interests and passions, but also refining your understanding of how and why he or she might give. In fact, if the donor is savvy about your field (and many are), you may learn information vital to your organization's successful growth.

Journalists will tell you that the best way to interview someone is to ask open-ended questions—questions that don't show off your expertise or imply a conclusion, but simply invite the other person to educate you. Depending on your nonprofit's work, you might ask such questions as: "What do you think are the most important components of a child's education?" "Which of our shows did you like best this season?" or "How do you think our project could be improved?" Find out about the donor's other interests, hobbies, and work. Ask what other organizations the supporter is actively involved in and what he or she likes about volunteering or other experiences there.

At some point, bring the discussion back to the purpose of the meeting. If you've brought written or visual materials, present these in a well-organized fashion. Lay out what your organization is up to and why its work, or a particular project or program, is worth investing in. But don't get too buried in your written materials. Always remember the things that get you personally excited about the organization. Draw on these and the inspiring conversations you've had with other staff and volunteers to build the supporter's interest. Although good written materials can buttress your pitch, your enthusiasm for the cause will usually be more convincing than a briefcase full of budgets and brochures. Also try to incorporate specific details, to distinguish your organization from the many others doing good work. Which of the following two statements would you find more persuasive?

- "Our program of reading aloud to children in shelters has been shown in statistical studies to make a significant difference to their psychological well-being and produced measurable improvements in their school performance."

- "I'll never forget the first time I participated in our program to teach at-risk kids to read. I was sitting on a mat on the floor at the back of the shelter on 17th Street with a homeless six-year-old whom I had been working with for a month. When one day she picked up a book and read 'Spot saw a cat,' I literally had tears in my eyes."

The first sentence is relevant, and might work (with a little paring down) in a grant proposal, or even as a subpoint in an annual report. But the second one tells your lunch companion what hooks you in, and will probably bring the work alive for him or her as well. It's all in the details.

Learning to Tell Donors About the San Francisco Girls Chorus

Sarah Clark, former Development Director at the San Francisco Girls Chorus, says she knew upon starting the position that she loved listening to the girls' performances—in fact, they sent chills up her spine. But to really develop her passion for the SFGC's programs, and to help her explain it to donors, the organization encouraged her to get even further involved.

Sarah took the time to attend an array of behind-the-scenes activities: from rehearsals to outreach performances (at which the girls perform at schools in order to encourage budding singers to join) to the SFGC's annual summer music camp. She remembers, for example, an experience she had watching the Level 3 girls (ages 10 to 13) being coached by Judaline Swinkles Ryan: "I saw how the teaching emphasized discipline and excellence as well as musicality. Judaline was clear and direct with the girls about things like not coming in late, and paying attention—she'd say, 'Look at me!' And it made a difference. At the beginning of the half hour I spent watching, they sounded okay. But by the end, they were a tight, focused unit—and they sounded great!"

Through these activities, Sarah also got to know some of the girls who participated. She enjoyed seeing how they could be lounging on the stairs, eating junk food, and giggling together offstage, then turn into serious, poised beautiful singers onstage. This is the stuff of which donor stories are made.

Before long, it will make perfect sense to start talking dollars. Candidly explain to the prospect exactly how much things will cost and how you arrived at that figure. Mention any in-kind donations that you've received, to show that you're trying to keep costs down, as well as any significant grants or other donations that have come in. This is a great way to tell your meeting companion that he or she isn't the only donor in town, but will join a respectable group of people who believe in your cause.

Finally, once the preliminaries are over, and you've built—or reinvigorated—the potential donor's interest in your case, look him or her in the eye and say something like, "We'd like you to consider a gift of $10,000, to bring us within a realistic distance of our goal." Or if you're asking for a slightly raised renewal of a past donation, you might simply say, "Can I put you down for a renewal at the $2,500 level?" or something similarly optimistic.

Then sit quietly and let the person have a chance to think. Try to look hopeful, while you resist the human urge to chatter or even apologize for a bold request. And make sure anyone who accompanies you respects the donor's need for time to think.

If the person agrees, say thank you and be enthusiastic, but keep your wits about you. You'll need to discuss when and how the payment will be made. For example, if the donor won't write one check, you'll want to explain various payment methods and ask the donor to commit to one. Also, offer a pledge card if the donor won't immediately be writing a check.

Now is also the time to talk about whether the donor is interested in any return gifts or recognition opportunities. But whether you're talking about a brick in a donors' wall, a listing in a program, or a name on the side of a building, you should put your recognition in terms of your desire to thank the donor, not as the donor's "payback" for giving. If the donor wants no recognition or wishes to remain anonymous, perhaps even in printed materials like your annual report, make a careful note of this and make sure your internal systems are geared to respect this wish. You don't want to be in your office the day someone who made an anonymous donation of $25,000 reads about it on your website.

If the person seems uncertain about whether to give, try to get to the heart of the ambivalence. Would he or she like more information about your organization? Does he or she need time to think about the purpose for your request or to consult with a key family member? Is there a slightly smaller gift amount the donor would be more comfortable with? At this point, your job is to try to learn what the person is thinking. Or put another way, you need to listen to the donor's concerns before you can sensibly respond to them.

But make sure you ultimately get a yes or no answer. As one experienced fundraiser told me, "I like to get to the point of hearing an actual 'yes' or 'no'—in fact, I'll follow up on a vague answer with a question like, 'Does that mean you can't make a donation at this time?' This makes it easier for the other person to respond directly, and allows us all to move on."

If the donor says no, don't take this as a flunking grade on your performance (unless you really did screw up the pitch, which is unlikely). Remember, anyone affluent enough for you to approach has a world of things to consider—how much he or she has given to other causes lately, how his or her own investment portfolio is doing, his or her child's expensive scuba diving hobby, and the request for a major donation from another worthy nonprofit the donor received yesterday.

Also realize that it's not easy for many people to say no, so it's actually part of your long-term development task to make the donor feel better! You might say something like, "I'm sorry this didn't work for you, but I can certainly understand where you're coming from. Of course, we'll keep in touch, and I'll look forward to seeing you at our summer event. Would you mind if I contacted you again next year?"

Some experts recommend trying to negotiate after a "no" answer—for example, by suggesting a lower amount. Obviously, it depends on how the "no" was delivered—sometimes the donor's voice and body language suggest that it was really a maybe, and sometimes you'll get a clear signal that no means no. If you conclude that you really received a flat-out no, it's best not to torture yourself or the donor by trying to turn it around. Thank the person for his or her time, and focus both your attentions on the positive aspects of your time together—you perhaps had an enjoyable lunch or meeting, the other person learned more about your work, and you probably learned something about what ignites or dampens donors' interests. The lessons of that meeting may help you land an even larger gift from this person or someone else further down the road.

> **TIP**
>
> **Is that your final answer?** Take the advice of Sophie Lei Aldrich, of Boston University, an experienced fundraiser who says that she never thinks of any "no" as truly final. The "no" is just a reflection of the supporter's inclinations and financial situation on that day. Thinking along those lines gives her the freedom to graciously stop the money part of the conversation, while refocusing on fostering her long-term relationship with the supporter.

In the unlikely event that your meeting experience was truly horrible, just remember this: It will make a great story at your next professional fundraisers' gathering.

Follow Up After the Meeting

As soon as you get back to your office, draft a thank-you letter. And do this whether the answer was yes, no, or maybe. Also, promptly enter the pledge and other information into your database, and follow through on any other promises—for more written information or a meeting with another staffperson, for example. And if a large gift was made, and you have either collected or put the process on automatic, don't forget to gather other staff and board members to celebrate your success.

Setting Up a Focused Major Gifts Campaign

Everything in life gets easier if you can share your tribulations and victories with others. That's why many organizations organize major gifts campaigns, in which staff and board members get together and schedule a series of gift solicitations. The basic task is the same as described in the previous sections: One or two members of your organization invite a prospect to a meeting or lunch, prepare supporting written materials, and ask for the gift. What's different, however, is that the campaign is time limited. While this typically sets you up for an intense fundraising push, it also lets you know in advance when the hard work will be over—something that can be very helpful when seeking to involve board and staff members. Most major gifts campaigns last for a few months, with each person going to approximately one meeting per week.

To organize all this activity, you'll want to:

- **Develop a list of potential donors.** Carefully go through your existing list of donors and prospects, and meet with board and staff members to identify new prospects, until you have a list of people that's sufficiently large and promising that their reasonably expected donations will be enough to meet your goal. Only about half of the people on even the most well-developed list are likely to give, so plan your goals accordingly.

- **Start off with a training.** Get all your participants together at the beginning for a rousing review of your organization's mission and work, any special goals involved in this campaign, and how to conduct themselves at the meetings. You could photocopy portions of this book for them to review, or bring in an outside trainer. And don't forget that this isn't boot camp—your training should be inspiring enough that it also serves to remind the participants of what is really important about your work and why people will want to fund it. It often helps to bring in a client who's been helped by your organization's work, or a program staff person who can voice how it feels to see the results of the work. This will rev up your volunteers more than a dollar goal ever could (or should).

- **Distribute materials.** The materials you provide to your asking team should include an internal summary sheet describing the campaign and their role in it, materials they'll take to meetings with prospective supporters, a contact list of participating volunteers, board, and key staff members, "visit record forms" to be filled out after every meeting for future reference, and stationery with envelopes to use for thank-you letters.

- **Assign donor meetings within the group.** As you plan who will visit each prospect, make sure your participants are allowed plenty of input and at least a reasonable degree of choice. And be sure your tracking system is good enough to guard against embarrassing mistakes, like more than one participant contacting the same supporter.

- **Schedule "check-back" meetings over the course of the campaign.** Every few weeks, participants should get together to compare notes, tally results, and exult over or complain about their experiences. This will allow you to fix anything that's impeding the effectiveness of your effort. For example, you might find that a tidbit of factual information was left out of the training, with the result that no one quite understands why a new piece of electronic equipment is absolutely necessary. Check-back meetings also prevent procrastination. And, perhaps more importantly, they're great morale boosters. People who got large pledges help others realize it can be done; and people who had disastrous meetings feel better after turning it into an entertaining story for the group.

- **Tally up your results at the end.** Write up a summary of costs and expenses, a list of who participated and who was visited, and any notes about why the campaign succeeded or didn't meet expectations. Put this at the front of a file labeled "[Date] campaign," and include all the visit record forms and copies of other written materials that were used or distributed.

- **Celebrate.** Particularly if the campaign went well, have a final meeting or party in which participants hear the final tally, relax with some food or music, and have a last chance to boast about their fundraising prowess.

> **RESOURCE**
>
> **Capital campaigns are slightly different.** The campaign described above would be part of your annual fundraising program. This book doesn't cover larger scale campaigns, including capital campaigns, in which your entire organization may mobilize around a particular project or monetary goal—often to fund something on a scale that dwarfs your normal fundraising activities, such as a new building. Because this book's focus is on smaller nonprofits and raising money for their usual course of business, capital campaigns aren't addressed separately here. For more on planning and carrying out such campaigns, see:
>
> - *Conducting a Successful Capital Campaign: The New, Revised and Expanded Edition of the Leading Guide to Planning and Implementing a Capital Campaign,* by Kent E. Dove (Jossey-Bass).
>
> - *Capital Campaigns: Strategies That Work: Aspen's Fundraising Series for the 21st Century,* by Andrea Kihlstedt (Jones & Bartlett).

What About Those Billionaires?

Even with slumps in the economy, many of the rich are getting richer—which means that the stock of big-time philanthropists should remain steady. And philanthropy has become chic, with stars advertising their affiliation with good causes, and rich businesspeople upping their "star quality" by being seen at gala fundraisers. The likes of Bill Gates, the Waltons (of Wal-Mart), George Soros, and Warren and Susan Buffett have become actively interested in finding ways to use their wealth to change the world. The results are dramatic and visible. For example, whenever I return to my home town of Seattle, I can hardly find my way around without bumping into new buildings—musical, medical, or other facilities—all funded by Microsoft money.

So where's the trickle-down to your organization? Or better yet, the fat check? Many of these new philanthropists say that they'd give away more than they already do if they could only find a worthwhile cause. But don't get too excited until you hear the catch. If you think that foundations and average individual donors are demanding in terms of accountability and results, you ain't seen nothing yet. The philanthropist of today tends to be:

- highly attuned to business models and success strategies
- focused on personal involvement in a cause, either directly or through his or her foundation, and
- eager to see results within a lifetime.

The 1990s were a time of huge wealth generation. The people who benefited the most still tend to believe that their own skills and know-how accounted for much of their success. They reckon that the business models they used should be applied to charitable settings, to actually solve problems rather than to bandage them over. They speak of "investing" in programs, not "contributing" to them. The approach vaunted by investment banker Paul Tudor Jones's Robin Hood Foundation says it all: "Since 1988, Robin Hood has targeted poverty in New York City. By applying sound investment principles to philanthropy, we've helped the best programs save lives and change fates." (See www.robinhood.org.)

If the work of your organization involves a problem that's just not likely to go away anytime soon—at least, not without a total overhaul of the U.S. economic and social structure—you might be hard-pressed to attract the attention of these ambitious philanthropic capitalists. Sadly, feeding the homeless or providing shelters for victims

What About Those Billionaires? (continued)

of domestic violence might be seen as programs that don't "solve" an ongoing problem. You'll need to have a vision that's groundbreaking, and can be implemented efficiently and effectively.

That probably means your organization will already have to be successful and stable—it's one of those classic "it takes money to make money" conundrums. The struggling nonprofit with inexperienced volunteers answering the phones, information scattered between various filing cabinets, and a website that was updated last year (if it exists at all) may inspire more scorn than interest. You may have better luck asking for support in the form of a loan or management advice, some of the alternative giving models that the new philanthropists are exploring.

You'll also find that many of the big-time philanthropists have moved beyond mere check writing, and have started their own foundations (though some of them close these down as soon as they discover how much paperwork is involved). If a foundation has been established, you can approach it much like any other foundation—most likely with a formal grant application (see Chapter 10) if it makes grants publicly available.

Many of these new foundations are trying to eliminate the middleman (that is, your organization) by directly funding grassroots projects (such as an overseas cooperative) or by starting programs of their own. For example, Eli Broad, founder of SunAmerica Inc. and KB Home, put $400 million toward his own educational reform strategy, helping train educational leaders and sponsoring a yearly competition among urban school districts to improve student performance—with a prize of $500,000 in scholarship money to the winning district. Or there's James E. Stowers, Jr., who founded American Century Services Corp., and pledged a whopping $1.5 billion toward the creation of a center to find a cure for cancer—a disease for which he, his wife, and one of their daughters have all been treated. Such philanthropists aren't content to sit back and write checks. They tend to believe that they've got methods or answers that haven't been tried before. In that sense, your organization's continued existence may be a strike against you. If you had figured out a way to solve the problem at issue, then you could have folded up your tent and gone home by now.

Still, as time goes by, some philanthropists are confessing to their own naïveté, noting the intractability of certain problems and the importance of experience at working a problem. We may yet see a swing back toward relying on existing organizations.

Funds From the Great Beyond: Bequests and Planned Gifts

Your fundraising efforts with individual donors will doubtless focus on obtaining gifts out of their annual income. However, over the course of a donor's life, he or she may also accrue savings, property, and other assets—and eventually, the donor will have to decide how to dispose of these things at death. While bequests to spouses, children, and other close family members will almost always predominate, many people also plan to leave at least a small slice of their estates to a good cause. And studies have shown that large numbers of other people, both regular donors to charity and not, would consider doing so if asked. This is where you come in.

By reminding longtime donors about the importance of estate planning, and by explaining how their testamentary gifts can benefit your organization, you help everyone achieve their goals. Most of the time, you'll want to start by letting potential donors know that if they fail to plan their estates, state law will direct that their property be distributed under a one-size-fits-all statutory formula (called intestate succession) that's unlikely to fully reflect their wishes. You'll also want to encourage them to include a charitable giving component within their larger estate plan—not only by demonstrating that your group will put their assets to good use, but also, for your wealthiest donors, by explaining how charitable bequests can reduce (or even eliminate) the amount of estate tax their beneficiaries will owe.

As your organization grows, and its development efforts become more sophisticated, you may want to offer donors a further giving incentive. Estate planning tools with names like "charitable gift annuities," "charitable remainder unitrusts," or simply "life income gifts" allow people to give assets to your organization for investment, but either continue to derive some income from those investments during their lifetime or give your organization the income but require you to return the principal to the donors or their heirs.

This chapter offers a primer on the rules and methods for making gifts through an estate—commonly called "planned giving," "gift planning," or "deferred giving." However, because of the complex financial and tax concerns involved, this chapter will primarily cover the basics. Most organizations that are large and established either hire planned giving specialists or attend intensive trainings when they're ready to move into this advanced area of fundraising. Nevertheless, this chapter will describe important steps that you can start taking right now, especially when it comes to accepting straightforward inheritance gifts. It's a time-efficient way to raise substantial gifts.

> **CAUTION**
> **Don't expect your planned giving program to be a quick fix for financial problems.** Because most supporters who include your organization in their estate plans will enjoy good health for many years to come, the typical planned giving program doesn't start yielding results for seven to ten years after its inception. And it may take even longer before you receive substantial income from these types of gifts. Once things get going, you should find that the return on your investment of time and effort far outweighs the return on any other sort of fundraising—but don't expect those returns to start rolling in right away.

For some fundraisers, the most difficult part of developing a planned giving campaign is to overcome the natural reticence to mention the word "death." This reluctance is so strong that until about 20 years ago, fundraisers had a tendency to wait around politely, unwilling to broach the subject but hoping for a surprise call from someone's lawyer. However, the tide has now turned dramatically—requests for planned gifts have become a normal part of fundraising requests, whether in person, in newsletters, or on websites. In fact, many nonprofits now offer special seminars to teach their supporters basic estate planning principles, as well as how charitable gifts might fit in with their plans. And all of these changes are having an effect. A survey by the National Committee on Planned Giving found that 11% of Americans have already named a charity in their will, or arranged another form of planned gift. But don't worry that you've missed the testamentary giving boat—Americans over the age of 60 will bequeath as much as $15 trillion over the next few decades, and some of that money can flow to your organization, if you put the proper systems in place to encourage and receive it.

To help you assess long-term planned giving possibilities, this chapter addresses:

- what kinds of organizations can attract planned gifts
- how virtually any organization can handle basic inheritance gifts
- how to roll out your planned giving program smoothly and effectively, and
- the basics of soliciting and handling more complex life-income gifts.

How to Attract Inheritance and Other Planned Gifts

Many people's aspirations to do something noteworthy—such as creating a work of art, making a scientific discovery, or helping to bring about peace in the world—are partly motivated by a desire to achieve at least a small measure of immortality. Of course, they know that they won't really live on through such acts. But, regardless of their religious beliefs, they may take comfort in thinking that their impact will be felt on this earth even after their death.

Your organization can play a role here, by becoming the vehicle through which otherwise ordinary folks can make a lasting difference. The emphasis here is on "lasting." Your goal should be to help donors achieve maximum impact (and recognition, if they want it) through their world-improving gifts. For example, bequests that include a plaque or inscription with the deceased's name are quite popular (though plenty of givers are content to go without such recognition). And other forms of remembrance—from published thanks to dedicating a building, program, or scholarship to the donor—are equally effective.

To be well positioned to receive bequests, your organization should have some or all of the following characteristics:

- **Your organization will still be around when the donor's Last Will and Testament is pulled out of the drawer.** This may be difficult for small or new organizations, as well as for those teetering on the edge of financial collapse. It will be impossible for organizations whose sole mission is to accomplish a certain goal and then close up, such as an organization created to build a bicycle trail or free a small group of political prisoners.

- **Your organization's mission, goals, and activities are momentous enough to appeal to someone's idea of a legacy.** For example, a donor would presumably rather imagine, "Upon my death, a new stretch of park will be purchased for my home city," than "My legacy will be to buy a year's worth of gasoline for the bowling league van."

- **Your organization can articulate how planned gifts will be spent.** Most donors prefer to see that your organization has a clear spending plan in place—preferably applying such gifts toward something lasting, such as an endowment or a capital project, rather than toward covering general operating costs. If your organization has thought about how gifts will be used in advance, the donor will know that you won't spend a large gift carelessly.

- **Your organization offers meaningful recognition opportunities for those who are interested,** such as naming a creek, building, or other long-lasting monument after the donor. Not every donor will want these, of course. As Audrey Yee, Associate Director of Planned Giving at Golden Gate National Parks Conservancy (www.parksconservancy.org), puts it, "While many donors appreciate public recognition, others prefer low-key thanks and anonymity. The motivations of those preferring anonymity vary: Some are modest, some don't want other organizations to see their name and solicit them, and a few have delicate family situations—for example, estrangements where a person left out of the will might be upset at seeing that the money had gone to charity."

- **Your organization inspires enough respect, and creates a sufficient sense of personal relationship with its donors,** that they trust you to use their gifts wisely—even though they won't be around to monitor your actions.

- **Your organization does its homework,** including internal education and discussion, so that relevant staff and board members can competently, confidently, and enthusiastically represent your planned giving program.

- **When you start to offer more complex planned giving options, such as gift annuities or charitable remainder trusts,** your financial management system will be in expert hands.

CROSS REFERENCE

Don't forget the qualities that bring regular donors to your organization. For more on these characteristics—such as a timely and viable mission, and a good reputation in the community—see Chapter 4.

To be sure, not every donor places "achieving immortality" as his or her primary motivation to make a planned gift. Some longtime supporters will simply see a planned gift as their final way of helping out. Those of more modest means may realize that it will be the first time they can make a gift of a substantial size. However, the characteristics described above are no less important to these people. After all, what donors really want to know is whether your organization can deliver maximum impact for their buck.

Once you've identified the great opportunities to create a personal legacy that your organization can offer, don't be quiet about it. You can and should market your planned giving options. At a subtler level, introduce messages into your mailed appeals, newsletter, website, or other communications materials that talk about your organization's long-term goals. An article, for example, on "How Our Work Will Affect Your Children's Lives" might allow you to offer some planned giving information, in a way that more immediate articles (like "Summer Basketball Camp Opens Soon") don't. But you'll also want to approach people more directly, through mailings, seminars, and personal meetings, discussed below.

Handling Simple Inheritance Gifts

Here is some good news for the small, grassroots organizations not yet ready to handle the likes of annuities, remainder trusts, and other sophisticated estate planning devices: The vast majority of planned gifts are made the old-fashioned way, through wills and simple probate-avoidance devices such as living trusts and beneficiary designations on IRAs, 401(k)s, and other financial and investment instruments.

Transfers of property made through wills and living trusts are known as "bequests." Fortunately, these legal devices are quite simple for a nonprofit to accept. When the will or trust maker dies, the person in charge of handling the estate (usually called an executor, administrator, or successor trustee) simply transfers the appropriate bequest to your organization.

It's perfectly reasonable for an organization to start a planned giving program by focusing on attracting bequests, and not worry about the more complicated arrangements until the bequest program is up and thriving. In fact, such an approach is advisable, according to Greg Lassonde, Gift Planning Officer with the San Francisco Symphony: "My advice to people starting a planned giving program is to keep it simple. You can start such a program with as little as 5% of your time—that's two hours a week. There's no point in getting too technical too fast."

Estate Tax Reductions Through Charitable Giving

Most of your donors (or, realistically speaking, their heirs) probably won't owe any estate tax at all. The estate tax is a tax that must be paid on the portion of a deceased person's estate that exceeds a statutory threshold. A federal law passed in 2001 radically changed the estate tax system, putting into place a gradual repeal. As of 2007, only taxable estates worth more than $2 million will owe estate tax. This threshold will continue to rise until 2010, when the tax will be repealed—for a year, at least (under the current plan, the estate tax returns in 2011, although Congress could certainly extend the repeal).

Clearly, this disappearing threshold will leave a lot of estates safe from tax. Even in the years immediately before the 2001 change, only about 2% of people who died in the United States left taxable estates. On the other hand, when you consider that in some urban areas, a modest house can be worth $1 million, you'll realize that some of your "average" donors may actually be subject to the tax (if they're unlucky enough to die before the year 2010).

For those estates that are taxed, the feds can gulp down nearly half of the amount by which the estate's value exceeds the threshold for taxation. The exact percentage depends on the size of the estate, but it can go as high as 45% for the years 2007 through 2009.

Because of these high rates, those who will leave taxable estates will be eager to find ways to reduce their tax burden—which is where you come in. All gifts to tax-exempt charitable organizations are exempt from estate tax, period. What's more, any amounts bequeathed or otherwise donated on death to charity are subtracted from the value of the estate to calculate the amount on which the estate will owe tax—and whether the estate will be subject to tax at all.

For example, if a donor dies with an estate worth $2.1 million, but leaves $150,000 to a tax-exempt charitable group, the estate will not owe any estate tax—the charitable gift brings the value of the estate below the threshold where the estate tax kicks in. A sizable charitable contribution could significantly reduce the amount on which the estate must pay tax—or eliminate its tax bill altogether. For your wealthiest donors, these are very strong incentives to include some charitable gifts in their estate plans.

> **CAUTION**
>
> **Don't cross the line into giving legal advice.** The information in this section is intended to help you approach donors and explain how gifts can be made to your mutual benefit. Some of them might not know the first thing about estate planning. However, under no circumstances should you help your donors actually write a will or otherwise plan their estates. You could be held liable for practicing law without a license, and the gift could be invalidated if your overreaching looks like coercion. If your donors need specific advice, they should see a lawyer or financial professional. Also, for help writing a will and engaging in more sophisticated estate planning, Nolo offers excellent and highly rated self-help options, including *Quicken® WillMaker Plus* (software with explanatory text, covering wills, living trusts, and more); *Nolo's Simple Will Book*, by Denis Clifford; *Plan Your Estate*, by Denis Clifford and Cora Jordan; and *Make Your Own Living Trust*, by Denis Clifford. You and donors can also get free information on wills and estate planning on Nolo's website, at www.nolo.com.

Gifts Made Through the Donor's Will or Living Trust

First, you'll need some basic information about wills and living trusts. A will is a document in which a person specifies what is to be done with his or her property when he or she dies, and names a friend or professional to oversee this process, as "executor." The person writing a will is usually called a "testator," and those who will receive property are called "beneficiaries." Wills are also useful for taking care of some nonproperty concerns, such as naming a guardian for young children, and stating who gets the pets.

A living trust does much the same thing as a will—that is, it allows someone to leave property to chosen beneficiaries. Instead of an executor, the trust maker (called a "trustor") names a "trustee." Usually the trustor chooses him or herself as trustee until his or her death, when the named "successor trustee" (usually a beneficiary of the trust) takes over. The successor trustee will oversee transfer of property after the trustor's death. The main technical difference between living trusts and wills is that the legal transfer of property ownership under a will happens only at the donor's death; with a living trust, this transfer happens during the trustor's lifetime. The trustor transfers his or her property into the trust, which

Report From a Fledgling Planned Giving Program

Berkeley Repertory Theatre, a 36-year-old professional resident theatre company based in Berkeley, California (www.berkeleyrep.org), can usually count on getting a "surprise" bequest every year or so. However, a few years back, they decided to institute a more formal planned giving program. Here's how Annual Fund Director of Development Lynn Eve Komaromi describes their first steps and early results:

"We rolled out our program with a brochure and an announcement, containing an invitation to join the Michael Leibert Society (named after our theatre's 1968 founder). We sent this package to our longest-time patrons, particularly those who'd been with us for around 30 years. No one who has subscribed for less than ten years was included. Our reasoning was that the longer-time patrons were not only loyal to the theatre, but likely getting to an age where estate planning was on their minds. A handful of people responded, as did some members of our board. We continue to let people know about the program, through our website, announcements at major donor lunches, and the like. Every year, some more people join.

"To acknowledge our society members, we host a lunch once a year, at which they meet someone special, such as the artistic director or someone who can bring them closer to the artistic process. We also include the names of every Michael Leibert Society member in every theatre program.

"Interestingly enough, everyone who has joined so far plans to make a gift through a will or living trust. We offer charitable trusts as well—and have advisors standing by in case anyone takes us up on the offer—but so far, almost no one has. Given that, like most nonprofits, our staff is already stretched in many different directions, I'm satisfied with people naming us in their will for now. I am, however, looking forward to further developing our planned giving program, including making time to meet with donors individually."

technically owns the property, although the trustor generally has the right, during his or her lifetime, to use trust property as he or she sees fit; to transfer property into and out of the trust; and even to dissolve the trust altogether.

Living trusts have recently been enjoying a surge in popularity, for the simple reason that they allow beneficiaries to avoid probate. Upon the trustor's death, the successor trustee will simply use his or her legal powers to obtain the property from whoever holds it, and then follow the trustor's instructions regarding who should receive it. Also, certain complicated living trusts (such as an "AB trust," often used by affluent married couples) help avoid estate tax. Even if they have a living trust, however, many people also write a will, to cover any property that they don't get around to transferring into the trust before they die.

Neither a will nor a living trust needs to be written in legalese, and neither requires the help of a lawyer. Your donor should have no trouble naming your organization as one of the will or trust's beneficiaries. The primary issue is simply making sure that whoever is handling the estate can clearly understand which of the world's many charities the deceased person had in mind to receive the property. Whether the donor uses a will or a living trust (or both), all the donor needs to do to leave your organization a gift is to:

- accurately state the full legal name of your charitable organization (for clarity, it helps to include your tax ID number, but this isn't required)

- state your organization's location (again, for clarity, it's good to state the address, but city and state are enough), and

- describe the gift, as well as what the donor expects you to do with it.

To help donors assemble the information listed in the first two bullet points above, prominently display it on your website, your newsletters, and any brochures or other communications related to planned giving.

CAUTION

Be ready for surprise gifts. The donor can do everything necessary to leave your organization a gift without your involvement—which means that you may not know about the intended bequest, or know how much it is worth, until after the donor has died. In fact, studies show that this is exactly what happens in one out of three cases. I'll explain how to encourage donors to advise you ahead of time.

Types of Gifts

Money is hardly the only asset transferred through wills or living trusts. Most people accumulate copious amounts of other property, far more than they themselves are aware of—everything from clothing to cars to jewelry to childhood journals. Therefore, when a person sits down to write a will, he or she will have to find a logical way to distribute both the money and the property. The donor has numerous options when deciding how to make this distribution. The possible types of gifts that might be made to you or others include:

- cash of a particular dollar amount (called a "general bequest")
- a percentage of the total value of the donor's estate (a particular type of general bequest called a "percentage bequest")
- a particular item of property, such as real property (land), personal property, such as a car, painting, or refrigerator, or a financial instrument, such as stock certificates (called a "specific bequest")
- a remainder of the donor's estate, after all the other gifts have been made to other beneficiaries, and all debts and taxes have been paid (called a "residual bequest"), or
- a portion of the estate that will go to your organization only if the originally intended beneficiary dies before the donor (called a "contingent bequest").

Restrictions on How Your Organization May Use the Gift

After the donor has decided what type of gift to give your organization, his or her next task is to specify how the gift must be used. For your purposes, it's best if the donor chooses the broadest possible drafting language, stating, for example, that the gift is "to be used for its [your organization's] general purposes." This is what's called an "unrestricted gift." Unrestricted gifts can be put toward any uses your organization thinks appropriate, within its mission. But few people will be willing to give you what amounts to a blank check. Instead, you'll have to respect the fact that many donors will specify particular purposes toward which the gift must be put (called a "restricted gift"). For example, the donor might state that the gift is to go toward your organization's endowment; that it can be used only for a particular program; or that even more conditions must be met, such as "to be used only for support of hatha-style yoga during the summer children's program."

You're legally bound to follow the restrictions stated in the donor's will to the extent possible, and to keep the gift funds separate from your organization's other (unrestricted) funds. I don't need to tell you, however, how frustrated your organization might feel when trying to follow a detailed set of restrictions or conditions, especially if some of them are inappropriate or incoherent. In the yoga example above, for example, suppose you no longer offer yoga? Or, suppose you do offer yoga, but have replaced your hatha program with Iyengar yoga? Although your organization may have some flexibility in cases where carrying out the donor's wishes would truly be impossible, you'll nevertheless need to consult a lawyer about any significant changes in how you use the gift.

If you have a chance to talk to the donor in advance about his or her intention to leave you a restricted gift, it makes sense to remind the donor of the potential difficulties of too narrowly describing the gift's intended purposes. Explain that while you'll do everything possible to respect the donor's wishes, hopefully many years will pass before the gift is actualized, and binding your organization to something that may no longer be important won't honor either your organization's needs or the donor's intentions.

Obviously you can't write the donor's will for him or her, but as an alternative, you might suggest tying the gift to more general purposes that the donor will nevertheless be excited about supporting. Another approach is for the donor to tie a gift to narrowly defined purposes, but ameliorate it by adding a sentence along the lines of, "If the gift cannot be used for these intended purposes, it may be put toward such purposes as the board of directors decides."

You can also encourage the donor to make a nonspecific gift to your organization while at the same time writing a separate letter, outside the will, in which the donor expresses his or her wishes for how the gift is to be used. While this type of letter isn't legally binding, it should help the donor feel that his or her voice will be heard by your group's board of directors when the gift is received.

CAUTION

Update your database or mailing list when a bequest donor has died. The last thing you want is for family members, who no doubt know of the donor's generosity to your organization, to receive one of your regular mailings, addressed to the dead person, requesting more funds.

Can You Count on Receiving This Gift?

Even if you have been told that a donor has included your organization in his or her will or living trust, don't forget that—as in those Hollywood scenes, where shocked family members sit around the table while a lawyer delivers the bad news—both wills and living trusts can be, and often are, changed. If, over the course of the donor's long life, the donor becomes bored or disappointed with your group, or simply shifts focus to another group, he or she might rewrite the will or living trust without telling you. Fortunately, such changes are relatively rare, especially because many donors make bequests to more than one charity in the first place. (This gives you an incentive to catch potential estate donors when they're relatively young.) Nevertheless, the prospect of donor changes of heart should remind you to never let up on your donor relationship-building efforts.

Another concern often expressed by nonprofit fundraisers is that disgruntled family members might go to court and contest the will. Rest assured that contested wills are also rare, particularly because the family member would probably have to prove either that the donor was mentally incompetent when writing the will or living trust, or that your organization used fraud or exerted "undue influence" on the donor. Both of these are presumably unlikely scenarios.

While chances are reasonably good that you'll get any planned gifts that donors have told you about, you can't count on them until they are sitting on your desk (or in your parking lot). Above all, don't enter such gifts into your organization's budget, break ground for the intended new building, or otherwise change your organization's plans in anticipation of a particular planned gift.

Gifts Made Outside the Donor's Will or Living Trust

Wills and living trusts are not the only methods by which estate gifts can be transferred. The simplest probate-avoidance technique is to name a person or an organization as the beneficiary, upon death, of specified property, such as a bank account, life insurance policy, or retirement plan. These financial instruments usually require the naming of a beneficiary, so the donor doesn't have to take any extra steps—except perhaps to fill out a change of beneficiary form—to choose your organization.

First Steps Toward Attracting Inheritance Gifts

Your organization could just go about its business, never planning for the certainty that key donors will eventually die, and hoping for surprise windfalls. Although you may receive the occasional gift this way, you'll be much more successful if you ask donors to actually consider including your organization in their estate plans.

Get Your Planned Giving House in Order

Your first step is to create a plan to attract bequests. Hold a meeting among your board, E.D., and development staff, to reach agreement on the following issues:

- **Your organization's ability to attract significant amounts of inheritance gifts.** Determine whether your organization has the characteristics that legacy donors are seeking. Also consider whether you have a large enough base of long-term donors—especially middle-aged and older people—to make this type of planning worthwhile.

- **Your organization's ability to actively solicit and appropriately handle inheritance gifts.** Also consider how far you want to go with your program— will it be limited to simple inheritance gifts, or is your eventual goal to offer your donors more complex giving arrangements, such as life income gifts?

- **The types of gifts you're willing to accept.** Cash gifts are a no-brainer, but what about gifts of stock in a private corporation, interests in a limited partnership, or other financial instruments? Unless you have a board member or staff person competent to deal with these types of arrangements, you could end up squandering a potentially valuable gift. Gifts of property are an even iffier proposition. Real property (land or houses) can certainly be valuable—but such gifts can also create problems and even substantial liabilities if they come with environmental problems, long-term tenants, or other baggage that makes a quick sale impractical. (Some nonprofits attempt to reduce their risk by limiting gifts to "marketable" property, but remember that donors may not realize the potential liability problems.) And, gifts of personal property can simply be a hassle, if you have to arrange for the property to be sold or hold an estate sale yourself.

- **How your organization will use inheritance gifts.** Remember, the donors will be eager to hear that their gifts will have a deep and lasting impact.
- **Your initial budget for staff time and training, explanatory brochures, volunteer mobilization,** and other costs of instituting the program and communicating with donors.

Plant a Seed in Your Donors' Minds

Step two is communicating your bequest giving plan to your donors. Some of them might need a reminder to plan their estates (though probably not your older donors—a whole industry exists to remind them). But you do need to remind your donors how satisfying it will feel to leave a world-improving legacy, via your organization.

At this point, you should be talking to all of your donors, not just the affluent ones. In fact, your low- to moderate-income donors might be eager to leave you a bequest gift, in part to offset their inability to make larger annual gifts from their income. As Audrey Yee of the Golden Gate National Parks Conservancy explains it, "I think of planned giving as a hybrid of the other individual giving models. You have your annual gifts, your major gifts, and your planned gifts, and you can view each in some respects as a subset of the other, or all of them as intersecting circles. For example, an annual giver might become a planned giver without ever becoming a major donor. This is especially common when an annual giver needs the money during his or her lifetime, but is sufficiently interested in your organization to want to help as soon as he or she can."

Greg Lassonde, with the San Francisco Symphony (www.sfsymphony.org), echoes this analysis: "I'd estimate that only about 10%–20% of planned gifts come from major donors. That makes planned gifts special—so much thought goes into them, by people who may have never before had the means or opportunity to make a substantial gift."

The simplest way to start conveying estate planning information is within your existing newsletter, brochure, or website. Make sure that any section that discusses general giving also mentions inheritance gifts. Many organizations simply insert a shaded box into every newsletter, containing the central message and key information, including:

- a reminder of the importance of estate planning

- a suggestion that supporters consider a planned gift

- the great uses to which their gift would be put

- any recognition or naming programs

- your organization's legal name, and

- who to contact for more information.

Others add a checkbox to their donation reply cards, saying something on the order of "Please send me information on how I can make a bequest gift to your organization through my will or living trust," or "I have included your organization in my will or living trust."

> **CAUTION**
>
> **"Planned giving" may mean nothing to your donors.** Although it's a common term in fundraising circles, your donors may not know what planned giving is. Therefore, your communications materials should avoid headings like, "Have you considered a planned gift?" Better to stick to plain English, with headings like, "You can leave a living legacy," or "Please consider including [*name of your organization*] in your will or living trust."

Another great form of encouragement is to tell them stories of other donors. For example, at the San Francisco Symphony, Greg Lassonde says, "We publish a regular planned giving newsletter ('Keynotes') that includes stories of our planned giving donors, and have found these stories to be very effective. Part of the reason is that it's not just our organization talking to people; it's another human being. The messages are highly personal, rather than technical, concerning the person's life, their love of music, and how they went about arranging the gift."

Again, such stories could go in your newsletter, on your website, or even in your annual report. They can be anything from lengthy profiles to small boxes with photos and mentions of the intended gift (particularly appropriate for your website, in the section describing donation possibilities). You'll need the donor's permission, of course, or that of his or her family if the donor has already died. But there's no need to wait until the donor is gone to celebrate a planned posthumous gift—many donors will be pleased to get credit for their generosity while they're still around to appreciate it.

Your anecdotes should briefly highlight each donor's personality, special interests, and values during his or her lifetime, and explain how the gift allowed, or will allow, these interests and values to be furthered. Make clear how your organization has made excellent use of the gift (if it has already been received), and that it will have a lasting impact. Positive quotes from family members are also reassuring to donors fearful of disappointing their rightful heirs.

The organization "openhouse," a San Francisco–based group (www.openhouse-sf .org) that works to meet the housing and health needs of elder lesbian, gay, bisexual, and transgender people, published a newsletter article in 2003 about receiving a $130,000 bequest. The donor was a gay man named Harold Baron, who'd been closeted for most of his life but regretted not having been more supportive of the gay community earlier on, and wished he'd had the chance to live in the senior housing community that openhouse was building. The newsletter included an engaging picture of Harold as a young man (shown below).

Some organizations attempt to foster more personal contact with potential legacy donors by inviting them to an estate-planning seminar. These seminars usually discuss what can be achieved through a will, living trust, or other estate planning arrangement, and then advise the audience about the relevant law and procedures for moving forward. It's best to have a lawyer or other professional lead the more technical part of the seminar. To avoid the possibility that the event will be seen as either an advertisement for the lawyer's services, or as exerting inappropriate pressure on the attendees to write their wills in your organization's favor, a couple of cautions are in order:

- **If possible, involve a lawyer who already supports your organization or its causes,** and will say up front that he or she is donating his or her time and not recruiting clients.

- **Be up front about your goals of attracting bequests to support your programs.** That means all promotional materials should feature your inspirational bequest options. And, at the seminar, you should outline exactly why bequests are so important to your group and its causes, and what you will do to recognize these bequests.

Senior community ▌living with pride
openhouse

Adventurer leaves openhouse $130,000 bequest

Harold Baron, a closeted gay man, had just moved to a Marin retirement home when four women approached him in the dining room.

"Mr. Baron," said one, "my friends and I have heard about the many amazing things you have done in your life. Would you be willing to come talk to us sometime about your experiences?"

Harold paused a moment. "Well, not ALL of them," he replied.

Harold was an astounding person by any measure. Once when he was home with a cold in his New York apartment, so the story goes, Marlene Dietrich personally made and brought him a bowl of chicken soup.

The world's greatest pianist, Vladamir Horowitz, was one of Harold's dinner guests. Other personal friends included people as diverse as Marian Anderson, Boris Karloff, and the Queen of Denmark.

Harold died in 2002 at the age of 89, and when his estate was settled last month, a major part of it—a nearly $130,000 bequest—immediately went to openhouse. More money will come to openhouse from his estate this Fall.

"Is that place in San Francisco ready yet?" he kept asking in the final months of his life. "I want to live there."

Harold didn't make it, but others will, thanks to his generosity.

Ironically, Harold decided to "come out" only at the very end of his life. "I regret that I haven't been more supportive of the gay community," he told us. "I want to make up for that now."

In his honor, a library space at openhouse will be named after his mother, Sarah Baron, who couldn't read English but who taught her children to value people of all cultures and races. Harold used to read to her every night by the candle on their kitchen table.

Harold's passions took him to many places. In the depths of the Depression, he traveled the globe as a crew member on a freighter. He read everything he could find, and he taught himself to write. He became Articles Editor of Redbook and Today's Woman, and an editor for Crown Publishing. He wrote for Reader's Digest, Look, This Week, Travel, Family Circle, and Woman's Home Companion. President Johnson personally hired him to research and write a report about the need for civil rights in the South. He taught writing at Columbia University and Queens College of the City University of New York. And then when he retired, he volunteered as an English teacher to at-risk children in one of New York's toughest neighborhoods.

continued on page 2

Harold Baron, 27, ready to change the world

What is openhouse?

openhouse is a bold, innovative, entrepreneurial initiative designed to meet the housing and health needs of lesbian, gay, bisexual and transgender (LGBT) elders, age 60 and above. Seniors of all sexual orientations will be welcome at our senior village, which will celebrate diversity.

openhouse is carefully preparing to construct a mixed-income, multicultural retirement village in San Francisco, with up to 225 units of senior housing, a wellness center and many other support services. This complex will be a popular destination with strong neighborhood connections, offering an array of social and cultural services.

openhouse will ensure that all senior residents—regardless of income level, gender, race, ethnicity, or sexual orientation — have a safe, positive aging experience.

openhouse has always been about more than just housing. It is also a community symbol, the recognition of a population—LGBT elders —that has historically been invisible. Building senior housing will help us become a truly intergenerational community that provides care for all of our seniors.

what's inside

winter **2003** vol. **1** issue **1**

- **Because affluent older people may receive a number of similar seminar invitations, you may do best if you partner with one or more other high-quality, like-minded organizations.** This should not only reduce any pressure felt by attendees to commit, but can also enhance the prospects of all groups. We are all judged in part by the company we keep.

Be Ready to Respond to Interested Donors

After you start putting the word out, you're bound to get some responses from interested donors. This is where some organizations fall down on the job. Perhaps because they never believed in the possibility of success, they fail to put together materials or a plan in advance. The result is that donors may feel alienated and/or lose interest in the whole enterprise.

The appropriate plan for your organization depends partly on the types of overtures you made in your marketing materials. For example, if people checked a box saying "please send me more information," then of course you'll want to have an explanatory brochure or other information at the ready. If you've asked people to check a box saying they'd like to be contacted to discuss this matter, then you'll want call right away to offer more information—whether it be immediate details over the phone, written materials, or a sit-down meeting to further explore the possibilities.

A brochure can be a sensible and cost-effective means to follow up with donors who want further information before naming you in their will. (If your budget is very low, a letter will do.) Your brochure can describe in greater detail how their bequests and other estate gifts will help your organization. You might also include basic information on procedures for preparing a will or living trust, and suggest appropriate language that they can use to make gifts to your organization. One good approach is to work with a planned giving consultant, who, for a reasonable fee, can help you create an appropriate brochure. Besides sending brochures out upon request, you can slip them into other mailed appeals, or into your newsletter mailing—once a year is appropriate. You can also design a separate mailing around this brochure, to be sent to all interested donors, major donors, and other donors whom you think are positioned to become major or planned-gift donors.

Approach Prospective Planned Gift Donors Who Haven't Expressed Interest

Consider how and whether to approach the topic of inheritance gifts with appropriate long-term or major donors who haven't spoken up, perhaps because your newsletter and other messages haven't made an impression on them. As with any major gift request, scheduling a personal meeting may be appropriate. (See Chapter 6 for more on arranging and holding personal meetings with donors.)

Planned giving isn't a topic about which you'll be scheduling a separate meeting with every donor, or even with every major donor. Ideally, you should approach donors whom you, or one of your board members, know well enough to comfortably offer this giving option. If you keep your ears open, you may pick up verbal clues. For example, Berkeley Repertory Theatre's Lynn Eve Komaromi remembers talking to a donor who lightheartedly said of her annual gift, "Well, I guess I'll keep doing this for as long as I live!" That gave Lynn Eve an opening to suggest that the donor think about giving even after she is gone—and they immediately scheduled a meeting to discuss it further.

Beyond the donors whom you're close to personally, the most likely ones to approach are those who fall into at least one of the following categories:

- **Committed supporters of your organization.** These may be major donors, with whom your organization has built a solid and warm relationship. Also look for donors who have been making gifts for many years, even if it's only $10 a year.

- **Donors age 45 and older.** This is the age at which most people write at least a basic will or living trust. And the younger they are, the more likely they are to include a charitable donation. (But not everyone will be ready for will-writing—statistically, people at age 45 can expect to live from 40 to 45 more years, and many won't yet be interested.)

- **Donors of any age who are affluent and childless or widowed.** Such folks are more likely to have considered their lack of natural heirs, and the prospect of a planned gift.

- **Donors with wealthy children.** The reason is obvious.

- **Younger donors who work in a field like law, accounting, or medicine.** These professionals are conditioned to be realistic about preparing for their death (although they may still be procrastinating about writing a will).

- **Homeowners.** Something about buying a house spurs people to write a will. And longtime homeowners in most urban areas are living in an appreciated asset, and will have a good-sized estate to plan around, regardless of their current income level.

As with all donor interactions, success in attracting planned gifts comes down to doing your research and understanding each donor's individual interests.

TIP

Meeting with prospective planned givers may jump-start their annual giving. According to planned giving professional Linda Solow Jaffe (currently with the John Muir Health Foundation of Walnut Creek, California), "I've had many experiences where I'm helping a donor who has never once made a major gift look into our planned giving options—and, as a result of the conversation, the donor's level of excitement about our organization rises so much that he or she begins increasing the level of his or her annual gifts, as well! The lesson is to make every donor aware of your planned giving program, if only through a mention in your newsletter or website."

In preparation for any planned giving meeting, write up a statement explaining how your organization will use a significant gift. Be specific about how the gift will be applied toward an important, lasting goal (such as opening a new wing to your clinic or saving a beach from development) or will support the donor's favorite programs and activities (such as a literacy program that will help bring reading to future generations). Your written statement should also briefly explain what sort of gifts your organization is in a position to accept (or can't accept, such as real property). If your organization offers more complicated giving vehicles, you'll want to work in these possibilities.

The end of a conversation about a posthumous gift is quite different from one about a current major donation, since the donor won't open up his or her checkbook on the spot. A good way to close the discussion is to ask anyone making a planned gift to stay in touch as he or she takes the various practical steps required, so that your organization can appropriately recognize the planned bequest. And, after your program has a significant number of participants, you will also want to invite them to join in events or groups geared toward honoring planned gift donors.

TIP

Get your board on board. As both committed members of your organization and potential major donors, your board members are good prospects for planned gifts. One effective way to enlist them is for one member to take the floor at a meeting, and say, "I've included this organization in my will—who else is willing to commit to this?" Assuming the eventual answer is quite a few, you'll want to ask board members to help recruit others. After all, a pitch that begins with the fundraiser's own story of setting up a planned gift to your organization stands a better chance of success.

Develop Meaningful Ways to Recognize Bequest Donors

Now that you've gotten your donors thinking about the benefits of leaving your organization a gift through their will or other transfer device, you need to find ways to thank them. It's an interesting situation, because the gift hasn't been made yet, and you may not know for sure how large it will be—yet waiting until the donor's death to recognize his or her generosity would be nonsensical.

First, you need to find out what inheritance gifts lie in store for your organization (whether from major donors or others). The only way to get this information is to actively solicit it. For example, your reply cards for fundraising appeals might include a box to check, saying, "I have included your organization in my will or estate planning arrangements." Follow up on those who check "yes," by calling to thank them and ask whether they'd like to discuss the uses to which their gift might be put and recognition opportunities. Your newsletter or website might also ask your donors to advise you if they've named your organization in their will or other estate planning arrangements.

Next, you need to find special ways to thank your bequest donors. Many of the familiar ways remain appropriate, including a thank-you letter or lunch invitation after you first hear about the bequest, and a mention in your annual report or event program. (Names can be removed a year or two after the gift is actually made.) However, you should also consider how to give unique recognition to this group. After all, they haven't merely given you a slice of their income; they've promised you a potentially substantial amount of their worldly goods, as one of their last acts on this earth.

Be Ready for Memorial Gifts

If a donor who cared deeply about your organization dies, his or her family members may ask friends to make a charitable memorial gift in lieu of sending flowers. Memorial gifts not only require special handling, but you'll also need to be ready to spring into action quickly. Your organization should be prepared to:

- give the donors a specially designed card that they can hand to or immediately mail to family members, offering condolences and advising that they have made a gift in memory of their loved one.

- if your website has an option to donate online, make this available to memorial gift donors. This need not require updating the website every time—you can simply add a box for donors to check indicating a memorial gift, followed by a space where they can fill in the deceased person's name.

- in addition to sending the usual thank-you letters to the actual donors, notify family members of the amount of each gift made in memory of the deceased.

- list memorial gifts under the name of the deceased in your annual report, newsletter, and website, as appropriate.

- If the deceased person was well known and the gift pool may be large, be ready to quickly establish an ongoing special fund in the deceased's name.

It's a good idea to add memorial gift donors to your mailing list, at least for a year or two. Even if they weren't interested in your cause before, their departed friend's commitment to it may inspire their interest. And they'd probably be interested in receiving your newsletters for a while, to see how their gift was spent. But don't be surprised if their gift was just a one-time deal—and be sure to remove them from your mailing list if they show no interest after a reasonable period of time.

> ### (!) CAUTION
>
> **Distinguish the living from the dead when creating your recognition lists.** If your annual report, newsletter, program, or website lists legacy donors by name, be sure to asterisk those who are already deceased, and explain this in a footnote. (Otherwise some people may assume everyone on the list is dead, a potentially very disturbing miscommunication.)

For gifts that are particularly large and might inspire future gifts, you might create a fund bearing the donor's name, dedicated to a particular purpose—the Warner Scholarship or the Guerin Endowment, for example. To ensure the posterity of the gift, it's often appropriate to make it an "endowed gift." With an endowed gift, your organization invests the gift, and uses only a portion of the interest earned to carry out the gift's purposes. Creating a named fund or endowment not only gives posterity to the donor's name, but also allows you to leverage the donor's gift, by using it to attract others.

For the larger pool of more modest gifts, an effective strategy used by many organizations is to create a special "society," with an honorary name.

What Should You Name Your Society?

For the unimaginative, a host of generic names are possible, like "legacy society" or "heritage club." It's far more compelling, however, if you follow the lead of those organizations that name their group after an honored person, such as one of the organization's founders, like Berkeley Repertory Theatre's "Michael Leibert Society" or The Women's Foundation's "Ruth McGuire Society." (This so-called "society" isn't a separate legal entity; it's just a way to name a segment of your donors.) An added advantage to naming your group after a known person is that some people treat this as akin to a memorial gift, and make bequests in the named person's honor. Other organizations choose a name that's inspiring for other reasons: as with the Golden Gate National Parks Conservancy's "Silver Lupine Society," named after its successful efforts to replant the silver lupine in order to create a habitat for the then-endangered mission blue butterfly.

Once you have your society in place—and even if you don't institute an actual society—consider these additional ways to honor your planned gift donors:

- invite them to an annual thank-you lunch, tea, or dinner, just for society members (the San Francisco Symphony, for example, holds an annual lunch at which the members listen to chamber music, meet the musicians, and receive a small gift such as a chocolate musical note)

- create membership certificates (yes, it sounds corny, but no one can help but feel proud at receiving such recognition, and many people display them)

- establish a walkway, wall, or other place where society members' names can be inscribed

- have your E.D. or a board member visit society members occasionally, especially those whose health doesn't permit them to attend events, and

- send greeting cards with news of your organization's doings, and perhaps a small gift, such as a pin commemorating their society membership.

You should also, of course, include your legacy society donors in the same activities and opportunities as your other donors, such as tours of your facilities and holiday parties. If, however, certain donors have made restricted gifts, try to tailor your efforts to their interests. For example, if the donor has promised a bequest for the free meals portion of your homeless services, make sure he or she is invited to attend during one of these meals.

Preview of Other Planned Giving Arrangements

As you've seen, gifts made via wills or living trusts require very little action from your organization. Most of the hard work is done by the donor, possibly (but not necessarily) with the help of a lawyer. After the donor's death, the estate's executor, administrator, or successor trustee will ensure that your organization receives its due. Life income gifts are another matter. Most of them are designed to take advantage of favorable but complicated tax laws. Typically, they involve a donor gifting money or property to your group in exchange for your commitment to pay the donor regular interest income for life. You'll need the help of a professional, either an in-house staffperson, or an outside consultant or bank, to set up and run this kind of program. For this reason, this section will simply give you a taste of the possibilities.

TIP

Your local community foundation may be willing to handle life income funds on your behalf. Many are already accustomed to creating pools of donor funds and handling complex financial arrangements for small nonprofits. Talk to the larger foundations in your area to find out what they have to offer.

Below are the main types of life income arrangements and their close cousins. Which one is best for any particular donor depends on the donor's current level of assets, need for predictable future income, and various income tax and capital gains tax considerations.

Charitable gift annuity. During his or her lifetime, the donor gives the nonprofit either cash or another asset (often real property), and the nonprofit in return pays the donor (or another beneficiary) an annual, fixed income (an "annuity") for life. The amount of the annuity is negotiated at the outset between the donor and the nonprofit. To produce the income that will hopefully cover the amount of the annuity, the nonprofit invests the assets or proceeds from the sale of property (or, in the case of real property with tenants, may manage and continue to rent out the space). When the donor (or other beneficiary) dies, the nonprofit becomes sole owner of the assets and can use them for its charitable purposes.

Deferred payment gift annuity. This is much like the charitable gift annuity described above, except that the donor decides not to start receiving annual annuity payments until a later date, usually at a specified age. This option is most often chosen for tax reasons, particularly by younger donors (they can claim a tax deduction in the year the gift is made, but don't have to worry about paying tax on the annuity payments until they are older—and presumably in a lower tax bracket).

Charitable remainder annuity trust. The donor gives assets over to a trust, and a trustee manages and invests the assets, then makes payments to the donor (or other beneficiary or beneficiaries) out of the trust's income and, if necessary, out of its assets. This continues for either a specified number of years or for the rest of the donor's life. The amount and rate of payments are established when the trust is set up. When the term of years ends or the donor dies, the nonprofit gets what's left in the trust. Though very similar to the charitable gift annuity, the charitable remainder annuity trust is preferable to some donors for capital gains tax reasons. (In particular, with gifts of securities or other property that the donor purchased a year or more ago and that have appreciated in value, transferring them to the trust completely bypasses the capital gains tax system. Contrast this with a donor who transfers appreciated securities to a nonprofit for a charitable gift annuity, who will still have to pay tax on a portion of their value.)

Charitable remainder unitrust. A donor gives assets over to a trust, and the trustee manages and invests the assets, then pays the donor an annual percentage of the trust's current value (meaning that the amount the donor receives may go up and down over the years, depending on how the investments are doing). After the donor dies, remaining assets go to the nonprofit. This has capital gains tax advantages similar to the charitable remainder annuity trust. The unitrust is also good for donors who aren't as interested in a fixed income, but are willing to gamble that the value of the trust will go up, and that their payments will therefore increase.

Charitable lead trust. This is sometimes called a reverse charitable remainder trust, and for good reason. The donor creates a trust, out of which payments are made to the nonprofit for a specified number of years or until the donor's death. When those years are up or the donor dies, the principal assets are returned to the donor or whoever else the donor has named as a beneficiary. Donors enjoy the same capital gains benefits as with other trusts, as well as estate tax benefits when the property is transferred to their heirs. A charitable lead trust is especially appealing to those donors who want to leave a particular piece of property to their heirs, but also want to put it to use both philanthropically and for tax purposes in the meantime.

Pooled income fund. A group of donors contributes assets to a particular fund at a nonprofit, and the nonprofit invests the pooled assets and pays out the earnings to the donors. When each donor dies, the nonprofit may withdraw that donor's share of the fund for its own charitable use. This is a good option for schools, hospitals, and other nonprofits whose donor base doesn't include many people with enough money to warrant setting up an individual charitable gift annuity.

Retained life interest. The donor transfers ownership of a piece of real property, such as a home or farm, to the nonprofit, but retains the right to live there for life.

RESOURCE

Need to learn more about bequests and other forms of planned giving? See the following resources (but realize that, because many of the benefits associated with planned giving are dependent on the tax laws, which change frequently, printed materials can fall out of date quickly):

- **the website of the National Committee on Planned Giving, at www.ncpg.org.** This is the standard-setting organization in this field, and publishes a quarterly magazine called *The Journal of Gift Planning.*

- **the website of consultant Phil Murphy, at www.plannedgivingcoach.com.** This site contains free information, including sample letters to prospects regarding both bequests and life income gifts.

- *Planned Giving Today,* a monthly newsletter written in plain English with a marketing focus, available by subscription at www.liebertpub.com/pgtoday.

- *Conducting a Successful Major Gifts and Planned Giving Program: A Comprehensive Guide and Resource,* by Kent E. Dove, Alan M. Spears, and Thomas W. Herbert (Jossey-Bass). ●

Special Events

Ask any professional fundraiser to name his or her best and worst fundraising memory, and you're likely to hear a story about a special event. Special events can be the highlight of your fundraising year—grand occasions that simultaneously mobilize volunteers, bring you into direct contact with your friends and supporters, and create a festive atmosphere for everyone involved. Unfortunately, special events can also set the stage for huge public embarrassments and spectacular losses of money. I know one fundraiser who still shudders when she thinks about the 600-person picnic where the person with the only restroom key disappeared.

Special events come in all shapes and sizes. Their common denominator is their uniqueness—by definition, they are occasions outside your nonprofit's usual activities, where your membership and/or the public is invited to attend and support your work, usually by paying an admission fee or buying things once they get there. The more common special events include dinners, auctions, fairs and festivals, lectures, benefit concerts, home and garden tours, tournaments, contests, sporting events, walk-a-thons, garage sales, and bake sales. Whole books have been dedicated to exploring the array of possible special events—and they still don't cover everything that an innovative mind might envision.

Rather than attempting to describe how to plan and put on every possible type of special event, this chapter focuses on how to make your special event serve the focus of this book: raising money. This is an important distinction, because not all special events are intended to serve primarily as fundraisers. As many experts will tell you, one of the first questions an organization should ask when considering a potential special event is, "Will this be a fundraiser or a friendraiser?" It's an especially legitimate question given a recent report by Charity Navigator, a watchdog group, finding that special events are an inefficient way to raise money, bringing in an average of $1 for every $1.33 they spent. The exceptions are often large groups with well-connected boards and a compelling cause.

Events that don't bring in any actual profits can still be valuable, particularly if they bring visibility to your organization, mobilize and expand its donor base, or highlight a particular issue of special importance to your members and/or clients. An open house, for example, when you invite your membership—and possibly a few prospective new members—to come see what you do and meet your staff, might serve important purposes beyond raising money for your group.

No matter what the purpose of your event might be, it's important to stay focused on your goals—especially during economically tough times, when it may make sense to rethink or even drop certain events because they tend to absorb so much valuable staff time and energy. With careful budgeting and planning, however, you may be able to turn a potential break-even event into a true fundraiser.

This chapter covers:

- types of special events and the fundraising potential of each
- how to choose an event that suits your organization
- creating a realistic budget
- creating a schedule of activities before and during the event
- protecting your organization from legal and financial liability
- tips for making your event go smoothly, and
- following up after the event.

TIP

Get their names. No matter what type of special event you choose, you'll have an opportunity to put your organization's name and work in front of new eyes—which means you'll want to be organized about getting people's names and addresses (including email) for your mailing list. If you won't know in advance who will be attending, create a sign-in sheet. But to make sure people don't breeze right past your registration table, professional events planner Laurie J. Earp (based in Oakland, California—see www.earpevents.com) suggests an even more effective tactic: "I like to create a door prize, requiring people to fill out their name and contact information or provide a business card. I've found that this brings in not just a few more names, but many times more names than I'd get with just a sign-in sheet." Also, be sure to have a table or other location featuring brochures, photos, and other demonstrations of your organization's work, so that new people realize that the event serves goals beyond their own pleasure.

Other Reasons to Hold a Special Event

Although this chapter focuses on the fundraising potential of special events, there are a number of other good reasons to hold one. This is particularly true of party-type events, where you have something important to celebrate. Here's a short list of good reasons to hold a special event where fundraising doesn't take center stage:

- **to raise visibility**—the promotional activities surrounding the event, as well as the new contacts you make with people who attend, will be of lasting benefit

- **to improve your organization's relationship with the public,** such as the residential neighbors around your shelter, or with a particular group of influential people (if you're a children's education group, for example, you might hold a reception for faculty members of the educational department of local colleges)

- **to mobilize volunteers**—and bring in new ones

- **to celebrate milestones and achievements,** such as your organization's anniversary, approval for a large grant, a staff or board member's departure, or the graduation of a group of students or trainees (though these can easily be turned into effective fundraisers)

- **to thank dedicated people who have helped your organization,** or

- **to kick off a membership or fundraising campaign** (although the larger purpose here is to raise money, the event itself may be primarily a consciousness raiser).

Survey of Special Events

This section takes a quick ride through the special events landscape, looking at the most common types of events, the major costs associated with them, and the keys to making them a financial success. Bear in mind that the biggest predictor of any event's success is the quality and energy of the people who work on it, as well as the size and dedication of your group's core roster of supporters. As you review this section, remember that you can combine certain types of activities into one event. To determine whether this is appropriate, see "The Virtues of Combo-Platter Events," below.

TIP

Watch the calendar. Keep tabs on events being held by other organizations in your area. This is important both to collect creative ideas and to make sure you don't duplicate something already happening nearby or at the same time. Also, keep an eye on important dates—you don't want to schedule an event on a Jewish or Muslim holiday, for example, particularly if you have members from these faiths.

Lunches, Dinners, and Other Food Events

The most common special event is the annual or special celebratory dinner. And, of course, luncheon, tea, or cocktail hour events are also typical. There are numerous variations on the meal theme—your basic hotel or restaurant sitdown meal (most often with your organization paying the costs, though some restaurants will cut you a deep discount as a donation); a small food or drink event at the home of a supporter; a meal for which your clients or supporters make the food, such as a themed or an ethnic buffet; a staged event where participants go to different houses or restaurants for drinks, appetizers, a main meal, and dessert; and a "tasting," where you arrange for local vendors, such as restaurants, wineries, or ice cream manufacturers, to send a representative offering samples (free advertising for them, free food for you).

Most meal events also try to incorporate some sort of entertainment or education, such as a speaker, musical performance, video presentation, or showcase of clients' talents or activities. If your organization doesn't regularly hold an annual dinner, then other effective event themes might include its anniversary or the retirement of a longtime E.D. or board member—especially because such occasions tend to bring back long-lost supporters who want to share memories or honor a favorite person.

The key to making a dinner event profitable is to understand that its main proceeds won't come from ticket sales. (In fact, "banquet fatigue" is an

The Virtues of Combo-Platter Events

To maximize both fun and profits during an event, it's worth considering whether mini-events can be dovetailed into the main one—combining, for example, a raffle with an open house, an auction with a dinner, or booths of food vendors at a sports tournament. As long as you're mobilizing your volunteers anyway, you may as well offer them alternative directions in which to channel their fundraising energies. You'll be surprised, too, at how often the very same donors are willing to spend money on a variety of things, even if they wouldn't have been willing to write one big check. (No one who arrived at your event willing to spend more should leave unsatisfied! At the very least, a booth where you sell your organization's T-shirts might be profitable.)

Also, combining activities often increases participants' enjoyment. At a dinner event, for example, many people will be too shy to mingle with strangers on the open floor, but will happily chat with them as they view the silent auction tables.

There are, however, two potential drawbacks to consider when combining events. First, if your event is already complex, and your pool of volunteers stretched thin, you can easily overdo it by piling on more responsibilities. (In any case, make sure your various activities don't get into one another's way—keep them to a strict schedule, and make sure, for example, that a silent auction ends before dinner starts.) A second possible drawback is that combining fundraising activities might exclude potential donors. For example, a friend of mine volunteers at her children's school, where a gala fundraising dinner was formerly combined with a raffle. However, the development committee realized that, because many of the parents are low-income, they couldn't afford the relatively expensive dinner tickets—but would have been quite willing to buy raffle tickets. So, the two events were split apart, and overall parental donations increased as a result.

increasingly common complaint among philanthropic types.) Although these receipts will be important to creating a fundraising success, the money you take in from ticket sales almost never catches up with the event's costs. Instead, you must make the event serve as a rallying point for a broader effort to collect individual and corporate donations. For example, a local business that might not give you a cash donation to support your programs might instead be willing to donate to your annual dinner, especially with your assurances that the event will receive press coverage, and that the business will be appropriately (and prominently) thanked in the printed event program.

Many dinner events also incorporate another moneymaking activity, such as an auction, a raffle, or a series of booths with items for sale. Involving a well-liked celebrity is also a good way to boost your dinner's fundraising potential—it will both elevate ticket sales and allow you to charge more for the tickets.

TIP

Seek donations of necessary items. Of course, it's always best to receive cash in hand, but you can also fund your event with donated contributions of time and materials, such as food, space, or labor. With these items covered, you can more confidently approach potential donors about your surefire success event. Because there's no limit to your creative imagination, there's also no limit on what you can request—flowers, balloons, other decorations, costumes for the waitstaff, music or other entertainment, a sound system, printing services, transportation for your keynote speaker, and more. It all depends on your organization's connections and the energy of your staff and volunteers.

There are other important ways of garnering corporate and other sponsorship. One widely used method is to sell space in what's known as a "tribute book" or "ad book," a small printed booklet distributed to event guests, with entries like "Joe's Plumbing congratulates City Youth Services on 50 years of community service." (Such ads can also be incorporated into your event program.) Another is to ask a business to buy an entire table's worth of tickets, which allows it to display its business name on that table. Your board member's employers and local businesses that your organization patronizes are your most likely buyers.

On the expense side of the ledger, you'll need to work hard to make sure your dreams for the event don't degenerate into a bucket of red ink. Food and catering costs alone can add up fast. One option is to have volunteers prepare the meal, but you'll probably have to bring down your ticket prices for a more homespun event like this. Also, you'll find that feeding large numbers of people requires special equipment, such as warming trays and coffee urns, not to mention space, tables, and chairs, that you may have to rent. After adding up all the extras, some organizations find it more cost effective to hire professionals.

Renting a private hall and hiring a caterer is usually cheaper than contracting with a hotel—the latter are famous for charging five bucks for a mediocre cup of coffee. If a hotel seems like your best option, you can bring down the costs by asking to include some separately donated items on the menu, such as wine or chocolates.

> **TIP**
>
> **Good food is critical.** Although your purpose is to raise money rather than to provide a gourmet dining experience, don't overlook the importance of giving your guests a good meal for their money. Participants will remember overcooked pasta or tiny portions years later. Worse yet, I heard of one event where a group tried to cook dinner for 500 people—who waited hungrily until 10:45 in the evening to be fed. If you're doing your own cooking, at least consult with a professional about how to pull it off. If not, try to sample all menu items before the event. Ask the hotel, restaurant, or other food preparer to prepare you the exact same meal as your guests will be served. Make sure the meal fills you up and tastes good—but isn't so decadent that health-conscious diners will stick to the parsley garnish. Also try to arrange options for people with special diet needs, such as vegetarian or kosher. Because of the variety of diets and allergies, it's usually easiest just to give your guests the name of a chef or other food-planning person to contact directly, and let them work out the details.

Auctions

An auction, whether silent or live, can be a stand-alone event or a part of another event, such as an annual dinner. For those unfamiliar with the distinction, a silent auction is one where people write their bids on a sheet of paper, usually in an area where the items up for auction are displayed, with little time pressure. People can go back to see whether they've been outbid, and then write in a higher bid if they wish. At an appointed time, you close the bidding, and later announce the winners or let people check for their names on the bidding sheets. A live auction, of course, is one where an auctioneer (preferably a professional) is at the helm, and people call out (or otherwise indicate) their bids. Which one you choose may simply be a matter of practicality—an important advantage to a silent auction, for example, is that it can be conducted quietly, without disturbing any other simultaneous activities (such as speakers or cocktail hour conversation).

If your choice between a silent or live auction will be based on which is more profitable, go with a live auction. Silent auctions usually bring in about half the market value of the items auctioned, while live auctions tend to bring in bids closer to or exceeding the items' market value. The reason may be that more excitement, or even frenzy, develops as people compete out loud. People may start out looking for a bargain, but end up saying, "Well, at least it was for a good cause."

No matter which kind of auction you hold, your overall profits will also depend on your audience. In the words of events planner Laurie Earp, "You have to know who your guests are going to be. Are they looking for a good bargain, or are they looking for a good bidding war, and willing to pay more than the retail value of the items? It's best to have a combination of both." Part of this will depend on whether your guests are existing organization members or donors, or are simply members of the community who attend for their own pleasure. If it's the latter, you may be able to tweak their consciousnesses and further open their wallets by reminding them of the purpose of the event—and by setting minimum bids higher than bargain basement levels.

Silent and live auctions can both be highly profitable fundraisers because, of course, you'll be auctioning off donated goods. Many businesses understand that donating something to an auction brings them publicity, and you'll be pleased to discover that many of them are willing to make a gift. Part of this willingness stems from the fact that they probably paid wholesale prices for the goods, while you will bring in something closer to their retail cost. You can also minimize how much you ask of any one business (and have fun to boot) by creating packages—the classic one being plane tickets to a holiday destination like Hawaii, with a week's stay at a hotel (or supporter's home), and meals at nice restaurants. Package deals don't have to be on such a grand scale, however—you could also create an auction package offering "A Day on the Avenue," and ask merchants along a popular commercial street to donate certificates for a spa visit or massage, lunch, movie tickets, and a latte. Or, you might create a food basket, with every item carrying a tag from its donor.

Some of the best donations come from your own supporters—for example, a ride on someone's sailboat, dinner at someone's home, a foursome at a private golf club, use of a vacation home, or use of professional services—from chiropractic to accounting to hairdressing. A friend of mine who happens to be a highly ranked chess player offered a free chess lesson as an auction donation. The most interesting auction I've attended was one selling paintings made by elephants—abstract paintings, of course. These particular elephants were on an animal preserve in Thailand, and the auction helped to raise money for their care. (For more information, particularly if you're unfamiliar with the phenomenon of artistic elephants, see the website of the Asian Elephant Art and Conservation Project, at www.elephantart.com.)

The drawback to using auctions as fundraising tools is that they take an enormous amount of time to prepare. Every merchant or other donor needs to be approached, the items need to be picked up, certificates may need to be created for the winners of intangible items such as dinner at a board member's house, packages need to be put together, and thank-you letters need to be sent out to every gift-giver. Obviously, these tasks are ideal for board members and other volunteers—but you'll need to set some parameters first, on the types of items you want and the potential sponsors or donors who should be approached. You don't want volunteers showing up at your office with donated kittens, or worse yet, carloads of used goods.

Make an effort to coordinate your volunteers so that the same donor isn't approached twice. Also make sure that all volunteers are armed with brochures describing your organization and a "Dear Friend" letter explaining the event and the recognition the donor will receive for making a contribution.

TIP

Raffles are a close cousin to auctions. Though they're not really "events," raffles are a great way to earn between $2,000 and $10,000. The principles of lining up donated goods are the same. You simply set a raffle ticket price that seems fair (and sufficient to make it worth your investment of time), create tickets with a stub for the buyer and a portion for you, where the buyer fills in his or her name, address, and email, then sell the tickets. Having kids sell raffle tickets is a surefire way to get things going. I have a friend who says, "All you need is three kids and a mountain bike." The concept is that you arrange with a sports store to buy the bike at cost, then post the kids (and the bike) outside the store or at another popular location, such as a coffee shop. They sell raffle tickets until they've earned enough to cover the bike plus a healthy profit, then some lucky ticket holder pedals off into the sunset.

The names and addresses you collect from your raffle tickets are yet another source of potential new members for your mailing and email lists. A caution, however: Some states separately regulate raffles—for example, by limiting the number you can have per year or the value or type of items you can raffle, or by requiring you to file a report when you're holding a raffle. Check with your state nonprofit-regulating agency for more information.

Fairs and Festivals

This category encompasses events like crafts fairs, carnivals, Renaissance fairs, music festivals, and other occasions that showcase a variety of vendors or talents. Some organizations invent their own theme festivals—for example, the International Crane Foundation, a Wisconsin-based center for the study and preservation of cranes, has held a Crane Fest, featuring bird-related activities like guided hikes, origami crane folding, bird-feeder building, and a performance of the play "Sadako and the Thousand Cranes" (see www.savingcranes.org). The key is to create an occasion where people can access things that they might not ordinarily find all in one place—such as ethnic artifacts and food, antiques, fun activities, or unusual musicians who come from far away or wouldn't be heard on local airwaves. With a nice location, a little music, decorated booths, and perhaps people in costume, you're also creating a destination that will attract people who are simply looking for something to do.

But don't try to undertake a large-scale fair or festival until you've had experience with other or smaller special events. There are plenty of ways to put on a small yet profitable festival. For example, if you hold an ethnic culture fair at a local church, no one is going to expect miles and miles of booths. You might increase profits by combining it with a silent auction. Make sure your publicity materials don't exaggerate what you'll be offering, of course. If you feel you must start on a larger scale, it may be worth hiring a professional—not only an events coordinator, but perhaps also someone with experience in the particular industry you'll be featuring, such as music or arts. If you work with a professional outside the nonprofit world, be prepared for him or her to charge a substantial fee, or to take a percentage of the proceeds.

Announcement for KPFA Annual Crafts Fair

Reprinted with permission

As the scale of your event gets larger, you can charge rent to both the exhibitors and the people who attend. Also, because a fair or festival is already a variety program, it offers you great opportunity to mix in other fundraising methods, such as raffles, bake sales, and the like. And, although costs start to go up as you look at larger venues and more equipment, the greater community benefit you'll be providing increases your chances of getting help from sources such as your city government (for example, with waived parking fees) or local businesses (for example, with loans of equipment). For a more detailed account of the process of shepherding a crafts fair from infancy to large-scale success, see "KPFA Annual Holiday Crafts Fair," below.

KPFA Annual Holiday Crafts Fair

KPFA, a community radio station in Berkeley, California, has held an annual holiday crafts fair since 1970. The purpose of the event is manyfold—it helps put a human face on KPFA, raises money, and has become a favorite holiday tradition unto itself. The crafts fair now includes over 200 crafts and nonprofits booths and food vendors, all occupying a large San Francisco festival space. It usually brings in about $150,000—but before you get too excited, understand that all but about $30,000 or $40,000 of this goes to pay for the fair.

Jan Etre has been coordinating the KPFA crafts fair since 1988. It's a half-time job for her, along with a part-time assistant, who primarily handles publicity. Here's how Jan describes it: "As an organizer, my job is to make a party happen. But it's all the work done in the prior six months that makes the fair a comfortable place to be. My job starts slowly every year, requiring about ten hours a week, but builds to about 60 hours a week in the days and weeks before the fair happens. My tasks include things like screening the artists and craftspeople who will sell their wares, setting up the website, organizing the venue, organizing food, entertainment, security, and shuttle service to and from nearby BART (subway) stations, developing promotional materials and posters, and actually promoting the event. In fact publicity and promotions are well over half of my job.

"The best advice I have for someone starting a crafts fair is to start small, and put the artists first. If you try to put on a huge event and it fails, word will get out—and if you've made 200 artists unhappy, they'll tell their friends, and you'll have fewer quality artists to choose from next year. On the other hand, if you start with a small number of artists and focus on making sure they turn a profit and feel happy about your event (even if it means keeping your booth fees artificially low at first), they'll return. What's more, they will bring other high-quality artists with them, and your event will grow naturally.

"Sometimes our philosophy of putting the artists first means we have to make some counterintuitive decisions. For example, there's been some pressure to allow imported goods into the KPFA crafts fair. However, we've refused, because this would undermine the prices that our U.S.-based craftspeople can charge—and they're trying to make a living wage from their crafts.

"One last thing that I like to remember is that every year's event is also a dress rehearsal for next year. It's an opportunity to learn what might be done better—and I'm still learning!"

Benefit Concerts, Lectures, and Other Presentations

Here's where your organization's personal contacts come in handy. If you know a celebrity, author, expert, or musical group that will offer to perform or speak for free or at a discount, and if the public would be interested enough to pay money for it, you've got yourself an event. It's crucial, of course, that the person or group be interesting or high-profile enough to inspire high tickets sales. This is worth some research—at least ask your friends, or kids, to find out which names generate excitement. Someone you've never heard of may pack the house, while a famous old warhorse may barely fill the first five rows. (See Chapter 13 for suggestions on getting media publicity before the event.) Depending on how many seats you have to fill, however, realize that you may not have to look for someone of national interest. If a local band, for example, has a devoted following—even if it's mostly family and friends—it may be enough to pack a coffee shop that donates its space for the evening. Or, a well-regarded local pianist could perform in a board member's living room.

You can also approach people with whom you have no personal connection, although it's much harder without a personal introduction. Most celebrities and groups have publicists who handle their bookings. The publicists are very experienced at diplomatically saying "no" to the many charitable organizations that approach them. Your job is to convince the publicist that your event will be good publicity for the person or group, that the person or group will be well taken care of, and that they may even enjoy themselves. Better yet, if you can contact the celebrity directly—for example, via a board member who is a personal friend—you may get a quick and enthusiastic "yes."

If you don't have any personal contacts, the celebrities who are most likely to be interested in participating are those with something to sell—in particular, authors. Upon publishing a new book, big-name authors usually go on a multicity publicity tour to visit bookstores, give media interviews, and make other public appearances. If there are any open spots in the author's calendar, the publicist will be eager to fill them—particularly if you can promise some time for the author to sit at a table, greet readers, and sell books. By watching the local bookstores' speakers schedules, you may be able to figure out who's coming. For a more efficient approach, simply contact a publishing company whose works would be appreciated by your audience, and ask to speak with one of its publicists. Explain your needs and approximate time frame, and see what he or she can suggest.

TIP

Avoid canned and rehashed speeches. "I try to create an event that otherwise wouldn't have happened, and preferably won't ever happen again," says Bob Baldock, Events Coordinator at KPFA radio in Berkeley, California. "For example, I ask authors to not simply read from their book, but to talk about how they're apprehending the world at this time. Or, I'll try to put together an interesting pair—or even a small group—of people. With enough ingenuity, you can create an event that will basically promote itself."

Although most arrangements for this type of event can be handled through letters back and forth, there are circumstances in which you'll want to protect your organization's interests by signing a contract. This is particularly true if you'll be covering a number of costs, such as transportation, hotel, room service, and the like. Your contract should clearly specify and limit the costs you'll cover, so that you won't be surprised by a bill for your celebrity's personal assistant's three-hour massage at the hotel spa after the event.

Benefit events can be reasonably good moneymakers, because you can control your expenses, including the cost of space, promotion and publicity, a sound system (always expensive, but not something you should compromise on), and refreshments. Expenses can mount quickly, however, if you're bringing in out-of-town performers—the cost of transportation and accommodations for your performers and their entourage can be especially high.

RESOURCE

Want to read more about events with celebrities? For a well-written, engaging guide with lots of information—and horror stories—about celebrity events, as well as sample contracts, see *Black Tie Optional: The Ultimate Guide to Planning and Producing Successful Special Events,* by Harry A. Freedman and Karen Feldman Smith (Taft Group). It's out of print, but you should be able to find it in libraries and nonprofit resource centers. The Freedman/Feldman Smith team has also written a more recent and very practical guide, called *The Business of Special Events: Fundraising Strategies for Changing Times* (Pineapple Press).

Walk-a-thons, Tournaments, Contests, and Sporting Events

Not every special event has to require a suit and tie; consider the many possible special events that get people out sweating or competing. Such events are particularly appropriate for organizations that have young memberships or are concerned with health issues. The various "a-thons" (walk-a-thons, bike-a-thons, swim-a-thons, 10Ks, and the like) are among the simplest ways to fundraise, because your primary needs include only a route or pool, some paper for participants to use as sponsor sign-up sheets, refreshments to hand out along the way, and a few prizes for those who finish first and/or collect the most in sponsorship money. Of course, larger events will need to incorporate more, including medical assistance, bike mechanics, and other support goods or services.

You should also try to solicit corporate sponsors. Fortunately, people are so accustomed to seeing corporate logos associated with sports events that you can prominently exhibit these without fearing that folks will think your nonprofit has sold out. The sponsors will probably ask for their logo to be displayed on the front of your promotional brochure, on banners at the event, and possibly on participant T-shirts. For an attractive example of a promotional brochure incorporating sponsor logos, see the National Multiple Sclerosis Society's 14th Annual Top Hat Classic brochure, whose first and last pages are reprinted below.

One problem with these various "a-thons" is their popularity as a fundraising tool. Because so many groups rely on them, the public is getting tired of participating, especially in the more boring ones. Some really do lack imagination—I remember participating in a walk-a-thon as a teenager, and thinking at approximately mile 16 that they couldn't have chosen a less interesting stretch of paved-over Seattle suburb for us to drag our feet through. Our energy would have been much better spent volunteering for the cause—and in fact, some groups now organize volunteer-a-thons, along those very lines.

However, it's also true that there are times when a walk-a-thon can be just the right fundraiser for an organization. Schools and other organizations with lots of kids and families, for example, find that they are a good way to tap into this donor group (with the added benefit that you start children on a tradition of philanthropy). Walk-a-thons and their ilk are also a good fit for organizations in low-income areas, where small amounts can be solicited from a large number of

MS Society's Top Hat Brochure

donors. And the press can be surprisingly interested in events like walk-a-thons, which could lead to increased visibility for a fledgling organization.

Organizations that do best with these events make it an inspiring experience for participants. For instance, the AIDS/LifeCycle is a bicycling event in which participants, some of whom are HIV+, train hard enough to ride all the way from San Francisco to Los Angeles. People camp side by side along the route, develop friendships, and get lots of support and cheering from route bystanders. Of course, this event takes place on a much larger scale than your average nonprofit is prepared to handle. Another fine example is the American Cancer Society's "Relay for Life" walk/run, which usually takes place around a track, with teams of people walking in shifts for a 24-hour period (and some camping overnight). The spirit can be compared to a mini-Woodstock. And the opening to the event is particularly moving—cancer survivors set out on one direction around the track, and their caregivers in the other direction. There's hardly a dry eye when they meet up.

Before you decide to do a walk-, swim-, or bike-a-thon, consider whether the people who would go out and seek sponsors could be utilized in more effective ways—for example, by canvassing for new members as described in Chapter 4, or approaching potential major donors, as described in Chapter 6. If a recreational event really is the best way to use your potential participants' time, be sure to put some imagination into your event, so you can attract the largest possible pool of supporters.

A close cousin to walk-a-thons are sports tournaments and contests, in which you raise funds either by charging an entry fee, relying on the more traditional individual sponsorship system, or both. You should also line up corporate sponsors. Groups that successfully organize such specialized events are usually already associated with the activity, such as a horse, vintage car, or motorcycle club might be. The lesson here is that it's important to involve someone in the planning process who truly knows and loves the sport or activity. You wouldn't want to plan a Scrabble tournament only to discover you'd brought the wrong kind of dictionary, for example, or plan a foot race on a route with significant air pollution.

> **TIP**
>
> **Contests make good media fodder.** Holding a contest is a great way to attract publicity. There's always a winner and, particularly if you've got cute kids involved, some good photo opportunities. For example, a kids' pet show is almost sure to be covered by local media. See Chapter 13 for details on how to access and notify the appropriate media outlets.

Home and Garden Tours

Organizing a successful home and garden tour usually involves convincing a group of private home or garden owners to open their space to members of the public—who then buy tickets for the privilege of wandering through these (hopefully) gorgeous inner sanctums. The themes can be refined almost infinitely, from kitchen tours to Victorian home tours, sculpture garden tours, or whatever else might fit the interests of your nonprofit and sell tickets.

Tours are a wonderful way to make money from something you get for free. The main costs are promotion (printing and advertising), supplies for the day of the tour (such as banners and ticket tables outside the various stopping points, and brochures describing the homes or gardens) and anything else you add to the process (such as refreshments). Tours also afford an opportunity to charge for extras, particularly if people will spend any time at a central location. For example, Park Day School in Oakland, California, holds an annual garden tour. After purchasing tickets, visitors start on the school campus, where they (as well as the general public) can browse and buy garden-related items such as ceramic pots, tools, and starter plants from a series of booths operated by local vendors. For an additional fee, participants may buy a box lunch.

The challenging part of putting on a home and garden tour is the massive amount of organizing required. You've got to start well in advance to find appropriate homes or gardens, and negotiate with the owners to make them available on the appropriate day. You'll also have to politely say no to some eager people whose homes and gardens just aren't worthy of a tour stop. After identifying a set of homes or gardens, you'll need to gather information about them and write up descriptions for a brochure that visitors can carry with them on the tour. Unless you're lucky enough to identify homes and gardens within walking distance of each other, one of your volunteers will have to drive to every destination and write up clear directions. (Don't rely on Mapquest alone—it may not provide all the information your participants will need, such as landmarks to look for along the way, temporary detours, and suggested parking areas.) Also, you'll need to organize a large group of volunteers for the day of the tour, to handle tasks like checking tickets at each stop and standing at key points to answer questions and make sure visitors don't step on the tulips or pocket the silverware.

> **CAUTION**
>
> **Stay in touch with homeowners.** There's nothing worse than having someone withdraw a week before your event because they must jet off to Rome, Italy, or attend their grandson's kindergarten graduation in Rome, New York. Staying in close touch with homeowners in the months and weeks before your tour will demonstrate how seriously you take their participation and help discourage last-minute defections.

Garage Sales, Bake Sales, Used Book Sales, and More

There's a reason why garage sales, bake sales, used book sales, car washes, and the like never go out of style. They don't require much time, money, or expertise to set up, and loads of people are happy to buy something at a reasonable price while simultaneously supporting a good cause. As a classic example, events planner Laurie Earp told me, "The third grade at our school spontaneously put together a garage sale in just over a week, and made about $1,100. This was with incredibly minimal effort—imagine if they'd started earlier!" And, if you also hand out pamphlets and collect interested participants' names, you may also get some long-term donors out of the event.

Anyone who has been involved in one of these types of events knows how crazy things can get, with goods, cookies, or soap suds flying everywhere. The key to making it all work is organization, before, during, and after the event. Even if your event is small-scale, it will probably take at least twice the volunteer time that you imagine. In addition, you'll always want to have an extra person on hand during the event to deal with unexpected questions or requests. ("Can someone help me count these puzzle pieces to make sure they're all here?" "Would you please load this into my truck?")

Used Goods Sales: Here are some tips on making used goods or book sales profitable. For starters, every item should have a price tag on it, so that buyers don't have to find someone to ask. Pricing is an art unto itself. Karen Garrison, whose years of garage sale experience are described in "Hill-Wide Garage Sale in San Francisco," below, says, "You have to designate someone as a pricing czar. Otherwise, you'll have your various volunteers coming around and saying, 'Oh no, I think it should be more,' or 'you're nuts, no one will pay that,' or unilaterally dropping prices." Ideally, all donated merchandise for garage or used book sales should be reviewed in advance by an expert, who can help you figure out which items might be antiques or first editions and worth setting aside in a special area at a higher price. If you know an antiques dealer, a used clothing expert, or a used bookseller who will volunteer to take a quick look, you're in luck. Failing that, you'll want to pick the most knowledgeable people available. After all, you don't want to sell a pair of once-worn Prada shoes for $3.50.

Your experts can also help you identify which items are junk, and should either be sold at a very low price or disposed of immediately. If you don't recognize and deal with the junk well in advance, two bad things happen. First, the worthless items tend to pull down the prices of the more valuable property. Second, your trip to Goodwill or the Salvation Army at the end of the day—an inevitable part of the event that you should plan for in advance—will be an even bigger endeavor than you'd anticipated.

> **CAUTION**
>
> **Accepting old clothing and household goods or furniture?** If so, the IRS now says that they must be in "good or better" condition for the donor to take a tax deduction. You can help the donors by providing filled-out receipts stating the products' condition, though few organizations have time for this. Experts also advise the donors themselves to take photographs of the goods in case of an audit.

Assuming you've priced things well, you'll probably want to hold fairly firm to those prices for at least the first half of your sale. Reminding people that this is a fundraiser will help deflect some of the more persistent bargainers. However,

Hill-Wide Garage Sale in San Francisco

Often, it's not the event you first choose, but what you make of it over time that will really dictate your fundraising success. Years ago, the senior services department of the Bernal Heights Neighborhood Center (www.bhnc.org) decided to try a fairly traditional fundraising strategy: a garage sale. It was a good choice to draw on the organization's existing assets: BHNC was already working to build community in this somewhat remote part of San Francisco, and had willing volunteers among the seniors it served (with classes, congregate meals, outings, and more). Since the original sale, however, this event has grown into an award-winning community tradition, involving as many as 120 registered garage sale sites at locations spread throughout Bernal Heights, and attracting thousands of customers, some from many miles away.

Karen Garrison, Director of Senior Services with BHNC, feels that this event might serve as a model for other organizations: "Normally we have a large garage sale here at the Neighborhood Center, so we're sort of the epicenter of the whole thing. Our volunteers also set up some food booths. People come to the Center and buy things at our sale, but they also pick up event maps, telling them where other sales are being held throughout the neighborhood. This gives us a few seconds—because people are eager to get going—to tell the visitors about BHNC's work, and suggest a donation for the maps (this brought in over $300 last year). The map is a surprisingly important piece of the picture. People who want their garage sale included on our map pay us $20. The reverse side of the map contains narrative information, including a reminder that the event is a fundraiser. Of course, some people don't stop for maps, and just drive around looking. The energy on the street is unbelievable—lots of people, lots of cars.

"We start planning for this event about two months in advance, but once we get going, it's very labor-intensive, including about 200 staff hours, and many more volunteer hours. Aside from sending out invitations to potential participants (and guidelines, after they sign up), coordinating volunteers, and creating the map, promotion is a big part of our preparation. We make use of all the community media outlets' opportunities for free announcements, do outreach within our own service network and at churches, and our volunteers place around 2,000 fliers in local store windows, coffee shops, and the like.

"Admittedly, the event doesn't raise a lot of money—about $4,000 last year, which is less than 1% of our budget. Profits come from a combination of map fees, our on-site

Hill-Wide Garage Sale in San Francisco (continued)

garage sale, and percentages of proceeds from other sales, which some participants voluntarily pledge. We're looking into ways to increase profits, such as getting local merchants involved with sponsorships and in-kind donations. Luckily, the costs are quite minimal, so we're virtually guaranteed to turn a profit. But what makes the event truly worthwhile is both the increased visibility for BHNC and the fact that it creates such wonderful community feeling."

you'll also want to decide in advance when to start dropping prices, to make sure you aren't left with too many unsold goods. For an all-day sale, late afternoon is usually an appropriate time to offer some bargains (allowing some discretion by your pricing czar, depending on how sales are going). Even then, try to drop prices according to a preset schedule, so you don't start giving things away for practically free, thus wasting your and your volunteers' time and efforts.

CAUTION

Decide how you'll deal with earlybirds. First, you'll have to consider whether to sell particular items to a professional antiques dealer or bookseller, particularly those who helped set your prices, and to your other volunteers who've no doubt been eyeing things they'd like, in advance of your sale—this might bring in guaranteed profits, but it also diminishes the public's perception of the quality of your sale. Next, you'll need to be ready to deal with the semiprofessional bargain-hunting community, which in most areas has become a force to be reckoned with. They're likely to show up at your sale well before it is open, demand to start shopping, and scarf up all the good stuff before you've even begun (goodbye Prada shoes). The aggressive response is to put up ropes and post no-nonsense volunteers until you're ready to open; the lower-conflict but somewhat unsatisfying alternative is to warn your volunteers that they should plan to start the sale around 30 minutes before it's officially open!

Bake Sales: Bake sales or other food sales are almost guaranteed to please a crowd. Even so, you've probably seen some of the problems that can reduce profitability—such as stingy or overgenerous portions or badly labeled items that are hard to identify. Also, with allergies and vegetarian or vegan diets increasingly on the minds of the American public, you need to be prepared for probing questions about what your food items contain. One good way to solve this is to have each of your food preparers list the ingredients in every item. Also, you'll want to be sure to stock at least some items without the most common allergens, including nuts, eggs, peanuts, wheat, and milk products.

Car Washes: Car washes are also a standby of grassroots nonprofit efforts. They can be particularly effective if you can put a hose or towel in the hands of the celebrity or two. Customers love to brag that their car was washed by Fiona Famous or Stanley Star. One perennial tension, however, is that it takes a fair amount of time to wash a car well. This can mean either that the nonprofit doesn't make much money, or that the customers end up dissatisfied, as the soap bubbles dry into spots on their windshields. To keep things moving along, it's essential to use an appropriate space, preferably one loaned by a gas station or another place with lots of hose hookups. (In many areas, these are also environmentally friendlier, since they drain to the sewage treatment system rather than through the storm drains to local waterways.) Then, to ensure some quality control, practice car washing techniques with your volunteers, and explain to everyone what you expect. Volunteers should work in teams of four or five so cars move in and out quickly.

Choose the Right Event for Your Organization

The first step in deciding what type of special event to hold is the same as the first step in planning your annual fundraising strategy—examine your organization's assets. (Review Chapter 3 for a reminder of how to plan your annual fundraising.) If you've got a large physical facility, think about events that might attract a crowd. If you've got an unusually large volunteer corps, consider events that require large numbers of people to prepare or run, such as an auction, fair, festival, or home tour. If you've got access to celebrities or experts, consider lectures, benefit concerts, or major donor parties to meet your stars (see Chapter 6 for details).

> ⓘ **CAUTION**
> **Make sure your intended special event is grounded in your annual fundraising plan.** When a volunteer in a good mood offers up a beautiful house for a party or proposes some other unplanned event, it's easy to say "yes" without considering all the consequences. Unless you can truly mobilize volunteers who weren't serving any other fundraising purpose—a rare situation, and one that should cause you to question why those volunteers weren't otherwise occupied—your special event is likely to divert time and attention away from potentially more profitable fundraising activities. This doesn't mean that you should never seize an unexpected fundraising opportunity, but you should do so only if it doesn't unduly disrupt your plan.

After figuring out what types of events you could offer, think about who is likely to show up. Although "paying customers" are your first priority, remember that your event is also an opportunity to pick up new support, which means that you'll want to attract people who fit your donor profile. For example, I once spoke with members of a suicide prevention group who started an annual golf tournament simply because one of the founders liked golf and could mobilize his friends—but its effectiveness sputtered out after a few years, as they realized that participants weren't interested in other donations or involvement.

Once you've got a brilliant event idea in mind, do some research to find out whether people will pay to attend (or pay for items once they're there). How much research you'll need to do depends on the size of your event. For a small event, it may require no more than talking informally to your major donors and other supporters. For events designed to bring in more members of the general public, however, you may have to find experts in the relevant area—such as the music business—to quiz about attendance estimates. Also talk to folks at other nonprofits that have done similar events (in comparable cities, if you're worried about being in competition with more local nonprofits).

The amount of time an event will take should also be part of the planning process. Because you should be conceptualizing the event as part of your overall fundraising planning, you should also have an idea of how much staff and volunteer time you've got to spend. It's hard to exaggerate how much time a good-sized special event can take to organize! Multiply your initial estimate by three.

WORLD's Fashion Show Develops from HIV+ Clients' Personal Interests

WORLD (Women Organized to Respond to Life Threatening Disease) is an Oakland, California–based information and support network by, for, and about women living with HIV/AIDS (www.womenhiv.org). In recent years, a highlight of their traditional dinner event has been a fashion show put on by HIV-positive women and their children. This is no mere ode to fashion—the women, many of whom are low-income and dealing with AIDS-related illnesses or the side effects of medication, conceived of the event as a way to celebrate their lives and their bodies.

This fashion show provides an excellent example of the wisdom of planning your event around existing resources. As WORLD's Board co-chair Sonja Mackenzie told it, "Not only did the idea of the fashion show start organically within this group of HIV-positive women, but it so happened that in its first year at WORLD, our organization had a useful connection—one of our donors had friends within the fashion industry. She was able to line up loans of some incredibly fancy outfits for the women and children to wear, from notable designers such as Jessica McClintock. The women (and children) looked and felt beautiful.

"Audience reaction to the show was indescribable, incredibly powerful. I think the show really hit on the core elements around HIV and being a woman with HIV. The audience included medical providers, family members, and members of the pharmaceutical industry. They were both moved and impressed by seeing their family members/patients in a new, powerful role.

"The second year that we did the fashion show, we no longer had our fashion industry contact. That made the planning a lot trickier. In the end we found a more local contact, an Oakland-based designer of African clothing. We also divided the show into differently themed sections, such as 'On the beach,' 'My heritage,' and others. The emcee (a local television personality) read each woman's brief autobiography, such as 'This is so-and-so, a 35-year-old woman who's been living with HIV for ten years. The most important thing in her life is her son, whom she wants to see graduate from college. She's on the beach in Hawaii today, because one day she dreams that she will be able to live there.'

"In the end—and despite my initial misgivings—the show was another huge success, largely because it included such powerful personal narratives. Nevertheless, putting the show on was an enormous amount of work, more than any of us ever imagined. Though we probably won't be able to repeat it at every dinner, we definitely plan to bring it back in the future."

For a big event, hiring an outside consultant or events planner can be an efficient way of ensuring that your staff's daily work isn't greatly disrupted. Although this is likely to cost you several thousand dollars, a good, experienced events planner can often earn back his or her fee and then some, simply by drawing on longstanding relationships with graphic designers, printers, musicians, local businesses that are proven donors, and others to keep costs down and minimize delays. They can also help you make informed decisions about what works to draw in and satisfy the public, and how to maximize profits overall. Just don't expect the events planner to do everything—in particular, soliciting donations from your own donors or even some local businesses is a task that should stay within your own staff and board, as part of your relationship-building efforts.

CROSS REFERENCE

Review Chapter 3 for more information on planning your fundraising strategy—its principles are also applicable to planning a particular special event. Also review the portions on getting buy-in from participants. Though you want to minimize the amount of time spent on meetings and process, deciding what event to hold should not be done unilaterally—those involved need to express their doubts or willingness to help.

Develop a Realistic Budget

There's no great mystery to creating a special events budget: You list all your anticipated expenses in one column, then enumerate what you expect to bring in from various intended activities in the second. Finally, you subtract your expected revenues from your anticipated expenses to give you a total. The trick, of course, is accurately projecting your expenses and income. Part of this involves taking your analysis to a micro level, so that you don't forget to budget for paper napkins and microphone rentals, for example. Another critical factor in the eventual accuracy of your budget is how faithfully your volunteers follow through on the activities your figures are based on. In other words, if you plan to keep expenses down by getting donated food and chairs, and to keep income high by getting corporate sponsorships, you've got to communicate this to whoever is in charge of doing these things, and make sure the tasks get done.

Every fundraising event creates financial risk. You'll have to cover most of your expenses before you know how much the event will bring in—or whether an unexpected snowstorm or other disaster will soak your balance in red ink. One great way to minimize risk is to stick to events that don't cost a lot to stage. Then, if anticipated revenues don't materialize for some reason, you haven't dug yourself a huge financial hole.

Estimate Expenses

There's no better way to understand the event budgeting process than to grab a pencil and paper. To make this easier, I've provided the expense worksheet below (sorry, the pencil is the first of your expenses). As you start to fill out the worksheet, you'll inevitably learn more about what you can afford, what key decisions need to be made (for example, how much you're willing to spend on advertising and promotion), and how many guests you'll need to attract. You'll also hopefully think up a few special items to add to the worksheet, based on whatever is unique about your event. And for every expense item, be sure to consider whether you can get needed items through donations, or cut the costs in some other way—by renting as opposed to buying, for example.

If you're new at this, assume that your final figure will be on the low side— some suggest adding at least 20% for unanticipated costs or occurrences. And always remember that staff time is a hidden cost—although it doesn't show up in the budget, it's a very important consideration. It's very easy for staff to get pulled away from important development or program responsibilities by the whirl of activity leading up to a special event.

> **CAUTION**
>
> **A cheap sound system can ruin your event.** We've all been at events where the electronic feedback made our fillings ache, or the speaker equipment was diabolically positioned to blast the VIP table. This isn't random bad luck—it can be overcome by paying a little more for your sound system. For example, in a large hall, it's best to connect speakers at points around the room rather than just line them up on the stage. Though paying more seems hard to justify at the abstract, budget-planning level, think of it as an investment against audience irritation or inattention.

Fundraising Worksheet 6: Projected Special Event Expenses

Expense Category	Projected Cost	Description of Reasoning or Assumptions, Particularly for Discount or Donated Items
Physical Space		
Room, building, outdoor space	$	
Chairs, tables, performance platform	$	
Site manager and other staff fees	$	
Heating or air conditioning	$	
Sound system, projector, screen, other equipment	$	
Traffic/parking permits	$	
Subtotal:	$	
Decorations		
Banners	$	
Lighting	$	
Flowers	$	
Candles	$	
Balloons	$	
Party favors, gifts, award plaques, and certificates	$	
Other	$	
Subtotal:	$	
Food and Drink		
Snacks or appetizers (for participants and volunteers	$	
Main meal	$	
Extra catering or corkage fees	$	
Alcohol, other drinks, ice	$	
Plates, cups, napkins, cutlery	$	
Waiters and bar staff	$	
Subtotal:	$	

Fundraising Worksheet 6: Projected Special Event Expenses (continued)

Performers/Speakers		
Performance fee or honorarium	$	
Transportation and parking (airfare, shuttle, rental car, cabs, or limousine)	$	
Hotel	$	
Meals	$	
Telephone and other extras	$	
Subtotal:	$	
Publicity		
Graphic designer and/or artist	$	
Printing (save-the-date postcards, invitations, posters, programs, ad books)	$	
Stationery, envelopes	$	
Postage (invitations, press releases)	$	
Professional mailing services	$	
Event photographer	$	
Subtotal:	$	
Miscellaneous		
Taxes on goods sold	$	
Photocopying	$	
Supplies for volunteer meetings and information packets	$	
Reimbursement of volunteers' expenses (i.e., gasoline, telephone)	$	
Unexpected or emergency expenses	$	
Subtotal:	$	
Total:	$	

Estimate Income

Correctly anticipating income is a bit more difficult, particularly in the first year or years of an event. Your crystal ball rarely reveals how many people will show up at an event, how much they'll buy, or how high their auction bids will go. Fill out the worksheet as best you can, but protect yourself from risk by starting small and getting lots of advance support from major donors and corporate sponsors. If the event becomes a tradition for your organization, however, your projections will become more accurate, aided by your experience and by last year's records.

Fundraising Worksheet 7: Projected Special Event Income

Income Category	Projected Amount	Description of Reasoning or Assumptions
Tickets	$	_____ of guests at $_____ per ticket
Ad books or ad space in program	$	_____ of advertisers at $_____ per _____
Exhibitors' or vendors' rental fees	$	_____ of exhibitors/vendors at $_____ per booth
Corporate sponsorships	$	
Sales of food or goods	$	
Silent auction or raffle proceeds	$	
Total:	$	

Compare Projected Expenses and Income

For a successful event, your income should exceed your expenses by a healthy margin. This is hard to quantify, but you should aim to earn at least five times your expenses—for example, kids selling a mountain bike worth $500 should attempt to bring in $2,500. Using this approach, even if you collect only $2,000 you're still doing pretty well. The actual dollar amount that you'll hope to earn depends, of course, on the size of your organization's budget and the size of the event. But if it's only a couple thousand dollars, think hard about how much staff time will be going into the event. Again, I didn't work this hidden cost into the budget worksheet, but when profits will already be low, staff time can make the difference between making and losing money

Make sure your projected budget still shows a profit if things go wrong. For example, try running the numbers with a third of the attendees showing up, and see what happens to your income. Once you've swallowed that bitter pill, think about which of your expenses you can put off incurring until you're sure of attendance figures. Hotels, for example, will generally ask for a deposit up front, then require that you confirm attendance and pay for a set number of meals by a certain date. Make sure to set your ticket sales deadline before that date!

> **CAUTION**
>
> **Tell donors exactly how much of their ticket price or other payments to your organization during an event are tax deductible.** You and they must subtract out the value of actual goods or services received by the donor. You'll need to give each donor a dollar figure stating how much of his or her payment is tax deductible. For more information on tax deductibility of donations, see Chapter 4.

Plan and Pace Event Activities

The success of your event depends in large part on what goes on behind the scenes in the months or weeks leading up to it. Allow plenty of lead time—the "classic" special event, such as an annual dinner, gala ball, or benefit concert, normally takes between six months to a year to prepare. Giving yourself a realistic amount of time will not only save your sanity, but also save your organization's money. For example, the costs of design and printing will go down if you give your designers and printers ample time to work the tasks into their schedules—and will go up just as easily if you ask for a rush job.

It's also important to get a head start on corporate sponsorships. Most companies make their decisions about sponsorships in either the last quarter of the preceding year or the first quarter of the year when the event will be held. This means that even for some fall events, you'll need to have gotten your sponsorship requests out in the previous year.

If you're working primarily with volunteers, however, it is often better not to launch your preparations until six months before the event. If you give more lead time, people won't feel any time pressure—and some of them won't get over this feeling until a few weeks before the event. Be warned, too, that volunteers may be heavy on the good intentions and somewhat lighter on the follow-through, so having leaders who can motivate them (as well as do a little friendly monitoring) will help make sure tasks get done on time.

> **TIP**
>
> **Help motivate participants by creatively announcing your progress.** For example, the Bernal Heights Neighborhood Center marks its progress toward its community-wide garage sale (see "Hill-Wide Garage Sale in San Francisco," above) in terms of how many neighborhood residents have signed up to participate. They regularly create a huge sign with the latest number (photocopy shops can create giant blowups for a few dollars) and prominently hang the sign at the Center for staff, volunteers, and passersby to see.

Some of the main preparatory tasks are covered below. However, when you've identified your event and outlined your goals regarding promotion and publicity, sponsorship, and the like, you may want to consult some more specialized resources for additional tips. You'll find some listed at the end of this chapter.

Create a Calendar of Activities

The time-tested way to figure out what needs to be done by when is to work backward from the day of the event. What are the final steps—such as picking up rental chairs and flowers? By when do these need to be ordered? By when do decisions need to be made about how many chairs and what type of flowers? Who will be responsible for the decisions? When should this committee meet? Similarly, if you'll have a featured entertainer, when must you choose this person to make sure that his or her name will be announced in promotional materials? How much time before this should you allow to negotiate and sign a contract for this person's services? How many weeks in advance should be allotted for approaching different performers? When will the committee meet to select potential performers' names? You get the drift.

Once you have worked out what needs to be done and by when, create an actual calendar. The bigger the better—in fact, for more complicated events, I suggest you create poster-sized calendars for each month leading up to the event. Write in the dates on which you or one of your volunteers must start the various activities, not the dates by which they must be completed. For example, "Last day to choose menu" is not a helpful calendar entry unless it was preceded by one advising you to begin the selection process.

Working with the dates you've entered on the calendar, create checklists for yourself and your committees, itemizing every task that needs to be done. You or your committee leaders should review these checklists regularly, ticking off items as they are completed, and calling people to confirm that they have completed their assigned tasks by the required dates.

Define Committees and Assign Leaders

Every special event needs a central point person to coordinate volunteers and keep things moving according to schedule. But one person can't pull off an event alone. By looking at your budget and other planning materials, you should be able to identify all of the activities that need to be attended to. Then, you'll want to create subject committees to match. For example, depending on the type of event you're planning, your committees might include some combination of the following:

- site planning
- meals or refreshments
- choosing exhibitors, performers, vendors, or home or garden tour destinations

- decorations
- transportation
- awards
- gathering auction or raffle donations
- obtaining corporate sponsorships
- event staffing and registration
- promotion and publicity (including graphics and printing), and
- cleanup.

Some of these activities are discrete enough that they may require only a single person, or a committee of two or three. In fact, at times it's best not to assign too many people to a task, lest the abundance of people give committee members the idea that little is expected of them. The two most important considerations are these: first, everyone must understand his or her responsibilities, including what needs to be done, by what deadline, and with whom to communicate about progress (or the lack thereof). Committee members should also understand the limits of their responsibility. For example, if you want the food committee to come up with a potential menu, but the E.D. will actually have the final say on what is served, this needs to be made clear from the beginning. Second, someone must monitor the situation conscientiously to make sure that all key tasks are really getting done.

> **CAUTION**
>
> **Communication between committee and other leaders is key.** The more committees you've got, the greater the risks of miscommunication. As Sonja Mackenzie, WORLD Board co-chair, put it: "I'm a strong proponent of open group process, but you still need to be clear about who the point person is, and keep the communication channels open to that person. If you've got a lot going on—for example, in WORLD's case, we combined a fundraising dinner with a fashion show—you'll find that the questions start multiplying, such as who picks up the microphone, and whether the dinner planners remembered to rent a venue that will accommodate a fashion show stage."

The point person should plan to be in regular contact with all committee leaders. Depending on the timeline and number of people involved, scheduling regular meetings or conference calls, where everyone will report on their progress and any difficulties they're facing, may be worthwhile. To save on unnecessary meetings, periodic email check-ins can also be useful—perhaps once a week early on, moving up to daily in the last week. You'll still need the occasional meeting, but you'll conserve time by saving them for important issues. In the name of good record keeping, the point person should ask for documentation of certain accomplishments, such as names of committed corporate sponsors, or copies of press releases. Excessive politeness has been known to lead to situations where volunteers assert that everything is going great, when in fact little or nothing has actually been done.

> **TIP**
>
> **Time to get organized.** Your event point person should create a note-book or system of file folders, to help keep track of important pieces of information and to ensure that nothing gets forgotten. Sections of the notebook, divided by easy-to-see tabs, should include your checklists, a month-by-month planning calendar, budgeting and finances, subject matter sections corresponding to each committee (and containing important documents such as contracts or notes on decisions and accomplishments), a master contact list of all vendors, volunteers, and other participants, and anything else relevant to the particular event. The leader should also work with the committee heads to help them get similarly organized.

Plan Promotion and Publicity

If you're hoping to attract members of the public to your event, especially members who are not on your organization's mailing list, you'll need to pay particular attention to promotion and publicity. (Loosely speaking, promotion is advertising that you arrange or pay for yourself, such as posters and invitations; publicity is media reporting, usually in response to your press releases or other contacts.) In fact, because the success of an event like a garage sale or street fair rides upon people hearing about and attending it, you should plan for promotional and publicity activities to consume the vast majority of your and your volunteers' prep time. It's helpful if you can enlist the services (preferably volunteer) of a professional public relations or marketing person.

Of course, step one in promoting your event is to tell your members and supporters about it. Your newsletter and website should start generating excitement about the event months in advance, mentioning the date, location, and contact person for more information or volunteer opportunities. To make sure that people make room on their calendars (even before you're ready to sell tickets, if any), it's traditional to send a "Save the Date" postcard approximately three to five months before the event.

Invitations, or opportunities to buy tickets, should be sent or announced six weeks before the event. In addition to sending these to your supporters, you might rent a mailing list of potentially interested people—for example, a list of members of a musical society if you'll be holding a concert. (See Chapter 4 for more information on the process of acquiring mailing lists.) Culling additional names is a separate and important task, one which you might assign to a committee. For example, all volunteers who get involved in the event should be given a piece of paper, and asked to write the names, addresses, email addresses, and telephone numbers of any of their friends who they think might be interested in attending. Similarly, any featured speakers or honorees should be asked for the contact information of friends or relatives who might wish to attend. (You'll need to develop a policy in advance regarding how many complimentary tickets your speakers or honorees will be given—normally tickets for a spouse or significant other and minor children should do it.)

> **TIP**
>
> **Each one bring ten.** Sometimes the simplest and cheapest promotional methods work the best. If you have a good-sized local membership, you might charge each member with recruiting ten friends. Especially if you include a fun contest (the winning recruiter gets a weekend at a donated vacation home, for example), this can be an incredibly cost-effective way to spread the word.

Event posters should be created for any event to which the public at large will be invited. If pressed for cash, this is something you can do in black and white with your own photocopying machine, but don't try this if you plan to charge high ticket prices or attract high-income attendees. Usually the help of a graphic designer is required, unless you have particularly artistic folks involved in your effort. An attractive poster can be a sought-after item, so that coffee shops, stores, and other public places will be more than happy to display it. Putting up posters is a good task to assign to a large number of volunteers, making sure that each is assigned a separate geographical area. Watch out for local ordinances concerning placing posters in public spaces or on telephone poles.

Your promotion and publicity committee should also consider which newspapers, magazines, or websites are most likely to be seen by your potential ticket buyers. An increasingly popular site for all kinds of events is http://eventful.com, and it provides a special page for charity and fundraising events. Instead of straining your budget for advertising, look for media outlets that offer free community calendars. In addition, you can get free publicity, and potentially reach a specialized segment of the public, by arranging for announcements within the newsletters of local churches or other groups, such as a bicycling or chess club.

The best advertising, however, is a positive media writeup or in-depth coverage by electronic media. See Chapter 13 on how to generate media attention for your event.

> **TIP**
>
> **Take photos of this year's event for next year's promotion.** Even if your event won't be highly photogenic, pictures of key speakers or people enjoying themselves are great for your website and promotional materials. If you'll be sending out a press release immediately after the event, photos will also increase the chances that your story will be picked up.

Create Corporate Sponsorship Opportunities

Despite the fact that many events charge admission fees, event profitability often depends on garnering money from outside sources, such as corporate sponsors. Sometimes, getting corporate sponsorship can be as simple as encouraging your board members to ask their employers to buy a table's worth of tickets for an annual dinner event. Other times, you will want to look for more major sponsorship—for example, by asking a company to be the lead name on your

10K run or whale watching tour, with its logo prominently displayed on your banners and publicity materials, in return for underwriting costs or supplying space, food, or other event necessities.

Either way, the important thing to remember is that businesses don't ordinarily sponsor an organization unless they feel assured that it will garner good publicity for the business itself. Be prepared to explain to any businesses that you approach:

- the nature of the event
- why it will suit their interests to be affiliated with it
- how many people you expect to attend, and
- what sort of publicity you're willing to give their business.

> **TIP**
>
> **Set up a system to display the logos of your sponsors.** Although it's fine to have a lead sponsor who pays for this prominent position, you'll rarely want to depend on one sponsor alone, unless that business is truly willing to make a major financial commitment. Instead, set aside space for a number of corporate sponsors—and let them know that their names will be front and center at your event.

Advertisements in your event program or an ad book are other popular ways of getting corporate sponsorship. I know of one organization that earned $125,000 on its ad book alone, which was prepared in conjunction with an annual dinner. An ad book is just what it sounds like—a small brochure that displays either traditional advertisements or small testimonials to the organization on behalf of the business or person buying the ad, such as "Bronze Medal Athletic Gear wishes to congratulate KidsClub for its 25 years of helping inner-city youth excel through physical activity and teamwork." Some ad buyers, such as sole proprietors or professionals such as lawyers, accountants, or music teachers, will simply want a copy of their business card in your ad book. Your graphic designer or printer should be able to help you set guidelines for planning and selling ad space.

Deal With Risks and Liability Issues

Because making your event profitable will require you to keep costs down, you must consider any minor or major disasters that might befall your event—such as a child getting injured on the site, a donor drinking too much and causing an accident driving home, or a thief taking your cash box or goods for sale. Because a special event is outside your usual course of business and may involve large numbers of people, you'll have to adjust your thinking to expect the unexpected—and plan to deal with the consequences.

There are three important steps you can take to forestall mishaps and disasters: First, make sure you've complied with all applicable laws and permit requirements; second, put your own sensible safety measures into place; and third, consider buying special insurance for the event. For smaller events, accomplishing steps one and two would probably be enough, but for large-scale events attended by many people you don't know, buying insurance may also make sense. And some event sites may require you to carry a specified type and amount of coverage as a condition of using their facilities.

Comply With Laws and Permit Requirements

Whether your event is on your organization's own site or elsewhere, unusual attendance or activities may bring up legal issues. Large numbers of people impeding traffic flow or parking in one area may require advance discussions with your local police department. If you'll be serving liquor, you may be required to obtain a license or permit, usually from your city. Whoever will be serving the alcohol may also be required to go through special training (to make sure they understand how to check IDs and when to cut someone off). Auctions (particularly of luxury items) and gambling activities may also require licenses or permits. As appropriate, talk to other nonprofits, your police department, or to a city official before proceeding. And, if you still have outstanding legal questions, look for a volunteer lawyer to help you find the answers.

Implement Appropriate Safety Measures

The best way to minimize damage is to avoid it in the first place, then create backup measures to deal with whatever can't be predicted or avoided. For starters, make sure that your event is well-staffed, and that every volunteer knows who to go to with a problem. If the person in charge will carry a cell phone, give every volunteer the number. Volunteers should wear something distinctive, so that members of the public know who to alert when the food has run out or they observe a burst pipe leaking in the direction of your sound system.

Also consider whether there are any rules that you want members of the public to observe. For example, if it wouldn't be appropriate to allow children below a certain age to participate, make this clear in your publicity materials, and be prepared to enforce it at the door. Similarly, if people shouldn't bring certain materials like alcoholic beverages or firearms, warn them in advance and be prepared to check for violations. This may require hiring a security person who is trained in dealing with such matters. I also suggest saying no to dogs, as well as to more exotic creatures—the cleanup problems are immense, and there's no upside unless it's an animal-centered event. (Working dogs, such as seeing-eye dogs, are of course an exception.)

Think carefully about who you're going to trust with sensitive tasks such as handling money, serving alcohol, or transporting people by car or van. Don't forget that these people will need to take breaks or spend some time enjoying the event themselves, so schedule additional people to spell them from time to time. Ask to see the license of every driver, and if they'll be driving a large truck or bus, make sure they're specially licensed for this as well. All volunteers carrying out sensitive tasks such as cashiering should be told that they can't just hand their responsibilities over to someone else; by the same token, other volunteers should understand the limits of their roles and responsibilities.

If you anticipate large amounts of cash changing hands, make sure to have a foolproof system in place for tracking it and keeping it secure. For starters, tell your cash handlers to put all large bills, as well as all bills in excess of what are needed to make change, into a special place—either under a plate in the cash register or, better yet, into a locked and hard-to-move box. It is also sensible to schedule someone to pick up cash at periodic points during the event. That person should keep records of exactly how much cash is taken from every cashier or box, in case questions arise later.

TIP

Take it to the bank. Picking up cash every hour or two solves one big problem, but creates another. Now you've got wads of money just waiting to be stolen or misplaced, with very little tracking as the day goes on. Instead of devising an elaborate security system, it's usually easier to simply deposit cash after every pickup in the bank's after-hours system.

Serving alcohol creates its own set of issues. You don't want to serve drinks to minors, you don't want people who've had too much to create a scene or a medical emergency, and you certainly don't want a drunk guest driving home to injure someone—who can then sue your organization for the damages you "caused." Even if your area doesn't require alcohol servers to be specially trained, servers should be ready to check IDs and tell patrons when they've had enough (or start mixing their drinks with nine parts soda). As the event winds down, someone should be stationed at the door to wish people farewell—and to offer a cab or other ride to anyone who seems to be staggering toward his or her car. To be extra-cautious, you could arrange with a cab company to have a couple of taxis waiting for this purpose, though they'd probably charge you for this service. One way to deal with all the above issues is to restrict alcohol events to restaurants, hotels, and other venues with experienced staff on hand.

Disability access is an important consideration, too—and one you should consider before contracting to use a particular physical space. Some buildings claim to have wheelchair accessibility, but it turns out to be a makeshift ramp at a precarious angle. Restroom accessibility is also an area where many physical spaces fall short. The last thing you want is a situation where helpful volunteers try to carry a disabled person up a set of stairs or into a bathroom.

These are just a few of the safety measures you can put into place. You may need to develop others based on the type of event, the number of people and type of activities people will be engaging in, any special needs that your guests are likely to have, and your own common sense.

Purchase Insurance

Contact your insurance broker or company and ask them to go over your policy with you, to explain how many of your activities will be covered. Chances are, there will be a number of gaps in your coverage. For example, someone who slips and falls while at your organization's office will probably be covered—but not if they slip while at a picnic in your local park. And injuries caused by staff members—for example, if your E.D. accidentally drops a case of wine on someone's foot—may be covered, while injuries caused by your volunteers may not be. Fortunately, event-specific insurance is available at a reasonable cost. Realize, however, that almost no insurance policy is a substitute for detailed planning, and most won't cover harm caused by reckless or intentional acts (for example, if one of your volunteers drives a car filled with balloons at 90 m.p.h. and ends up in a pile-up, or if a staff member gets into a wrestling match with a guest).

Last-Minute Tasks and Tips

The last days and hours leading up to the event are usually whirling-dervish time for even the most organized events planner or leader. Now you'll really want to put your checklists to work. Review them frequently and carefully, and double check that all of your committee leaders are communicating with one another as needed. Although the precise tasks to be accomplished will depend on the type of event you're having, here are some things no event planner should forget:

- **If you are the event leader, delegate shamelessly to make sure that your list of assignments for the actual day of the event is blank.** As Jan Etre, KPFA crafts fair organizer, says, "You should be completely available for answering questions and putting out fires. Someone will tap you on the shoulder, and you never know what's coming next—perhaps a lost child, or a parking problem." Sometimes just walking around your event can be important. One year, Karen Garrison took time out during the BHNC community-wide garage sale to walk the neighborhood, and discovered a number of "renegade" sites that hadn't paid for inclusion. After gently reminding them that this was organized as a fundraiser, she collected more fees.

- **Take a last look through your notebook, to make sure nothing got lost in the shuffle.** Make confirmation calls to any important speakers or vendors to whom you haven't spoken in a while. Make sure that all money owed to you has been paid, and that you have paid all the appropriate vendors. You don't want to be signing checks and working out small disputes over financial matters during the event itself.

- **If you're having a sit-down lunch or dinner event, take your final list of ticket buyers and create a seating chart of who will sit with whom.** Create an easy way for people to find their way to their table, such as a number on a flag in the centerpiece. And be sure the registration staff know what to do if someone shows up without a ticket.

- **Pack any items that could possibly be useful in a pinch, such as adhesive tape, petty cash, a stapler, trashbags, paper towels, first aid supplies, and the like.** Of course, you should also have created a checklist, and started packing, those items you know you will need for the event, such as food and equipment.

- **Buy snacks and goodies for your volunteers, and water for everyone.**

- **If you've rented space, make sure you'll be allowed to get in with enough advance time to set up, decorate, arrange silent auction items, and the like.** These tasks always take longer than you think they will—three to four hours is usually considered the minimum for a "typical" event.

- **Double check that your registration tables will be adequately staffed and provided for.** Believe it or not, a whole book could be written about the event registration process. Your goal is to have people registered and into the event within a few minutes of arriving. Depending on how many attendees you anticipate, this may require a whole bank of registration tables, with easily visible letters of the alphabet if you wish to divide people by name. Make sure all your volunteers know your policies on issues such as check acceptance and dealing with lost tickets.

- **Create handy contact lists of key people and vendors that you and other lead staff or volunteers can keep in their pockets or purses.** This will help reach someone in case they've forgotten something or you need emergency help.

- **Create a final list of who needs to be publicly thanked (hopefully, you kept a running list, and will compare your final list against those of other event leaders).** At some point during the day, a key staff member or volunteer may have an opportunity to address the crowd. If so, that person should start by effusively thanking the people who did the most to bring about the event. Relying on memory has obvious dangers. If the names are too many to list one by one, refer to committees or groups, and make clear that there were many helpers who must remain unnamed.

> **TIP**
>
> **You can't prepare for everything.** Some final thoughts from events planner Laurie Earp: "Life happens, and you've just got to be ready for surprises—the caterer who doesn't show up, entertainers who bring lighting that's not bright enough to see them by, or equipment cables too short to reach electrical outlets. If you think on your feet, you'll find a way around the problem, and the event will be great in the end."

After the Event

A day or two after the event, you'll probably be dying to return to the other tasks you've been ignoring—those letters piling up in your in-box, those unreturned emails. However, if you don't tie up loose ends now, you may never get to them. This is the time to send out thank-you letters, assess the event's overall success (financial and otherwise), and assemble clear records for anyone who might handle the event in the future.

You already know the importance of thank-you letters when dealing with individual donors, but after a special event, you'll have whole new lists of people to thank—and each one is critical. If you haven't already, send personalized thank-yous to every committee head, volunteer, sponsor, individual donor (including donors who bought things at auctions, because part of their payment was a contribution—but not including people who purchased items from independent vendors at craft or art fairs), and business donors. Remember to note the amount of any financial contribution, minus the value of anything received in return, for IRS purposes.

If the story of what happened at your event is media worthy, then you should immediately send out a separate press release—for example, describing and quoting the contents of your famous speaker's presentation, complete with his or her photo, or announcing the winners of your bicycle race.

Even if your event was a roaring success, there are no doubt many lessons to be learned from it. And, if there is any possibility that you might repeat this or a similar event, you'll want to collect all relevant information about what worked and what didn't. Assemble your committee leaders, and potentially the entire committees, to collect impressions of what they felt went well or could have been done better. Alternately, you can simply distribute paper or email surveys. For example, after the Bernal Heights Neighborhood Center garage sale described above, they collect written evaluations from everyone who held a garage sale at their home that day, asking them what worked and what didn't.

When holding meetings to assess how things went, remember to keep the focus positive. Although there will undoubtedly be touchy areas where people would love to shift or assign blame, the important thing is to constructively figure out how similar problems can be prevented in the future.

One of your most important tasks is to draw up a final event budget and compare it to the original budget, to see how well your projections ultimately matched up with reality. After you've collected all your information, write up all of your narrative and budgetary conclusions, and put them into your event folder for future reference.

Finally, imagine that this time next year, you and all your committee leaders will be enjoying Brie and baguettes at an undisclosed Parisian location. Meanwhile, back at the nonprofit, some poor soul will be trying to recreate your smashingly successful event. Will your notebook and files be enough to tell the whole story of how the event was done, who helped out, who was invited, who did the graphic design and printing, where to advertise, which media outlets were responsive, what other vendors to contract with, and the rest? This is not an idle exercise—nonprofit turnover rates being what they are, you really could be somewhere else next year, or you might have simply forgotten all the details that seem so deeply burned into your brain right now. Go through your notebook and add any documents that are floating around elsewhere, making sure every section is complete, and writing memos to explain important issues that aren't otherwise covered by the documentation.

The Importance of Recognizing People's Efforts

Dr. H was a successful businessman with a comfortable cushion of inherited wealth. His family had a tradition of philanthropy, and he gave generously to a number of causes. When a local charity hosted a fundraising dinner, Dr. H bought tickets for an entire table, filled it with his friends, and made sure that his table set the evening's record for spending the most at the auction.

After the event was over, Dr. H promptly received a thank-you letter—but it was the same letter that everyone else involved in the event received. A form letter. It made no mention of the special efforts he'd made or the amount he and his friends had given. He felt sufficiently let down that he cut his contributions to that organization, and has not attended any further events. He doesn't even return their phone calls—and they're still scratching their heads about it.

RESOURCE

Want more information on special events? The following are helpful, well-written guides offering further detail on the process of holding special events:

- *How to Produce Fabulous Fundraising Events: Reap Remarkable Returns with Minimal Effort,* by Betty Stallings and Donna McMillion (Building Better Skills). Includes a diskette containing form letters, lists, budgets, and more.

- *Special Events: Proven Strategies for Nonprofit Fundraising,* by Alan L. Wendroff (John Wiley & Sons).

- *The Business of Special Events: Fundraising Strategies for Changing Times,* by Harry A. Freedman and Karen Feldman (Pineapple Press). ●

Raising Money Through Business or Sales Activities

There have been times—usually late at night, when struggling over a grant proposal—when I've wondered whether it wouldn't be easier to just stand by the nearest bus stop and sell cookies. With all the time a fundraiser spends trying to engage people's hearts and minds, an anonymous transaction in which you engage little more than someone's taste buds can look like a welcome relief.

Of course, my idea isn't an original one. There is a time-honored nonprofit tradition of hawking cookies, T-shirts, and tote bags, as well as conducting raffles, garage sales, and even car washes to augment other fundraising activities. Sometimes the only thing that stops a nonprofit from going into one of these or similar businesses is fear of the unknown—or of the IRS, which can investigate and ultimately shut down nonprofits that stray too far into the profit-seeking world.

On the other side of the coin, a growing number of nonprofits are taking a full plunge into commercial enterprise, by starting major side-businesses, such as restaurants or retail shops, in some cases enlisting their clients' help, or entering into relationships with for-profit business ventures. Although some of these businesses have prospered or been spun off into successful subsidiaries, a daunting number have failed miserably, and some have indeed dragged the nonprofit into trouble with the IRS.

TIP

Business is business, whatever the terminology. A lot of highfalutin terms have been coined to describe profit-making efforts by nonprofits, including "social entrepreneurship," "social purpose enterprises," and "social enterprise." The trouble is, there is little agreement as to what these terms really mean. For example, "social purpose enterprise" is sometimes used to describe a business staffed by clients to further the mission while at the same time raising money, while other times it's used to refer to any business run by a nonprofit. And "social entrepreneurship" is sometimes used to describe nonprofit business activities, but in other instances to describe philanthropists who "invest" their dollars in a social cause. To steer clear of all this semantic confusion, I'll simply refer to all of these activities as business ventures run by nonprofits.

It's impossible to draw a firm conclusion as to whether small-business ventures make sense for a particular nonprofit. There are just too many variables to come up with a clear rule, and much depends on the skills, interests, and energy of the people involved—you might as well ask whether an ordinary person who wants to make money should open a business. Experience has shown that nonprofit-run ventures are no guaranteed pot of gold—even nonprofits that enjoy significant success in the business realm have to overcome major challenges, some of which inevitably take time and energy away from their altruistic concerns. But one generalization seems to hold true—starting a business is not a good strategy for a nonprofit that's desperate for cash, because a significant return on initial investment usually doesn't come for a few years at best.

On the other hand, for those nonprofits able to find a profitable market niche, their ability to draw funds from outside the usual donor pool can contribute mightily to their growth and long-term survival. The YMCA, for example, whose central mission remains to nurture young people, earns about 70% of its revenues from health club membership and other program fees—many of these paid by affluent adults who just want a good place to work out.

Business revenues offer entrepreneurial nonprofits a way to break out of heavy reliance on grant funding. And they can simultaneously make funders more excited about your operation's long-term growth prospects, and therefore more likely to fund you in the future. In fact, the prevailing belief among many funders is that the very process of starting and running a business venture can transform a nonprofit into a more effective and efficient operation.

Driven by these and other reasons, nonprofits are entering the business world like never before. In fact, those attempting comprehensive surveys of new entrepreneurial efforts by nonprofits usually have to give up on the "comprehensive" part—the pace at which nonprofit businesses are being started is too rapid to keep up with. On the other hand, many of the startups one hears about seem to drop off the map after a year or two—it's a field that's littered with empty storefronts and dead Web links.

RESOURCE

Want to know more about other nonprofits' experiences with business activities? For valuable case studies, survey results, and an itemization of the most important lessons learned by nonprofits attempting business ventures, see the website of Community Wealth Ventures, a consulting firm that works with nonprofits to develop business ventures and corporate partnerships, at www .communitywealth.org.

So, the question becomes, would marketing goods or services to the general public give your nonprofit a fresh way to bring in significant dollars from sources outside your donor base—better yet, funds with no strings attached? Or would it drag your staff into spending precious time on activities outside your core mission that end up producing little return—and may even lose money or jeopardize your tax-exempt status? This chapter will help you answer these questions, by considering:

- how much business activity the IRS permits without penalty
- lessons that can be learned from other nonprofits' business successes and failures
- how to come up with a business idea that's a good match for your nonprofit
- how to compare your business ideas with market realities
- how to create a business plan, and
- whether partnering with an existing business makes sense.

> **CAUTION**
>
> **Is your accounting house in order?** Unless and until you've got a good internal bookkeeper and an outside accountant, who have together successfully implemented a system for efficiently tracking your existing costs and cash flow, don't even think of launching a small business. The dollars will be flying around a lot faster once you start a business, and you'll need to be ready to keep up.

Tax Rules for Business Activities

Your organization was granted its 501(c)(3) status—and therefore allowed to avoid paying taxes—because its founders said that it would engage in charitable activities, not in for-profit business like the rest of the corporate sector. And the IRS will hold you to your promise, by taxing certain business activities and even revoking your tax-exempt status if you start to look more like a for-profit business than a charitable organization. But the prohibition against nonprofits engaging in business is far from absolute. As long as a nonprofit stays away from ongoing profit-making activities that don't further its purposes and don't personally benefit any individual (other than a client), it's usually not at risk of losing its 501(c)(3) status. This means that a nonprofit can engage in one-time or irregular business activities, or business activities that fall squarely within its mission, as long as all profits go to the nonprofit and don't benefit insiders, such as staff or directors.

Sounds simple enough. But what understandably confuses many nonprofit managers about the federal tax law is the large gray area that exists between those activities that are absolutely prohibited and those that are clearly permissible. Much of this confusion stems from the fact that nonprofits can, in some circumstances, engage in business activities beyond the limits of their tax-exempt mission, or that are ongoing, without risking their existence as a nonprofit, as long as they pay corporate income tax on the business profits.

To understand how IRS rules might apply to your nonprofit's possible business ventures, it's helpful to separate business activities into the following categories:

- clearly allowable activities
- activities that raise income on which tax is assessed, but that nevertheless do not endanger the nonprofit's 501(c)(3) status, and
- business activities that the IRS considers excessive or inappropriate, and therefore undermine the group's very 501(c)(3) status.

CAUTION

Never use nonprofit income for noncharitable purposes. Though there's a lot of gray area in the tax rules regarding how money comes into your nonprofit, there's very little ambiguity about how it's supposed to be spent. Profits generated by a nonprofit business may not, repeat not, be used for the private benefit of any person or organization outside the charitable organization.

Activities That Will Never Raise IRS Eyebrows

Take a look around you—plenty of nonprofits are selling goods and services without so much as a peep from the IRS. Chances are that in storefronts near you, you'll find the Goodwill, Salvation Army, and perhaps a local church-run thrift shop. Your local museum or hospital may run both a cafeteria and gift shop. And, of course, you have the Girl Scouts selling cookies, your local public TV station peddling calendars and coffee cups, and half a dozen environmental groups offering calendars, T-shirts, and tote bags.

What makes these and similar merchandising activities legally acceptable? For the most part, they're viewed by the IRS as falling into one or more of the following allowable categories:

- activities within the organization's mission
- activities that are not part of an ongoing business, or
- income or activities that are subject to a special IRS exception.

Activities Within Your Mission

If your sales of goods or services are in some way tied to your organization's mission, you're probably on safe ground, tax-wise. Museum gift shops, for example, stay within their mission by selling items to educate or interest people in the subject on display—such as animal magnets at a wildlife museum or art reproductions at an art museum. Even so, these shops may be required to pay tax on some of the items they sell. For example, the IRS says that an art museum shop that sells souvenirs of the city in which it is located will have to pay tax on those items.

Organizations such as Goodwill further their mission of employing needy people through selling used goods. Goodwill uses its shops as a training and employment center, as do many other nonprofits that run businesses such as bakeries, bicycle repair shops, and more.

Activities That Are Not Part of an Ongoing Business

A normal, for-profit business needs to keep its doors open on a fairly regular basis, or risk having customers go elsewhere. To maintain a clear separation between these businesses and nonprofits, the IRS allows nonprofits to make sales that occur irregularly, or a few times a year. For example, the Girl Scouts sell cookies only once a year (to the frustration of many a sweet-toothed consumer), so their cookie sales are not part of an ongoing business. They could probably sell cookies more often than once a year and still be fine—as long as the sales aren't as frequent as a commercial business would conduct in order to survive and prosper.

Other examples of irregular nonprofit sales abound—including auctions, bake sales, benefit concerts, car washes, garage sales, calendar sales, and more. Most of these tend to be specially scheduled activities, outside the nonprofit's usual day-to-day work. The one area where you need to be careful, however, is with activities that are sporadic by nature—for example, if you run a catering business that is hired only every few weeks or so, you may look very much like an ordinary catering business—although not a wildly successful one.

Activities That Fall Within IRS Exceptions

You might be encouraged to learn that the IRS has created numerous exceptions and exclusions: Activities or income that fall within these categories are automatically considered nontaxable. Smaller groups that sell the occasional T-shirt or coffee mug (as much to encourage organizational solidarity as to raise money) will be delighted to learn that they needn't report annual earned income amounts less than $1,000. Such small amounts don't even require the nonprofit to file a tax return, even if the business activities were clearly outside or unrelated to the group's mission. The other major exceptions include business activities in which:

- substantially all of the work of providing the services or creating the products is done by volunteers (for example, if you sell volunteer-created baked goods or crafts, or your volunteers can be hired as translators)

- the product or services are primarily for the convenience of the group's members, students, patients, officers, or employees (for example, an on-site cafeteria or pharmacy)

- the nonprofit accepts money from a company that sponsors its educational, fundraising, or other event, and displays the company's name or logo on its premises or publications in return. But it's not okay for the nonprofit to provide the company with advertising or allow it to use the nonprofit's logo in company periodicals. (For example, you can't devote a page of your newsletter to a company ad, or accept payment for having your logo appear in company materials, without paying tax on any income you receive.)

- the nonprofit sells merchandise that was donated to the organization (an important exception that allows for the many thrift shops, donated goods auctions, and used-car resale businesses run by nonprofits)

- bingo games are used as fundraisers (as long as bingo is legal in the nonprofit's area, and is not played in a hall that's also used for commercial bingo gaming)

- a nonprofit exchanges or rents its membership list with another nonprofit, or

- entertainment is provided to attract people to a fair or exposition that promotes agriculture or education.

The IRS also excludes from tax any income that comes from:

- dividends, interest, annuities, and other investment income

- royalties earned from allowing use of the nonprofit's trademark, trade name, copyrighted material, or other valuable rights (but not personal appearances or services)

- rents from real property (such as land or buildings; but see IRS Publication 598, *Tax on Unrelated Business Income of Exempt Organizations* for the various exceptions, for example if you're also providing personal services to the renters, or if you've got a mixture of real and personal property, such as equipment)

- income from research grants or contracts, and

- gains and losses from selling property.

SEE AN EXPERT

Get answers to your questions about unrelated business income. This section summarizes the IRS's definitions, exclusions, and exceptions dealing with unrelated business income. However, before you make any final business decisions, you'll want to read IRS Publication 598, *Tax on Unrelated Business Income of Exempt Organizations*. You can get a copy by calling the IRS at 800-829-3676, or on the IRS website at www.irs.gov. Consult an attorney if anything remains less than completely clear.

If you can think of an activity that would both serve your mission and bring in funds, you're in great shape. For starters, any fees that you charge for special events or client services are no problem—you don't need to worry about the federal tax implications, and you can even charge market rates. If there aren't any natural ways to raise funds within your mission, then your next step is to consider raising revenues on an occasional basis, or starting up an activity that fits within an IRS exception. Any revenues you earn from any of these ventures will not only be safely within the rules of your tax-exempt status, but will also earn you tax-free revenue.

Activities That Will Be Taxed

What happens if your nonprofit's business activities don't fit within one of permitted categories just discussed, and instead constitute an "unrelated trade or business"? As long as you're churning 100% of the profits back into your charitable activities, they are still permitted, with one big catch. You'll have to pay corporate income tax—to both the feds and possibly your state government—on any profits ("unrelated business income" or UBI) of more than $1,000 per year. (You pay the tax using IRS Form 990-T; if you earn less than $1,000, there's no need to file the form.) In fact, if it looks like your total tax payment (not income, but the amount you'll owe) will be $500 or more, you'll have to pay quarterly, estimated taxes even before the usual April tax time rolls around.

The IRS definition of income from an unrelated trade or business is remarkably free of tax-code gobbledygook. They call it:

. . . income from a trade or business that is regularly carried on by an exempt organization and that is not substantially related to the performance by the organization of its exempt purpose or function, except that the organization uses the profits derived from this activity.

Of course, it wouldn't be the Internal Revenue Code if there weren't a couple of terms that need defining.

- **"Trade or business"** means selling goods or services in order to produce income. If you think you're in a trade or business, you probably are. For example, if your organization charges non-clients for consultations on organic landscaping, you owe tax on the profits. And the IRS is quick to point out that you can't hide a trade or business by burying it within your exempt activities—for example, a nonprofit hospital pharmacy that sells drugs to its patients (within its charitable purpose) would still have to pay taxes on drugs it sells to the general public. As another example, selling commercial advertising in your organization's newsletter would be considered an unrelated trade or business, even if the rest of the newsletter contains reports on your nonprofit's programs.

- **"Regularly carried on"** is another term that has been the subject of much learned discussion by nonprofit tax experts and the IRS. Whether your business is "regularly carried on" (or, hopefully, is only occasional and therefore exempt from tax) depends on whether it's run with the same frequency and continuity as a typical profit-making business. Like any business, however, your own commercial viability may depend on running a continuous operation. So, for example, if you're planning to run a bakeshop, there's no point in closing it on odd days and times in an effort to make it "irregular"—you're better off just paying the taxes. And note that you can't necessarily get around the requirements by choosing a business with "irregular" operations, such as a catering company. If your company caters functions with the same frequency as a commercial catering company, your income will be taxable.

- **"Substantially related"** business activities—those that contribute importantly to your nonprofit purpose—are entirely tax exempt. If you're thinking that any fundraising helps you accomplish your charitable purposes, I'm sorry to report that the IRS is one step ahead of you—and specifically rules out this line of reasoning. The IRS appears to grant tax-exempt status to programs in which products or services are a spinoff of the nonprofit's existing activities or a direct result of its charitable activities. For example, if your organic agricultural research nonprofit sells milk produced by your herd of experimental dairy cows, the profits are not taxable—but once you start turning that milk into ice cream and the like, it stops being an activity that contributes to your charitable purposes, and you would have to pay tax on any profits.

Here are some of the IRS's examples of activities that are taxable as a trade or business that are not substantially related to your charitable purposes:

- selling your membership list to a for-profit business

- using your school facility to run a summertime tennis club open to the general public

- selling handicrafts made by local members of the public (even if they're sold alongside handicrafts produced by your clients)

- renting studio apartments with dining room services to artists even though your organization's main purpose is to sponsor art events

- offering pet boarding and grooming to the public (even if it's by an organization dedicated to preventing cruelty to animals)

- offering travel tours that don't include an educational component related to your group's purpose, or

- charging for the use of your organization's name on product endorsements.

Activities That Risk a Nonprofit's 501(c)(3) Status

Paying tax on your unrelated business activities is not as good as paying no tax at all, but it's greatly preferable to engaging in activities that call into question your nonprofit's 501(c)(3) tax status. Unfortunately, you can face this unhappy situation if doing business becomes the focal point of your nonprofit's activities. This is doubtless one reason your local YMCA works so hard to raise money for its charitable programs, despite all the profits they are likely to make from fitness centers. Unfortunately, there's neither a bright line nor a numeric amount (such as a percentage of total income or a flat dollar figure) at which the IRS automatically finds that your profit-making business is too large in comparison to your tax-exempt activities. However, if your programs are shrinking but your business is growing, it's time to take a closer look. And even if both your business and nonprofit activities are growing, if you're lucky enough to enjoy substantial business profits, it may be time to spend some of that money on a nonprofit lawyer who can evaluate the situation for you.

TIP

Consider creating a separate tax-paying organization. If your business activities threaten to overwhelm your nonprofit purpose, you might want to make the business a separate, for-profit venture. For example, if your education-centered nonprofit publishes calendars and books that become hugely popular and profitable, it might make sense to spin those activities off into their own business entity. This way, the business could channel its profits in your direction, without threatening your 501(c)(3) status. You'll need a lawyer's help for this.

Learn From Other Nonprofits' Experience

To help you get a sense of the range of business ventures that might work for your nonprofit, this section takes a closer look at how other nonprofits have fared. Although only a minority of nonprofits engage in any significant business activities, the creativity and range among those that do is inspiring. Nevertheless, a number of hard lessons have been learned along the way—which gives you an opportunity to avoid relearning them.

As a broad generalization, nonprofit businesses fall into two categories:

- enterprises centered on client training and employment, and
- sales of goods and services produced by nonclients or outside sources, sometimes but not always with a thematic connection to the nonprofit's mission and work.

Although hybrids of the two models certainly exist, each category is covered separately below, so as best to highlight their advantages and challenges.

Client-Based Businesses

The ultimate in mission-based enterprises is to involve your clients in some part of the business. Sometimes called "social purpose enterprise," this strategy has been utilized by numerous nonprofits to teach business, vocational, or life skills to low-income, disadvantaged, homeless, recovering, or disabled clients. Instead of training the clients and then sending them elsewhere to get "real" experience, such organizations bring the world of business in-house. The clients use their newly acquired commercial skills to do everything from selling Christmas trees and moving furniture to woodworking, mechanics, cooking, landscaping, computing, and much more. Typically, they either create things for sale or operate businesses serving the general public. As a result, consumers can now purchase everything from coffins to salad dressing to Web design services for a good cause.

Ideally, social purpose businesses will earn enough to be able to pay the client-employees a salary or stipend, thus reinforcing the larger point that work is rewarding. In rare cases, it might even bring in profits to the organization.

> **CAUTION**
>
> **Operating a client-based business is probably not the best way to raise funds.** While businesses that use clients as workers may provide the clients with excellent training and life skills opportunities, such businesses' chances of doing much better than breaking even are slim. They're a fine idea if your main goal is to create a setting where clients can gain real business experience, but a poor choice if you need to raise extra funds to cover other programs.

The biggest advantage to running a client-based business occurs when clients are already at the core of your mission and will benefit from your business activities. If the client-based business raises funds you would have otherwise had to get from foundations, individual donors, or other fundraising efforts, you're already far ahead of where you would have been without the business—and probably running a more exciting and educational program to boot.

One reason why client-based business can work well is that you've probably got a built-in labor pool—something nonprofits that don't provide direct services to just-released prisoners or recovering alcoholics might envy. And you create an opportunity for your organization—and hopefully its clients—to meet, and raise awareness among, people beyond your usual donor base. Especially if your customers are satisfied with what you sell them, and if you make sure they understand the role your nonprofit played in bringing this interaction about, you may turn your customers into donors.

However, if starting this type of business will represent a significant expansion or alteration of your existing programs, you'll also need to take a close look at the disadvantages—and they can be many. Organizations with experience in running client-based businesses—even successful ones—have identified the following unique challenges:

- low worker efficiency and high turnover, as compared to for-profit businesses
- difficulty in finding professional-level managers to oversee operations
- heightened risk that business failure will harm the lives of client workers, and
- conflicts between mission-related goals and business goals.

Let's start with the most hopeful scenario: Your new client-based business has been well planned and managed, and breaks even almost from the start. Best of all, your clients are learning a new skill—perhaps baking or bicycle repair. Customers appreciate the quality of what they're receiving, and are returning for more—and sending their friends. Your client workers enthusiastically complete their training in a matter of months, and find better-paying jobs in the private sector. But unfortunately, you now have a new problem—you've just lost valuable, trained workers, while you must continue pleasing your growing customer base.

Even with good planning, this problem doesn't always have an easy solution. Assuming that part of your goal is to help your clients develop job skills, you certainly don't want to discourage them from moving on, both to better themselves and to make room for new clients. But the inevitable result is that unless you can carefully phase your "graduations" so as to always have a decent number of experienced workers, you'll always be trying to run a business with new or only minimally trained workers.

Of course, quick success probably won't be your biggest problem. If you honestly consider who your clients are, you may also have to face the very real reasons that they're not already in the workforce. Sometimes a second chance is all someone needs, but often it's not that easy. As worthy of help and respect as they are, your clients may lack not only tangible work skills, but other personal qualities customers have come to expect. Unfortunately, many nonprofits operating with good hearts and high hopes have come to realize that a few weeks of training aren't necessarily going to turn around a person's lifetime of habits. Basic things like showing up regularly or on time and interacting appropriately with others can sometimes be a significant problem, depending on the client's personal background and ongoing medical, family, or other needs. For clients with cognitive difficulties, completing tasks will obviously take longer—which can become frustrating to the clients if they're put under pressure. And clients with criminal backgrounds may even fall into old habits around your inventory or cash register. To some extent, you can factor these issues into your business planning, by choosing a type of business that is easy to run, doubling up on personnel on any given shift, and providing extra supervision and separate counseling, for example. But no matter which way you slice it, your business efficiency will be reduced.

If extra supervision is required, you may need some luck to find it. Your existing staffers may be highly skilled in client training and support, but not necessarily in the business aspects of supervising a staff, much less in other business management techniques. You may well have to hire additional staff—but finding a person who has the full plate of business and client interaction skills may not be easy, especially at a salary you can afford. To some extent, this is a dilemma you already know well. Any professional person in your nonprofit could probably be earning a lot more elsewhere. Hopefully, you can compensate with other benefits, such as quality of life, the satisfaction of doing meaningful work, a job title and range of experience that will enhance one's resume, and long vacations. But, as you also probably know, this isn't always enough to keep someone at a job over the long term—and once again, high turnover isn't going to help a fledgling business. There is some hope on the horizon, though—as more and more business schools introduce nonprofit management programs, the field is receiving growing attention and interest, so the pool of applicants may expand. And when you do find a skilled person, he or she will probably have knowledge and talents to lend to other aspects of running your nonprofit.

If your client-based business doesn't turn a decent profit—and it probably won't in the first few years—conflicts may arise between your organization's goals and needs and the business's requirements. For example, what if you're attempting to pay your clients a salary—but having trouble paying them the minimum amount that will allow them to stick with the program? If neither your business profits nor your agency's budget can accommodate such expenditures, you've got a conflict. Or what if one of your client workers is going through a personal crisis, and others feel that the first priority should be to listen to and support him or her—even if it means setting the work aside? A steely-eyed businessperson might take a more draconian approach to these issues than you can—or should. But you may find yourself choosing whether the organization as a whole or the business suffers—with the added frustration that the business may have been budgeted to be self-supporting.

In the worst case, your business may head toward failure. While this is a reality that every business faces—and it does not mean the end of the world—failure of a nonprofit-run business may nevertheless spell unusual rupture and economic difficulty for its client workers. If your business provides the sole source of

Juma Ventures: Doing It for the Mission

With its Ben & Jerry's franchises, a lodge in Yosemite, and high-volume concession operations at the San Francisco Giants and 49ers ballparks, all providing training and employment to youth from low-income communities, Juma Ventures is considered one of the Bay Area's social-purpose-enterprise success stories. (See www.jumaventures.org.) But ask Jim Schorr, E.D. from 2000 to 2007, whether social purpose enterprises are the way to nonprofit financial independence, and his answer is unequivocal: "Nonprofits that consider starting a business venture in order to generate money for overhead and other such expenses are likely to be sorely disappointed.

"We're serving a double bottom line: our social goals and financial needs. Many of the challenges that others have identified are very real, such as relying on employees who present significant challenges, and finding multiskilled business/social program managers. Also, many of the business types that are simple enough for a nonprofit to operate well—such as a retail shop—will never, even under the best of circumstances, turn a large enough profit to be anything more than self-supporting. At Juma, we fundraise to cover our businesses' social costs and to close the gaps in what our business ventures earn.

"In the meantime, we consider Juma Ventures to be one of the world's most efficient social programs. Our businesses are employment programs that self-fund about 85% of their costs. It's great work, and extremely worthwhile, but we don't want to perpetuate any of the myths that seem to be going around about how social purpose enterprises are an easy or short-term solution to pulling nonprofits out of financial need."

support for clients who are already on the economic margins, layoffs may, in an instant, push them back toward homelessness, substance abuse, personal crises, or precisely the traps that the program was meant to help them out of. Even if the business merely reduces hours, such cuts can dampen your client workers' morale—and lower their paychecks—at a time when they're vulnerable. You might need to plan ahead for the extra client support that such a scenario would require. You might also find yourself scrambling to find other funding to plug the holes in the failing business.

RESOURCE

Want to learn more about client-run enterprises? Two publications, *Social Purpose Enterprises and Venture Philanthropy in the New Millennium* and *From Opening Doors to Closing Shop: A Case Study on Youth Industry's Impact on Homeless Youth and the Organization's Decision to Close*, both provide a sobering, but valuable, view of the problems that can beset client-based social purpose enterprises. They are available from the Roberts Enterprise Development Fund (REDF), at www.redf.org.

Other Sales of Goods and Services

If you don't have clients to involve in your business, or you've concluded that business activities wouldn't be a good use of your clients' time, that shouldn't stop you from creating a small business that sells goods or services created by your own staff or by others. In fact, clients may still participate in some way—for example, by creating the art designs for a set of greeting cards—but this section covers only situations in which your clients aren't actually involved in business staffing or day-to-day work. (For a discussion of the process of producing greeting cards, see "Children's Hospital at Oakland's Holiday Card Sales," below.)

Nonprofits operate small businesses at nearly every scale imaginable, from selling the occasional mug, to huge national events such as Girl Scout cookie sales, to ongoing operations such as thrift shops and website sales. Some of these business types are covered in more detail below—but first, here are some of the general advantages and disadvantages of running this type of business.

On the plus side, this kind of project can energize people who are tired of feeling like they're begging for money. Your business venture may be just the place to direct the skills or energies of particular board members—like those who drag their feet when asked to do other types of fundraising. If you're really lucky, you may be able to tap into the artistic, culinary, or other skills of existing staff members or volunteers. Also, selling goods and services gives you an opportunity to reach out to people beyond your usual donor base. Everything that you sell with a tag or label on it should loudly proclaim what your organization is about and how the buyer is helping an important cause. The interested buyers may eventually turn into donors as well.

On the minus side, you're launching into an area that is probably outside the expertise of most of your staff. And, while the energy of staff and board members may be high at the beginning, their enthusiasm may flag when it comes time for the real work—or receive the first customer complaint (complaints being inevitable), or don't see profits coming in at the rate you'd anticipated.

As with client-based operations, another inevitable disadvantage comes up when conflicts arise with your mission-based activities. In fact, these conflicts can look even starker when you're selling something that has very little immediate benefit for your mission, because it doesn't employ or train a client. For example, what if the business needs a cash investment in order to get past a difficult period or produce some inventory, but cash is tight, funding has been cut for one of your other programs, and you're already deeply in debt? Or, what if you're counting on a staffer to write a book for sale, but a pressing environmental or social concern makes it urgent for everyone to spend their time mobilizing your membership instead? If everything is happening under the same roof—or with the same people—tugs of war are inevitable.

Fortunately, there is a wide variety of business types and models for you to consider. At the most minimal end of the scale, many nonprofits offer souvenir-like products, such as T-shirts or mugs, showing their logo or something thematically related to the work that they do, such as wild animals for an environmental group. (There are scads of companies that will quickly print your organization's logo, a photo, or other design on just about anything you want, for you to resell.) Many nonprofits make such items available as a small thank-you gift for donations, but in part because the unit costs for these items are far cheaper when they are purchased in large numbers, nonprofits often end up with a garage full of items they need to sell separately. Most nonprofit fundraisers will tell you that these small-scale sales are not a good way to raise money, but they keep the sales going for other reasons, such as getting the organization's name into the public eye and increasing membership. Nevertheless, with the right kind of sales strategy and perhaps volunteer commitment, you can turn anything into a moneymaker if you sell things for significantly more than you pay for them. For more on the collateral advantages to retail sales, see "Human Rights Campaign Uses Retail to Draw in Members," below.

A Human Rights Campaign "Action Center & Store"

Reprinted with permission

Human Rights Campaign Uses Retail to Draw in Members

Take a look at the offerings on the website of the Human Rights Campaign (HRC), a Washington, DC, group working for gay, bisexual, and transgender equal rights, at www.hrc.org (click "Support HRC," then "HRC Store"). They've used their symbol, an equal sign ("="), as the aesthetic basis for a tantalizing array of products, from glycerin soaps to paper message cubes to beach towels. These are available both online and in retail stores (combined with "Action Centers") in Washington, DC, Provincetown, Massachusetts, and San Francisco, California.

Sales are strong, in part because these products allow their members and other buyers to express a commitment to the group's message. But do they work as a fundraiser? According to Don Kiser, former Director of Retail Development, the short answer is, "No." But you also need to hear the rest of the story.

Don says: "Our retail operations finance themselves, but they are not actually a profit center for HRC. Before you even start selling, 50 cents of every dollar goes toward the cost of goods, and that's too high to fit into the traditional fundraising model. Sure, we could find ways to lower costs, but quality is an important concern—if someone buys a towel from us and it falls apart on the third wash, they're going to think we're a low-quality operation, too. We also try to make sure our goods come from reputable sources, not sweatshops, and that means higher prices.

"But, there are reasons that we've gotten as deeply into retail as we have: It enhances our visibility and helps build our membership. We began offering these goods as a service to our existing members, and to help fulfill our advocacy role. (In fact, our mail-order marketing is still limited to existing members.) But we've also found that our merchandise attracts potential members who might not have found us any other way. For instance, when we set up a Pride Booth at a festival, some people will come up just because they see a pretty purple sweatshirt—people who might never have stopped just to pick up a brochure—but we give them a brochure too, and tell them about what we do. This becomes their first step on the giving ladder.

"Naturally, we ask all of our customers if they're interested in receiving future email communications from us. Then we follow up, not only with product promotions, but with issue-based emails, for example about gay parenting, issues of concern in the person's home state, and more. Recipients can always opt out, but many opt in, and become long-term donors."

Another common nonprofit enterprise is small-scale publishing of books, reports, or classroom materials, produced by the groups' own staff or supporters. The tricky parts are not so much the writing and publishing—although, done well, these are harder than most people credit—but the marketing. A huge amount of material makes it into print these days but very little of it finds a sufficient audience to be profitable. In a world where information is increasingly delivered electronically, large publishing companies are finding it difficult to maintain profitability. Nevertheless, if your experts really do have valuable information on an issue that people want to know more about, you may be able to realize some profits from publishing it. The Immigrant Legal Resource Center (ILRC), in San Francisco, California, is a good example of making this niche marketing work. The ILRC's mission includes making legal and social services available to immigrants, a mission which it serves primarily by providing support—including on-call advice attorneys, regular email and printed updates, and legal seminars—to legal staff and other nonprofits serving immigrants. Because of its in-house expertise and connections to the broader immigration community, the ILRC is uniquely positioned to create manuals encapsulating its expertise, for use by immigration attorneys and advocates. Over 20 manuals and videos are now available for sale at prices ranging from $15 to $165, and are common sights on the shelves of immigration attorneys.

TIP

Pay more to print less. The biggest mistake publishers make—whether profit or nonprofit oriented—is to fall for the printer's siren song that unit costs drop fast when volume goes up. The printer may be right, but very few organizations will be able to sell 5,000 (or even 3,000) copies of anything. Better to keep your print runs short, and charge enough to cover costs and allow for a profit. (A good example of how to solve the not-big-enough-audience issue is the corporate sales mentioned in "Children's Hospital at Oakland's Holiday Card Sales," below.) A small group that could partner with local businesses, for example, might have a hope.

Yet another significant niche is selling products that you've sought out or commissioned in order to serve the particular interests of your clients or the larger community that cares about the issue you serve. For example, SightConnection, in Seattle, Washington (www.sightconnection.com), sells products that help the blind and partially sighted. It offers everything from magnifiers to full-spectrum lamps to talking clocks. SightConnection's revenues support Community Resources for the Blind and Partially Sighted, a group that works to help vision-impaired people maintain their independence and well being. (This is also an example of the for-profit subsidiary relationship mentioned above.)

And let's not forget the variety of cards and posters depicting art or animals sold by museums, arts, and environmental groups—the Sierra Club calendar is famous, even among people who don't otherwise support the Sierra Club. However, you should also take a lesson from the Sierra Club's recent closure of retail stores—they've found it more cost-efficient to sell online or through distribution to bookstores. You're not likely to achieve large sales unless you're either a national group with a large audience, or have a killer marketing plan. See "Children's Hospital at Oakland's Holiday Card Sales," below, for more information on the early phases of marketing printed materials.

Marketing is the area where most nonprofit businesses fall down. I learned that lesson the hard way myself, while I was a legal staffer at an immigration nonprofit. I got involved in a project to create greeting cards that featured photos from the four continents, with a regional recipe on the back. I and other staffers had a wonderful time collecting the photos, trying out the recipes,

Sample Children's Hospital Holiday Card

Reprinted with permission

and admiring the cards once we'd spent a few thousand dollars having them professionally printed. The trouble was, we didn't have a solid marketing plan in place, and at a certain point, we could no longer spare time from our client service work to pound the pavement in search of buyers or distributors. I still think the cards look beautiful—and I get to see them often, when my mother-in-law, who kindly bought several packs, uses them to write to me!

Children's Hospital at Oakland's Holiday Card Sales

The Children's Hospital Foundation of Oakland, California, has, for the past five years, created and sold holiday greeting cards to help support Children's Hospital & Research Center at Oakland. (See www.chofoundation.org.) Sales have been steadily growing, but not without some lessons learned along the way. Here's how Cathy Meyer, Director of Philanthropy for the foundation, describes the process:

"We first started the holiday cards because we saw that other hospitals were doing this successfully. Still, I was cautious—I didn't want to spend any more money than we had to. I literally started by using some pictures drawn by children being babysat by one of our staff members.

"Since then, the process has gotten much more organized, as well as time- and staff-intensive. One of the biggest jobs is holding a contest to get images drawn by children—our submissions are up to about 500 to 700 entries, from children all over the Bay Area. (We decided it wasn't practical to gather artwork from the hospital's patients.) The contest is a great way to raise community awareness about the hospital, on the theme of 'Kids Helping Kids Get Well.' Sometimes whole classrooms will participate.

"I'd say the biggest lesson we've learned is that you need to have a staff person devoted to marketing and taking orders for the cards in advance. It took a few years, but when I was finally able to budget for a marketing person, our income rose by one third. Having this person on board allowed us to move beyond our usual constituency, and seek out corporate customers, namely local businesses that send out holiday cards. Even now, however, the profits aren't great when you consider the staff time and other expenses—but the other benefits, in terms of outreach and visibility, make it worthwhile."

Develop Your Own Great—And Low-Risk—Business Idea

If, after hearing about other nonprofit experiences with developing products or services for sale, you're still enthused about this approach to fundraising, you'll need to decide what to offer. Look for a business idea that will yield a solid return with a minimal risk of failure. If that sounds painfully obvious, reflect on the fact that many fledging for-profit entrepreneurs follow the opposite strategy—they bet their money (and often everything they can borrow) on the Next Big Thing, with the hope of making millions. It's best to leave them to their fantasies. Though one of them may create the next Beanie Baby, Pokemon game, or Jamba Juice, a far greater number will fail. And one thing should be absolutely clear—no nonprofit needs the added burden of a business meltdown.

To minimize risk, you'll need to think about what goods or services your nonprofit is best able to provide, and what the public wants. So that you won't be doing all the thinking alone, I also provide a plan for brainstorming as a group.

> ! **CAUTION**
>
> **Risk is inevitable.** If a risk-free business niche existed, someone else would have long since filled it. However, the existence of risk shouldn't be a new pill for your nonprofit to swallow—if you're careful, starting a relatively low-risk business should be little different than the risks you take with other fundraising efforts, such as sending out a direct mail package or holding a special event.

What Goods or Services You Can Offer

Looking for a side business for your nonprofit is a little like looking for a night job for yourself. For example, if I wanted to pick up some extra money, the last thing I should do is apply to be a car mechanic or a pet groomer, having spent my life at various research and writing jobs. Conceiving of an added career for your nonprofit should operate on the same principle—don't stray too far from what you or your inner circle know best.

In fact, your best starting point for a business or sales idea is the very asset list you drafted to create your fundraising plan in Chapter 3. (If you skipped that chapter, go back and look it over now.) Many of the items on your asset list will be relevant to planning a business as well, including your nonprofit's physical facilities, in-house expertise, or reputation in the community. You can also add to that list any assets that you might not have thought of while you were focused on fundraising—perhaps a contact who could offer you commercial space at low rent, a board member with mail-order-business expertise, or clients who would enjoy creating sale-worthy items. Look hard at what your nonprofit is already doing, and at what types of expertise or activities could be expanded or marketed to a larger audience.

The most successful nonprofit businesses often draw heavily on existing assets. Good examples are all around you—every hospital that opens its cafeteria to the public, every museum that sells reproductions of its artworks, and every public radio station that sells tapes and CDs of its programs, makes use of assets it already had or owned as part of its mission.

Similarly, some organizations identify a good or service already being offered to its clients—such as a seminar on recovering from addiction or learning how to budget—and make it available to the general public for a price. You can get even more creative with your existing expertise, as the Red Cross did in designing First Aid Emergency Preparedness Kits for sale (in partnership with Target; see www. redcross.org). Similarly, various environmental organizations offer test kits for radon, arsenic, and other home and garden toxins.

What Customers Want or Need

There's no point in having a great product or service unless someone will buy it. Customers can be fickle, but you can stay in the safety zone by focusing on goods or services that you know are already needed or wanted. (Especially if your organization is dedicated to protecting the environment, it should avoid selling unneeded junk that will further deplete world resources and quickly end up in a landfill.)

Taking the for-profit business world as a model for the moment, you might notice that some of the most successful, as well as socially responsible businesses, are not begun with the primary motive of making money. Instead, they were born when someone noticed a gap in existing products or services—sometimes out of personal dismay that they couldn't find what they needed—and took steps to fill that gap. For example, Anita Roddick, founder of the Body Shop, says she got her idea of producing natural cosmetics that didn't demean women with false promises of eternal youth from her own irritation that she couldn't find such products. (See her book, *Business as Unusual* (Thorsons), for more information on how her U.K.-based company created a business revolution by treating its employees well, seeking out small, nonexploitative suppliers, and investing its profits in human rights and other campaigns.) Another example is Yvon Chouinard, the founder of Patagonia, a blacksmith and mountain climber who was disturbed that the very steel pitons he was creating were contributing to damage to the wilderness. He started by creating alternate, aluminum gear, then branched into clothing and other supplies, and Patagonia was born. The company now supplies high-quality mountain gear, much of it using organic cotton and recycled plastics, gives its employees two-month internships to volunteer for environmental causes, and invests in other environmental campaigns, described on its website at www.patagonia.com. And finally, let's not forget Nolo, the publisher of this book, begun by legal-aid lawyers who saw that sky-high legal fees meant ordinary people were going without basic legal services and protections, like getting a divorce or writing a will. They published a pamphlet explaining how to do your own divorce, and the rest is Nolo history. (See "About Nolo," at www.nolo.com.)

If you aren't poised to fill a gap like this, your next best bet is to identify goods or services that people already need or are buying, and that they'd be willing to buy from a different source. Food is the classic example here: We all need food—or can at least justify buying it—every day. This is yet another reason that those Girl Scout cookies have been around for so many years. (In fact, anything containing chocolate seems to rank high on the list of what people regard as "necessary.") The salad dressings, popcorn, and spaghetti sauces sold by Newman's Own (which donates all profits to charity) are the stuff of fundraising legend, having earned over $150 million for good causes since the company began in the early 1980s. In 2003, Newman's Own achieved perhaps the ultimate mainstream success, by contracting with McDonald's for use of Newman's Own salad dressings.

Though choosing to sell food means that you'll always be competing with other providers, you have a big potential edge: As Paul Newman tells it, "If you can make people aware that things are going to charity, and if there are two competing products on the shelf, maybe people will grab the one where some good will actually come of it" ("Newman's Own: Two Friends and a Canoe Paddle," by Jon Gertner, *The New York Times*, November 16, 2003).

Food is not your only possibility, of course. People also need clothing, though perhaps not a T-shirt or baseball cap from every nonprofit they support. Fleece jackets and other athletic wear seem to be the nonprofits' current clothing sales item of choice. Be cautious however, in considering the potential profit margins—you'll essentially be reselling something that someone else has put all the labor and materials into, which means that they'll have to charge you a reasonable amount unless they're exploiting someone. If the only thing that makes the clothes that you're selling unique is a logo from your nonprofit, you'd better have a large and enthusiastic membership. You might have better luck, however, if one of your volunteers is willing, for example, to produce hand-dyed scarves for sale.

People also need shelter. You may not be able to sell them a home, but my college alumni association came up with an interesting idea, by setting up a bed-and-breakfast network. Traveling alumni were linked up with other alums willing to open up their homes, and the B&B fee went straight to the college.

People may not "need" recreation, but they are willing to pay for it. This accounts for the many tours run by nonprofits, in particular colleges, environmental groups, or groups with an international focus. You don't have to plan an overnight, or an international tour—a simple day trip, on a bus, boat, or on foot, can be a great way to start. (Chapter 6 describes the canoe tours offered by Save The Bay, in Berkeley California—also featured on their website at www .savesfbay.org.) One advantage you have as a nonprofit is that more and more travelers are actually searching for something more meaningful than a margarita-on-the-beach outing. If you can offer a combination of scenery and education, you may attract people who are genuinely interested in your nonprofit's work, and will pay to get involved in it.

CAUTION

The IRS closely scrutinizes travel tours. In the IRS's view, tours by nonprofits compete closely with those offered by for-profit businesses, and may be required to pay tax accordingly. Still, if you introduce a unique educational component, you should be able to operate tax-free. Consult a lawyer for information and advice specific to your tour idea.

People also need information. Because many nonprofits occupy forgotten niches of our society, they have developed expertise in areas that no one else gives much thought to. You might use your in-house expertise to offer classes, or create books, classroom materials, or other printed materials for sale. Just be sure you truly do occupy a specialized niche, or have information that would be in wide demand—as mentioned earlier, the world is becoming saturated with free information, so it isn't always feasible to make money from selling it.

The lesson here is that the most solid business ideas begin close to home. But you'll still need a little brainstorming and inspiration to come up with an idea custom-fitted to your own organization, as discussed next.

Engage a Brainstorming Group

Like your fundraising plan, thinking up a business is not something you should do on your own. If you're seriously considering a business or sales venture, pull together a small working group (under ten people) of staff and board members to generate ideas. You might also ask people from outside the "usual suspects" list to join the group—perhaps donors or vendors with experience in the type of business you're contemplating, or in sales or marketing. (This type of short-term commitment is ideal for many volunteers.) Ask the group to come together for a brainstorming meeting.

In preparation for the meeting, write down, on a chart or blackboard, the assets you identified on your fundraising list, and any additional assets specific to generating business. On a separate chart or half of the blackboard, write down the community needs that your organization recognizes based on its unique expertise and community position. These might be things like "weekend activities for kids," "nutrition counseling," or "morning coffee."

Start by asking your group to help add to both sides of the chart, by suggesting ideas that will utilize or rely on your organization's assets. Also see whether your list of known community needs points to any assets that you forgot your organization had. Tell people to feel free to suggest ideas that will require some outside expertise or help—that may be inevitable. Also be clear that at this point, you're not talking about any particular size or scale of business— everything from an annual sandwich sale to a nationwide Web-design service is a potential candidate for consideration.

Be open to, and write down, all the ideas that come up. By starting with the assets list, however, you've made the message clear—any idea worth its salt is going to have to have some grounding in what your organization is already doing (or is capable of doing) without too far a stretch.

After you've brainstormed, take a break (or even close the meeting for that day). Then come back later and evaluate your ideas. Ask your group to help you draw arrows between the assets and community needs, to see whether there are any obvious linkages. Those with linkages should be the first up for consideration. Assets without arrows to known needs should be reassessed, to determine whether they can be linked to a need you hadn't thought of. Listed needs with no assets in place to meet them should be tossed. Take notes on each idea's advantages and disadvantages. See how many of the items below you can answer "yes" to—the winning ideas should have the most "yeses." (Your group may not know the answers to all of these questions, but should do the best it collectively can.)

- ✓ Does your organization have special assets, expertise, or potential partners that can be used in this business?
- ✓ Can the up-front costs be kept to a minimum?
- ✓ Can the business be started relatively quickly—preferably in less than six months?
- ✓ Is the business likely to generate enough profit to support other program activities, or, alternately, is your organization content to start a social purpose enterprise that will be self-supporting while it achieves an important mission-related purpose?
- ✓ Is there one person within your organization who can enthusiastically dedicate most of his or her time, thought, and energy to this project (a factor widely cited as vital to a nonprofit business venture's success)?
- ✓ Will you be able to deliver a product of high enough quality to compete in the marketplace?
- ✓ Does the business steer clear of high-risk, potentially high-liability activities such as working with hazardous materials or caring for children?
- ✓ Will your intended customers really be able to find your product and be willing to pay for it? (For example, starting a fancy sit-down restaurant in a fast-food neighborhood is almost certainly a bad idea.)

✓ Can your existing staff spare enough time to help launch and run the business? How else could they be deployed to raise money if you didn't start a business?

✓ Will the activities involved in starting and running the business be meaningful—or hopefully even enjoyable—for the participants and affected staff and board members?

✓ Can the business be started on a small scale, so you won't be forced into higher overhead costs or production runs than you can necessarily handle?

✓ Is the business likely to stand the test of time, rather than fade due to changes in fads or technology?

✓ Can your organization survive if the business doesn't live up to expectations?

✓ When all is said and done, could you make more money with a simple auction or raffle? Though this sounds facetious, the expenses and effort of running a small business often cancel out many of its profits, while mobilizing your volunteers and collecting donated goods will often reliably produce a one-time major cash influx.

At the end of this meeting, an idea or two may emerge as promising. Remember, this isn't a final decision. You'll need to do some more research on costs and demand, and talk to others. You'll also want to reconsider the financial questions on this list with your core group of leaders and accountants. In the end, realize that there's no shame in deciding that your organization isn't in a position to launch any sort of business at all. Better to acknowledge this at the start than to take on an expensive proposition whose inevitable doom could have been foreseen.

Measure Your Ideas Against Reality

Once you've got some agreement on likely business prospects from the key members within your organization, it's time to do some real-world research. Do not skip this step! Running any kind of business involves risk—an estimated three out of four will close in the first five years. This chapter has already discussed what's most likely to go wrong with the various types of nonprofit business ventures. Now let's move on to some realistic ways of measuring your chances of success in the world of small business generally, including customer research, price research, and competition research.

After you've done the research described below, reevaluate your business idea to see whether your basic assumptions are sound—namely, that there's a solid group of customers out there who would be willing to buy products from your organization at a price that will make you profitable. If so, it makes sense to carry on with more detailed business planning, as discussed further on in this chapter. If not, go back to the planning stage to make sure your results were correct; often, the best business decision you'll make is not to start a particular endeavor. Alternately, you could define your business more narrowly, for example, by scaling it down from retail to online catalogue sales, or by selling by advance order only.

Customer Research

By now, you should have identified a product or service that you reasonably believe your customers could benefit from. But the big question remains, will they buy it? For example, many of us need funeral plots, but how many of us plan to shop for one in the near future? And if your business sells something new or innovative, its existence may be so far from any customers' imagination that they don't think to look for it. Fortunately, multitudes of business and marketing experts who've gone before you have turned customer research into a science—and you can benefit from their proven approaches without having to spend too much on the process.

Here are some great ways to research your market. Use as many of these methods as it takes to get you a set of consistent, logical answers:

Talk to owners of similar businesses. Look for businesses that do what you'll do, in a similar locale. To avoid future competitive problems, focus on those outside your own neighborhood or city. If you can find a business being run by a nonprofit, all the better. Be open about who you are and what your goals include, and ask them to spend a few minutes telling you about what's worked, what lessons they've learned, who their best customers are, what kind of marketing has been most successful, and how long it took their business to get on its feet. You'll be surprised at how eager some businesspeople are to talk, once they realize you're serious and that you respect their need to protect their own interests. Even local business owners may reveal more than you'd expect if you stop by, as a customer, and simply ask, "How's business?"

Observe customers of similar businesses. If you'll be operating a business that people visit in person, spend time there. Let's say you'll be opening a bagel bakery. If you stop by a bagel bakery in a nearby city and munch slowly on your cream cheese and lox for an hour or two, you should be able to pick up scads of relevant information: the going prices, number of customers, number of employees, favorite flavors, number of people who buy sandwiches versus a dozen to take home, discounts the bakery offers in order to boost sales, sources of customer complaints, and amount of leftover inventory at the end of the day. (Remember that if you visit during lunch hour or a busy time, it doesn't represent the entire business day.) An even more effective approach is for someone in your organization to volunteer his or her services working in the business for a week or two. Yes, it's time consuming, but there is no better way to learn a lot quickly.

Talk to, or survey, your most likely customers. It may be that your customers are people already known to you—for example, patients at your clinic, patrons of your museum, or participants in your classes. You can either talk to them informally or ask them to fill out a survey, perhaps when visiting, or via email. Ask simple questions like, "Would you be interested if we made (a café, gift shop, etc.) available?" "Would $___ be a reasonable price to pay?" "How often would you be likely to purchase this?" "Is there a related product or service that you wish we'd offer instead?" Also talk, or send surveys to, any sympathetic friends, family, or supporters of your organization.

If your customers are not likely to be people with whom you're already in contact, you'll need to start by defining who you think your customers are most likely to be. Try to create a portrait of your typical customer, such as "middle-income teens involved in sports and living in the nearby suburbs," or "wealthy urban vegetarians with pets." Likely characteristics around which to define your customers include (depending on your business type) age, gender, income level, profession, family size or composition, ethnic background, geographic location, education level, media preferences, buying habits, and hobbies or activities.

Once you've created your customer profile, you can—probably by going through friends, and friends of friends—pull together a group of people who fit that profile and are willing to serve as a focus group. Ask them to test your product (if you have it available already) or to offer their opinions as prospective customers. If possible, try to offer choices—would they rather you located your service here or there, do they prefer doughnuts or pancakes, what kind of people do they think would buy your product, and the like. Although commercial operations pay people to serve on focus groups, you have every right to ask for volunteers—but should treat them well, and probably serve snacks!

Research demographic data. Using your developing sense of who your customers are most likely to be, research how many of them are around. If your likely customers are clients or visitors to your nonprofit's office, counting them up should be easy. If, however, you're seeking a new customer base, you'll probably need to rely on sources such as the U.S. census (www.census.gov) or the Internet. Your local reference librarian can be a great source of help with such research.

Price Research

If you'll be selling goods or services, a basic question you'll need to answer is whether you can sell enough of them, at a hefty enough markup, to make a profit. Once you add the costs of purchasing or producing the goods or services, plus an adequate profit margin, you may be shocked at how much you have to charge. Although this may result in your developing a new sympathy for small businesses trying to compete in a Wal-Mart world, it may also cause you to conclude that, like so many of them, you simply can't charge a competitive price. No surprise there—the low prices consumers expect to pay for many items are based on low-wage overseas workers, highly automated supply chains, and high-volume discounts at the wholesale level, none of which are available to you.

But one thing you can and should do, if you plan to sell goods and services beyond a small circle of maniacal supporters, is be sure the price you plan to charge is within the realm of reasonableness. Fortunately, it's easy to compare prices on the Internet, or by calling the merchants you find in your local Yellow Pages.

Even if you find that your survival depends on charging slightly above-market rates, don't despair. For starters, remember that you have no obligation to sell things on the cheap (despite common myths about nonprofit law). And, if enough of your customers will buy from you rather than the bargain warehouse down the block, you may still do well. But, all of your advertising and other materials should clearly explain that by buying your product or service, the customer is supporting a good cause. See "Stand By Your Price," below, for an example of how one nonprofit learned this lesson.

Competition Research

Even if you think you know who your likely competition is, double check this with some research. The purpose is to discover how many other similar businesses there are in the area you plan to serve. (If you'll be selling online, then that area is nationwide and potentially worldwide.)

> **CAUTION**
> **Don't ignore businesses that have recently closed their doors.** It does you no good to be the only business of your type if your predecessors tested the waters and drowned. See if you can contact the proprietors to find out what went wrong—people love to share a tale of woe.

What is a "similar" business? For the most accurate research, you'll want to look not only for businesses that provide the exact same thing, but for those that satisfy the same market segment. For example, if you plan to open a bagel bakery, and there's no bagel bakery nearby, that's good so far—unless there happens to be a bread store on the same block. Both of you may be satisfying the market segment of "fresh-baked goods and sandwich providers," which may be more than the local demand can support.

Again, you don't need an M.B.A. to research the competition. Your telephone book, the Internet, and your local Chamber of Commerce should all provide ample amounts of information. On Excite.com's business Yellow Pages, for example, you can enter a type of business and a city, and get a complete listing of names and addresses. If your business will have a storefront and will rely on walk-in traffic, you should also drive around the area to get a sense of where else your potential customers might go.

Create a list of all your competitors, containing their names and addresses, a brief summary of what they offer, and, where possible, price information. If

Stand By Your Price

The DAMAYAN Migrant Workers Association came up with a fundraising idea that its volunteers and new members were excited about: to set out a table at the Asia Pacific American Festival in Union Square Park, New York City, and sell homecooked Filipino treats. (DAMAYAN is a young nonprofit membership organization that organizes Filipino domestic workers in the New York area to fight for their rights and welfare; www.damayanmigrants.org). Here's how Amanda Vender, board member, describes the event:

"It was a beautiful, sunny day. We unfurled our newly painted green banner, propped up the photo display of recent events, and put out stacks of brochures. Most of the table was filled with trays of cassava cake, biko rice cakes, and empanadas—all on sale for two dollars each. Festivalgoers flocked to our table.

"When the time came to pack up, the organizers found the food trays empty and the brochure stack mostly full. And when all of the cooks were reimbursed for the ingredients, we found that we had only broken even. What happened?

"It turned out that a few festivalgoers were more resourceful than we were. They negotiated down the price of our sweets and empanadas, saying that they were cheaper at other tables. And as the day went on, our volunteer salespeople rushed to get rid of the perishable goods. Two dollars apiece became $1.50, then $1.00, then 50 cents, then three for a dollar, and finally four for a dollar!

"We had obviously forgotten an important element: to sell our organization, not just the empanadas. With the help of a fundraising consultant, we learned that we should have been telling customers: 'Your donation of two dollars helps to support our organization. We organize Filipino domestic workers—some of the most isolated and exploited workers in the city—to know their rights and to fight for better conditions.'

"Before our next fundraising event, we've resolved that everyone involved will practice and roleplay our fundraising pitch, and will hand out a DAMAYAN flyer to every customer."

you'll be relying mostly on local customers, plot out your competition's locations with pins or dots on a map. Then try to learn more about your competitors, to see how much of a threat they really pose. Perhaps their businesses are doing well, and they in fact have more business than they can handle. On the other hand, if they're hurting for customers in an oversaturated market, you'd do well to back off. Also evaluate the quality of their goods or services—if yours is higher, you may be able to woo away customers.

Final Planning and Test Runs

If your research has shown that your business is likely to succeed, it's not yet time to open your doors or launch into production. You need to map out your exact plans and expectations, as discussed below. You may also want to ease into a mini or test version of your planned business, as described under "Minimize Risk by Starting Small," below. And you may need to be ready with some initial cash, as discussed under "Finding Start-Up Money," below.

Create a Meaningful Business Plan

Up to this point, you've been conceptualizing your business and researching its prospects for success. Now it's time to sit down and plot out its future, for approximately the next three years. (Don't bother projecting farther—too much guesswork is involved.) This may or may not involve preparing a written business plan. Although some MBAs and consultants will warn you that few businesses can succeed without a written plan, including an extensive narrative, charts, budgets, and projections, the truth is that for many small nonprofit enterprises, such plans consume more energy than they're worth. Worse yet, they may produce an artificially rosy picture of the future, leading to a false sense of security. ("How can we fail, when we've got two inches of paper saying all will be well?")

What your organization needs to arrive at through planning is a deep understanding of what your business is about. In other words, you must think through every element of starting and running your business. Even if you don't plan to write it up in a fancy document, you should be able to summarize it in a succinct report. To do this, you and the other wise heads in your organization should consider the following:

1. What will the business sell or do, and for what types of customers?

2. Who will your most likely customers be, and what's your basis for believing they'll be interested in buying?

3. Who will be responsible for what tasks, using how much of their time?

4. How closely connected will the people who do the work be to your nonprofit "mothership"?

5. How much initial investment will be required to start the business?

6. How much will it cost to run the business and produce the goods or services on an ongoing basis?

7. What's your "break-even" point—how much will you need to bring in to cover your running costs and pay back the initial investment?

8. At what price will you need to sell your product in order to not only cover your costs but to make a profit?

9. How will you deal with any significant foreseeable legal, insurance, or tax concerns?

10. How will you market (tell the world about) your goods or services?

11. What's your profit timeline—how many months will you go without a profit, when should you expect to see profits, and at what levels?

12. After your start-up investment is spent, will your incoming cash flow be enough to cover your costs month by month, or are you likely to require loans or other cash infusions?

Take the time to write up a brief planning document covering these issues. Include the specific research sources or bases upon which you projected any financial figures, market demand levels, or other external facts and figures that may affect the business's success.

Next, bring your marketing and accounting experts into the process. Ask them to help you create forecast budgets for the following three scenarios:

- **The best case:** if everything goes right, you keep your costs down, and your customers respond as well as can reasonably expected.

- **The break-even scenario:** often best calculated backwards, to see how much you'd need to purchase or produce and sell just to cover your costs. (For more information on how to calculate this, see the article entitled "Will My Business Make Money?" free on Nolo's website at www.nolo.com.)

- **The worst-case scenario:** what will happen in the case of such foreseeable problems as product cost increases, failure to obtain donated equipment or labor, and, most important, a disappointing customer response.

If the best-case scenario doesn't look too exciting, your business idea may not be worth the effort. Same story if the worst-case scenario would result in losses that would cripple your organization. The break-even scenario should help you determine whether the business is realistic—and hopefully lead you to further planning of how to push it to true profitability.

> **CAUTION**
>
> **Never hand the entire business-planning process over to a consultant.** It's your business and only you can determine whether it will be viable. Business consultants can help you make this decision, but don't turn the whole job over to them—chances are that all you'll get in return is a long and expensive document that you don't really understand.

You can, of course, develop a much more detailed business plan. In fact, if you plan a large business that will require either major support from donors or foundations or commercial (most likely bank) loans, you'll surely have to do so. Such a business plan should include narratives and formal financial reports, including a break-even analysis, a profit-and-loss forecast, a cash-flow projection, and a start-up cost estimate. See the resource box below for good information on how to draft such a plan. Also contact local business schools—many of them sponsor classroom projects in which students evaluate potential new businesses. You can get a great deal of free, personalized, and expert attention to your business planning process this way.

> **RESOURCE**
>
> **Need help drafting a business plan?** For a quick introduction to what belongs in a formal business plan, see the free article "The Essentials of a Business Plan," at www.nolo.com). For in-depth information on drafting a business plan, I recommend *How to Write a Business Plan*, by Mike McKeever (Nolo), which offers easily digested, plain-English guidance on general business plans. The following articles specifically discuss business planning for nonprofits: "A Brief Tutorial on Business Planning for Nonprofit Enterprise" and "How to Build a

Business Plan," both by Cynthia W. Massarsky and available online at www .ventures.yale.edu/library.asp.

Minimize Risk by Starting Small

If your nonprofit is as cash-strapped as most, it literally can't afford a business failure. Before attempting a high dive into full-scale production, it's worth dipping your toes into—and testing—the business waters first. Three good ways to do this include:

- starting with borrowed or temporary resources
- running a test version of the business, and
- lining up customers before you create the product.

As a nonprofit, you have a huge advantage when it comes to minimizing your risk: You're accustomed to getting by with less and being creative about filling your daily needs. For example, the file folders that a corporate office might recycle after one use probably have, in your office, been relabeled so often that you could perform an archaeological dig on the layers. Don't drop these thrifty habits once you enter the business world. A surprising number of new businesses spend far too much, far too soon, precisely because their owners get caught up in creating the appearance of a successful businesses—complete with a pricey address, cherrywood desks, a glossy catalogue, and an extensive product or service line. In short, they quickly spend themselves out of business. The more you can get by at the beginning with existing space, staff, and resources—at least while you're getting started—the better. Assuming you succeed, you will have the resources to pay for expansion, something you'll need to do quickly on the staffing front, because few nonprofit staff members have much spare time in their already busy days.

If you can't use existing resources, think about how you can avoid expensive investments. A surprising amount of equipment can be borrowed or leased short-term, rather than purchased outright. You may even be able to line up donated facilities, at least for the short term—for example, a restaurant's kitchen on a day when it's closed for business, a church's basement for initial product assembly, or an undeveloped lot for purposes of starting a garden. Look into these possibilities well before you've committed to a business venture.

If you'll need to purchase some products or inventory, see whether the most expensive items can be donated. Talk to local businesses, especially those that you or your clients already patronize. As discussed in Chapter 2, many businesses see charitable donations of goods or services as a normal part of their annual financial cycle—though you may need to catch them early in their fiscal year, before they've made all of their planned donations.

There are limits, of course, to this "just getting by" philosophy. The two most important are that you shouldn't compromise the quality of your goods and services, and the process of soliciting donations shouldn't take more time than it's worth. For example, customers might not mind a hand-printed label on your jar of homemade applesauce, but the applesauce itself should be of top quality. Fortunately, another advantage that you have as a nonprofit is that no one expects you to look like the corporation next door. In fact, because supporting a nonprofit may be part of your customers' incentive in giving you their business, they may actually be put off by an up-market address or the latest, shiniest equipment.

It's usually best to start small, which can include beginning with mini, test versions of your business. If, for example, you're thinking of opening a crafts business, why not try setting up booths at a few fairs first? Or better yet, avoid the costs of retail altogether and sell by mail order or online. This will not only keep your costs down (opening storefronts is notoriously expensive) but will also tell you a lot about whether your staff and/or clients can handle the production and service end of the business. You'll also be learning what your customers like and respond to—or don't. You may even decide that a small-scale operation is all you want to pursue for the moment.

Another excellent strategy when you're starting out is to avoid committing resources to anything until you're sure you've got customers lined up—preferably paying in advance. In some cases, this will be easy—for example, customers who sign up for a class, workshop, or tour usually understand, or can be warned, that the event is subject to cancellation for low attendance. (Just make sure you're ready to return their deposits or payments immediately!) See "Women's Studio Workshop Summer Arts Institute," below, for an example of a successful use of this "keep it small and get advance commitments" strategy. Or, if you take orders for goods, you can tell customers how long they'll have to wait before delivery, and use that time to create the goods. (This is another advantage to not opening a store, where you'd have to have a full supply of the goods on hand.) In other cases—particularly for large or expensive orders—you may need to negotiate with the customer and sign a contract, asking them to pay in full in advance but to wait several weeks for delivery.

Women's Studio Workshop Summer Arts Institute

For most of the year, the Women's Studio Workshop (WSW, at www .wsworkshop.org) in Rosendale, New York, focuses on providing arts residencies to people making a career out of art. During the summer, however, they use their 6,500 square feet of professional studios (for printmaking, papermaking, photography, book arts, and ceramics) to offer classes in traditional and experimental studio techniques. Practicing artists and the arts-interested public from across the country participate in workshops, which run from two to five days and cost from $270 to $650; there is also a scholarship program.

The Institute's classes are a good example of building a small business using existing resources. According to Anita Wetzel, Development Director, "Part of the reason this works for us is that we already have the facilities. We are known in the field, and have established connections to artists who teach. Also, we keep our plans small scale, while being flexible enough to expand on short notice. A full class is about six to eight people, allowing participants a lot of hands-on time in the studios and one-on-one interaction with the instructors. We make sure that, at a minimum, we have enough people to pay for the teacher's salary, and transportation to get her here. Then, if more than the maximum number of students sign up, we do our best to create an additional class section."

The one catch to this strategy is that small steps into business won't gain you large returns in the long run. At some point, you'll need to either invest or risk some real money in order to make money.

Finding Start-Up Money

If you need more start-up cash than you can scare up from existing sources, you'll have to look to major donors, grantmaking foundations or corporations, or bank lenders. Because none of these sources can ordinarily give you overnight returns, be prepared for at least six months' effort in lining up commitments. For some nonprofits, it has taken one to two years.

Starting up a business provides an interesting focus for a major donors campaign. Your pitch to them is that their gifts will go farther than ever, as they'll help to launch a profit-making enterprise. As you'll remember from Chapter 6, launching a campaign requires your leadership and board members to devote a period of several weeks to meeting with various donor prospects and asking for their financial support. You'll want to show the prospects your plans and forecasts, and demonstrate that your organization is ready to launch into this new venture. With the right presentation, this can give you a chance to approach existing donors in a new way, with a new message, to reinvigorate their support. If your efforts don't lead to sufficient amounts in outright gifts, also consider asking major donors to support you with low-interest loans.

An increasing—though not yet overwhelming—number of foundations will make grants to assist you in starting a small business. As with the major donors, you're in the happy position of offering them something new to support—and as you've probably learned, foundations are much more receptive to new projects than to ongoing support of the "same old thing." At the same time, your track record of good communication with funders and measurable outcomes on past grants will be an important way of demonstrating your chances of business success.

Be aware of—and receptive to—a preference by some foundations to give you technical assistance, such as educational or consulting opportunities, in business planning and setup, rather than an outright cash grant. Some foundations are also developing funding alternatives that are something short of a cash grant, such as revolving lines of credit or loans that are forgiven when certain benchmarks are reached. See Chapter 10 for more on researching and approaching foundations for support.

As a last resort (given the risks that come with carrying a debt burden), you could also approach banks for small-business loans. Bank loans are certainly one of the primary methods used by for-profit entrepreneurs. You're at a bit of a disadvantage here, however, if this is your first business effort. The bank will want to see not only a formal business plan, but also evidence that you're capable of getting a small business off the ground and repaying the loan. This is a good time to enlist the help of any board members and other volunteers who will be participating in this effort, and emphasize their experience, business knowledge, and ongoing role. For more information on approaching banks for loans, see the resources listed at the end of this chapter.

Licensing, Sponsorships, and Other Relationships With Existing Businesses

Rather than developing and implementing your own business idea, you may be able to generate revenue in cooperation with, or through sponsorship by, an existing business. For example, universities can make significant sums by licensing their names and logos for clothing and all sorts of other products. In return for a business's sponsorship or other payments, the business would normally expect one of the following from your organization:

- **your organization's name or logo,** which the business would license from you, in order to give its products a stamp of socially conscious approval. Just open your newspaper for examples—tea and coffee companies sometimes state their commitment to fair trade and other socially responsible growing and harvesting schemes, backed up by a reputable nonprofit's logo.

- **your organization's name or logo on a product again, but with a different fee arrangement,** where a certain percentage of the profits goes to support your organization. This is known as "cause-related marketing." It's similar to the licensing arrangement, but takes it one step farther, not only because of the percentage payment, but because you might also be asked to encourage your organization's supporters to buy the product. The Gap, Saks Fifth Avenue, Apple Computer, and Motorola all offer cause-related merchandise. Affiliate credit cards, which are now widely available, are another example—check one out on the World Wildlife Fund's website at www.worldwildlife.org. WWF has partnered with Chase to offer a Visa card featuring WWF's name, logo, and a picture of a wild animal—in return for which WWF receives

"Shop to Give" Websites Don't Generate Much Income

Among the many fundraising innovations spawned by the Internet is one involving a partnership between commercial websites and businesses. Various businesses now offer to give a shopper's favorite charity a cut of the profit on the shopper's purchase if the shopper accesses the business's website through an online charity mall or the nonprofit's own website. (See, for example, iGive.com or dogreatstuff.com.)

Although well-intentioned, this appealing model hasn't lived up to expectations. In fact, many of the websites begun for this purpose have gone out of business. The model's effectiveness is reduced because:

- The percentage given to the nonprofit is usually minimal, typically 2.5% to 8%. As a result, a donor who buys a $250 television may feel he's given a lot to your charity, not realizing that his gift amounted to no more than $20.

- The merchants don't usually tell you the identity of the shoppers, which prevents you from building a deeper relationship with these donors.

- Many of the businesses big enough to enter into such a deal may be selling items that are inconsistent with your mission (guns, alcohol, or overpriced self-help videos, for example).

Does this mean that every group should avoid these online giving sites? Not necessarily—for very little work, you might see a little boost in your budget. In fact, small groups with minimal fundraising staff, who can mention this opportunity in their newsletter or other publicity materials, tend to be happiest with these services, because the rewards are significant relative to their overall budget. Just don't expect to see big bucks roll in. And, as always, do your research before choosing a service—ask other nonprofits about their experiences.

0.55% of all purchases. (Note: Because of the quid pro quo arrangement, the business cannot deduct from its taxes the amounts it gives your nonprofit.)

- **your display of the business's logo**—for example, in your publications, on your website, on team shirts, or on banners—in return for the business sponsoring an event or activity. (Also see Chapter 8, on special events, and Chapter 13, on media, for more on the most likely uses of corporate sponsorships.)

- **your assistance with a joint business venture,** in which both you and the business provide a portion of the expertise or services, and share in the profits.

As a practical matter, larger, more established nonprofits—with recognizable names and logos—are the ones in the best position to enter into licensing, marketing, or sponsorship arrangements. That shouldn't stop smaller groups from thinking up creative possibilities, however. This is an expanding area of opportunity, with the corporate world's realization that supporting charity gives a company a competitive advantage. Or, you may need to set your sights on smaller businesses, those that more closely match the size and reach of your organization. For example, a local sports bar might sponsor your little league team, or a local print or photo shop might be happy to say in its catalogue, "We're the choice of environmentally conscious organizations such as [*your organization*]," in return for either a fee or a discount on their services.

The arrangement that will require the most creativity is that of a joint venture, in which both you and the business take some role in business activities. However, having already considered your assets, needs, and business concepts, you may have already identified an area in which an existing business could take part. For example, a local grocery store might partner with you in a catering venture. Or, you might consider short-term ventures. Your bonsai club might arrange to give classes at a local nursery—the nursery would do the advertising through its mailing list, and you would both reap the profits. Or, if you are a cancer-care organization, you might arrange for a local hat store to come to your nonprofit and offer advice and discounts on attractive headwear for people undergoing chemotherapy—and give you a share of any profits from sales.

Cause-Related Marketing as a Win-Win Situation

Looking to the U.K. for inspiration, Ireland's SuperValu grocery stores (www .supervalu.ie) was one of the finalists for the 2003 award for cause-related marketing given by a group called Business in the Community (a network of socially aware businesses, at www.bitc.org.uk). SuperValu had entered into a partnership with a cancer-awareness group called Action Center. Here's how it worked: Action Center would bring its mobile cancer detection unit vehicles to the parking lots of SuperValu. This allowed Action Center to bring its services and information about breast and cervical cancer to women in underserved rural areas. SuperValu provided not only the parking space but also electricity, water, public relations, and marketing. Both SuperValu's and Action Center's names and services were promoted in the public relations efforts, including posters, sales promotional leaflets, and joint branding on SuperValu's shopping bags.

Everyone won in this effort—Action Center got a chance to spread its name and reach out to new service recipients, at low cost, and SuperValu got an immediate source of potential walk-in customers, plus good publicity.

Approaching a business or corporation has one important thing in common with approaching an individual—there are no preset rules, and you'll need to do your research first. By learning about the business's values, how it's doing financially, and who the right person to approach is, you'll vastly improve your chances of success. Be prepared to be quite open with the business about what's in it for them—perhaps an increase in their customers, access to a new customer base, or a boost to their public reputation. Before embarking on any plan, make sure your arrangement is written up as an agreement, signed by a representative of both parties. This doesn't have to be in legalese—the important thing is to use words and phrases that both sides understand and feel comfortable with. If the business provides a document, perhaps drafted by its legal staff, go over it carefully. There's no shame in asking, "What does this mean, and why does it need to be here?"

One of the most effective ways to interest a business in partnering with you is to find points of commonality between your two messages or how you want the public to view you. For example, in 2004, the American Diabetes Association announced that it was entering into a sponsorship arrangement with the makers of Splenda, an artificial sweetener. The match is obvious—diabetics need to avoid sugar, and certain artificial sweeteners can allow them to enjoy desserts without too much effect on their insulin levels. In fact, part of the sponsorship arrangement allows Splenda to contribute recipes to the ADA's website (http://diabetes.org), no doubt using you-know-what sweetener. Other matches are sometimes based on a company's need to overcome a negative aspect of their reputation—for example, a number of car manufacturers sponsor Mothers Against Drunk Driving (MADD, at www.madd.org).

With all of these business arrangements, there are ethical issues that your organization will need to discuss and consider before the deal is signed. You're not tainted just by association with businesses—many of them are no more or less moral than your average nonprofit. However, your reputation may start to suffer if you've got corporate logos plastered all over your website and publications. And, of course, you'll need to think hard before helping a company that creates harmful products to try to save its reputation. There's something to be said for letting them atone for their errors through your organization, but at least make sure it's a sincere effort, not a cynical marketing strategy.

The Next Steps

Hopefully, this chapter has guided you toward the front door of your new business, but you'll have to walk through it on your own. A book of this size couldn't possibly advise you on all the aspects of running your small business—issues like obtaining permits, choosing a business name, avoiding trademark disputes, leasing space, managing employees, dealing with customers, paying business taxes, marketing and advertising, riding out hard times, and more. For compact guides to all these issues and more, see *Legal Guide for Starting & Running a Small Business,* by Fred S. Steingold (Nolo), and *Marketing Without Advertising*, by Michael Phillips and Salli Rasberry (Nolo). It's perfectly appropriate for you to be reading books that aren't geared only for nonprofits at this point—you'll need to play by the same rules as other businesses do, with only a few exceptions. Still, I recommend developing relationships with other nonprofits pursuing business activities, and with organizations that support them, to keep up with new knowledge and developments in this quickly changing area of endeavor.

RESOURCE

Want more information on nonprofit business ventures? For more detailed but eminently readable information on the issues covered in this chapter, see *Selling Social Change (Without Selling Out)*, by Andy Robinson (Jossey-Bass, Chardon Press Series) and *Venture Forth! The Essential Guide to Starting a Moneymaking Business in Your Nonprofit Organization*, by Rolfe Larson (Amherst H. Wilder Foundation, at www.wilder.org). You'll also find high-quality information on a website created by the Yale School of Management, at www.ventures.yale.edu (you'll need to register, but it's free).

Seeking Grants From Foundations, Corporations, and Government

The world of grant funding is surrounded by a somewhat unwarranted mystique. Novice fundraisers tend to imagine that if they can only come up with the right combination of words, money will rain down upon their organization. Actually, the truth is more complicated. On the one hand, it's not terribly hard to write a grant proposal—no magic set of talents, other than solid research, writing, and organizational skills, are required. On the other hand, experienced insiders realize that there's a lot more to getting a grant than writing a compelling proposal. While good grantwriting skills are valuable, they rarely, in and of themselves, determine which organizations will receive a big check. Indeed, as this chapter explains, writing a good grant amounts to no more than composing a tasty entrée—but who wants to skip the salad and dessert? Here is the recipe for creating the whole meal:

- understand who gives out grants in your field

- narrow the list by researching your grant prospects

- understand the entire proposal process, from initial inquiry forward, including how to write a targeted grant proposal

- follow up with the funder, and

- apply for grant renewals.

Understand the Funders

There are two primary sources of grants to nonprofit organizations: foundations (private and public) and the government (local, state, and federal). Each source has unique purposes and requirements for granting funds. For example, a large, corporate-run foundation may seek to have its name associated with a certain positive image; a private family foundation may be primarily motivated to carry out the very personal interests of the family that founded it; and a government grantor may be fulfilling legislative requirements. To improve your chances of winning support, you'll need to know a lot about any funder you approach—particularly when it comes to private foundations, whose organizational personalities can be, and often are, as distinct and quirky as those of any individual donor.

Characteristics of Private and Public Foundations

Most nonprofits find that public and private foundations are their best bet for obtaining grants. A foundation is essentially another form of charity—in fact, their tax status, like yours, is covered by Section 501(c)(3) of the Internal Revenue Code. Over 70,000 grantmaking foundations are active in the United States today. Collectively, they granted about $40 billion in funds in 2006, a huge rise from previous years. One of the best things about foundations is that they don't just give out money because they want to; many of them give it out because they have to! Depending on their particular tax status, "private" foundations must spend at least 5% of their investment assets on philanthropy every year; this includes money spent on reasonable administrative expenses such as salaries, facilities, and travel.

Tax laws also affect the foundations' essential character and way of working with you. Private foundations are usually in the hands of a single source of money, such as a wealthy family or a corporation. (The Bill & Melinda Gates Foundation is a well-known example.) Many private foundations were funded by wealthy philanthropists, seeking to change the world to fit their vision. Some of these organizations are quite small, or narrowly focused. For example, one of the Charles and Helen Schwab Foundation's main initiatives addresses childhood learning disabilities, in large part because Charles Schwab himself grew up with dyslexia. (See www.schwabfoundation.org and www. schwablearning.org.)

Some family-based foundations are so private that you might think that they want you to just go away and leave them alone. In fact, a few do want just that—as evidenced by the fact that they don't even publish a website. Others are long-established, high-profile players in the foundation world. Whatever their size or provenance, most family foundations tend to focus on one major substantive interest area and two or three other minor ones. This makes it hard for most groups to get in the door, but relatively easy to stay inside once you cross the threshold.

Corporate-sponsored foundations also normally fall into the private foundation category. Although they account for approximately $4 billion of the foundation money granted every year, this is only 29% of the $13.8 billion that corporations give to nonprofits annually. That's because most corporate giving isn't channeled through foundations alone, but instead is given out directly by the parent corporation. (See "Nonfoundation Corporate Giving," below.) Any consumer would probably recognize the names of corporate foundations—the Levi Strauss Foundation, the Ford Foundation, and the Merck Company Foundation, to name a few. Some of these make grants that explicitly tie to their company product or philosophy. For example, the Aetna Foundation lists its first giving priority as health—a fitting choice given that its creator company, Aetna Inc., is one of America's largest sellers of health insurance. The Sun Microsystems Foundation gives out educational grants, particularly encouraging students to further their studies of math, science, technology, and engineering. Other corporate foundations simply try to promote the interests of the communities in which their customers live. For example, the Sara Lee Foundation's website says: "We are committed to doing what we can to improve the communities where we do business." (See www.saraleefoundation.org.) (People living in hunger are presumably less likely to buy Sara Lee cake!)

RESOURCE
To see the tax reports that foundations file with the IRS, look for the Form 990-PF filed by private foundations and Form 990 filed by public foundations. These are available using the Foundation Finder function at www.foundationcenter.org.

Public foundations, which usually have to forage for their own funding sources in order to turn around and make grants, are slightly different animals than the private ones—hungrier ones, to be precise. Unlike private foundations, which are usually funded by one or a few families or corporations, public foundations must beat the bushes for funds, typically trying to aggregate lots of small donations. The United Way or the Red Cross are examples of public foundations, as are local community foundations. Many public foundations also pursue those not-quite-super-rich philanthropists who would like to give away a little of their largesse, but don't have enough to form their own foundations. In this regard, community foundations position themselves as liaisons between such philanthropists and nonprofits, helping the philanthropists learn more about community needs, and efficiently taking care of the administrative aspects of giving.

Nonfoundation Corporate Giving

Corporations don't grant money through foundations alone—in fact, many of them find it easier or more advantageous to give by other means. And, of course, not all companies that make charitable gifts are organized as corporations—sole proprietorships, partnerships, and limited liability companies (LLCs) can also be generous with their profits.

In fact, especially if yours is a small, local nonprofit, it's key to realize that the majority of business giving available to you will be through nonfoundation avenues, such as employee volunteer or matching gift programs, in-kind donations of services, goods, or facilities, event sponsorship, cause-related marketing (where their advertising mentions your nonprofit and cause), or cash gifts.

Because most businesses prefer to keep their giving local (sometimes even at the neighborhood level), and because companies can set their own rules for their gift programs, you should research the companies operating in your area to see what they have to offer.

Here are some tips for tailoring your approach to businesses that don't operate a foundation:

- **View this as another relationship to be built.** Look for existing contacts between your staff and volunteers and the company's employees. For example, perhaps several people from a local company have adopted animals from your shelter, giving you a good entry to ask the business for support.

- **Ask yourself what's in it for the company.** Unlike at corporate foundations, your contact person at a local business will quite possibly be in the marketing department. This means you must focus squarely on how you can improve or advertise the company's image or enhance quality of life for its customers or employees. For example, if you want businesses to contribute a gift of attractive products for your silent auction, be ready to tell them how you'll publicize their donations.

- **Think creatively.** Few rules for business giving are written in stone. Thus, you might approach a small food producer that has never given anything to charity before by proposing an exciting way to partner—for example, featuring their rice-based desserts at a county-wide event directed at people with gluten intolerance.

- **Be prepared to sign a contract.** The fact that no formal grant is involved doesn't mean there won't be paperwork. In some cases, particularly with event sponsorship, you'll

Nonfoundation Corporate Giving (continued)

need to sign an agreement with the company, specifying such things as where you'll mention their name and feature their logo.

- **Don't approach a company in financial trouble.** Do your homework before getting in touch—read the business pages and do some online research. You want to catch them when they're feeling generous.

For more information on where to find corporate support, see:

- *National Directory of Corporate Giving* (Foundation Center). Gives descriptions and guidelines for over 2,500 corporations that make gifts directly or through a foundation.
- *Corporate Giving Directory* (Taft Group). Profiles 1,000 of the largest charitable giving programs.
- *Matching Gift Details* (Council for Advancement and Support of Education). Profiles of more than 10,000 companies with matching gift programs, in print or online.
- *Giving by Industry: A Reference Guide to New Corporate Philanthropy* (Aspen Publishers, Inc.).
- **www.hoovers.com.** Use this website to check on a company's health, or to look up companies by industry category.

For your organization, this means that working with public foundations will help you get around the narrow grant guidelines that otherwise plague the foundation world. Public foundations need you to feed them exciting new ideas that they can use to stimulate their donors' interests. In fact, some grant decisions won't be made by the foundation itself, but will be based purely on the donors' choices. This can add up to some serious money in the case of donor-advised funds, in which major donors pool resources and make their own decisions about who to fund and for what purposes. Of course, you're at a particular advantage if your nonprofit works in "fun or popular" fields like education, health, or the environment. Even if you don't, however, it's well worth courting your local community foundations' favor, because those that lack immediate grant opportunities may be intrigued enough to link you up with an interested donor later.

People Who Staff Private and Public Foundations

After learning how foundations work, your next task is to understand who works for them. Obviously, you won't expect to find the person after whom the foundation was named sitting behind a desk (although this sometimes happens). The main people you'll interact with are a foundation's "program officers." They typically are responsible for reading and evaluating proposals and presenting the ones they like to their boards of directors—who usually make the final call (although program officers may have discretion to approve small grants on their own).

Many program officers cut their teeth in nonprofit jobs, including fundraising, so you can expect them to be fairly savvy about who you are and what you can reasonably expect to achieve. Above all, most are extremely interested in seeing that their money is invested well. So, it will always be important to present your organization as solid, well organized, and able to produce results.

> **RESOURCE**
>
> **Want to read a humorous take on who goes into foundation work?** Check out *Bobos in Paradise*, by David Brooks (Simon & Schuster). Brooks coined the word "Bobo" from "Bohemian Bourgeois," by which he means a meritocracy of people who have money, an elite class background, or education, but who also have artsy or creative aspirations. According to Brooks's view, many members of the meritocracy with a tough or "predatory" bent become lawyers or businesspeople, while those who like to nurture may end up in other careers—including foundation work. If you're presenting a proposal to one of society's insiders, it may help to have staff or a board member with a similar background be the spokesperson for your application.

Government Grantmakers

Government grants are made by local, state, and federal agencies. Statistics are hard to come by, but it's a good guess that nonprofits nationwide get about 12% of their revenues from the government. However, the distribution is uneven, with some nonprofits in certain fields, such as health services or education, relying almost completely on government funds, while others receive none at all. If you are one of the lucky ones that gets funded, the amount granted is likely to be quite substantial—the feds, in particular, rarely mess around with pocket-change grants. Although the purposes of government grants have traditionally been fairly narrow, they are now turning toward outsourcing and privatization, which means that grants will increasingly be available for a broader range of purposes. But before you leap clapping from your chair, you should know that the government tends to be very risk averse, so new organizations and untested projects will have a tougher time getting funded.

Government grants can also be affected by the political goals of the current administration or party in power. For example, during the George W. Bush administration, family planning projects whose primary focus is anything but abstinence became difficult to fund through federal sources.

While you're more likely to be funded by your local and state grantors, especially if you have projects that will improve a local community, the federal government also gets into a surprising number of grassroots projects. For example, I've written proposals that yielded a few hundred thousand dollars' worth of federal grants for an immigrant youth project designed to help curb teen violence, not something everyone might have expected the feds to fund.

TIP

The more reproducible your project, the more likely it is to be funded. Especially with innovative programs, the federal government loves to see evidence that your program will serve as a pilot and model for others to follow. After all, in a huge country, there is little to be gained from pouring huge funds into creating one local success story. But if you can show that your effort— whether it be curbing gun violence, teen smoking, or accidents on the farm—can be rapidly rolled out in other communities across the nation, you are much more likely to receive a big check.

A big downside to any government grant is the overwhelming amount of red tape involved. The application alone can be more than some nonprofits can handle. Your federal grant application may well stack up to two inches or more once you've completed all the forms, narrative, statistical information, lists of collaborators and advisory committees, and the like. Worse yet, federal grant opportunities are often announced a mere six weeks before the applications are due. State and local grant applications are less onerous when it comes to paperwork, but often include other requirements, such as mandatory attendance at dull meetings with large groups of other applicants or grantees.

People Who Staff Government Grantmaking Offices

The administrators with whom you'll interact on a government grant may be far away geographically, and may not seem attuned to the nonprofit world. Their background is likely to be more state university than Ivy League. They may have worked their way into their current job from another branch of government— and, as a gross generalization, government workers tend to be highly attuned to rules, requirements, and obedience to orders from higher up. So don't expect your prospective grant administrator to overlook deficiencies in your application based on its wonderfully creative concept. None of this is meant to say, however, that you shouldn't try to establish human contact with government grant administrators—their very remoteness means that you can set yourself apart from the pack by picking up the phone and trying to get to know them, as well as keeping in regular contact after you receive your grant.

Research Grant Prospects

Researching your most promising funders, and the grants that they offer, is a critical part of the grantseeking process—and sadly, one that too many people zoom though. While different funders report very different success/rejection ratios, all agree that they receive scads of applications proposing programs that are 180 degrees away from their stated purposes or guidelines—in other words, that are completely unfundable. Though it's impossible to know for sure, the common wisdom is that a mere one of each ten submitted grant proposals gets funded, with a significant portion of rejections attributable to the applicants' failure to understand the guidelines.

> ⓘ **CAUTION**
>
> **Receiving an unsolicited grant application form doesn't materially improve your chances of getting a grant.** Especially once your nonprofit is established, funders may mail you grant applications out of the blue. Many funders do this as a courtesy. However, this doesn't mean that your application is

any more likely to be accepted once you complete it and send it in. Unless your application is both competitive and relevant to the funder's mission, you'll just be joining the ranks of all the other nonprofits who send out grant applications cold.

To get your application to the top of a grantmaker's in-box, take the time to do some basic research. Your object is to make sure your proposal is a likely match for the funder's stated—and in some cases, unstated—interests and priorities. Begin your research with some library or online work, but be ready to follow up by acting like an investigative reporter, determined to sniff out the real-deal grant opportunities. Your research progression should typically go something like this:

- decide what you're looking for
- research public information
- make personal contacts with funders, and
- create files to track funders.

Choose a Goal for Each Research Project

If you've read Chapter 3 on creating a fundraising plan, you understand the importance of carefully planning before you leap into the next exciting-sounding funding possibility. As discussed in more detail there, you must have a solid sense of your agency's mission and your fundraising "sub-mission" *before* you set out to raise the money, not after the applications are in the mail.

Seeking grant money is probably the area where the "plan first, act second" approach gets violated the most. If you get a Request for Proposals (RFP) from your local city government inviting you to apply for funding, you shouldn't start by writing a proposal, but by first figuring out whether your group is any more likely to be funded than the multitude of other groups in town who received the same solicitation. (If a "can't-pass-it-up" RFP comes along, you can, of course, alter your fundraising plan—but be realistic about the costs that come with every grant you pursue.)

Sticking to Your Mission
During her time as Development & Communications Coordinator with the World Institute on Disability (WID), Marisa Lianggamphai became all too familiar with the temptation to apply for grants that don't quite fit. "WID focuses primarily on issues affecting adults with disabilities, at the policy level. Although several of its programs have components that serve youth with disabilities, they are not the main focus of the organization. Unfortunately, there are a lot more funding opportunities for youth with disabilities than for adults with disabilities. I often thought it would be great if WID could change its programs to go where the funding is, but that really isn't WID's purpose. Every possible funding opportunity must be run through the question of 'Is this within our mission?' Otherwise, an organization's strength and purpose gets watered down."

Once you're clear on your funding goals, break them into categories and fill out the chart below for each grantseeking effort.

Most of the chart's criteria should be fairly self-explanatory. Your **clients or issue** depends on how you've defined your fundraising goal. Your answer could be as broad as the entire populace served by your agency, such as the homeless, the blind, or wild birds, or as narrow as the purchase of a new drinking fountain for your dance studio. The **greater goal** would be all or part of your agency's mission, such as "reducing maternal mortality" or "ending youth violence." This goal is important because it should dovetail neatly with goals set out by a funder.

Set yourself a **minimum grant amount**, or at least have an idea of how many grant proposals you're able to write in order to reach your funding goal. You don't want to stretch too far and end up preparing 15 small grant proposals to raise $30,000, when two larger ones would have done the same job. **Geographic area** is a common limitation placed by funders, so you'll need to know exactly what area your agency plans to cover, bearing in mind any future plans for expansion. The funding source will no doubt define other **restrictions** on what you can do with the money, so be clear about which ones your organization can't accept. Prohibitions on legislative advocacy or prohibitions on working with certain populations are common ones. For example, in the immigrant services

Fundraising Worksheet 8: Grantseeking Chart

Clients or issue to be served:	
Greater goal being pursued:	
Minimum useful grant amount:	$
Geographic area served or covered:	
Any unacceptable restrictions:	
Any unacceptable sources of funds:	

field, certain governmental funding sources will not give support to agencies whose clients include undocumented ("illegal") immigrants, which makes it virtually impossible for agencies serving immigrants to accept this money.

Some organizations also struggle with whether it's moral to accept money from a **funding source** like a drug or tobacco company. It doesn't mean you're crass or ruthless if you don't set such limitations—plenty of nonprofits figure that it's time these corporations gave a little back, and that it's nearly impossible to find money that wasn't raised through someone's exploitation in the not-too-distant past.

> **TIP**
> **Don't hide what you're doing.** Occasionally, you may be able to get around funders' limitations by casting what you're doing in a different light. For example, if you work with a mountain biking association that seeks to have more trails opened to bikes, and you apply to a funding source that funds education, not advocacy, you may nevertheless be able to develop a fundable program to educate the public and governmental decision makers as to why biking doesn't necessarily harm trails. However, if you have to resort to hiding part of your activities or mission to get a grant, it will backfire. Even if you get the grant, the grantmaking community is a tight one—and if your transgression is discovered, word will spread quickly, hampering your ability to get any future grants.

With your Grantseeking Chart in hand, it's time to start researching individual foundations and other grantmakers. Although you could just use the chart as a general checklist to identify good matches, it's better to go one step further and assemble detailed information on the most promising-looking funders. To do this, use the following worksheet; you can, of course, add to and customize the worksheet to fit your organization's needs and interests. The information on this worksheet will help you decide whether the possible grant is a good fit for your organization and what your next steps should be.

Fundraising Worksheet 9: Grants Worksheet

Basic Information	
Foundation/funder's name & address:	
Foundation's stated mission and purpose:	
Contact person:	
Contact person's telephone, email:	
Names and titles of other staff members:	
Names of board members and trustees:	
Total grants made annually:	$
Eligibility Information	
Grant subject matter:	
Grant eligibility requirements:	
Geographical limitations:	
Other limitations:	
Maximum grant amount:	$
Funding duration:	
"Good Fit" Indicators	
Other organizations that have received grants for similar work (name the organization(s), list how much received and for what work):	
Typical grant amount:	$
Limitations on overhead/administrative costs:	%
Prospects for grant renewal:	
Special considerations:	

Fundraising Worksheet 9: Grants Worksheet (continued)

Application Process	
First steps:	❏ query letter? ❏ full proposal?
Printed application form or guidelines:	❏ available? ❏ obtained?
Next application deadline(s) (if any):	
Board meeting dates:	
Likely to hear answer by:	
Research Trail	
Have checked	
❏ Website	
❏ Directories (name them):	
❏ Form 990	
❏ Annual report	

Most of the information on this worksheet is self-explanatory. Taking a look at the funder's application deadlines and schedule for answers will also help you decide whether the grant prospect fits into your annual fundraising plan. You're likely to wait three or four months for an answer to your proposal, but some funders can take up to a year—which is a problem if you were counting on this grant to fill a particular, more immediate need. Also, not all funders set specific application deadlines—some accept applications on a rolling basis. However, they're likely to make decisions at one of their board meetings. Therefore, if you can find out when their upcoming board meetings are, you can put yourself in the best position by submitting your proposal two to three months in advance of that date.

The entry regarding "similar grants given to other organizations" is there as a reality check. No matter what the grantor says it wants to fund, the grants it has actually made tell the real story, helping you interpret what they mean by generalized phrases like "vocational training" or "leadership development."

For example, a foundation that says it funds environmental projects may really be interested only in water issues or forests. Part of your job is to find out the funder's unspoken, internal guidelines.

Public Information About Grants and Funders

Researching grant opportunities isn't difficult. A number of nonprofit-support organizations and public libraries are dedicated to assisting nonprofits, and the Internet can bring a wealth of helpful information right to your desk.

The Foundation Center (www.fdncenter.org) is an excellent organization with lots of helpful funder information. It has main branches in Atlanta, Cleveland, New York, San Francisco, and Washington, DC, and affiliate relationships with hundreds of "cooperating collections," so chances are good that information is available near you. Many of these centers offer personal or group orientation sessions to help you best use their research materials. If you have ready access to such a resource, you can skim the rest of this section, which covers:

- printed and CD-ROM directories, and
- online resources.

Printed and CD-ROM Resources

Though the Web has almost taken over the research process, printed resources aren't yet obsolete—and may be a great choice if your only time to research is while sitting on the bus going home. Even better (but more expensive) is to purchase a searchable CD-ROM directory.

For general compilations of foundation funding sources and requirements, the best printed and CD-ROM resources include:

- *The Foundation Directory* (by the Foundation Center). Part I of this guide covers the top 10,000 foundations in the United States, based on giving levels. Part II lists the next 10,000 foundations. The *Directory* will tell you most of what you need to know about a given foundation—who's involved, what they give, how to apply, and more—and it has an extensive subject index. Their 2007 edition cost $215 for Part I and another $185 for Part II. Available through www.fdncenter.org (there's also an online version, at a monthly subscription cost) and your local funding library.

- *FC Search: The Foundation Center's Database on CD-ROM,* a searchable guide to over 88,000 U.S. grantmakers, including private and public foundations as well as corporate givers. Includes links to websites and Form 990-PFs. The subscription cost in 2007 was between approximately $1,195 and $3,395, depending on the number of users. It may also be available at your local funding or public library.

- **Also see** *The National Directory of Corporate Giving* (the Foundation Center), a guide to grants and direct giving by over 3,700 corporations and corporate foundations. The cost in 2007 was $195.

For government grants, see:

- *The Federal Register's Notices of Funding Availability* (federal grants only). The Federal Register, which is printed daily and is available at many main larger public libraries, is also available online at www.gpoaccess.gov/fr/index .html. Unfortunately, reading it every day is hardly practical—you're more likely to find out about good opportunities through other sources, such as a nonprofit-related newsletters, magazines, or listservs.

- *The Catalog of Federal Domestic Assistance* (federal grants only), also available online at www.cfda.gov.

Numerous specialized guides to funding opportunities also exist. Here are some of the most useful:

- *Grant Guide series* (the Foundation Center), a collection of directories focusing on the major funders in specific subject areas, such as education, health, religion, and the arts. If you know you're interested only in grants in a certain subject area, using one of these guides cuts your costs and your research time.

- *LGBTQ Grantmaking by U.S. Foundations* (a report by Funders for Lesbian and Gay Issues, www.lgbtfunders.org).

- *Directory of Research Grants* and *Directory of Grants in the Humanities* (both published by Greenwood Publishing Group, www.greenwood.com).

Subscribing to newsletters or magazines that keep abreast of the funding world is also a great way to learn about grants. Many of these will advise you of funding opportunities and changes in the grantmaking world, and most also include material on broader issues, such as nonprofit management or other types of effective fundraising. Especially for development people in growing organizations, these publications are a rich source of ideas:

- *The Chronicle of Philanthropy,* at http://philanthropy.com.
- *Grassroots Fundraising Journal,* at www.grassrootsfundraising.org.
- *The Nonprofit Quarterly,* at www.nonprofitquarterly.org.
- *TheNonProfitTimes,* at www.nptimes.com.
- *Nonprofit World,* at www.sngo.org.

Online Resources

A fair amount of information is available free on the Internet, from websites that collect information on funders, from listservs and email newsletters, and, once you've got a prospect in mind, from the funder's own website. As your resources expand, you may well want to invest in a paid online subscription service. Here's some of the best of what's out there, free or by subscription:

Websites:

- **The Chronicle of Philanthropy,** at www.philanthropy.com. Contains news on the foundation and nonprofit world. A limited number of articles are posted for free, but you must subscribe to their print or online version to see the remaining articles and access their grants database.

- **Community Foundation Locator,** sponsored by the Council on Foundations, www.cof/locator.org. This website displays a map of the United States, where you can click on your region to pull up a list of its local community foundations and links to those foundations' websites.

- **The Foundation Center,** at www.fdncenter.org. This stellar website pulls together much of what you'll need—substantive advice, research studies, a "Foundation Finder" that lets you look up basic information on foundations whose names you already know (including their IRS Form 990 or 990PF), a "Philanthropy News Digest" that archives news articles on foundations back to 1995, and links to myriad other helpful sites.

- **FirstGov,** at www.firstgov.gov/Business/Nonprofit.shtml#fundraising. This U.S. government website has helpful information for nonprofits, from available federal grants (including grants by federal agencies, such as the Environmental Protection Agency) to U.S. Postal regulations.

- **Guidestar,** at www.guidestar.org. This Web service offers information on all kinds of nonprofits, foundations included. You'll need to register for the advanced search capabilities, allowing you access to Form 990s, 990-PFs, and other publications, but registration is free.

- **The Grantsmanship Center,** at www.tgci.com. By clicking "Funding Sources," you can find links to today's *Federal Register* and to community foundation websites, accessible state by state.

- *The Philanthropy Journal* (a publication of the A.J. Fletcher Foundation), at www.philanthropyjournal.org. Contains news about foundations, and recent surveys about fundraising trends and other nonprofit issues.

Information From Funders

Although general information from printed directories or independent websites can be helpful, they're only the start of your research (and the information you find there may be out of date). Your next step is either to call the foundation or agency to request a copy of its annual reports and grant guidelines or to go online to view and download them.

The annual reports are useful not only to get a sense of the foundation's personality, but also to find out what programs the foundation is proud to have funded and who has received grants in the past. Many reports present useful lists of every group funded, including the amount of the grant and a brief description of its purpose.

The funder's grant guidelines will provide more detail than secondary sources about the foundation or government agency's eligibility requirements, funding priorities, types of projects funded (for example, new or pilot projects, research or direct services only), submission requirements, and timelines for decisions.

> **TIP**
> **Bookmark the funder's website.** No matter how much information you think you've gleaned, requirements and opportunities may change overnight. The funder's website will be your most up-to-date source of information—short of personal conversations with the grantmakers, covered next. Stay current by visiting the website regularly.

After you've researched funders through the various sources described above, you should have some good information on your most likely grant prospects.

For the hottest prospects, create separate files containing your summary worksheets, notes, and any application materials or other information and instructions that you've photocopied or downloaded from their websites.

Make Personal Contact With Funders

By now you should have a short list of the hottest prospects—and you are probably champing at the bit to start working on your proposals. That will get you points for enthusiasm, but not for common sense. As perfect a match as your organization and the funder seem to be on paper, any experienced fundraiser will tell you that there is always more to the story. Your next step is to make telephone or personal contact with a decision maker within the foundation or other funder's office.

Now is where the real detective work begins. That "contact person's telephone number" entry on your summary worksheet is probably still blank. And for good reason: Grants officers could spend all of their days and nights talking to people seeking funds—most of them for proposals that will never get off the ground. While there are exceptions, many foundations are about as accessible as a 14th-century fortified castle.

It may take perseverance and even a little luck to get the needed phone number, but you can usually do it. First, get a list of the foundation's grant officers and board members, and circulate it among your staff and board. If your people know anyone on the list, that can be your critical link. As you gain experience in the development world, every conference, meeting, or special event will be an opportunity for you to meet people who work for foundations, or colleagues who can tell you the right person to call. And never think of this as just a preliminary step to your "real" work—making contacts and establishing relationships is your real work. There's no need to be surprised, or worried, if you spend large amounts of time on it.

> **EXAMPLE:** Iris, a development director, is looking for funding for a needle exchange program—never an easy sell. She spends part of one morning reading her email listservs and the *Chronicle of Philanthropy*. Though much of the information doesn't help her, she does notice that Dave, a program officer at an area foundation that has previously funded her organization, has moved to a large foundation—and because it works in health areas, the new

foundation is on Iris's prospect list. Unfortunately, Dave is now in charge of grants for children's issues. Iris starts by calling someone she knows at Dave's old job to get his new number. She gives him a call, schmoozes a little, and then pops the key question: "Who's the best one to talk to about our needle exchange program?" Dave suggests Iris talk to Radhika, and gives Iris her direct line number. Bingo. And because Dave thinks Iris and her organization do good work, he volunteers to pave the way with Radhika. A couple of days later, Iris has a cordial conversation with Radhika, learns how to structure the grant to meet several explicit and not-so-explicit foundation guidelines, and receives funding.

Sometimes the first person you get on the phone may be an administrative support person or a receptionist. Don't treat this person as a low-level gatekeeper (though gatekeeping might indeed be part of his or her role). Your goal is to develop a long-term relationship with this and every other person in the foundation. Support staffers can be invaluable contacts later—for example, if you have a last-minute question, or need to know whether your proposal arrived by the deadline. In addition, if you needlessly alienate these frontline folks, your organization may develop a reputation for rudeness—one you never find out about, but that may come back to haunt you.

As shown in the example above, knowing a friend or colleague of a foundation staffperson can often be your password to a constructive conversation. This isn't simple nepotism (although sometimes it can also be that), but a reflection of the fact that all funders operate, at least in part, on trust. They don't want to spend their time—or, further down the line, a chunk of their foundation's money—without knowing that it's going to a legitimate, responsible organization. If the grants officer trusts someone who thinks your organization deserves attention, you have a solid reference—someone who says "this group is okay, there's no need for us to look for a quick excuse to hang up." (Of course, this will be harder to achieve when your organization is young.)

TIP

What if foundation guidelines prohibit phone calls? Many funding organizations' websites and printed materials warn applicants not to call about grants. But everyone answers the phone. In most cases, this rule really means that the foundation doesn't want unsolicited phone calls from strangers. If you've already done your detective work, preferably have been referred by a trusted intermediary, and have some real questions to ask, by all means give it a try. If the person hangs up on you, it won't set your group back (as long as you take the rejection graciously).

If one of your staff or board members knows someone at a funder's office, he or she may be the best person to make the initial call. Your E.D. is the next best bet. The development director is a reasonable choice too, but some grantmaking officers will take the E.D. more seriously.

The initial conversation should be brief and to the point: "Hello, my name is so-and-so, your colleague so-and-so suggested that I call you. I'm the [position] with [X] organization, and I'd like to talk with you a bit about our [X] program." Your opener shouldn't last longer than a minute. If the officer seems harassed or perhaps even hostile, ask if there is a better time for you to call. Assuming your initial verbal sally is well received, give a very brief overview of your program's purpose and goal—making sure to convey your enthusiasm about it. Then ask your specific questions. This should break the ice with all but the stuffiest grants officers.

If you can get the grants officer chatting, you have done your job. Remember, you're not applying for a grant on the spot. You'll rarely get an outright "no" to funding over the phone, unless your program doesn't fall within the foundation's guidelines, in which case now is the best time to find out. One of the good things about starting with a telephone call is that the person you're talking to probably doesn't have enough information to justify telling you that funding is impossible. By the same token, because a written proposal (or even a query letter, discussed under "The Proposal Process, From Query Letter Onward," below) is very easy to reject, calling first is a great way to introduce your request—and help ensure that it will receive some consideration once you submit it more formally.

If the conversation goes well, you and the officer might agree to meet, or you might be asked to submit a query letter. Meetings are usually held at the foundation offices, though in rarer cases the officer might start with a site visit. If you've got an exciting chance for the officer to come view what your organization is doing—such as Save The Bay's canoe outings, discussed in

Look Solid, But Needy

In any interaction with funders, consider what kind of impression you want to make. First and foremost, you want them to realize that you're a solid operation—not one that will take their money and patch up a few holes in your circus tent before folding it up and leaving town. On the other hand, you want them to know that you genuinely need the grant.

The first requirement is the harder to prove, because it depends partly on intangibles and things beyond your control, like your organization's reputation both on the street and behind the closed doors of the funding community. However, some things that will help bolster your professional and dependable appearance include:

- well-designed stationery (but don't use fancy paper)
- a compelling annual report (but avoid full-color and high gloss) (see Chapter 11)
- audited financial statements
- newspaper articles quoting or describing your organization
- a relatively up-to-date, engaging website (see Chapter 12), and
- letters of recommendation from those who have funded you in the past.

In your narrative, refer to evidence of your organization's good reputation, steady income, and staying power, such as "Our core funders, who include so-and-so and so-and-so, have been supporting us for [#] years."

Demonstrating that you need the money is the easier part. After all, what nonprofit couldn't use three or four times the amount it has? To distinguish your group, focus not on your abject need, but on how the foundation's funding will help your group meet a documented community need. If possible, also try to show how the grant will fill a particular project gap—something along the lines of "We have everything in place to make this a go except $xx." The bottom line is, you want to appear to be the most effective program to accomplish a goal that the funder strongly supports.

Chapter 6—this may even be a good time to extend the invitation (depending on the tenor of your conversation, of course). If you are invited to the foundation's offices, it's best to take two people along—a funding person, such as the E.D., development director, or board member, and a program person, who can describe how the funding will be used. This isn't much different from meeting with an individual supporter, as discussed in Chapter 6. You'll want to bring along written materials, such as your organization's brochure, annual report, project description, and budget.

At any meeting, whether at lunch, your program site, or the funder's office, you'll want to spend a fair amount of time listening. Try to find out what the grants officer's interests are, where he or she sees the greatest community needs, what types of program successes the officer gets particularly excited about, and the like. Also, remember that the officer probably doesn't have the last word on funding your organization (unless he or she is a senior officer and your grant application is small). If you submit a proposal and the officer likes it, he or she will probably have to present it to the foundation board or at least to their director for approval. This isn't entirely a bad thing; once a foundation staff person agrees to support your proposal, he or she will usually coach you on how to present it to the board. Hopefully, you can do this in a way that will actually strengthen your program, not turn it inside out just to fit the foundation's goals.

At the end of your meeting with foundation staff, you may be invited to submit a proposal. By now you understand that this is not your first step, as many novice fundraisers believe, but a milestone well on your way to your goal.

Keep Files to Track Funders

Your research process should be ongoing. Starting with the information you gather to submit your first proposals, you'll want to build a system that not only tracks the foundations that fund you, but also profiles those most likely to do so in the future. Anytime you read something of interest in the *Chronicle of Philanthropy* or your email listservs—such as a new grants officer, a new program focus, or a particular grant made to another organization—make a copy or printout for the appropriate file. Similarly, if you attend a social event and meet someone from a foundation on your A-list or someone who has relevant information about it, promptly enter all relevant facts in your database.

Although it may take time, eventually this attention to detail will help you develop an insider's view of your funding prospects and put you in a better position to plan and execute a targeted fundraising strategy.

As part of this process of keeping current, you'll want to do your best to maintain cordial relationships with grants officers—even those who haven't yet funded you! Jim Lynch of CompuMentor tells the following story: "I had developed a phone contact with an officer at the Crocker Foundation. Every year I called, to ask what they had going, and every year the officer told me that it wasn't a good fit. Finally, one year I called, and something did fit—and we got the grant! I think the officer was partly relieved to be able to give me some good news for once. All this had happened without the two of us having met. But when we finally did meet, we fell on each other like long-lost friends."

The Proposal Process, From Query Letter Onward

Lest you get overwhelmed by all the details of the grant application process, this section leads you through it step by step. Depending on the foundation's guidelines and preferences, your path to funding will probably include some combination of the following:

- a query letter
- a written grant proposal
- a site visit
- a presentation or meeting with the funder, and
- grant approval.

Query Letters

A query letter is often the first written communication between you and the funder (particularly if you're dealing with a foundation rather than the government). Other names for a query letter are "letter of interest" or "letter of inquiry" (LOI). The letter's purpose is to give the recipient foundation a quick sense of who you are and what you're seeking, and to find out whether you should take the next step in the proposal process. A sample query letter from a fictional organization is provided below.

Many foundations require you to submit a query letter as the first step in the funding process. In some instances, as discussed earlier in this chapter, the grants officer may have asked you to send a query letter. And, of course, there may be times when you have tried but failed to make personal contact, and decide to send a query letter as your next best alternative.

Before you fire up your word processor, find out whether the foundation publishes guidelines for the query letter (on its website or in its printed guidelines). If not, don't worry: Query letters are short (one to three pages) and follow a fairly standard format. But this doesn't mean you should dash yours off without careful thought. Even within the expected or required format, you can and should write an excellent letter—one that inspires the foundation and grants officer to ask for more information. Because your goal is to impress your readers, you shouldn't hold back good material to include as a "surprise" in the full grant proposal. Unless you highlight your best points in your query letter, you probably won't be invited to submit a full proposal.

The key elements of a query letter are:

- **Your purpose.** In the opening paragraph, give your organization's name and an overview of the reason for your letter: namely, to seek a particular amount of funding for a purpose or project that you briefly describe. Don't be coy—they are funders, and they expect people to ask for money. And don't beat around the bush when explaining why your proposal fits within the funder's mission and guidelines—explain directly how your project will help the funder further its own goals. You will also briefly want to establish that your organization will be able to accomplish the proposed project. To do this, it's helpful to mention the names and qualifications of key project staff. If someone in the foundation knows your organization and thinks well of it, this is also worth mentioning.

- **Who you are.** In the next paragraph, briefly describe your organization's mission, history, and current programs. Your focus should be on establishing your organization's credentials, in particular its ability to identify and meet community needs. If prominent board members have helped drive your efforts, mention their names.

- **Who or what needs your help.** Here you get to the heart of the matter: the community need that your organization seeks to address. Find the most powerful way to establish that a need exists, whether by statistical data, vivid examples, or both. Be precise about the who, what, and where of those you'll be serving, always looking for ways to tie your project to the foundation's purposes and the people it hopes to serve.

- **How you'll help.** Present a detailed and convincing account of what you'll be doing and how it will meet the stated community need. Explain how you'll measure the project's success. If you haven't already done so, this is a good place to include names and titles of the main project staff, who will bring your project to fruition.

- **Other supporters.** If you've gotten commitments from other grantors or donors, mention them here. You might also mention who else you'll be approaching for support.

- **A wrap-up.** Briefly recapitulate the goal of the project. If possible, briefly mention a few new facts, such as planned future steps or mutual contacts, and thank the potential funder for considering your request.

The letter should preferably be signed by your organization's executive director or board chairperson. Don't weigh it down with any attachments unless the foundation's guidelines request it. Send the letter by regular mail, not by fax or email.

Oakland African-American History Project
123 1st St.
Oakland, California

The California Historical Foundation
321 6th St.
San Francisco, California

Query Letter

Dear Ms. Officer:

I'm writing to you at the suggestion of your colleague Bob Everbuddy, who is familiar with our work at the Oakland African-American History Project. Our organization has, since 1995, taken the lead in collecting and cataloging the personal histories and documents of Oakland's African-American community. We are particularly interested in African-American migration to California during the late 1800s, when many came to work for the railroads. Our organization is currently seeking $65,000 to support a new project—interviewing the children of this migratory generation to preserve their oral histories, before their generation also passes into history. Given your foundation's special interest in collecting histories of California's diverse communities, we ask you to consider a full proposal for support of this project.

Our organization's mission is to preserve Oakland's African-American history, for the education of future generations as well as the inspiration of its existing African-American community. The enthusiasm and commitment of our Board members, including such community luminaries as [names], helps drive all our efforts.

We pay special attention to getting young people involved in our projects. In fact, a component of this new project will be to work with schools, churches, and youth groups to locate and train high-school-age volunteers to help out. With the historical information we collect, our staff and volunteers regularly prepare photo brochures and catalogs, and maintain an educational website. However, we do not maintain the collected materials at our offices, but rather place them with Oakland's public libraries and museums to ensure that they are preserved and made widely accessible to the public.

Without oral history projects such as the one we propose, personal perspectives on historical events are often lost forever. In fact, as earlier mentioned, we must act quickly to preserve the memories of the remaining members of this aging population. Our research specialist, Stella Amanuensis, Ph.D., has collected the names of over 30 potential interviewees, and believes there are at least as many more out there. However, the average age of these interviewees is 78 years, and some have significant health problems. In addition, the project will serve a secondary community need—to excite African-American high-school student volunteers about their community's history, and train them in historical research methods. Studies have shown that Oakland's high school students perform poorly in history as compared to other courses, and seldom study history in college.

Our plan is to have our staff and volunteers visit each interviewee at least three times, spending 90 minutes per visit. They will ask the interviewees questions about their early home life, stories their parents told them about where the family came from and why they left, family traditions and recreation, basic household economic issues such as what they ate, when and how they bought or made clothes, how many people shared living space, and more. We'll also focus on the steps migrants took to forge new community ties within the Oakland area, and how these ties have developed or changed over the years.

By the end of the project, we intend to have trained at least 10 volunteers, met with at least 35 interviewees, recorded the interviews on MiniDisc, and transcribed the interviews into hardcopy for public reading. We also plan to publish a paperback book containing photos and excerpts from the various interviews.

The $65,000 we intend to request from The California Historical Foundation will cover staff salaries, recording equipment, and promotion and incidental expenses associated with finding and visiting interviewees. In addition, we have a commitment of $5,000 from a board member to allow our ten most committed volunteers to attend a special oral history training seminar at a local college. A local printer has also agreed to produce the final publication at no cost.

The beauty of our proposed project is that it has both present and future benefits. In the short term, it will teach the student volunteers important research skills, help them understand and take pride in their place in history, and bring them in touch with an older generation. In the long term, it will gather important information about a critical time in African-American history, and make it available for this and future generations. Thank you for your interest in our project. We look forward to hearing from you.

Very truly yours,

Carter Pastime

Carter Pastime
Executive Director

Grant Proposals

The next step in the process—or in rare cases, the first step—is to submit a full grant proposal. A proposal usually contains a written narrative explaining who your organization is, the project for which it seeks funds, and the reasons why the project is important and will succeed. This narrative will be backed up by a budget, proof of your 501(c)(3) status, and other relevant attachments.

By this time, you should have obtained a set of guidelines and probably an application form from the funder. These will be your most important resources as you draft the proposal. The guidelines will specify the format, length, content, and documentation required. If the guidelines or form are more than a month or two old, check the funder's website or call to make sure the materials are current.

Start by carefully reading the guidelines, highlighting the most important information. Then, sit down in a quiet place and read them again. Do this even if the funder provides a checklist for you, and even if you have written a pile of grant applications. Too many grant applicants skim, rather than read, the guidelines; as a result, they submit proposals that are not exactly what the funder requested. And any little item you forget decreases your chances of getting funded. Foundations continue to report that many proposals don't get funded because the writer didn't follow the directions. If you take the time to really study the guidelines, your chances of success will materially increase.

TIP

Don't use a small type font to jam in extra material. As you try to fit the required content into the maximum number of pages, you may be tempted to use a ten-point font—even if the funder's guidelines asked for 12-point. This would be a mistake. The people who work at foundations have to read dozens of proposals and will immediately see what you are doing. They may even punish you for straining their eyesight, by setting your proposal aside. If you've got too many pages, edit your proposal ruthlessly to eliminate redundant and nonessential material.

With the guidelines as your main resource, use the information that follows to help:

- use the right tone and style
- respond to all requests for information, and
- polish your final draft and compose a cover letter.

Writing Style

Clear, communicative writing is important in almost every fundraising endeavor, but it's especially crucial when drafting grant proposals. Here are some tips to keep in mind:

- **Know what you want to say before you begin.** A surprising number of organizations whip out grant proposals without any sense of the program or project they're proposing. But, as professional grantwriter Susan Messina (based in Washington, DC) puts it, "You can't write what you don't know." Susan adds, "People forget that it's a two-step process; first you plan, then you write. Often I'm handed a proposal project where I have to go back to the organization and work with them on the details of program planning."

- **There's a human being at the other end.** In your effort to respond to the foundation's guidelines and to set a professional tone, it's easy to write a proposal that reads like a Master's thesis and is just as turgid. In addition to respecting the foundation's guidelines, remember that your audience is a real person who will surely appreciate it if you convey the passion and conviction you feel about your organization's work. This person wants, above all, to be inspired and moved—something that's easiest to accomplish if you are able to write directly and clearly.

- **Convey authority.** In addition to writing convincing and moving prose, you must also demonstrate that your organization can handle a seemingly overwhelming task. Try drawing the reader deep into the world your organization understands best. For example, if your work consists of assisting people in administrative hearings to claim disability benefits, make sure that the reader understands the expertise you've developed in analyzing doctors' reports, interpreting Social Security regulations, and coaching the applicants in preparation for their hearings. Also show your organization's business acumen—even using some business vocabulary may help show that your organization has a well-thought-out plan for success, understands how it stacks up against the competition, and is prepared to make good and efficient use of the funder's investment.

- **Use their jargon.** Every funder has its favorite words; ones like "authentic," "outcomes," or "personal empowerment." They've chosen these words because the meanings resonate for them. No need to confuse the issue by substituting your own words, such as "novel," "successes," or "self-sufficient." It's a good idea to identify the funder's key words and echo them back in the course of your proposal—just make sure not to overdo it, and always use the words in their proper context.

These tips may at times seem contradictory. But the beauty of writing is that you can, with a little practice, weave many strands of thought together into a cohesive and convincing whole. In the words of WID's Marisa Lianggamphai, "The more personal, yet professionally conversational I can make the proposal, the more likely I am to reach someone."

> **TIP**
>
> **Find a good editor.** There's not a writer in the world whose words can't use improving, or who will catch every last typo, ambiguity, or other glitch. Leave time for a talented writer within your organization, or even a freelancer, to review and edit your draft proposal.

Responding to the Standard Application Questions

A grant proposal may remind you of a college application, with questions that require you to write mini essays. Fortunately, as you gain experience, you'll see that most funders ask for similar information, which allows you to reuse good material you've written in the past. Funders usually ask for:

- a title page and table of contents
- an executive summary
- a background statement and/or list of your organization's qualifications
- a statement of community need

- a description of your project's grand goals or purpose
- a description of the project's more immediate objectives
- an action plan or project description
- a timeline
- an explanation of the methods by which you'll evaluate the project's success
- a budget (sometimes with line-item explanations)
- an explanation of where future funding will come from, and
- various attachments containing the facts necessary to convincingly back up your assertions.

> **CAUTION**
> **Don't get bogged down on the introductory sections.** According to professional grantwriter Susan Messina, "The number one mistake I see my nonprofit clients making is spending way too much time writing the perfect statement of who they are and what they've done. These issues are important, but what you really need is a program plan that makes sense, an evaluation plan that's rigorous, and a budget that's detailed and complete. These can be much harder than describing how fabulous you are as an organization."

Title Page and Table of Contents

The title page normally lists basic information like your organization's contact information and the project title. Give your project a name that's short and catchy, but still descriptive. The table of contents simply lists the various headings and page numbers. Be warned, however: Some funders count the title page and table of contents toward your page limit.

Executive Summary

The executive summary should outline all the key segments of your proposal, from background about your organization and a clear statement of the good work you hope to do, to your proposed solution. The summary shouldn't be more than two paragraphs long. You may even be able to use language from your query letter.

Background and Qualifications

Here's where you show that your organization is the best one for the job. Your mission, history, major programs, reputation, receipt of awards, and particular strengths may all be worthy of mention. If your organization has been around for a long time, emphasize its experience and ability to weather the tests of time. If your group is relatively new, emphasize how innovative, exciting, and responsive to current needs it is. Also name the key players in your organization and describe their qualifications, interests, and experience. For example, if your new E.D. just came on board after running a similar and noteworthy program in another part of the country, be sure to mention it. Even your physical facilities may be worth a mention—a state of the art research boat, learning lab, or health clinic, for example.

This can also be a good place to mention where you fit in with the "competition"—that is, with other organizations doing similar work. Understanding the competition has become an increasingly important concept in funding circles, so don't be squeamish about addressing it head-on. Funders will be most interested if you don't present your competition as groups to be elbowed out, but as worthy organizations working in a slightly different niche.

> **CAUTION**
>
> **Never badmouth another nonprofit.** Even if some of your competitors don't produce high-quality results, you have little to gain by pointing this out— except perhaps a reputation as a backstabber. If a competitor really is doing poor work, funders will figure it out fast enough on their own. This means it makes sense for your group to quietly position itself as a reliable alternative that can pick up the pieces, if necessary.

Statement of Community Need

The section on community need provides an excellent opportunity to establish your organization's professionalism. Though the community need may seem very real and obvious to you, it's probably much less so to a busy foundation officer inundated by other "crucially needed" funding proposals. In short, you'll want to describe exactly what the need is—and what the consequences are of not acting promptly to meet it. One way to do this is to run all your statements through the "so what" test. For example, "There are no suicide prevention hotlines in our city" may seem like an important need to you—but a "so-what" skeptic might ask whether such hotlines actually make a difference, or whether callers can simply use national hotlines instead. So to really rivet the funding officer's attention, take your explanation one step deeper, and express the need like this: "Citizens of River City who might call the suicide hotline we hope to establish have absolutely no other access to this highly effective method of suicide prevention. As a result, many deaths will occur that our program could help avoid."

Statistics, results of reliable studies, other information from neutral sources, and your own organization's surveys should all be assembled and presented concisely and coherently to support your assertion of need. Depending on the funder's guidelines, you may want to add charts or graphs within the text, or as attachments at the end.

Especially if yours is a local or regional organization, finding recent and appropriate statistics can be a challenge. But with a little imagination, you can usually patch together credible numbers. For example, if you're working to straighten out drug-involved youth, it may be impossible to say how many kids abuse drugs in your area. But you can find out the number of teenagers in your area and the percentage who didn't complete high school, which is a significant indicator of drug-related problems. To this you might add the percentage of kids in the country as a whole (and possibly in your state) who regularly use drugs, and perhaps a quote from a local high school principal pointing out that local teenage drug use is a serious problem.

If no numerical or statistical information is available, you'll have to fill this section in with more anecdotal material—but make a note to ask your program leadership to put more effort into finding ways to quantify the need for your services for future proposals.

RESOURCE

The U.S. Census is still one of the best sources of statistical information. Check it out online at www.census.gov.

Project Goals or Purpose

The purpose or goal of your project should be presented broadly and optimistically. To do so, answer this question—if all goes well, what will our organization have achieved? For example, "reduce teen drug addiction" is a goal or purpose; "provide counseling" is not. Don't get too lofty, however. While working to save Riverfront County's historical buildings is a measurable and realizable goal, "saving the world" is neither. Also make sure your goals are consistent with your mission statement.

Objectives

In your "objective" statement, you tell the funder exactly what you plan to use its grant money to accomplish. Objectives should be tangible, and should include numerical targets and other signs of success. An example might be "provide job training and counseling that helps 40 developmentally disabled youth develop and market their skills."

In picking hard numbers, it's well to follow the old adage "underpromise and overperform." Otherwise, you may find that your organization can't achieve the goal you set, no matter how hard and effectively it works. For example, if you were to say, "provide job training and counseling that results in 40 developmentally disabled youth finding jobs," you may have given your program staff an impossible task, especially if the job market turns sour. That's why I recommend that program staff carefully review the objectives section of your proposal to make sure you have chosen realistic milestones that will also satisfy the funder.

Another reason to beware of choosing overly optimistic numerical goals is that they can actually result in your organization taking on only the "easy" cases, because the tougher ones are less likely to show measurable results. I know this trap all too well, from my experience working at a nonprofit that helped immigrants. Our clients included people who'd fled persecution in many of the world's most violent regions. To stay alive, they needed to obtain political asylum in the U.S. We could never predict how many cases would be granted—that depended on multiple factors, such as how talkative and convincing an often traumatized client was, whether a doctor could confirm the client's experience of torture and other mistreatment, and the attitudes and prejudices of the immigration officer who decided the case. Yet, until we got wise to dealing with objectives, our promises to some funders included "political asylum gained for ten clients," and the like. If we had succeeded in only seven cases as we neared the end of the funding year, the pressure was on to find at least three more likely winners.

Some funders will accept outcome measurements based simply on your organization carrying out the steps in its action plan—for example, giving five workshops or meeting with 50 clients. Others will insist that your outcomes relate to your overall goals, such as protecting a natural resource, establishing a cultural center, or opening a recreational facility for elderly veterans. Even in these latter cases, however, a little creativity may yield a way to style your outcomes conservatively. In the job training for developmentally challenged youth example, you might promise to serve 40 youth, but predict job placement for only 20 of them. Incidentally, we eventually followed a similar approach with our immigrant services project, by explaining to one funder that our goal was to take on a certain number of the most challenging cases requiring such a high level and investment of legal expertise that the clients probably would likely be rejected elsewhere. By first establishing the difficulty of our task, we were then able to show that the number of people served and the number of cases won were impressive.

> **TIP**
>
> **If possible, promise more results than the funder's money will cover.**
> Many projects have multiple funders, or include money or in-kind contributions from individuals. If you're in this situation, never hesitate to set projected outcome at the total project level, not just for the donor's portion. Funders will be pleased to see that you plan to enhance the bang for their buck.

Action Plan or Methods

The action plan (also called the "methods" section) is the most fun part of the proposal. Here, you get to bring your organization's work to life. To do this, explain what, when, and why your organization has chosen particular activities to meet its goals and objectives. And don't forget to mention behind-the-scenes aspects of the work, like staff training or client selection.

The "what" and "when" of your work are the easiest, because these will summarize your daily activities, such as establishing curricula, planning field trips, mounting events, and explaining how staff will interact with clients or the public. If you aren't asked to include a project timeline elsewhere, you'll also want to fit that in here.

For the "why" of your activity, avoid repeating the old "need plus your project equals success" equation. Instead, explain why your chosen approach was elected over other possibilities. For example, if you've found that your antibullying project works best if you arrange group sessions with the children away from the school campus, explain this. This helps show your organization's expertise and thoughtful approach. Also, be sure to give the project staff credit for any challenges they've learned to overcome—past failures can be advertised as important learning experiences! Make your plan sound effective without making it sound easy.

Timeline

You'll no doubt be asked for a project timeline, whether in a separate section or as part of the action plan. This is fairly self-explanatory. Don't feel that you have to wrap the project up by the end of the funding cycle, but be prepared to say what you will have achieved by that time, and what milestones you expect to reach along the way.

Evaluation Methods

Providing a solid explanation of how you'll evaluate the results of your project affords you another chance to set your organization apart from the rest. Foundations are used to a certain "flake factor" in this area—a mushiness about accounting for results. They also know that many nonprofits regard data collection as a bothersome task that's imposed upon them by foundations. (See, for example, "Creating a Culture of Inquiry: Changing methods—and minds—on the use of evaluation in nonprofit organizations," a report by the James Irvine Foundation, downloadable at www.irvine.org.) This means that if you can propose a serious and effective system of project evaluation and outcome reporting, you are likely to really impress your readers.

Unfortunately, it's not easy to achieve tight, accurate evaluation and reporting. Nonprofits tackle some of the toughest, most intractable problems society has to offer. They're not like businesses that can tell their shareholders, "We sold 400,000 wombits, hired 200 new workers, and increased profits by 200%!" So how do you shine in this tough endeavor? If you've been more realistic in establishing objectives, your task of evaluating the project as a success will be easier—but may at the same time be more labor intensive, because you'll likely have to do more than just present raw numbers of people fed, books read, or acres of land preserved.

Creating methods for evaluating your projects will require input and cooperation from program staff. It's not something that you, as the proposal writer, can simply dream up. But working together, and depending to some extent on what your organization does, you usually will want to choose from a couple of broad evaluation methods.

One is to keep the focus on what you did, reporting on numbers of people served or tasks accomplished. If you adopt this approach, you shouldn't have too much trouble developing a systematic and reliable method of data-gathering. (See Chapter 2 for resources on developing a computer database for this purpose.) Even if you don't have sophisticated technological capabilities, you can still point to a well-organized office system and set of written records, typically including forms completed by clients, schedules of meetings, your employee supervision system, minutes of board meetings, and the like.

Your other main evaluation alternative is to focus more subjectively, by trying to answer the question, "How did we do?" This could involve as simple a method as passing out evaluation forms to your clients, trainees, or participants in activities. Such an approach might be particularly appropriate in a setting where you aren't working with people over the long term, or toward a major life turnaround. If, for example, you go to high schools and show an antismoking videotape, the funder may be less interested in how many kids sat (or slept) in a darkened classroom than in how they reacted to your message. Of course, you can and often should mix and match numerical and judgmental evaluation methods, as appropriate. For example, the funder would certainly be interested in knowing that you showed the videotape in more than one classroom, to more than one student.

RESOURCE

Want more information on evaluation techniques? To learn more about selecting realistic results measurements and methods where none seem possible, see:

- *The Grantseeker's Guide to Project Evaluation,* by Jacqueline Ferguson (Capitol Publications)

- **"Three Funders: Process or Outcome?"** Foundation News & Commentary, vol. 37 (March-April 1996): pp. 46–8

- **"Basic Guide to Program Evaluation," and "Basic Guide to Outcomes-Based Evaluation for Nonprofit Organizations with Very Limited Resources,"** both by Carter McNamara, M.B.A., Ph.D, available online at www.managementhelp .org/evaluatn/fnl_eval.htm and http://www.managementhelp.org/evaluatn /outcomes.htm, respectively.

Budget and Budget Narrative

The person reading your proposal is likely to turn to the budget section first. Never mind all your fancy explanations: It's the raw numbers that many of them feel tell the real story. Though you'll probably be asking for a nice round number, you'll have to show more precisely how you arrived at this figure and how this money will be spent.

Often the funder will provide a budget form or format. Usually, the breakdown will include salaries, office and other project supplies, and a miniscule amount for administrative overhead (usually no more than 15%). Your project budget should reflect not only new expenses, but also existing costs for staff (at full time or a percentage of their time), supervision, office space, and the like. If the funder to whom you're applying isn't going to be the project's only source of funds, you should list other prospective or actual grantors, as well as in-kind donations such as volunteer time. Funders are always delighted to see that their financial input will be leveraged in these ways, especially if your individual donors will cover administrative expenses so that all foundation money can go directly to programs.

> **TIP**
>
> **Think big.** I asked the former head of one of America's most prestigious foundations what he considered to be a grant applicant's biggest mistake. "Asking for too little," he immediately responded. "Once you sell a foundation on the worthiness of your proposal and your ability to carry it out, it's only logical that most will want it to be bigger, not smaller."

I'm assuming that you are not your office's chief budgeteer, and that someone in the accounting department will actually run the numbers, after consultation with you and with program staff. Just be sure to give this person plenty of advance warning! And remember to consult with both your program staff and your accountant to arrive at a consensus about how much money is realistically required and what the numbers mean.

Many funders will ask not only for columns of numbers, but for a narrative explanation as well. Having consulted with program staff, you should be ready to do this in a way that brings your numbers to life for the potential funder. Along the way, be sure to explain any expenses that might seem unusual, and highlight any ways that you've managed to keep costs down. Keep it short: You don't need to rehash issues like the overall need for the project.

> **RESOURCE**
>
> **Want additional help with your budget?** Check out the Foundation Center's tutorial on developing a project budget for grant proposal purposes, at http://fdncenter.org (click "Get Started," then "proposal writing" (under "Learn About"), then "Proposal Budgeting Basics").

Future Funding Sources

More and more funders want to make sure that they're not just going to create a bubble project—one that will burst as soon as its funding stops, without having achieved anything. And, given that renewals are anything but guaranteed (especially because of the current penchant among foundations for funding new, innovative, start-up, or pilot projects), this should be a real concern for your organization as well. (The exception, of course, would be if you truly are proposing a project with a limited time span, such as restoring a community fountain.) Hopefully your leadership has thought ahead about the sustainability of the project you're proposing and how it fits into your overall strategic plan.

Of course, you can hardly guarantee where this year's funding will come from, much less next year's. Your best bet when writing the proposal is to describe your carefully constructed development plan (see Chapter 3). You might also mention the development office's record of success—for example, that you've increased individual contributions in the past year or years and can project continued success in this area. If you can name particular funders that you believe are likely to fund the proposed project in the future, great—but don't just toss names around. More likely, you'll simply want to describe the types of funding, whether from foundations, individuals, or others, that you'll be trying to obtain.

Attachments

Most funders will require supporting documents to accompany your grant proposal—at a minimum, a copy of the IRS letter proving your 501(c)(3) status. Though these may come at the end of the proposal, don't wait until the last minute to look at the funder's requirements. For example, an innocent-looking form may require you to assemble names of influential people willing to serve on a project advisory committee, which can take weeks or months to accomplish. And, if you're applying to the federal government, the attachments will dwarf the narrative part of the grant proposal, and require input from program staff and others.

You may also be permitted to attach documents of your own choosing. Your brochure and latest annual report may be relevant and helpful. Strong and convincing letters of support from funders, city officials, or other influential people can be particularly helpful. Such letters should describe your track record on past projects and express the letterwriter's great confidence in your ability to carry out future projects. Depending on your field of work, you could also get letters of support from other figures of authority, such as someone in the administration of a hospital or school with which you're affiliated. Such letters won't arrive on your doorstep spontaneously—you'll have to ask for them. This is an accepted and traditional practice, however, so your friends and funders should not be surprised to hear from you. In fact, many of them will be pleased that you are applying for additional money to expand your programs.

TIP

To reduce bulk, refer the funders to materials on your website.
Your annual report, media coverage, Form 990, and other materials may all
be available on your website—and your funder may well appreciate reducing the
amount of written material that lands on their desk. Find out their preferences
in advance, but then consider using technology to slim down your submission.

Final Preparation and Cover Letter

The last few steps in preparing your grant proposal are too easily forgotten.
First, run your proposal past the executive director and anyone else who needs
to approve it (you certainly don't want to have to amend it after it's submitted).
You'll also want to include a short, optimistic cover letter addressed to the
appropriate program officer or other contact person, and typically signed by
your E.D. Refer to any past grants or positive history with the funder. Make
sure that the letter indicates who in your organization the funder should
contact for questions, follow-up, and its response. Provide that person's direct
line phone number and email address. When the proposal is in final form, copy
it for your files.

Though I could tell you to plan ahead so you won't be working on the
proposal until the last possible minute, that's the sort of advice that rarely
changes anyone's behavior (including my own). If you are able to get things in
before the deadline, however, you've got an advantage—foundations think of the
deadline as the "last possible day," not as a simple due date, and are delighted to
have an opportunity to read a package that comes in before the flood.

CAUTION

If you're a latenik, research mailing options in advance. Create a list
with the addresses and hours of all U.S. Post Offices, Federal Express, or other
delivery offices, and put it on your bulletin board. There's nothing worse than
finally packaging up your proposal on the eve of the deadline, realizing you've
missed the closing time at the nearest post office, and making frantic calls as
evening turns into night.

Site Visits

A site visit is just what it sounds like—one or more people from the prospective funder's office schedule a visit to your program site to see for themselves what's going on. Usually this happens after your proposal has been received by the funder and gone through one or more layers of review. If your prospective funder requires or is willing to make a site visit, let out a cheer! This is one of those "picture is worth a thousand words" opportunities—and it indicates that your proposal is under serious consideration.

Grant Din, Executive Director of Asian Neighborhood Design (www.andnet .org), can testify to the great opportunity a site visit gives your organization: "Back when I worked as a grants officer at a foundation that had very limited funds, I well remember how heart-wrenching it was to say no to a good project after a site visit. Perhaps we weren't cutthroat enough, but we sometimes ended up giving out many small grants just to avoid rejecting a group outright. Now, as a nonprofit E.D., I do everything I can think of to get funders to visit us. Besides the usual query letters and personal contacts, we like to hold open houses, for example, when we launch a new training program. Our invitation list includes not only current grantors and donors, but prospective future funders as well. And it works—our success rate at getting a grant after a site visit is very high."

The site visit will be scheduled in advance. So don't worry that a black limo will pull up full of people wearing white gloves—you'll have time to plan. If possible, try to schedule the visit for a time when your organization is at its most active, seeing clients or engaging in field work. You want to give the visitor a hands-on experience, to the extent possible. Your chances of success go up if they can meet your clients, handle an art project, savor a tomato in your community garden, or do anything else that involves something other than talking to the E.D. and meeting board members. Remember, you've already engaged their minds with the grant proposal—now is the time to more fully engage their hearts. If the most interesting work of your organization isn't at its central office, then take the visitors where the action is (unless it's a wilderness trek, a toxic dump site, or some other dangerous or messy spot).

Advise all program staff and any relevant clients of who's coming, and ask staff to tidy up their workspaces. Also ask staff members or clients to be ready to talk to the visitors about their activities and, if appropriate, to do a "show and tell" presentation—with the emphasis on "show."

But keep things low-key. The visitors want to see your site as it really functions, not turned into a theater. Foundation officers say that one of the biggest mistakes nonprofits make during site visits is putting on a show rather than engaging in business as usual. Ron Rowell, a program officer with the San Francisco Foundation, told me, "Having worked in the nonprofit sector myself, I understand the urge to stage things for the funders' benefit. But now that I'm in the foundation world, the most important thing to me at a site visit is honesty. If all I hear is that everything is just peachy, one success after another, I start to worry about what's really going on."

On the other hand, foundation officers tend to like it when the organization doesn't spend all its time passively waiting to be judged, but actively asks the foundation officers what they're interested in, how their proposal can be improved, and the like. (In fact, if the site visit is conducted before your written proposal goes in, this is an ideal chance to pick up some tips on how to present the relevant information most effectively.)

When the visitors arrive, the executive director should take the lead in showing them around. Make sure you've got enough clean mugs ready to offer coffee or tea. Depending on how long they'll be staying, snacks or a light lunch might also be appropriate. Most site visits last from two to three hours.

> **TIP**
> **Out-of-town site visitors need more attention.** Though they'll probably book airplane and hotel reservations on their own, you'll want to be ready with several recommendations if asked. Be sure you supply detailed directions to your facility, and tips on good restaurants and entertainment. There is usually no need to be a tour guide, but be ready to suggest or join in on dinner plans if appropriate.

Meetings With the Funder

Some funders will ask members of your organization to come to their offices for a formal presentation or question-and-answer session. Again, this is a good sign, and a grand opportunity to put a human face on your work. Make sure to find out exactly who will be at the meeting—it may or may not be your main contact person. The United Way, for example, brings in volunteers who help decide what gets funded. Though the volunteers are briefed beforehand, they'll require a lot more background and introductory information than a foundation staffperson with whom you've been in contact for years.

Be careful in choosing who will attend this meeting—the proposal will be judged, in part, by the personality of the person or persons attending. A foundation officer once told me that he was quicker to grant money to an average project with good leadership than to a great-sounding project with leaders who didn't inspire confidence.

Though the executive director should definitely attend the meeting, there will probably be room for some additional people. Ironically enough, the development person who wrote the proposal may not be the best one to go along, because foundations often regard development staff as hired-gun salespeople. A program person is usually the best choice—someone who is actually doing the work and can articulate, passionately and in colorful detail, what it involves. If your program person isn't used to such activities, sit down with him or her beforehand. Work together on organizing a short presentation, if one is required or expected. Often the program person takes the lead here, relating events from his or her own working experience: how a client was helped, how an arts project was received by the public, how a research project was undertaken, and the like.

The Funding Decision

After more time than you'd probably like—usually from three months to a year after you submitted your proposal—you'll receive an answer. If months have passed and you haven't heard anything, it's okay to call your contact person to check in.

If the funding decision is negative, the E.D. may want to call and politely ask why. Not all foundations will be candid about why you were turned down, but if they are, it's important to listen carefully to the answer and not argue. Remember, a "no" doesn't mean you'll never be funded by this funder. It may be that your proposal didn't quite fit the mix of grants the foundation was trying to achieve or that they misinterpreted some element of your proposal for some reason that would never occur to you. Either way, be alert for information that will help you approach them next time.

If the decision is positive, congratulations! This is one of those moments that makes the stress and long nights of fundraising worthwhile. Be loud about your joy. Board members and staff can always use some good news, and will be especially gratified if they had any hand in preparing the proposal or in supplying the information that went into it. If it's a truly substantial grant, or will fund something that's story-worthy, consider trying to get some local media coverage (see Chapter 13). The funder may be willing to help in this effort.

And don't forget to thank the funder! Many development pros make it a habit to send out a thank-you letter before even cashing the check. In addition, having your E.D. or board chair call the funder to say "thanks" offers a good opportunity to get feedback that may help you craft your follow-up reports. In particular, try to solicit information about which part of your proposal was most persuasive and what could have been done to make it even better. Don't skip this important step! There's no better time to get constructive feedback about how to improve your proposal writing than when everyone is in a good mood.

TIP

If your overall funding falls short, try to renegotiate the terms of the grant. Nonprofits will often approach more than one foundation simultaneously, asking each to pitch in enough to reach the total needed for the project. However, if some foundations say "yes" and others "no" to your grant request, what do you do? It's rare that a nonprofit would have to decline the grant money in such circumstances. Your first choice is to ask the foundation or foundations who approved your request to grant a bit more to cover the shortfall. If that doesn't work, ask them to accept a scaled-down version of the project, or reduced outcomes.

Follow Up With the Funder

As you surely know, your grant work doesn't end when you deposit the check. All funders follow up, to find out how their money has been spent and what results it has achieved. As soon as you've got the grant paperwork in hand, make sure that the people in your organization understand their role in this process. Program people will typically need to track their activities and outcomes for progress reports. Your accounting department may need to track expenses, particularly if the funder operates on a reimbursement basis. Someone will have to set aside time on the calendar for drafting a progress report. Though these reports won't be as time consuming as the initial grant proposal, they often ask for similar information.

If progress reports are to be drafted by a program person, make sure that a development staffperson or the E.D. gives it a thorough review before it goes out the door. The object is to scrutinize the report to make sure that promises made in the grant proposal are being kept, or at least that there's an explanation for any changes to the action plan. It's also important that your organization speak with a consistent voice.

This required follow-up should not be pushed to the back burner. Maintaining strong and cordial relationships with funders is crucially important. Not only are you more likely to get a grant renewal if your reports are well-organized and timely, but demonstrating your ability to perform may also result in a number of other benefits. For example, the foundation may feature your organization on its website or in its annual report. In addition, a foundation that sponsors donor-advised funds may recommend your organization to individual donors looking for a group that fits their philanthropical inclinations. And, last but not least, because funders talk to each other, your reputation can be burnished or tarnished on the basis of your follow-through.

Beyond just complying with the funder's reporting requirements, think of ways you can use your reports to increase their interest and involvement. Start by treating the contact person at the foundation as you would an important individual donor—who appreciates receiving the occasional positive news clipping about your work or even an invitation to participate. For example, the Zen Hospice Project invites foundation representatives to its monthly donor

Women's Studio Workshop Uses Regular Letters to Reach Funders

The Women's Studio Workshop (WSW) is an artist's residency and educational program located in idyllic Rosendale, New York (in the Mid-Hudson River Valley). While WSW already provides visiting women artists with studio and living space in which to explore their voices and visions, its ambitions go beyond this—they'd like to routinely pay women a reasonable wage to come to WSW and do art. To this end, foundation funding has been an important resource. In particular, the Andy Warhol Foundation for the Visual Arts has offered WSW significant support.

As Anita Wetzel, Development Director, describes the course of WSW's relationship with the Warhol Foundation, "WSW had received a good-sized grant from Warhol in 1992. In 1998 a two-year award from the foundation helped us make a big leap forward, increasing the number of funded opportunities we could offer artists. In 2002, WSW received another two-year grant to fund artists working at WSW.

"Part of the reason we got this most recent grant may have been that I'd been sending the Warhol Foundation and our other major funders regular letters—about once every three months—telling them what's been happening. For example, my letters might talk about an international artist spending time with us, or describe a session of the Arts-In-Education program, where kids from Kingston City Schools come and develop their art skills. In fact, the program officer remarked on the letters when she came to visit.

"It's funny, because no one ever told me to start writing these letters. Like many people, I happened into fundraising because I wanted to make our project happen. But I had come to realize that you need to reach out to anyone giving you a significant amount of money. And, I enjoy writing the letters—it's a chance to tell people what we think is interesting and important, instead of always just answering the questions on their required reports. Also, by writing regularly, I can highlight colorful information before we've moved on to the next project and forgotten the details."

lunches, an informal event at which volunteer caregivers often share their experiences before they tour the residential house. Also see "Women's Studio Workshop Uses Regular Letters to Reach Funders," above.

> **TIP**
>
> **While things are going well, ask for a letter of recommendation from your funder.** A generic letter of recommendation from an influential funder can be very useful when you apply for other funding. The best time to ask for this is after you have submitted several progress reports detailing how you are successfully spending the funder's money.

Grant Renewals

Putting "renewals" in the title of this section is a bit misleading, because only a minority of foundation grants come with any expectation of a renewal (or in nonprofit lingo, "re-upping" the grant). In fact, many funders specifically prefer that after your one-, two-, or even five-year grant period is completed, you go elsewhere for subsequent funding. Though you may be lucky enough to locate a funder who makes a tradition of long-term support, such funders are getting more and more rare. Nevertheless, having invested time and effort in educating the funder about your work, it's worth inquiring whether a new grant is a possibility.

Even though re-upping may be difficult to accomplish with a particular funder, it may nevertheless be easier than finding a new funding source. By now, you have the advantage of personal contact with someone in the funder's office. For a one-year grant, the time to bring this up is no longer than nine months into your grant, when things are hopefully going well but you're not yet desperate about how you'll continue. Have a frank talk with your contact person. Ask for his or her views on whether the foundation might be interested in funding continuation of your program or another part of your activities.

The funder may require that your next proposal contain something new and different. (In fact, you should be ready with some ideas before holding any conversations.) Finding or creating something new to propose can be tricky, especially if you provide ongoing services that don't culminate in anything. This is one of those times when you need to be especially wary of letting the funding stream determine the program—altering or expanding your services just to get a grant can lead to trouble down the line. But realize that not everything about your proposed activities needs to be new. The funder may be happy to support a new phase of your program, an increased focus on the needs of certain members of your clientele, a collaborative effort encompassing existing services, or a heightened need for your services due to new legislation or social or environmental pressures.

If the funder truly can't support your organization any longer, ask for recommendations to other funders. Don't forget to take down the names and telephone numbers of the contact people!

RESOURCE

More information on the grant process. For more extensive, well-written information on researching, preparing, and submitting grant proposals, see the following resources:

- **The Foundation Center's website** at http://fdncenter.org.
- *Secrets of Successful Grantsmanship: A Guerrilla Guide to Raising Money,* by Susan L. Golden (Jossey-Bass). You'll find much helpful guidance here on researching and developing relationships with foundations.
- *Storytelling for Grantseekers: The Guide to Creative Nonprofit Fundraising,* by Cheryl A. Clarke (Jossey-Bass). This book places special emphasis on developing a compelling narrative for your proposal.

Creating Printed Communications Materials

Every organization needs certain printed materials on hand—such as a well-written, professional-looking brochure—to educate the public about its mission and activities. Newsletters and annual reports are also great for this purpose. And because these materials are not designed primarily as fundraising tools, they can have great credibility with your current and potential supporters. Once you have an attractive, up-to-date publication, you can send it to existing supporters, use it to inspire new ones, and hand it to people you meet at conferences, meetings, or fundraising events. Like a businessperson handing out his or her card, these publications are an instant way of showing that your organization is ready to be taken seriously.

Although producing a high-quality brochure should be well within the reach of virtually every nonprofit, creating newsletters and annual reports can be far more time-consuming and costly. The audience for these publications often expects something with higher production values than the everyday letter— although most donors aren't looking for something as slick and costly as your average corporate report. So if you're on a bare-bones budget, you'll do just fine producing these items using decent page layout software (such as PageMaker), supplemented by a copy machine and stapler. But if you have the financial resources, a modest investment in professional design and print services can be well worth the expense.

This chapter covers:

- brochures
- newsletters, and
- annual reports.

 RESOURCE

For more detailed information: See *Every Nonprofit's Guide to Publishing: Creating Newsletters, Magazines & Websites People Will Read,* by Cheryl Woodard & Lucia Hwang (Nolo).

How a Newsletter Paid for Itself

Kate McNulty, then with Sacred Heart Cathedral Preparatory School, described this "happy ending" to the school's production of its newsletter. "We've been putting out a newsletter to our donors reporting on how our capital campaign to fund the new Student Life Center is going. The newsletter itself costs a couple of thousand dollars to produce, and contains investor profiles, a construction report with photographs, and a fundraising update. After we sent the last newsletter out, one of our major supporters took an interest in one of the naming opportunities we listed. He pledged $15,000, and in recognition will have his name on one of our Campus Ministry Offices. He had been cultivated and asked earlier in the campaign for a gift, but it was the newsletter that clearly tipped the scales—and thereby paid for itself."

Brochures

As emphasized above, every organization should have an up-to-date brochure on hand. You simply don't want to be in the room when a prominent visitor or potential supporter asks for more information about your organization and you're caught empty-handed.

Your brochure should explain what your organization is and what it does. It should include information on:

- why your organization was founded and continues to exist (your basic mission, but spelled out in compelling language)
- what activities your organization currently carries out to address your mission
- your organization's hopes and plans for the near future
- how your organization is funded, and
- how readers can become involved or make contributions.

The simplest brochure is an 8½" by 11" piece of paper folded into thirds, which gives you six panels to fill with text and graphics. It's even smarter to use an 8½" by 14" sheet of legal-sized paper folded into fourths, which creates eight panels. Either size allows you to turn the right-most panel into a tear-off reply or donation card. But with the larger version, a professional can do something even snazzier—attach a tear-off reply envelope.

Because you want your brochure to have a reasonably long shelf life, you should include only general information about your group. Avoid adding dates or detailed descriptions of time-specific projects that will soon be in your rear-view mirror. Instead, focus on continuing programs and long-term results. Keep the text short and snappy—bold headings and bullet points will make your points far better than long-winded explanations. Photos are also an excellent way of giving readers an instant understanding and appreciation of your work.

The brochure is also a good place to provide key information for people who might need to contact or make use of your organization—perhaps your address and phone number, website address, hours of operation, a map to your facilities, fees for services or admission, and the like.

> **TIP**
>
> **Hiring a freelance designer can be a bargain.** Like a well-designed tool, vehicle, or building, a visually pleasing brochure will be far more attractive and effective than a slapdash one that's thrown together without much thought or skill. In just a few hours, a freelance design professional can turn an amateurish effort into something you can be proud of.

Below are some sample pages from an elegant and effective brochure, from the Haas-Lilienthal House in San Francisco. You'll see the front page, which shows an attractive photo and the necessary contact information, as well as the tear-off membership/donation page. Note that this page points out both the importance of donations and the various benefits to which membership entitles the donor.

Haas-Lilienthal House Brochure

The Haas-Lilienthal House

Photo © Douglas Keister

A property of
San Francisco Architectural Heritage
City Landmark No. 69
National Register of
Historic Places

2007 Franklin Street
San Francisco, CA 94109

House Information Phone: 415.441.3004
SF Heritage Phone: 415.441.3000
House Rental Phone: 415.441.3011
Fax: 415.441.3015
Email: info@sfheritage.org
Web Site: www.sfheritage.org

MEMBERSHIP REPLY CARD

Become a Member – San Francisco Architectural Heritage depends on membership dues and contributions to support its education and conservation activities. Membership and donations are tax deductible.

Benefits include:
- Our bi-monthly newsletter, *Heritage News*
- Free admission for you and your guests to the Haas-Lilienthal House, and on regularly scheduled walking tours
- Free admission to the Holiday Open House
- A 20% discount on educational events and book store items
- Advance invitation to special events

JOIN TODAY!

Yes! I'd like to join!
Please sign me up at the following level:

☐ $45 Senior/Student
☐ $60 Individual
☐ $75 Family
☐ $125 Supporting Member
☐ $250 Contributing Member
☐ $500 Sustaining Member

Name

Address

City/State/Zip

Phone/Fax/Email

We accept checks, VISA, MasterCard and American Express. If paying by credit card:

Account Number   Expiration Date

Signature

Tax exempt status: Heritage is exempt from Federal income tax under Section 501 (c)(3) of the Internal Revenue Code and has been classified by the IRS as a public foundation. Heritage is exempt from California State franchise or income tax under Section 2370 (d) Revenue and Taxation Code.

Please return to: San Francisco Heritage, Attn: Membership, 2007 Franklin Street, San Francisco, CA 94109

Designed by: PTI, Printers for Nonprofits
Reprinted with permission

Newsletters

Many nonprofits send out regular newsletters as a way to communicate with their supporters. Although newsletters take a fair amount of money and effort to produce, they can provide a series of ongoing tugs designed to pull donors toward deeper engagement with your organization. Your newsletter can take many forms, but probably the most common consists of three to four double-sided 8½" x 11" pages, sent out from one to four times per year, containing photos and substantive stories about your organization and its work. Wealthier organizations might produce a magazine, complete with a glossy cover. More and more organizations now send their newsletter by both print and email. Encouraging your supporters to choose the email option can be a great way to save print costs, but it also means that fewer people will actually read it—after all, it's hard for subscribers to put an electronic newsletter in their backpack or on their kitchen table to read at their leisure.

While one person in your organization—or, if you can afford it, a cost-efficient freelancer—should edit your newsletter, the articles can be written by anyone. In fact, writing newsletter articles makes a fun—and educational—project for board members and other volunteers with the necessary skills. Take a look at other organizations' newsletters to see what types of format and content appeal to you. The first pages of some eye-catching ones are shown below. One is from WildCare Marin, a California organization that provides care for ill, orphaned, or injured wild animals (www.wildcaremarin.com). The other is from Environment California, which focuses on protecting California's air, water and open spaces, by speaking out and taking action at the local, state, and national levels. (See www.environmentcalifornia.org.)

The stories in your newsletter don't have to sound like they were written by hard-nosed reporters—a certain degree of hominess is okay, as long as your pieces are interesting, timely, and appropriate. For example, your taxpayers' rights organization might appropriately run a story about waste in the mayor's office, but not a board member's long poem about freedom. Take a look at Chapter 13 for information on what the professional media considers a worthwhile, attention-grabbing story. It also helps to keep your newsletter's mission in mind. For example, is it meant to update people about what's

Newsletters From WildCare and Environment California

Winter 2005

WILDCARE

TERWILLIGER NATURE EDUCATION AND WILDLIFE REHABILITATION

Whoooo's News

ENVIRONMENT CALIFORNIA
Clean air. Clean water. Open spaces.

Fall Report

Taking clean energy to Capitol Hill

Getting D.C. to follow states' clean energy leadership

Americans know it's time for clean energy. Scientists and innovators have proven that our potential for renewable energy is unlimited. California and other states have proven that the political will is there. A country with a track record of setting ambitious goals and reaching them—like sending a man to the moon—surely has the ability to shift to clean energy.

Bolstered by advances at the state level, Environment California is pushing Congress to pass a strong renewable energy policy for the nation. On Aug. 4, the House of Representatives passed a bill to require 15 percent renewable electricity nationwide by 2020, thanks to the hard work of our staff, our members, our broad coalition and, most notably, Speaker Nancy Pelosi, who made it a top priority. The policy garnered more than 236 votes, including bipartisan support from California Reps. Brian Bilbray (San Diego) and Mary Bono (Palm Springs).

"Renewable energy standards are the most powerful tools for taking control of our energy future," said Bernadette Del Chiaro, clean energy advocate with Environment California. "This was a landmark vote and one of the strongest clean energy policies to pass the House of Representatives in years."

It is now up to the Senate to agree with the House and send the bill to President Bush's desk for his signature. As governor of Texas, Bush signed a similar law.

▲ A windmill generates clean power in northern California.

In the meantime, decision-makers here in California, and in dozens of other states across the country, continue to lead the way with local renewable energy standards. Environment California kicked off the effort by passing the nation's strongest renewable electricity standard of 20 percent by 2010 and establishing the Million Solar Roofs Initiative last year. This summer, we are working to expand California's solar power market to solar water heating systems (see Recent action, page 2). In addition, 22 other states are promoting renewable energy.

"The states have raised the bar for strong renewable energy policy and it's time for D.C. to develop renewable energy nationwide," said Del Chiaro.

more online ➡

Links to additional content are posted in the online version of this newsletter: www.EnvironmentCalifornia.org/newsletters

◀ **Day of action:** Volunteers planted pinwheels on state capitol lawns across the country to promote clean energy.

Everyone Loves Animals

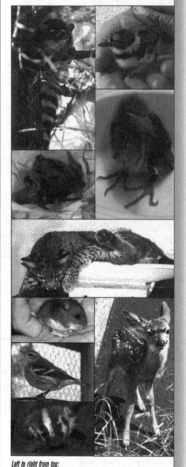

ANIMALS TREATED

In 2003 WildCare treated over 220 differe
species of wildlife and gave 3,998 ill, injur
or orphaned animals a second chance.

Left to right from top:
Ringtail, M. Piazza; Killdeer, A. Davis; House Sparrow nestlings, M. Piazza

Reprinted with permission

happening within your organization, or to educate them about the cause you work on? The latter is usually more effective—especially if you are providing information that isn't readily available elsewhere.

Remember the golden rule about readers: Everyone loves stories about people and animals. For example, if your environmental organization includes a photo and a profile of one of your clients, staff members, or rescued animals (as in the piece from WildCare's newsletter, to the left), I guarantee that more people will read that piece than a well-researched and highly informative article about your global warming campaign. To share your most important information with the largest possible number of readers, combine the other types of information—for example, your environmental organization will want to work as many key global warming points into your rescued-animal profile as possible.

Also be sure to include stories that follow up on any plans, projects, or emergencies that you've already described in mailed appeals. For example, if your donors were sent an emergency appeal for funds to deal with the aftermath of a flood, and your subsequent newsletter doesn't mention what happened next, your donors will lose interest in your stories at best, or at worst may become suspicious that you exaggerated or even fabricated the emergency to convince them to write a big check.

From a direct fundraising standpoint, your newsletter is also a good place to advise readers of any upcoming special events and other opportunities to get involved. If warranted, you can also include a tear-out or cut-out slip of paper to facilitate donations, and enclose a reply envelope.

Annual Reports

You don't have to produce an annual report, but it can be very effective for purposes of fundraising, educating others about who you are, and helping satisfy various nonprofit watchdog organizations that your group is on the up-and-up. (See "BBB Wise Giving Alliance Recommendations Regarding Annual Reports," below.) Unlike a newsletter, which often contains articles that zoom in on particular things your organization has done, your annual report should provide a wider-angle picture of your organization and what it stands for. The report should be published soon after the close of your fiscal year.

Somewhat like a corporation's annual report, yours should concentrate on a one-year period—usually your fiscal year—and include detailed financial reports, often straight from your auditors. Also like a corporate report, your annual report will play a role in marketing your organization. Thus, it makes sense to reserve some space for glowing coverage of your achievements, as well as information about your staff, volunteers, and donors.

Try to make your organization's work look attractive and effective, through interesting photos, graphics, and other design elements. But don't exaggerate or try to "spin" the true story. If you experienced both successes and failures in the past year, report on both. And don't be too self-congratulatory. After all, individual and foundation donors won't be motivated to support your work in the future if they feel that you've already succeeded in achieving your mission.

> **CAUTION**
> **Start preparing your annual report near the beginning of the year.**
> Deciding on your annual report theme, and then gathering the appropriate photos, stories, financial reports, and lists of donors to reflect that theme and convey your work over the past year, is a big job. Add to that the work of writing, editing, designing your report, and getting it to the printer, and it should be obvious that you'll have to start early. For a detailed overview of the elements and production process of an annual report, see *Publishing the Nonprofit Annual Report*, by Caroline Taylor (Jossey-Bass).

BBB Wise Giving Alliance Recommendations Regarding Annual Reports

The BBB Wise Giving Alliance, a nonprofit affiliated with the Council of Better Business Bureaus, has established itself as an industry standard-setter when it comes to nonprofit fundraising practices, disclosure, and more. Although the Wise Giving Alliance Standards are voluntary, their widespread use as a tool by which to judge your work makes them worth heeding. The group includes the following recommendation among its standards for charitable accountability:

"[The charity should] [h]ave an annual report available to all, on request, that includes:

- the organization's mission statement
- a summary of the past year's program service accomplishments
- a roster of the officers and members of the board of directors
- financial information that includes (i) total income in the past fiscal year, (ii) expenses in the same program, fundraising and administrative categories as in the financial statements, and (iii) ending net assets."

For the complete list of standards, see www.give.org (click "Charity Standards").

The key elements to include in your annual report are:

- **An attractive cover.** Make sure your organization's name, as well as the year the report covers, are clearly displayed. Include a visual image that both conveys your organization's personality and identity and makes people want to open the report—perhaps a photo, collage of images, or artwork.

- **Your mission statement.** Your organization's succinct and compelling mission statement should appear on the inside of the front cover or in some other highly visible spot.

- **Message from the top executive.** A short "letter" from the executive director or chairman of the board (or both) is traditionally included near the beginning of the report. This is the executive's chance to put a personal stamp on the report, expressing his or her vision about the core message the

Annual Reports From Bryn Mawr College and The Women's Foundation

Reprinted with permission

Reprinted with permission

report conveys. It's often wise to accompany the letter with an appropriate personal photo—the executive should look reasonably professional, but not too formal. A picture that speaks to your organization's mission also works well, such as showing your executive on a project site or next to the people you serve. See, for example, the introductory letter in Slide Ranch's annual report (go to www.slideranch.org for more information on this agricultural and environmental education center), below.

- **Short descriptions of the major projects or endeavors that your organization took on during the year.** You don't have to cover everything, but highlight important or successful work that supports the overall message of that year's report. If you began an exciting new initiative, be sure to cover it, even if it's still in the start-up phase.

Sample Letter From the Executive Director

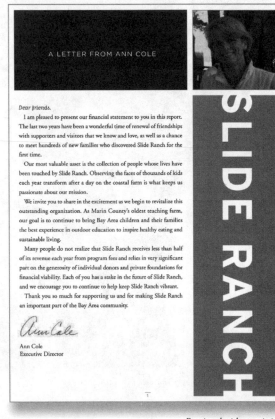

Reprinted with permission

- **Work that remains to be done.** There's no need to imply that you wrapped up all of your projects in a neat package by the end of the year—in fact, it works against your ultimate fundraising interest to suggest this. Your report should highlight ongoing challenges and projects, and problems you are still working to solve.

- **Photos or illustrations.** People read reports much like they read magazines, often thumbing through for items of interest. Pages of pure text aren't likely to catch anyone's eye. Including photos of your organization's work (with good explanatory captions) as well as drawings, graphs, or charts conveying relevant information will help reel in the readers. It will also make your organization's work seem more interesting, real, and believable. See, for example, Slide Ranch's creative use of a carrot to show where its income came from (in its Financial Statement below.)

- **Where the money came from.** Now's your chance to give credit to the various foundations, donors, and others who supported your organization over the past year. You might include narrative descriptions, charts (for example, a pie chart showing the amounts that came from foundations, donors, and other types of sources), and an explanation of any changes in your pattern of support from past years. And whatever you do, don't fail to include a list of individual donors, usually ranked in categories of gift levels. A standard breakdown would include a top category that matches your highest current level of support. For example, if you are lucky enough to have several big donors, you might start with $100,000 and above, and then drop to $50,000 to $99,000; $25,000 to $49,999; $10,000 to $24,999; $5,000 to $9,999; $2,500 to $4,999; $1,000 to $2,499; $500 to $999; $250 to $499; $100 to $249; and $1 to $99. If you've received anonymous gifts, mention them; this not only demonstrates your full range of support, but it also shows that, on request, you will you respect your donors' privacy.

> **TIP**
>
> **Never leave out your donor list.** Every donor who receives your newsletter will look for his or her name, and check to see who else gave at the same (or higher) levels. Others will scan the names even if they didn't give, out of sheer curiosity. So be absolutely sure to spell names correctly, include spouses and

significant others (if their names are also on the check), and don't leave anyone off the list inadvertently.

- **Where the money went.** Be sure to include audited financial information. In addition, you'll want to supply an explanation of what the numbers mean for the budgetarily challenged. Readers will be particularly interested in the ratio of program versus administrative costs and in interesting stories of donations of good or services or money well spent. You would normally commission audited financial reports from outside auditors and drop them in whole, usually near the end of the report. If you don't have audited financials (or won't have them by the report's scheduled publication date), hold up the report until you get them. An annual report without a financial statement just isn't an annual report.

Financial Statement in a Slide Ranch Annual Report

2000 Financial Statement

For a complete financial report, audited by Markle Stuckey Hardesty & Bott, contact Slide Ranch's Development Office.

Statement of Activities & Changes in Net Assets

Revenues & Support

Foundation Grants	89,885
Corporate Grants	20,870
Donations (from Individuals)	248,198
Program Fees	116,860
Farm & Merchandise Sales	8,194
Interest & Other Income	9,482
Total Revenues & Support	**$493,489**

Expenses

Annual Fund Program Services	211,266
Annual Fund General & Administrative	57,047
Capital Campaign Fund raising	145,434
Total Expenses	**$413,747**
Change in Net Assets	79,742
Net Assets – Beginning of Year	488,885
Net Assets – End of Year	**$568,627**

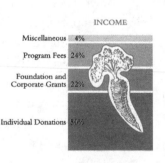

INCOME

Miscellaneous 4%
Program Fees 24%
Foundation and Corporate Grants 22%
Individual Donations 50%

EXPENSES

Capital Campaign Fundraising 35%
General and Administrative 14%
Program Services 51%

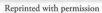

Reprinted with permission

- **Introduction to your staff and board members.** Even though you and many of your longtime supporters obviously know your key staff, not all readers of your report will. And, of course, staff members come and go, meaning that introductions are always necessary. If your organization is large, you may want to include only your key staff. In general, however, readers love to see the faces of those involved with the work, even if they are interns or part-timers. So include lots of photos of staff if your people will agree to them. This section usually goes toward the end of the report.

- **A reply device.** An envelope and fill-out form for donations is not required with your annual report, but it's never a bad idea to add one.

A high-quality newsletter or annual report can cost you anywhere from $5,000 to $25,000 to produce. A bare-bones (but still useful) report can be produced for considerably less, especially if you can tap volunteer labor. Either way, it is worth some investment, especially if you've got a good-sized audience that will judge your organization (at least in part) based upon the report. The report will probably look best if an outside professional creates it—although you don't want to send the message that you spent lavishly to produce it. However, if your cash situation is extremely tight, it's better to produce a homemade annual report than no report at all.

> **TIP**
> **Your publication should look as good read backwards as forwards!**
> When you read a magazine, do you always start at the front page and proceed straight through? Not if you're like most people, who dip in here or there, or in some cases start from the back. As you plan the layout of your newsletter or annual report, make sure that every page has something appealing on it, or a way to draw people in, just in case it's the first page they happen to flip to.

Tips for Keeping Down Design and Printing Costs

Designers and printers who have worked with nonprofits should be thoroughly familiar with how to produce the frugal but competent look you are after. But, if you are working with a volunteer or graphics person who is not sensitive to nonprofit sensibilities, be sure to educate him or her. The last thing you want is a highly produced, glossy report that conveys that you are flush with cash and willing to spend it promoting yourself. Even worse, you don't want to spend precious dollars on a report that looks unprofessional, fails to convey the spirit or accomplishments of your organization, or otherwise falls short of the mark.

Here are some tips that will help you make the most of your relationships with publishing professionals:

- **Before choosing a designer or printer, ask for references, and find someone you can trust.** Ask other nonprofits for recommendations—in every urban area there are designers and printers who specialize in working with nonprofits.

- **Especially on your first job, work closely with your designer and/or printer.** Be ready to visit his or her office, look over samples, express your opinion on paper and color, and more. You may be able to nip expensive propositions in the bud, and find out about lower-cost options you wouldn't have heard about otherwise.

- **Don't take offers of free services at face value.** For example, a free layout may not be such a great deal if you are overcharged for paper, ink, and printing.

- **Plan your year's printing needs in advance, to maximize what can be printed in one lot**—for example, don't have new envelopes printed for every mail appeal.

- **Find out the costs of mailing—and weigh a prototype of your package—before producing it.**

- **Don't print anything until you have a plan in place for distributing or marketing it**—otherwise you could end up with a pile of expensive material in your closet.

- **Always bid out your good-sized printing jobs, such as your annual report, and get estimates from at least three printers.** Nothing will cost you more in the long run than making a "best friend" out of the printer.

- **Avoid full color unless money is no object; even then, you'll have to consider whether your donors will see it as too costly.** A single shade of ink plus black on a well-chosen color of paper can look great and allow for legible, attractive photographs. Ask your designer or printer for suggestions.

Designing Your Website to Draw in Donors

Every nonprofit that can scrape together the necessary funds and talent should set up a website. Because people now use the Web as a telephone book, research tool, contact method, and much more, your absence in cyberspace makes about as much sense as deciding not to have a telephone. Given this reality—and that most nonprofits have long since gotten at least a bare-bones website up and running—I don't cover the mechanics of establishing a website (see the resources listed below if you need such help). Instead, this chapter will help you make sure that your website helps you effectively achieve your fundraising goals.

The checklist below gives you eight simple ways to assess your website's ability to help you raise money. Each of these topics is discussed at greater length in the sections that follow. If you are still in the organizational start-up phase, it will obviously be most efficient to address these various issues during the design of your website. But these strategies can help you even if your website is already up and running—particularly if it's running in the wrong direction. At least as far as your fundraising goals are concerned, there is always plenty you can do to improve matters without going back to square one.

CAUTION

Few websites attract random donors. In the early days of the Web, nonprofits hoped that generous people would surf the Net, looking for worthy organizations. But this rarely (if ever) happens, so you should assume that most of your website's visitors have some previous connection to your organization. They may have heard of it through a news story, a member friend, or the interesting written materials you've produced. True, some people interested in your area of concern may find you through a Google search, but even when this happens, they are unlikely to become contributers until they establish personal—not just cyber—contact with your group. Don't let that discourage you. It's worth being ready "just in case." After Hurricane Katrina, for example, many service-providing organizations saw their online fundraising increase a thousand-fold.

Fundraising Worksheet 10: Check Your Website's Fundraising Effectiveness

❏ **Basic Contact Information:** Does your website clearly state what your organization does, where it's located, and every possible way to get in touch with development and other staff?

❏ **Your Organization's Personality:** Does your website convey your organization's personality in a manner that's consistent with your fundraising and other marketing materials?

❏ **Freshness:** Does your website appear current and up to date?

❏ **Content:** Does your website present interesting content about your organization's cause?

❏ **Donation Information:** Does your website lead viewers easily to information on how to donate or get involved?

❏ **Information on Where the Money Goes:** Does your website tell donors how their money will be spent?

❏ **Funder and Donor Information:** Does your website find space to publicly thank funders and donors?

❏ **Tracking Users:** Does your website allow you to track where viewers go within the site and how successfully you're leading them to donation or involvement options?

After you've created a website that meets as many of these criteria as financially feasible, don't keep it a secret. Your website should become one of your principal communication devices. Post the address prominently on business cards, stationery, brochures, T-shirts, and every printed document you put out. Encourage newsletter readers to check your website for further information or updates on issues they're reading about. And include links to your website within emails sent to supporters, allowing them to click for further information or to donate online.

RESOURCE

Need more information on building a website? Check out these resources:

- **TechSoup, at www.techsoup.org.** Check out "Web building" under the "Learning Center" tab.
- **Network for Good (www.groundspring.org),** a San Francisco nonprofit that offers handbooks, training, and services nationwide , and links to Web-building resources.

Basic Contact Information

In the course of writing this book, I looked at countless nonprofit websites. Although many were very good and others were at least decent, I couldn't believe how many were truly awful in the sense that they lacked even the most basic information about the organization. In some instances, I couldn't even tell what city or state the nonprofit was located in, much less find its actual address. My personal pet peeve is when I click the "Contact Us" button and receive only an email popup, without a phone number or any hint of where the organization is located outside of cyberspace. Do these groups really expect visitors to undertake extensive research just to figure out where they should send their checks?

Your nonprofit's full name, address, telephone number, and email address should be prominently displayed on your website's home page, and on the bottom of every other page. If yours is a national nonprofit, or affiliated with one, there should be easy-to-find information on the nature of the affiliation, and links to any national, subsidiary, or sister offices. A one- or two-sentence statement of what you do should also appear somewhere on the home page. You can use your mission statement, as long as it's clear, concise, and readable; if your mission statement is lengthy, create a more succinct version for your site.

How far you go to explain who's who in your organization is partly a matter of your workers' privacy preferences. However, you'll really help supporters feel personally connected to your organization if you provide links to its staff, with bios, photos, telephone numbers, and email addresses. This personal approach encourages people to get in touch with you. It has the added bonus that, due to human curiosity, many viewers will read your staff members' biographies, which may enhance their confidence in your organization as well as their sense that you're all like-minded people. To get Web visitors to the right page, most groups post an "About Us" link on the home page. The next page may include a detailed description of (or links to) the group's mission and activities, contact information, and job openings—as well as a link saying "Meet Our Board and Staff," "The [*Group Name*] Team," or something similar.

Your Organization's Personality

Remember, your organization is trying to build a personal relationship with donors—and that's going to be a tall order if the donor perceives that your organization has a multiple personality disorder. Hopefully, you already have an idea of what image your organization is trying to present, whether it's traditional, scientific, homey, offbeat, ethnic, left, right, center, or whatever. Take a look at the fundraising materials you've been producing—your letters to donors, grant proposals, newsletters, annual reports, and so on. Ask yourself what personality is emerging. Then look at your website and make sure it's got the same one.

You can present your organization's personality through the use of colors, graphics, words, photographs, and more. It's a broader issue than I can cover in this book—the important point here is to look for consistency. If your website seems to be reflecting a personality you don't recognize (perhaps that of your Web developer!), it may be a simple matter of borrowing images or text from your other materials to get it back in line.

For an example of a consistent presentation, compare the website and other marketing materials produced by Slide Ranch, an agricultural and environmental education center located on the Pacific Coast in California's Golden Gate National Recreation Area. Children and others come to Slide Ranch to learn respect for animals, plants, the earth, and each other, through hands-on farm and wilderness experiences. As you can see, photos of the children take center stage in Slide Ranch's website and materials. The organization's beautifully designed sheep and chicken logo is always prominently displayed. And, if we could only bring you color illustrations, you'd see that bright green is used as a unifying color between the website and many of Slide Ranch's other printed materials.

Another way to create consistency is to treat Web visitors in a manner true to your organization's mission and ideals. An organization that works with the elderly, for example, shouldn't use a tiny text font. An organization working with the disabled should ensure that its website is accessible to its clientele, as discussed below.

Slide Ranch Home Page

Sample Slide Ranch Printed Materials

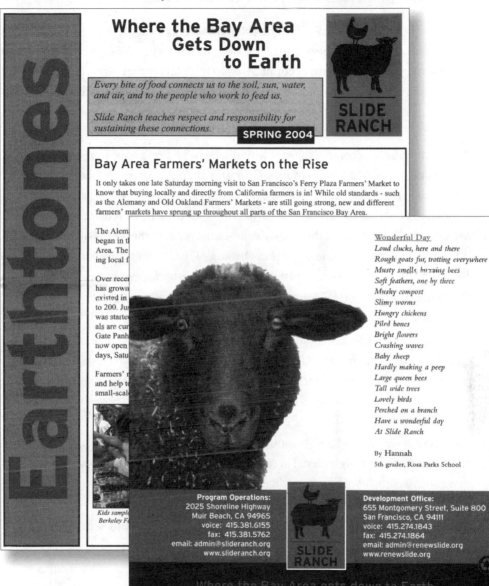

Where the Bay Area Gets Down to Earth

Every bite of food connects us to the soil, sun, water, and air, and to the people who work to feed us.

Slide Ranch teaches respect and responsibility for sustaining these connections.

SPRING 2004

SLIDE RANCH

Earthtones

Bay Area Farmers' Markets on the Rise

It only takes one late Saturday morning visit to San Francisco's Ferry Plaza Farmers' Market to know that buying locally and directly from California farmers is in! While old standards - such as the Alemany and Old Oakland Farmers' Markets - are still going strong, new and different farmers' markets have sprung up throughout all parts of the San Francisco Bay Area.

The Alem[...]
began in th[...]
Area. The[...]
ing local f[...]

Over recen[...]
has grown[...]
existed in[...]
to 200. Ju[...]
was started[...]
als are cur[...]
Gate Panh[...]
now open[...]
days, Satu[...]

Farmers' [...]
and help to[...]
small-scal[...]

Kids sampl[...]
Berkeley F[...]

Wonderful Day
Loud clucks, here and there
Rough goats fur, trotting everywhere
Musty smells, buzzing bees
Soft feathers, one by three
Musky compost
Slimy worms
Hungry chickens
Piled bones
Bright flowers
Crashing waves
Baby sheep
Hardly making a peep
Large queen bees
Tall wide trees
Lovely birds
Perched on a branch
Have a wonderful day
At Slide Ranch

By Hannah
5th grader, Rosa Parks School

Program Operations:
2025 Shoreline Highway
Muir Beach, CA 94965
voice: 415.381.6155
fax: 415.381.5762
email: admin@slideranch.org
www.slideranch.org

SLIDE RANCH

Development Office:
655 Montgomery Street, Suite 800
San Francisco, CA 94111
voice: 415.274.1843
fax: 415.274.1864
email: admin@renewslide.org
www.renewslide.org

Where the Bay Area gets down to Earth

Reprinted with permission

Making Your Website Accessible to Visitors With Disabilities

If your nonprofit happens to work with disabled persons as a clientele, website accessibility should obviously be a top priority. But other organizations would be smart to take accessibility into account as well. Don't forget that 10%–20% of Americans have some form of disability. One of your supporters might be a bestselling author who's legally blind, or a venture capitalist with carpal tunnel syndrome.

Making your website accessible to users with disabilities doesn't have to require fancy programming or cost a lot of money. Often, it's a simple matter of choosing to do things one way rather than another. In fact, the complex, expensive websites with lots of graphics and video are sometimes the hardest ones for persons with disabilities—and for plenty of people without disabilities, as well—to navigate. In the words of Anthony Tusler, Coordinator of the Technology Policy Division of the World Institute on Disability, "An easily navigated, well-designed website is better for everyone."

Exactly what steps can you take to make your website accessible? The following tips will get you started; see below for further resources:

- **Allow users to move via key commands, rather than a mouse.** For people with limited use of their hands, navigating via mouse can be impossible. Yet some websites require that you use a mouse, for example to cursor between different boxes to fill out a form. By simply allowing users to hit the TAB key to move between boxes, you avoid this problem.

- **Don't use moving text.** Although your Web designer may be tempted to present news updates and other timely material in text that scrolls down the screen, you're better off without it. People with learning disabilities may not be able to follow along, and the screen readers of blind persons still can't decode moving text.

- **Avoid flashing lights and flickering images.** These can trigger epileptic seizures and migraine headaches.

- **Don't rely on color coding.** Many people suffer from color blindness, or have difficulty distinguishing colors that are similar in shade. If, for example, you ask users to "click the red button," be sure to put some sort of label within the button as well.

Making Your Website Accessible to Visitors With Disabilities (continued)

- **Use "alt tags" to caption your graphics.** Your website designer will understand what this means; basically, it involves writing up a little caption to describe any graphic image on your site. That way, blind persons using a screenreader to access your website will receive your description of any pictures you've put up. (Alt-tag captioning also helps people who simply have a slow modem: they'll see the caption before the picture.)

- **Caption any audio/video content.** If you add a video to your site where people need to listen to a soundtrack to understand what's going on, you'll leave hearing-impaired persons out of the loop unless you also provide captions.

RESOURCE

Want to know more about accessibility? For more information on making your website accessible to disabled persons, see the website of the World Wide Web Consortium's Web Accessibility Initiative (WAI). Go to www.w3.org and click "WAI." There you'll find information on what types of disabilities make using the Web difficult and detailed guidelines on how to design a website that's accessible without being boring.

TIP

Once you've got an accessible website, you can advertise that fact by displaying a WAI conformance logo (see www.w3.org/WAI/WCAG1-Conformance. html for details). The logo looks like this:

Freshness

Yes, it's important to have a website—but your Web presence can actually work against you if your organization bites off more than it can chew. I've seen many a website where the nonprofit clearly went through a major push to get material online—articles, descriptions of their projects, upcoming events, volunteer opportunities, and the like—and then left them up unchanged for months, while the projects were completed and the events became history. A potential donor who sees all this stale material is likely to think that the organization is stagnating as well.

The ideal, of course, is to keep your material up to date, and to replace old items with new ones as soon as possible. With enough interesting and timely content, your website can become a draw for people who are tracking or researching the issue you cover, as discussed further on in this chapter. Becoming a regular news source, or providing a favorite blog, is one of the few ways you might be able to turn anonymous Web visitors into eventual donors.

If you can't reach the ideal of regular updating, however, your next best bet is to simply avoid putting time-sensitive information on your website. Your organization probably has plenty of stories or information to share that aren't likely to become dated, such as its history, its sociological or scientific approach, success stories of particular campaigns or clients, and more. You don't have to write these from scratch: Look at your other communications materials, such as your annual report, for materials that you can borrow or adapt. You should be able to cull enough material to make your website seem meaty, without drawing attention to the fact that it's unchanging.

If even that seems like too much to tackle, you might reasonably create a website that presents nothing more than your organization's "name, rank, and serial number"—that is, an explanation of its identity, location, mission, and activities. This sort of website isn't going to wow anyone, but at least it won't turn them off.

Know Your Organization's Limits When Planning Your Website

Leanne Grossman, Director of Communications at the Global Fund for Women (www.globalfundforwomen.org), was integrally involved in their website's redesign—no small task for a site that includes 500 pages, with multilingual portions for French, Spanish, Russian, Arabic, and Portuguese speakers. According to Leanne, "The biggest caution I would give people concerns putting up content that will need updating. Any time you have to change content, it can be expensive and time-consuming. I spend about 10% of my time keeping up our current Web content—and we do a yearly review and overhaul—but I still feel like we could do more.

"One solution is to have some portions of your website that can stand on their own, without facts, figures, the 'new this,' or the 'new that.' It also helps to be clear when defining your website's parameters. We've had some donors ask us to locate and post articles with content pertinent to our mission, but as an alternative, we've provided links to relevant articles on other websites."

TIP

Use clever wording to avoid sounding dated. Sometimes, a simple solution like using the word "recently" instead of "last July" or "July 24th" can save a Web article from imminent staleness. Also avoid telling phrases like, "with the holidays coming up" or "as the birds begin their annual migration."

Should Your Nonprofit Blog?

Everyone seems to be talking about blogs—that is, "Web logs," or online diaries of news or commentary that may include photos and a place for readers to post comments. Though anyone can start a blog (and nearly everyone has—approaching 80 million at last count), they're becoming an increasingly respected and popular information source. Pat Joseph, current affairs editor and blogger at the Sierra Club (www.sierraclub.org), adds that blogs are "the best way to keep fresh content up on your site. It means there's always something new, no matter when you stop by. We get over 10,000 visitors to our blog each week."

Of course, if your nonprofit is already having trouble keeping its website up to date, blogging may not be for you. For example, Pat Joseph says maintaining the Sierra Club's "Compass" blog is the biggest part of his job. "But," he explains, "I post at least once a day, and usually three or four times a day."

Still, from a technical standpoint, blogging is much easier than actually updating your website. Many nonprofit bloggers sign on with a Web-based blog supporter such as Blogger, TypePad, or WordPress. They've made it so easy that, once you've set up the blog, you can basically type in your content and press "submit." (Your blog will appear on the provider's website, not yours, but you can link back and forth fairly seamlessly.)

Assuming you can't devote a full-time staffperson to blogging, look for someone who can post material once or twice a week—preferably someone with interesting opinions and good writing skills. The person might discuss everything from the work of your nonprofit to national news affecting your topic of interest. A captioned photo of your organization at work is a great way to add color.

As with everyone new, there are aspects of blogging that will take getting used to. One is the reader comment feature, assuming you choose to include it. Yes, anyone can potentially post anything on your blog, for the world to see. Pat Joseph explains, "You can set the program up so that you have a chance to approve comments before the public sees them, but that discourages people from commenting (they lose the satisfaction of seeing their posting right away), and it makes the blog seem less real. I've set mine up so that I can delete comments after the fact. Fortunately, I've received very few hostile comments."

Another concern is the stream of consciousness element. Whoever writes your blog should be careful to avoid late-night rants that might, for example, offend a funder or sound overly political, thus jeopardizing your nonprofit status.

Content

The best websites contain substantive information, preferably information that the reader might not get elsewhere. This information usually falls into one of two broad categories. First, readers might be interested in your nonprofit's current activities—such as news about ongoing projects; follow up stories on issues they've heard about before, such as whether a park has been saved from development or how your research was received at an international forum; or details and signup information for upcoming events and classes. (Remember that you can easily post copies of your press releases online.) The second category is information that doesn't derive directly from your nonprofit, but that you've either written or collected for your readers, such as articles about relevant national or local news issues, updates on the state of the environmental, legal, health, or social issues with which your nonprofit is concerned, and the like. This may seem a bit far from the fundraising theme, but studies have shown that readers place substantive content number one in importance when evaluating a nonprofit's website.

The Greenpeace USA website provides a good example of how to use news to draw people in (www.greenpeaceusa.org). When you go its home page, the first thing you'll see (below the customary tabs) are current news articles, with bold graphics that practically jump off the page. The Disabled American Veterans website, at www.dav.org, also does a good job, by simply putting headlines in a box, with photos.

Netarts, Treated at the Wildlife Rehab Center of the North Coast

I have a feeling this guy is going to have a name soon. We don't usually name our patients, but never have we had a bird with such personality. This pelican loves Sharnelle. He dances and flirts with her. In this photo he is doing what we think is some sort of greeting dance. Hi will open his beak and flare his pouch a bit and then sway and weave his body back and forth in front of her. If this pelican proves able to adapt to people, he will become an educational bird. Unfortunately, right now he nips at anyone who gets too close to Sharnelle, so he will have to be broken of that first.
Update, 2-12-01 - Yup, he's got a name: Netarts, for the town where he was rescued.

Significant content doesn't always have to mean weighty or heady stuff—perhaps your website can offer viewers a fun reason to stop in. Many wildlife rescue sites, for example, put up photos and stories concerning the animals they rescue. Meet, for example, a flirtatious pelican named Netarts, treated at the Wildlife Rehab Center of the North Coast in Astoria, Oregon (www.coastwildlife.org), pictured above.

Some websites take their news-provider role one step farther and offer readers regular email newsletters or news alerts. If your organization is able to do this, it's a great way of collecting email addresses of potential future supporters—whom you can cultivate with other electronic communications. And, there's no harm in including a line or two within every emailed newsletter mentioning donation and volunteer opportunities and providing links to your website for further information.

Donation Information and Opportunities

As a general rule, everything on your website should be easy to find—and, from a fundraising perspective, finding information about donating or otherwise getting involved should be especially easy. Again, I'm assuming that your viewers aren't random visitors who were searching the Web, but people who already have some history with your organization. They may be visiting your website for any number of reasons, including catching up on your activities or checking out a special event—but they still might be one mental step away from donating, given the right opportunity.

At the same time, you don't want to rush people to the payment page, especially without giving offering them some background information about why, how, and how much to give. Give careful thought to your organization's home page, introductory donation or support page, the nondonation pages of your website, and the possibility of offering online credit card donations, all of which will help boost the ease with which viewers can fund your group—and the likelihood that they will do so.

The Home Page

If you look at other nonprofits' websites, you'll see that a fairly standard set of home page tabs and links is emerging. Most nonprofits place a set of tabs across or alongside their home page, with links to such topics as "About Us," "Contact Us," "News," "Upcoming Events," "Publications," and—the important one for this discussion—"Support Us." Other examples I've seen for that critical "Get Involved" tab include "Get Active," "Become a Member," "How You Can Help," "Join Today," or "Support [*name of organization*]."

In addition, many display a separate button saying "Give Now!" or something similar, for viewers who are ready to make a donation that instant. This is not the time to get creative: Go with the system that has worked for others. (By the way, you may also notice something that is disappearing—fancy graphics and entry screens that look pretty but take a long time to load. Their usual result was to annoy rather than tantalize users.)

Not everyone uses a separate "donate" button. Some simply title one of their tabs "donate"—which fulfills the requirement of an easy link, but may turn away people who were hoping for other ways to get involved with your organization.

Introductory Support Page

Unless your viewers have decisively clicked a "donate now" button or link, it's best not to confront them too quickly with a credit card or other payment form. In many of the best websites, if you click on a link called "How You Can Help," "Get Involved," or something similar, you're led to an introductory page explaining how different dollar amounts will help the cause, as well as other relevant links, such as "Make a Donation, "Leave a Legacy," "Events," "Donate While You Shop," and "Volunteer/Intern." There's no need to write a book about donation purposes and possibilities, but now is the time to orient donors to their options—and to any premiums or benefits they'll get in return for their support—before proceeding to the bottom line.

There are alternate ways to design this introductory page, depending on your organization's strengths and range of giving options. Many organizations start the page with a brief introduction, then subdivide the remainder into summaries of various memberships or other options, each of which contains a link to further information. The organization Feed The Children goes straight to a description of how different giving amounts will help needy families, as shown below. Notice the page's attractive layout, with a large photo and not too much text—but a link called "Financial Accountability" for anyone who wants to know more or to see Feed The Children's audited financials.

Feed The Children Introductory Donation Page

Just don't make things too complicated—at the top of any range of options should be a basic procedure to give a modest amount of money, without frills or fanfare.

Links From Other Pages

Reprinted with permission

Websurfers may take a crazy ride through your website, clicking on items at whim, and often forgetting how they got to their current landing spot. Where does that leave them if their intent was to make a donation? No matter where someone is on your website, the pages should either repeat the home page tabs (though they can be relocated), contain a "donate" button, or provide another link to opportunities to get involved.

If you can invest a little more time, review the text of the nonfundraising sections of your website and add sentences where relevant. For example, in a description of a particular program, you could add a linked sentence saying "To find out how you can support [*name your client base or issue*], click here." This type of customized linking—assuming it's tastefully done—can be very effective in drawing people to your donation page.

Option for Online Donations

Any user who is Web-savvy enough to check you out online is likely to be comfortable giving online as well, using a credit card. In keeping with the fundraisers creed of making it easy to give, your organization should seriously consider investing in an online credit card donation service. This is best done through an application service provider (ASP) such as 4Charity.com, contribute .com, or entango.com. (The task of processing online donations in-house can be onerous—and lead to delays and frustrated donors.)

Ideally, you'll find (or already have) an ASP that offers a package deal, including such other services as website maintenance, donor tracking, email messaging, event registration, and more.

TIP

If you truly can't afford an online donation system, tell website visitors how to donate. Whatever you do, don't skirt the issue! You can, for example, offer a downloadable page that contains all the information on your regular reply card, along with information on where to fax or mail the completed form.

Once you've got an online donation system in place, mention its availability in all of your organization's printed, electronic, and other fundraising materials. Online giving may be preferable to some people who are reading your materials on paper but find it easier to turn on their computer than to fill out a check and lick an envelope. That means you'll also be enticing supporters to your website, where they'll read further information about your organization, giving you yet another opportunity to impress them.

Your online donation page should contain the following elements:

- **The usual places for donors to fill out their name and address, credit card number, and the like.** Make sure the donor knows whether your organization's name will appear on his or her credit card statement—some services that handle donations can only arrange for their own name to appear on the statement, which could easily confuse and alarm your donors.

- **An explanation of the measures you've taken to ensure the safety of online donations.** (Though transferring money online is usually quite safe, one still hears stories of hackers stealing credit card numbers.) Be able to truthfully assure them that donations are made through a secure server—in other words, that their personal information is put into code before it goes flying through cyberspace. You can also apply for seals of approval from groups such as VeriSign (www.verisign.com), BBB Online (www.bbbonline.org), or TRUSTe (www.truste.org).

- **For new donors, an explanation of your commitment to keeping their personal information confidential,** and an opportunity to opt out of having their email addresses shared with other organizations.

- **Non-Web ways to give money.** Maybe they'll change their mind about giving online at the last minute. If website visitors would prefer to fill out a form and send money via the U.S. mail, you should have full instructions and a downloadable form available online for this purpose.

> ⊘ **CAUTION**
> **Online donors expect an immediate thank you.** Without the lag time provided by the U.S. mail, electronic donors expect to hear from you right away. Most ASPs will instantly email a message of thanks, but make sure that this is part of their package of services. You should then follow up with a mailed thank-you letter, which looks more formal and guarantees that the donor will have something in print for tax record keeping.

Information on Where the Money Goes

Where and how supporters' gifts will be spent is a topic worthy of a separate page on your website—and it's a page that should be easy to find. Remember, supporters want to know that their money is funding worthwhile projects and programs. Studies have found that users rank information about how donations are spent high in importance when visiting a charity's website.

The Trust for Public Land (TPL)'s website at www.tpl.org shows an efficient and effective way to convey this information. After clicking a link on the home page called "Support TPL," you're brought to some introductory text about why to donate. This includes bullet points that mention TPL's achievements and awards and offer further links to media articles in which TPL was ranked highly as a financially efficient charity (by *Forbes, SmartMoney,* and others). These links are eye-catching, newsbreaking, and perfectly placed to allay any last-minute donor doubts.

Not every group will be lucky enough to make it into the national press, but that shouldn't stop you from reporting your own news. If you've received a high rating from one of the various watchdog organizations, such as the BBB Wise Giving Alliance or Charity Navigator, make that your link (and take advantage of the watchdog's offer to use their logo on your site). Or, simply prepare your own report and title your link, for example, "How Each Dollar Is Spent," "Financial Highlights," or even "Click here to learn more about our budget and funding." This portion of your website should also include links to your annual report (if available online) and Form 990.

Information About Funders and Donors

If you've been scrambling to find ways to publicly thank your foundation funders and major private donors, a website can really take the pressure off. Many organizations add a simple link to "Our Funders," whether on their home page or a deeper page within the site. Your annual report may contain this information, and it may be posted online. However, this shouldn't stop you from separately repeating some of the most relevant information—not everyone knows to look in your annual report.

Mentioning your funders and donors online serves purposes beyond recognition. It's also a way to build trust in your organization. You want Web viewers to think, "If the ABC Foundation and So-and-So support this group, they must be okay."

Some nonprofits go further than merely listing their funders and donors, and post profiles of individual donors, complete with photos and personal accounts of why they give. (You would, of course, have to get permission from the donor first.) Again, this is a way to inspire potential supporters to realize that others "just like them" have been moved to give, and to rally them to join the club.

Tracking Users

Up to now, I've been talking about the parts of your website that users see. But let's shift gears and consider what's behind the scenes. It doesn't take particularly advanced technology for your Web designer to add a feature allowing you to keep "site traffic statistics." This information tells you not only how many people are visiting your site, but also where your site visitors came from (what website) and where they go within your site—what links are enticing them to click, what pages they're leaving unviewed, what they're downloading, which page they most commonly exit from, and the like. If your site was set up without such a feature, you can install Web-tracking software or use an online service, such as Extreme Tracking (www.extreme-dm.com/tracking). (Some of the online services are free, but beware that they may irritate your viewers with pop-up ads.)

Once you make a habit of collecting and interpreting your traffic statistics, they can be invaluable for measuring and enhancing your website's fundraising effectiveness. The numbers will look particularly meaningful as you monitor them over time, leading you to evaluate, for example, the comparative success of an email campaign, the drawing power of a press release, or who your best referral sources are.

> **TIP**
>
> **Get to know your referral sources.** If another organization or website is referring a lot of visitors your way, perhaps with a link to an article on your site or an outright recommendation of support, it may be worth contacting them to talk about ways to deepen the relationship.

You might also learn where not to waste your energies. If, for example, you're putting a lot of time into writing updates on your organization's latest project or research, but no one is reading them—or, worse yet, users are exiting your site from that page—your time might be better spent on a more productive task. (On the other hand, maybe your updates just need better drafting or promotion.)

Your Website's Not Your Only Place in Cyberspace

Have you been hearing words like "social media" or "viral fundraising" lately? These refer to peer-to-peer uses of online technologies, like when someone posts a message online saying, "Help me support this cause," or "I've created a fundraising event, please come." They might do this on their own website, or on an existing one like MySpace, Facebook, Planypus, or Flickr (for photos).

Take a look at these websites and any new ones you hear about. That way, you'll be ready to support the efforts of any (probably young) staff or donors who want to use them to connect potential supporters to your organization. But don't feel too pressured to, for example, start your own page or post things on your own. Remember, this is about friends connecting with friends. It's okay to remain relatively hands-off and let things happen spontaneously (with the occasional check-in to make sure your organization's name isn't attached to events or efforts you feel uncomfortable about). Of course, if you've got a great video involving your nonprofit that would make a big splash on YouTube, go for it.

Media Outreach

When sending out fundraising materials like donor letters, grant proposals, or newsletters, you're trying to communicate with people one by one. Though this technique can be effective, it has obvious limitations—not only is it laborious to reach large numbers of people this way, but those you do reach may not believe your message regarding your organization's importance and effectiveness.

Wouldn't it be nice to reach lots more people far faster in a way that also enhances the believability of your message? That's where the media can help—by giving favorable coverage to your organization's work, in print, on the radio, and on television. Media coverage allows you to greatly increase public knowledge about your organization and your cause—and thus keep your existing supporters informed and excited about what you do, while you also gain new supporters.

Many organizations put no energy into media outreach, which gives you a greater opportunity to attract public attention and compete for that seemingly limited donor pool. Of course, you'll want to be sensible and appropriate about your media efforts. The last thing you want is negative public attention.

How do people, including those working for nonprofit organizations, get stories into the media? Not by sitting by the phone waiting for it to ring. Far more media coverage than you might ever imagine is generated by the group being covered; few journalists have time to wander the streets in hopes of witnessing an event in progress. Businesses, politicians, authors, and yes, even nonprofits that understand this simple fact learn to place stories about their activities. Some large, well-funded nonprofits even hire communications directors—it's a legitimate full-time job. Smaller nonprofits often rely on their E.D., program experts, board chair, and sometimes media-savvy development staffers to maintain appropriate media contacts.

To help you develop a smart and effective media strategy, and learn to make your own news, this chapter will address:

- what stories attract journalists' attention
- how to get to know your local media
- how to pitch or place stories, and
- how to protect your organization's reputation and interests in media interactions.

Buying Ads Outright Isn't Usually Cost Effective

Purchasing advertising space, whether in print, on the radio, or on television, can run into the four, five, and six figures before you know it. In a world barraged by advertising, you're not likely to make much of an impact—even businesses that advertise have learned that they must run their ads over and over, week after week, to make an impression on the audience.

As with every rule, however, there are creative ways to break it. One is to get corporate sponsorship for your ad. For example, in November 2003, Accion, a nonprofit that helps make small business loans to people working their way out of poverty, took out a nearly half-page ad in *The New York Times*. Most of the ad was devoted to a dramatic photo and description of Accion's activities—but the bottom contained the JPMorganChase logo, and an explanation that JPMorganChase had sponsored the ad, and was a proud supporter of Accion.

Another gutsy example was provided by MoveOn.org, which in early 2004 sponsored a campaign to create "Bush in 30 Seconds" ads (mock campaign ads indicting the Bush administration), then asked supporters to contribute funds to buy Super Bowl time to run the winning ad. Needless to say, the process itself generated a great deal of media coverage.

TIP

Track the buzz on your organization. You may be getting media coverage you don't know about, including mentions in blogs. A handy way to find out is using Google alerts, which will send you regular emails covering a broad variety of online sources. Go to www.google.com/alerts.

What Makes a Good Story

Engaging the media will require a shift in how you think about portraying your organization. A pitch that you might make to a donor—for example, "For 20 years our organization has been offering tutoring to homeless children," or

"We do great work tracking the misuse of campaign funds," is likely to fall flat with reporters. They want a story that's newsy, contains drama, is different, or, most often, is closely connected to a current issue or event. Many organizations simply don't understand that the word "new" and "news" are virtually identical. This helps explain why they call reporters and say, "I'm so-and-so, my organization is doing great work, how about a story?" Needless to say, this kind of approach won't lead to any headlines or airtime. Not every story has to be actual "news," but it will have to tie in with the public's current interests.

The bottom line is that very few media outlets will do straight profiles of nonprofit organizations; if they do, it will usually be because the group is already in the news. Instead, think about how your group or its work could fit into a larger story. Again, most journalists are looking for a "hook" or unusual angle with which to entice the audience into reading or viewing the particular story right then and there. You'll also need to be aware of the different types of stories that the media produces, from hard news, to gossip about personalities and do-it-yourself information, to community interest features—and style your publicity pitches accordingly.

Come Up With a Hook

When I say that journalists look for stories that have a "hook," I'm not just describing some subtle or subliminal process—most journalists will immediately ask themselves, "What's the hook?" as they evaluate a potential story. It follows that you have to know the answer to this yourself before you pitch a story. Here's how Nick Parker, Communications Director at the California School Age Consortium, an educational nonprofit concerned with issues of hunger and poverty, puts it: "When I worked in the film industry, we had to condense ideas for a movie into one sentence, like, 'The earth's computers have been taken over by aliens, and humans have 24 hours to get them back before our planet is blown up.' Getting a nonprofit-generated story into the media is not much different: You've got to be able to quickly sum up the central conflict in a way that grabs their attention."

Common hooks involve conflict, shock, laughter, something new and different in your community or the world, identification of a trend, a marking of time, such as with an anniversary or holiday, or a "first," such as the first person to be cured of a disease, or the first sighting of a supposedly extinct bird. The most obvious hook is that something that just happened in your organization really is "news." But, of course, it must be news to plenty of people beyond your little organization. Receiving a small grant may be big news to you, but of little interest to anyone else; receiving a large grant to build a new community center or start a noteworthy local program may warrant at least local coverage.

And, it's important to understand that not all good stories involve breaking news. Think of it this way: A true hook, for a news story or any other kind, involves a shift in how the audience views the world. Kids and animals, while they don't really fall into this pattern, also seem to be perennially interesting to the public. So, for example, your small grant might actually be newsworthy if it came from a group of grade school kids who dressed up as angels to deliver it to your homeless center.

Also realize that the media seems to develop its own internal trends regarding what it deems exciting. They all read, watch, and listen to each other, and borrow madly. Certain fads and cycles develop, some of which you may be able to take advantage of. For example, the early 2006 media frenzy about the Duke lacrosse team alleged rape case was an opportunity for groups concerned with violence against women, racial justice, prosecutorial discretion, and media coverage or bias to weigh in and get their own stories out.

No matter what the current media mood, certain stories are always difficult to pitch and gain coverage for. One is the depiction of the endless train of human suffering. With the globalization of the media in the last few decades, we have been horrified by hunger, disease, and injustice all over the world, with the result that compassion fatigue often sets in. Many people take long breaks from reading the newspaper or watching television, figuring that they've heard enough bad news—and the ever-ratings-conscious media knows it. As a result, many media outlets try to leaven this doom-and-gloom coverage with hopeful material. Thus, an area newspaper is more likely to cover a story about how a local group helped homeless mothers find shelter for their children than they are to do yet another feature on the root causes of homelessness.

What are the most likely hooks for a nonprofit-generated story? If you work with people or animals, you've got an advantage. (This is where keeping in touch with your program staff is important, so you are on top of personal news tidbits.) Sometimes the story you'd like to tell just needs a good angle. For example, if your shelter has been growing an organic garden, that's nice, but probably not quite enough to interest the media by itself. However, a story about your shelter celebrating its first Thanksgiving with all organic, homegrown vegetables might interest a reporter, as might a story about how your garden helps low-income people just say "no" to the unhealthy food sold at area fast-food outlets.

Even if you aren't providing direct services, your organization probably has an area of expertise, or opinions on things going on in the world. Take a step back and recognize what aspects of your work are new, different, or shed some light on current news or thought. In fact, if your organization conducts studies and publishes reports, these can often be rejiggered and put forth as news—particularly if you can identify a trend or some societal change. When dealing with dry facts and numbers, it's good to put them in terms that people can understand. For example, the Straphangers Campaign, a New York City–based group that advocates for improved public transportation on behalf of subway and bus riders, gives out an annual "Pokey Award" (a golden snail on a pedestal) for NYC's slowest bus. In describing the 2006 winner's rate of speed, the group noted that it wasn't much faster than a pedestrian. (See www.straphangers.org for more information and links to its press releases.)

How the Media Presents Stories

Though virtually every potential story needs a hook, you also need to recognize the different categories of stories that the media feature. For your purposes, the three most important story categories include:

- breaking news
- feature stories, and
- arts or other events.

Breaking news means just what it sounds like—something that's in the headlines. Journalists who are devoted to breaking news tend to be news junkies who think everything else is mere fluff. A nonprofit can make its own breaking news. For example, your group's successful boycott of a corporation's products resulting in its decision to stop using an endangered type of Southeast Asian

Making Agricultural Studies Interesting

The central activities of many nonprofits are not headline-grabbing stuff—research into economics or science, monitoring social or environmental trends, and the like. But sometimes all it takes is a little creativity to recast a seemingly humdrum issue into something with a powerful news hook. Food First, of Oakland, California (also called Institute for Food and Development Policy, at www.foodfirst.org), is among the organizations trying to stir up media interest in stories that contain dense content and not much hype. Food First's primary activities include preparing books and reports discussing health and social justice issues in modern agricultural production, such as genetic modification.

So, how does Food First get news coverage? Here's how Nick Parker, then–Media Coordinator, described it: "First of all, we try to consider the journalist's point of view—why would they be interested? Often we try to tie things to stories that are already in the media, but you've got to be fast on your feet, before the story gets stale. We also try to put a new twist on things. For example, let's say that proponents of genetically modified foods are claiming they will end world hunger. If we could legitimately headline a press release 'GMOs will cause starvation,' that might get some attention. It creates a little controversy, and the media loves controversy.

"Another strategy that we've used is to create a media event around existing issues. One of our most successful ones was an 'Economic Human Rights Bus Tour.' The theme was the human right to work and feed oneself. We rented buses, and invited journalists, politicians, activists, and others to ride with us on a most untraditional 'tour.' If you can get politicians to attend—which we did by offering them a chance to deliver comments—you increase the chances of press coverage.

"We visited places like SROs (single residence occupancy hotels for the homeless) in downtown Oakland, a soup kitchen, strawberry fields in Watsonville, and—to add a hopeful note—an organic farm. At the various stops, people gave testimony about the conditions of their lives or work. The details were particularly moving—for example, when you hear about the machines a strawberry picker has to work with, the lack of water, the condition of the bathroom facilities, and all that, it's far more revealing than statistics."

hardwood is certainly newsworthy. A demonstration or protest is always news; although whether it's big or interesting enough to cover might be another question. Some cities see protests so regularly, particularly in the same part of town such as city hall, that the media loses interest. And if the media perceives an event as solely staged to make news, many reporters will ignore it.

Releasing a study or report can be news, especially if your conclusions break new ground. Thus, if an animal rights group's well-planned study concludes that properly trained pitbulls are less likely to bite than your average cocker spaniel, media outlets will line up to cover it.

Alternately, you can tie your work or insights to a story that's already in the news. For example, if one of your elderly nursing home clients attempts suicide, that's probably not news by itself. But if you can legitimately present it as part of a pattern of suicides caused by reductions in public health care benefits and patients' fears of being kicked out of nursing homes, you've got yourself a news story.

Feature stories are a different animal, and are usually handled by a different set of journalists. Though feature stories may tie into news of the moment, they usually take a more reflective view of their topic, and go on at much greater length. (Think about the human interest stories that fill the middle sections of your local newspaper, or hour-long radio interview shows as opposed to quick, sound-bite news reports.) Feature stories allot enough print space or air time to give some background and flesh the topic out, often with the help of named experts.

Possible nonprofit-based feature stories might include:

- how years of your campaign picking up beach litter has contributed to the resurgence of tidal pool life
- local teens' attitudes toward smoking or sex, complete with interviews of teens at area high schools
- how an unusual and interesting method of mental health counseling plus high levels of physical activity is achieving success without drugs among your organization's severely depressed clients, or
- how the improving regional economy is affecting the lives of migrant farmworkers.

The point is that many, if not most, nonprofits have the raw material necessary to present the media with an attractive feature story. But again, the key to getting coverage is almost always to develop and polish the story yourself, not to wait for the media to discover you.

Nearly every type of media devotes separate attention to arts, literary, and social events. These might include everything from the opening of your fall music or theatre season to a small lecture, dinner, or garden tour—though you'll find that some media outlets report only on events of a certain size or perceived quality. If you ask for coverage, you may have to open yourself up to the world of critics, with their ability to make or break a show's success—but even criticism is a form of publicity, and at least a portion of the public has learned to take critics' rants with a grain of salt. Also, remember that there are other types of arts coverage. With some advance planning, you can get feature articles and interviews that focus on what the artist has to say or show. (If you land a radio interview, think about offering free ticket giveaways as a way to inspire audience interest!) Such stories give tacit encouragement to the public to check things out. You'll find more about how to invite the press to attend your events later in this chapter.

Who to Approach With Your Story

Let's assume now that you've got a story that's just dying to be told, and you've determined how you'll pitch it (what kind of hook you'll hang it on). Now you need to decide who to contact. Because most media operations work against deadlines and on a low budget, there's a very real risk that if you simply prepare a press release and mail or email it out, your effort will land in a dead file, unread. To greatly increase your chances of success, you need to understand how the media is organized to accept stories—and specifically who you need to reach within each media outlet. The sections that follow will:

- look separately at how print media, radio, and television are organized, and
- suggest methods for acquainting yourself with the appropriate journalists and media outlets serving your area.

How the Media Is Organized to Accept and Produce Stories

Most media outlets are more structured about who covers what type of stories, as well as when, where, and how the stories will be presented, than the public realizes. Obviously you'd never think of sending a press release about your litter pickup day to a newspaper's cookbook editor—but realize that you could be committing as absurd an error (and hamper your credibility as a result) if you send it to a reporter who covers only legislative and political news. This section will help you grasp the various distinctions, and learn who your first points of contact should ordinarily be.

Print Media Contact Persons

At a newspaper, your usual contact point, particularly for straight news stories, is a reporter. The "byline" on a story will tell you the name of the reporter who wrote it. That person may be a staff reporter or a freelancer (freelancers are more likely with a weekly or monthly newspaper or magazine). On bigger city newspapers, reporters are assigned a particular "beat," such as arts, education, environment, religion, or city/community issues. If you follow the news on issues similar to those that your nonprofit would like to weigh in on, you'll see the same names popping up regularly.

> **TIP**
>
> **Your nonprofit can be covered in the business section.** Business reporters are often hungry to cover something more interesting than the bottom line. For example, an organization that rehabilitates drug addicts by offering training in how to cook for—and run—a restaurant, is likely to attract the attention of the newspaper's business journalists. And, your nonprofit is itself a business, so your own creative strategies for success may inspire media interest.

When reading newspaper bylines, you'll see that a number of stories come either from a wire service such as the Associated Press (AP) or Reuters, or from another paper, such as *The Los Angeles Times*, through syndication. It follows that to get your story covered in a number of newspapers, you'll want to send it to major wire services, most of which have regional bureaus. Typically, you'll have to contact the news editor, unless you know a specific reporter interested in your subject matter. But be sure the story you're presenting will truly be of broad interest to a national audience—for example, your tips to parents on choosing a good summer camp might get picked up, but your ratings of local summer camps certainly won't.

Another possible news contact point at a newspaper is an editor. On large papers, editors are usually assigned to a particular topic (the business section editor, for example), with considerable control over the reporters who work on that topic. However, they're less likely to pick up on a story than the reporter who'll write it, meaning they're your second choice. You should be aware of their existence, however—their preferences can override the reporters' when it comes to which stories actually make it into print.

Newspapers also contain various articles and features that don't fall into the category of news—if you want to pitch a story like this, you may need to separately contact the responsible staffperson. For example, feature writers may cover even more specific areas than news writers, such as food, fashion, travel, or entertainment. Or, in some cases, if an event would make a great photo feature, you might contact a photo editor with newsworthy photos—say, of your blind child clients who have learned to make sand castles, or of loggers cutting down old-growth trees right next to a national park. Or put another way, it can sometimes pay to reverse the normal news-gathering process, which uses photos to illustrate a story, and instead offer a photo so evocative that a newspaper will want to feature it as an attention grabber—with or without a story.

Another non-news alternative is to offer the newspaper an editorial or op-ed piece, in which case you would separately contact the editorial page staff. Some newspapers also have columnists devoted to covering events or society happenings, whom you can contact to promote your organization's theatre, arts, or dance pieces, or other major special events. Also look for newspapers that have regular opinion columnists (although many editorials are provided by national news syndicates). They're always looking for something new to opine about—with a quick phone call, followed up by your expert factual materials, you may provide that very something.

Magazines tend to rely on submissions, often approved in advance, from freelance writers. Many freelancers regularly work for the same publications, however, so if you see a name appearing often, that person is probably your best contact. He or she would then approach the magazine. If you're up for a little more work, you could try writing a story for magazine publication yourself—the submission guidelines can usually be found in the first few pages of a magazine or on its back cover. Most magazines ask you to send a query letter before submitting the entire article. That makes your initial task easier, but can make getting the go-ahead difficult if you don't have a writing track record.

Radio Contact Persons

At a radio station, your contact point depends on the type of show. For news shows, reporters or news directors are your best bet. (Listen carefully, though— many stations license news programs from national outlets, such as National Public Radio (NPR) or CBS Radio News, and are therefore less accessible for locally generated news stories.) It's best to keep your ears open for the local news shows, especially those with a one-hour format. You'll notice that much of what they cover is not really hard news. For example, if your group works with architecture students at a local university to build excellent (but affordable) housing out of recycled materials, and then donates the housing to a low-income family, you may get plenty of coverage.

For public affairs or talk shows, the host is rarely the best one to contact— especially for more popular shows, it's the producer's job to select and schedule guests. Often the producer's name is mentioned briefly at the end of each show or you can identify him or her by calling the station. Especially if you can find a producer interested in your line of stories, you're in good shape, because producers tend to be easier to reach than hosts. In some cases, however, hosts do assume at least some role in deciding whom to interview, so it can also make sense to contact the host directly.

If anyone from your organization will be visiting another city, think about contacting radio journalists there, as well. Although telephone technology allows you to be interviewed from anywhere in the world, the sound quality and general ambience aren't as good as if you are there in person. For example, if your clean air group has just released a study on pollution from coal-fired power plants and you are planning a holiday visit to your parents in the Midwest or Northeast, chances are good that you can set up radio interviews there.

Many radio stations also have community calendars open only to nonprofits, a sort of public-service function that helps the station stay connected to its audience. If you've got an event, find out who coordinates the calendar, and how and by when to submit an announcement. If any important terms or names in your announcement are difficult to pronounce, put the correct pronunciation in parentheses and quotation marks after the word.

Television Contact Persons

At a television station, who to contact depends on the type of show and the size of the station. In general, you'll have the best luck with local stations. If you're seeking rapid attention to breaking news, such as an eviction, or the birth of an otter in captivity, ask for the "assignment desk"—that's where producers tell their crews, "Go to this location, now." For news events with a little more lead time, you'd normally talk to the planning desk or assignment editor. Some television programs have less news-oriented formats—for example, focusing on consumer affairs, local events, or travel. If you're interested in placing a story with one of these, contact the station and ask to talk to a producer of that show.

A number of local television stations also offer community event alerts, usually flashed on the screen now and then—call the station and ask for the appropriate contact person, then request submission guidelines and eligibility rules.

> **CAUTION**
>
> **Be nice to the intermediaries.** No matter what type of media outlet you're dealing with, support staff and interns are likely to be an integral part of the story selection process. Opening the mail, screening phone calls, and dealing with email are tasks commonly delegated to people whose work is rarely credited by name. It goes without saying that it can pay big dividends to be polite to these news department foot soldiers, whose opinion and enthusiasm may carry a lot more weight than their titles suggest.

Locating Contact Information

As far as how you actually get a journalist's contact phone number or email, it's usually easier than you might expect. For starters, newspapers, radio, and television stations all have a main phone number, and they have every incentive to keep it accessible. Typically, the receptionist will willingly pass you along to the appropriate person's line. Though you may not be given the person's direct line right away, someone will probably listen to your message and respond if they're interested.

Also look at the bottom of articles in your local newspaper: Many journalists include their email address there, and read what comes in. Most print publications will also list additional contact information on the first page or two. Also, at the end of a radio show, you'll often hear a phone number or email address for suggestions or comments. This is usually a more general box than their actual host's or producer's, but again, it's a start. In addition, always check the outlet's website for contact information.

RESOURCE

Use the Internet to find your contact. Some news outlets actually publish materials or guides on how to access them. For example, check out San Francisco television station KRON's "Media Access Guide for Non-Profit Organizations," at www.kron.com/Global/story.asp?S=510446&nav=5D8D5Bzu.

Because you may not be with your organization forever, you should create a media file for others to use. Creating a physical file with your notes, or better yet, a computer file of media contacts and information, will lay the groundwork for a lasting relationship between your organization and the media.

To get started, check out the national media list maintained by FAIR (Fairness & Accuracy in Reporting) at www.fair.org/index.php?page=111. However, unless you're with a large, national organization, your most fruitful contacts are likely to be with local media.

Educate Know-Nothing Hosts

In both radio and television, many show hosts—often called "talent" by real journalists—aren't personally familiar with the stories they cover. In other words, though they may look good, sound good, and project an aura of celebrity, they won't have read your study or, in many instances, even your press packet. For example, a friend of mine had long respected a San Francisco television talk show host—but when he finally appeared on her show, he was dismayed to hear her ask, with just a few minutes to air time, "So, what are we talking about today?"

Fortunately, unprepared hosts are only a problem if you aren't ready for them. Don't bug the producers for advance contact with the host, or withhold your best information for when you get to talk to him or her. Instead, fully cooperate with the producers, to get them excited about the topic, and to help them develop materials and questions that will fully prepare the host to sound like an informed expert. In addition, it pays to have a short list of potential questions, together with your name, organization, and information on how people can reach your organization. In appreciation of your efforts to make the host sound like an expert, many hosts will not only follow your suggestions, they'll also toss in several plugs for your activities.

Get to Know the Media Serving Your Area

Journalists are not all as remote as they might appear. Although a few broadcasters think they're movie stars, most of them, particularly at the local level, have chosen their life's work because they are genuinely interested in people and information. Add to that the fact that all news people are always on the lookout for a good story, and it's easy to see that they need you as much as you need them. But, as with any relationship, you've got to hold up your end. Even if you never talk to some of these journalists personally, doing your part to understand what they cover—so that you can, someday, knowledgeably say to one of them, "I've got a story that's perfect for you"—can make all the difference. It's a matter of matching journalist's names (many of which may already be in your media file) to personalities, interest areas, and even job descriptions.

Background Research

Your first step can be done in relative comfort, on your couch or in your favorite coffee shop. Simply observe what types of stories the media serving your area cover, and who's writing or producing the pieces. Probably the simplest way to learn is to scan a broad selection of local newspapers—not just the big dailies, but also special interest papers and free weeklies or monthlies. Even neighborhood papers, shopping center publications, and community association newsletters can work brilliantly for local groups.

Take a similar survey of magazines, particularly special interest ones. And don't forget magazines and newsletters produced by other nonprofits or public-oriented groups—they too are on the lookout for new material, and may be interested in an opportunity for cross-publicity. For example, if your nonprofit group promotes chess in the public schools and is sponsoring a regional tournament expected to attract students from hundreds of high schools, a regional group working to improve public education might be excited to cover the event in its newsletter.

Also get to know your local ethnic newspapers, particularly if cultural or immigration issues are relevant to the work you do—immigrants are a growing part of the U.S. population, and studies show that more and more of them rely primarily on ethnic or non-English-language media for their information. (Reading the non-English media will obviously be harder, but some provide translations or mix in some articles in English.)

Next, start listening to a variety of radio shows, especially locally produced news and talk programs. Large AM outlets are usually a good bet, as are your local public radio stations. Make sure you tune in during "drive time"—about 6:00 through 10:00 in the morning, and 3:00 through 7:00 in the evening. During these hours, radio stations put on their heavy-hitter news and talk shows, knowing that they've got a captive commuter audience. Try to figure out the stations' and hosts' interests and biases. Also, think creatively—for example, an all-sports station may not be approachable with your everyday story, but may be interested in your bike-a-thon, your recently published study about the effects of steroid use, or your rescue of a dog who loves to skateboard. And don't overlook college stations—they may not have a very far-reaching signal, but especially if you need volunteers, their listeners tend to be open-minded and interested in getting involved.

Television is another important outlet—and it may be more accessible to you than you think. Reviewing a weekly television guide should help you identify news and other special interest shows that might be interested in featuring some aspect of your organization's work or inviting one of your in-house experts to participate in a story. And don't skip over local cable access channels—they can be among the most accessible of television stations, because they often have time to fill. Especially if you can gain coverage before or after a widely viewed city council or school board meeting, you may reach a surprisingly robust audience.

Try to listen to or watch every potentially interesting radio or television program at least once, to understand its personality and format. If you don't have time to do more than that, find out whether the show has a website. Scanning the show titles may give you an idea of which journalists or outlets are interested in what. As you read, watch, and listen, pay attention to what subjects get covered the most, as well as how they get covered. Even if a particular media outlet doesn't have a stated theme, you'll notice that most media have favorite topics—and subjects that they steer clear of. You may notice some political bias, as well—very few media are as objective as they claim or hope to be.

Be on the particular lookout for stories that bear any relation to ones that you might want to place. Then, write down the names of the people who wrote or produced these stories, and add them to your media file. Also keep an eye open for the names of nonprofits and people who make it into the news, and ask yourself how the news producers found them. It probably wasn't in the Yellow Pages. Think about how you would have pitched the same story, and what aspect of it may have caught the reporter's or producer's attention. You may also start noticing the same experts' and groups' names cropping up over and over again when certain issues are covered. If they're talking about the area of your expertise, this may be annoying, but it should also give you encouragement—it may be time for fresh voices on a subject the media already covers.

Also be alert to show formats, which may dictate how you pitch a story. For example, if a particular public interest TV show frequently produces its material on location rather than in the studio, you'll have an edge if you can pitch an interesting event at an attractive location. If your guide dog for the blind group schedules a training at a seashore park, the station may be more interested in covering the event than they would be if you held the training in a roped-off parking lot.

If you decide to make a major commitment to courting the media, look for ways to travel in the same circles. See if any reporters will be speaking publicly (many of them write books and need to publicize them). Then attend, and introduce yourself. Or, sign up for area conferences or events on media issues—and be sure to wear your glasses so you can read the nametags. In some metropolitan areas, nonprofit media groups even provide training for media workers interested in peace, justice, education, and social responsibility, ever a likely place to meet professional journalists interested in your work.

> **TIP**
>
> **Even after your initial rush of media research, try to keep an eye on who is doing what.** Be sure to keep your media contacts list up to date. Journalists move between stations, publications, or assignments fairly frequently, and you won't help your cause by misaddressing your press releases.

Make Your In-House Experts Available

After you've figured out which media venues might be interested in covering your nonprofit's work, you should let them know about your group, and about any experts you have available to help them. The most prized possession of most journalists and media producers is their "experts" list—often maintained on an old-fashioned Rolodex. Therefore, your goal is to get your name, or the names of your organization's staff and board, on to those lists. Then, when a news story hits—say, the federal government's plan to spend more money on highways—there's a good chance that the E.D. of your rapid-transit-oriented organization will be called and have a chance to point out that the money could be far better spent on light rail alternatives.

> **TIP**
>
> **Make your experts available on short notice.** When news breaks, journalists often need to reach experts in minutes or, at most, an hour or two. If you can provide the expert's cell phone and home phone numbers, you are far more likely to see their names—and the name of your organization—in the news.

Pitching and Placing Stories

Once you know which media cover particular types of stories, and perhaps have made some initial contacts with journalists and producers, you can begin trying to place stories. The best ways for nonprofits to approach or attract the media include:

- press releases
- publicity for special events
- staging a media stunt
- phone calls about breaking news, and
- letters to the editor and op-ed pieces.

You'll notice that press conferences don't appear on this list. Unless you're the U.S. President or a well-known spokesperson for a very large organization, press conferences tend to be more trouble than they're worth. You'll spend a lot of time getting the word out (it usually requires a press release a few days in advance, then an advisory on the same day), assembling speakers, and preparing a statement—and you'll be lucky if more than one reporter shows up. But, of course, there are exceptions to every rule. If you've got an issue that's burning hot, or access to a location where lots of reporters will already be buzzing about, you may want to give it a try.

> **TIP**
>
> **Alert your supporters and colleagues to your organization's media appearances.** If someone from your organization will be appearing on television or radio, it's a perfect time to send an email to your membership (not to mention your friends and professional colleagues) giving them a heads up. For radio call-in shows, ask them to phone in with questions—to tip the balance against less sympathetic callers!

Press Releases

Anyone can write and send a press release. You don't have to have any special credentials or invitations. You simply write up the story you want to convey, preferably in one page or less, and send it out while it's still fresh and interesting.

If you've got some spare minutes, you'll also want to tweak your basic wording to better fit the interests of your different news targets.

Craft your release to grab the reader's attention within a few seconds. All journalists receive more press releases than they can read or cover—many remain unopened altogether. If you're lucky enough to have someone glance at the contents of your envelope (or fax or email), you want to give the journalist (or his or her assistant or intern) a reason to keep reading before sending your release to meet its comrades in the recycle bin. And your first reader is often looking for a reason to reject your release (and therefore, clean one more item out of his or her in box)—any obvious errors, such as a misspelled name or title, may provide just the excuse your reader needs to toss out all of your hard work.

> ⓘ **TIP**
>
> **Press releases aren't only for the press.** Make your press release do double duty—by publishing it on your website. This gives Web viewers a sense that your organization is a "happening" place, because you're busy disseminating up-to-the-minute information to the media. It also helps educate the broader public about your organization's work and the underlying issues. Remember, a Web search for terms related to the issues you work on might bring an Internet surfer straight to your press release.

Formatting and Drafting Your Press Release

For the appropriate format for a printed press release, see the template below and the sample following that, an actual press release from the Asia Society (a New York–based educational nonprofit that promotes awareness of the Asia-Pacific region, through art exhibitions, films, lectures, seminars, and more; www.asiasociety.org). Your press release should be no more than two pages long (one is better).

When preparing the hardcopy version (which most journalists with whom I spoke still prefer), use ordinary white 8½" by 11" paper, and print in black (unless your organization's logo is in color). If you need to include more information than fits in this format (such as background information or a list of plaintiffs in a class-action lawsuit), add an attachment that supplements, but is separate from, the main release. If the story warrants photos, black and white glossies are best, or you could email photos in digital form. Don't include other attachments, such as videotapes, unless they're essential to producing the story, and you've called to make sure that they will be welcome.

Slip the release into a plain folder with pockets, or a folder with a logo if your organization has one. Then put the folder into a 10" by 12" manila envelope—preferably not a padded envelope or a canister, because these are sometimes delivered later by mailrooms, and cause annoyance because they take up valuable space. And definitely don't use a business-size envelope, which will require you to fold up your press release. No one likes opening piles of mail, and they especially hate having to unfold the contents.

View From the Radio Newsroom

Harry Lin, former news anchor at KQED, an NPR affiliate station in San Francisco, told me the following about the many press releases he received from nonprofit organizations: "Since we covered local news on a daily basis, we received press releases from nonprofits all the time. Much of my daily routine, in fact, was sifting through releases . . . deciding which ones to toss, which ones to file as 'just background info,' which ones to give reporters to follow up on, and which ones got tacked to our communal bulletin board so that we could all laugh at them. All of which is to say that news organizations are swamped every day with releases, so to cut through the clutter and stand out is not easy. However: No matter how flashy or elaborate one's release, you can bet that someone else sent in something even flashier. So, the trick to getting noticed isn't to send in the wackiest, weirdest, loudest, most unorthodox release.

"For example, I can still remember the freshly baked icing-covered chocolate cake that was messengered to our newsroom one morning accompanied by a press release about . . . well, I can't remember what the press release was about, but we ate the cake in two seconds flat, and no, we didn't attend the event the release was touting.

"The most important factor is actually the most basic: The headline must be relevant, intriguing, timely, and newsworthy. News organizations aren't interested in anything that smells old, already-happened, or historical."

Press Release Template

[Your organization's name; preferably with logo]

FOR IMMEDIATE RELEASE

Contact: *[Name of one or preferably two persons they can call]*

[Date]

[Phone number of contacts]

[Email address of contacts]

[Centered title of press release, in larger font]

[Your state, in capital letters, such as "OKLAHOMA"]

[Text of press release, in short paragraphs, ending with a brief description of your organization and references to where they can obtain more information, such as on your website.]

###

[traditional signal of end of text]

NRDC Press Release

NATURAL RESOURCES DEFENSE COUNCIL

Media Center
Press Release

Main page | Archive

FOR IMMEDIATE RELEASE
Press contact: Julia Bovey, 202/270-0768 or Elizabeth Heyd, 202/289-2424
If you are not a member of the press, please write to us nrdcinfo@nrdc.org or see our contact page

NRDC Sues EPA for Failing to Ban Two Highly Toxic Pesticides

WASHINGTON (February 28, 2007) -- The Environmental Protection Agency has failed to protect the public from exposure to two highly toxic pesticides -- DDVP (dichlorvos) and carbaryl -- found in common household products that have been demonstrated in laboratory studies to cause severe neurological and developmental harm, according to a lawsuit filed today by the Natural Resources Defense Council (NRDC).

The action charges that EPA has missed its congressionally mandated deadline to finalize a comprehensive reevaluation of carbaryl, failed for 20 years to finish an expedited review of DDVP, and failed to respond to a petition calling for a ban on the chemicals.

"EPA is needlessly jeopardizing the health of our children," said Dr. Jennifer Sass, an NRDC senior scientist. "The agency should ban DDVP and carbaryl. There are safer alternatives on the market today, and we urge consumers to avoid any products that use either of these two pesticides."

DDVP -- commonly used in pest strips, aerosol sprays and pet collars -- is one of a class of the most dangerous pesticides on the market, called organophosphates, which derive from World War II-era nerve agents. Studies have shown DDVP causes cancer in laboratory animals. California lists DDVP as a known carcinogen, while the World Health Organization and the EPA list it as a possible human carcinogen. DDVP already is banned overseas, including the United Kingdom, Denmark and Sweden.

Carbaryl -- a highly toxic pesticide used in large-scale agriculture, lawn products, commercial garden centers and pet products -- is particularly toxic to the developing nervous system in fetuses, infants, and young children. EPA acknowledges that carbaryl can overstimulate the nervous system, inducing symptoms including nausea, dizziness, confusion, and even death in extreme cases.

"EPA has known about the risks of these chemicals to human health for decades, and has dragged its feet while allowing exposures to continue," said Mae Wu, a staff attorney at NRDC

The lawsuit is being filed in the U.S. District Court for the Southern District of New York.

As mentioned in "View From the Radio Newsroom," you should spend some time on the title of the release. This doesn't mean being so clever that you obfuscate the meaning—but it also doesn't mean a tired-sounding scholarly title. For example, let's say you work for an environmental organization that's reporting on new findings about ocean temperatures and otters. As possible headlines, "Hotter Otters Make Shark Fodder" would be silly and incomprehensible. At the other extreme, "Recently Published Studies Show that 0.75% Increases in Ocean Temperatures Negatively Impact Otter Populations and Increase Vulnerability to Shark Predation" would make readers eyes glaze over. A nice middle ground might be "Otters in Hot Water as Ocean Temperatures Rise"—it gets the main point across with a pun that isn't too annoying, and could itself be used as a newspaper headline.

Journalists love to lift words straight from press releases, to help them meet their ever-looming deadlines. To make their job easier and increase your chances of publication, write the body of your release in the same style you see in newspaper articles. It's best to start with a colorful story or set of facts, move to the background information, and wrap it up quickly with a snappy closing line. Don't forget to include the "five W's" early on—what, when, where, who, and why. Don't use long sentences or ponderous words—the person reading your release is going to be skimming it amid the noise and bustle of a newsroom, not reading it word for word. Most news sources figure that their audience members haven't finished high school, so eloquent literary language is not what they're looking for.

TIP

Line up colorful interviews in advance. Because reporters know that people like to read about people, most feature stories rely on anecdotes about—and quotes from—real folks. Thus, if your press release is about a summer program that teaches wilderness skills to inner-city kids, you'll want to include some names, photos, and contact information about your star pupils. And don't forget to prep them so they say something appropriate should a reporter call.

Be sure to include accurate contact information on the release. One of a reporter's pet peeves is getting a release that lists "Contact Person X," then calling the number and getting no answer, or being led into voicemail purgatory.

At that point, the reporter is likely to kiss the story goodbye and move on to one that can be finished before the deadline. Ideally, journalists hope that the phone will be answered by a live voice—if not the actual contact person, then someone who can connect them to that person quickly. On the positive side, according to Keven Guillory, of KQED radio in San Francisco, "A grassroots nonprofit can help put itself on an equal footing with larger nonprofits by having people who are easily reachable even during nonbusiness hours, and a front desk that will give top priority to media calls."

Sending Out Your Press Release

Once you've prepared a catchy press release, you'll need to carefully consider where, when, and how you'll send it.

Where to Send

Don't just send your press release out scattershot, or as a hand-scribbled fax. Be selective. The evening news probably doesn't want to hear about your upcoming garage sale fundraiser, unless it's of a truly staggering size. Your community newspaper, however, might be willing to give it a mention. You'll preserve your credibility with the media by demonstrating that you send them only stories that fit their area of interest. (You'd be amazed at how many people don't follow this rule, so journalists tend to get swamped and stop reading the releases of the serial senders.) By developing a track record of carefully placing stories, you'll increase the chances that journalists or producers will pay attention to your really hot story when it comes their way.

When to Send

Different outlets have different schedules, and it can be just as bad to send something too early as too late. If you're targeting daily news outlets, they work a day or three ahead, tops. If you send a release about something you want covered two or three weeks from now, you'll be long forgotten once that time rolls around. On the other hand, feature stories and talk-radio interviews often need a week or two of advance notice. Monthly magazines often need a lead time of three months, and they sometimes want high-quality photos to go with your story, so plan and send accordingly. As you establish contact with members of the media, ask about their schedules. Or, you can simply call the front desk of the news outlet and ask.

How to Send

There are several ways to send your press release. The traditional printed, mailed copy is still used, and still effective. You may, however, want to double up on your methods—for example, by combining U.S. mail with email or fax. Email and fax are both good for getting the word out quickly, but both are also easy for journalists to delete or ignore. One journalist told me that he always opened press release packages sent via by Federal Express or another courier first, even though he knew that the extra expense didn't necessarily translate into a better story.

Because you never know what's getting read and what's getting tossed, it's a good idea to follow up on your press release with a phone call, particularly to journalists whom you know should be interested in the story. Ask whether they saw your release, take a few seconds to pitch the story and make it sound exciting, and be ready to send another copy right away.

Check Out Media Watch Groups

A handful of nonprofits and other organizations are dedicated to keeping an eye on what news the media covers and how often with an implicit critique of the lack of coverage of issues in which your nonprofit may be interested. While these groups probably can't help you directly, you may learn more about the media from them, and they sometimes offer training or tips on getting underreported issues into the public eye. For example, check out:

- **www.alternet.org.** AlterNet, run by the Institute for Alternative Journalism, maintains an online database of alternative, public interest, and opinion stories to help feed the media.
- **www.media-alliance.org.** Media Alliance, based in San Francisco, is a resource center for media workers. It also offers training to community organizations and activists in media skills and advocacy techniques.
- **www.fair.org.** Fairness & Accuracy in Reporting, or FAIR, is a media watchdog group that works with both activists and journalists to critique existing news coverage and help get underreported stories into the news.

Publicity and Press Invitations for Special Events

An event that your organization sponsors or participates in is, by its very nature, "news." Whether it's interesting news is another matter—a theater piece will probably attract wider attention than your annual spring car wash. If you think your event is sufficiently colorful, will attract enough people, or fits an existing media outlet's area of interest, then by all means send out press releases and get in touch with your favorite media professionals to get the word out.

At the very least, many media outlets collect information on events for their entertainment or community calendars. It won't take much research for you to find out who carries these calendars, their criteria for submission, and—perhaps most important—how far in advance you need to advise them of a certain event. And don't forget events calendars on cable access channels.

The best way to get journalists to pay attention to your event is to invite some of them to attend—for free, of course. If your group or event is large enough, you might even set up a separate press night, prescreening, or the like (they'll love it if you include free food). Don't just send press members a stack of tickets, or you won't know how many to expect. Instead, contact selected journalists (by press release, phone call, or email) and tell them about the event. Include an invitation to call you for free tickets or a press pass. Remember to offer two tickets to each journalist, so that he or she can bring a companion—few people like to attend an event alone.

Will a journalist who attends your event necessarily do a story about it? No. Many consider freebie invites to be a perk of the job. But even if no story is forthcoming, this is a valuable way to build relationships. A journalist who doesn't think your current concert, fair, or seminar is worth a story will still probably develop a warm feeling toward your group, and may look for a way to cover you later.

Hosting Members of the Press at Events

When inviting members of the press to theater, musical, or other major events, it's customary to ask them to pick up their ticket at "will call"; or, if enough journalists will be attending, at a special "press table," usually in the lobby. When they arrive, you can give them not only a ticket and program, but also a "press packet"—a folder with additional background information, and copies of any other media coverage. Having a press table also gives you an opportunity to make personal contact and gently nudge the journalists about when and whether they're planning to feature your event or the artists or other participants—with the emphasis on gently. Mostly, you should just be welcoming. If it's a sit-down event, and seats aren't otherwise assigned, be sure to reserve seats for the journalists. They don't have to be in the very front row, but seat them close enough to appreciate what's going on.

TIP

If you're hosting a musical event, invite radio DJs. Local radio stations may be interested in playing music by the group you're featuring, along with mentioning the upcoming event on the air. If you offer the DJ free tickets and CDs for audience giveaways, your odds of coverage go up even higher.

Staging a Media Stunt or Direct Action

If your organization has an activist bent, you may want to create an event with an eye towards attracting the media—such as a protest, march, hanging a controversial banner, or delivering something humorous or damning to a government or corporate office. And fortunately, you don't need to court arrest to score lots of ink—something as innocent as staging a one-day count of migrating birds in Central Park or seals off the Oregon coast can garner loads of media attention.

Doing something that's visually interesting—for example, with costumes, signs, puppets, or props—will help you attract television coverage. This strategy is particularly useful for organizations that don't have visually interesting clients or activities, but have a message that needs to be heard. However, because many of the standard stunt techniques have already been tried (very few ears perk up at the mention of another protest march), you will need to think up something clever and creative.

One California group came up with a headline grabbing—and conveniently low-budget—stunt by cleaning up a clothing-optional beach while wearing nothing at all. At the other end of the fabric spectrum you'll find the Raging Grannies, a group of women who dress up in aprons, shawls, and old-fashioned hats and sing humorous—and sometimes shocking—songs to promote global peace, justice, and economic and social equality. The idea started in Vancouver, British Columbia, but different groups have sprung up in U.S. cities from Seattle, Washington, to Rochester, New York. And, they've attracted major media attention, from *The Washington Post, The New York Times*, and C-SPAN.

Another favorite stunt tactic is to deliver something unpleasant to a corporate or other wrongdoer. For example, in winter of 2003, Greenpeace offered its members the opportunity to donate enough to send a personalized bottle of polluted Bhopal well water to a Dow Chemical facility. You can adapt their strategy to something less confrontational and more local—for example, a group advocating the continuation of high school sports in the face of budget cuts could send 50 kids to a school board meeting carrying deflated soccer balls.

If you're planning to stage a media stunt, you'll need to promote it just like any other event, usually with a press release plus follow-up phone calls. The catch is that if you're planning to surprise anyone, giving advance notice may not be safe. In such a situation, it's best to tell only your most trusted journalist contacts, and place last-minute phone calls to others. Alternately, you can simply arrange for your own footage and photographs of the event, with written materials, recorded interviews, and contact information for follow-up interviews, and offer it to the media immediately afterward.

RESOURCE

Want to know more about media stunts? For more information on staging nonviolent direct actions, see the manuals and other information on the website of the Ruckus Society, at www.ruckus.org (look under "Resources").

Phone Calls

There are times when a full press release isn't appropriate. For example, maybe you've got a simple tidbit of colorful information or gossip—such as a tip regarding a natural event or a local politician—to pass on to an interested journalist. Or perhaps you're watching an event that merits immediate media attention—a beached whale, or a face-off between demonstrators at your family planning clinic, for example. Don't waste time writing a press release—just pick up the phone.

Phone calls also make sense when you're contacting someone who won't write an in-depth story on your issue—for example, an opinion or gossip columnist whom you hope will mention your organization or cause if you can pitch it well. For example, if your anti-noise group learns that your highly obnoxious anti-environment mayor has just bought the loudest type of motorcycle, which he drives home from city council meetings at midnight, it might be worth a call to your newspaper's "On the Town" columnist.

Whether you get the journalist or a message machine, be brief and to the point. Start with your name and phone number. Have the important information written down in front of you so that you won't forget anything. Above all, don't ramble, and stay positive—journalists get irritated and lose interest when forced to listen to extraneous detail, editorializing, or even worse, whining about the fact that no one is covering your story. If you reach the journalist in person, be ready to provide follow-up information, but don't expect or insist on a commitment. You may, in fact, get a blunt rejection—which probably just means that the story doesn't fit the media outlet's current priorities or interests.

TIP

Provide independent experts. To avoid looking hopelessly self-promoting, tell journalists when they should talk to people other than your E.D. and staff—perhaps a person at another nonprofit with which you cooperate, or one of your advisory council members, or just an expert you happen to know about. As long as this person is respected, you'll impress the journalist as an objective—and well-connected—source for future stories.

RESOURCE

Need more information on dealing with the media? For an excellent and practical guide to planning media events and interacting with the media, full of stories from the author's own experience and interviews with members of the press, see *Making the News: A Guide for Nonprofits & Activists,* by Jason Salzman (Westview Press). Also check out Jason Salzman's website at www .causecommunications.com.

Ask Your Funders About Joint Media Efforts

Not all foundations have a media strategy, but some understand that helping garner publicity for their grantees helps everyone in the long run. It brings in publicity and possibly increased donations for the funder and its grantees alike, and lifts a burden from the shoulders of nonprofits trying hard to deliver services.

One of the leaders in this effort is The California Wellness Foundation, which published a 2003 report titled "Reflections on Communications Strategies that Accent Grantees." The Foundation asserts: "We strongly believe we owe it to our grantees and the people they serve to use our non-grantmaking resources to tell their stories. So our entire communications program is focused on our grantees and their work." (The report is available on the foundation's website, at www.tcwf.org.)

Letters to the Editor and Op-Ed Pieces

Instead of waiting for someone else to write a story about you, try writing your own. Letters to newspaper and magazine editors and op-ed (opinion-editorial) pieces are great ways to demonstrate your organization's expertise and affect public opinion on issues of importance. And, the piece will be all in your own words (probably minus a few after it goes past an editor), unmediated by the bias or boredom of a reporter.

Letters to the editor are shots in the dark—you'll have to prepare and send them with little or no guarantee that they'll get printed. However, the fact that your letter will represent your organization, which presumably has some expertise on the topic, increases your chances of publication. Another way to improve your odds is to carefully follow the publication's guidelines regarding letters, particularly word count. The upward limit is often 200 words. You can often further boost your odds by sending a letter when your topic is in the news. In that case, you may want to style your letter as a response to or commentary regarding an article the publication (probably a newspaper, in this instance) printed. Fax or email your letter within 24 hours of the story you're responding to. The gamble of sending in a letter to the editor can pay off nicely—such letters are one of the most widely read parts of the newspaper or magazine.

Op-ed pieces are different from letters to the editor—they're usually given a special spot on a newspaper's editorial page, essentially as a guest editorial. For this reason, there's little to be gained by just sending one in. Instead, it's best to contact the editor of the relevant page in advance. Your chances of acceptance are best if you're willing to take a reasonably controversial (but not totally wacky) stand on an issue—including one that the newspaper doesn't agree with, but doesn't mind printing to stir up a bit of excitement. For example, an editor might print an article by the E.D. of an education-oriented nonprofit opposing affirmative action, but would be unlikely to print one advocating segregated education. Again, you'll need to jump on any hot issues quickly. If timing permits, the newspaper may arrange to place your op-ed piece next to one written by a person representing the other side.

Protecting Yourself in Media Interactions

Like anything else, there are downsides to taking on publicity efforts. Being aware of the most serious potential problems should help you take steps to avoid them. The risks are greatest in cases where you don't initiate the publicity or place your own story, but respond to a request for information or an interview. Here are the primary sources of difficulty you might encounter in working with the media:

- **You may spend a lot of time for little reward.** Once your organization's name is out there, your staff may get calls from reporters asking for information that may never be attributed to you. There's no point in getting mad—helping reporters write stories you are left out of is simply part of the investment it takes to play the publicity game. But once you know this, you'll want to avoid doing too much work. For example, never agree to write large portions of text for a print journalist without a mention of your organization's name. Also, be wary of freelance journalists who are shopping an article to publications without a firm commitment. Either way, you can spend many hours with no payoff.

- **The article or piece may be careless, wrong, or unflattering.** Print journalists are famous for talking to you by phone, scribbling down some notes, then putting quotation marks around something that you don't remember saying. Or, you may provide information that the journalist feeds into an unflattering piece about your organization or issue. In any personal interviews, try to speak slowly and carefully, avoid sarcasm or parodies that could be quoted out of context, and never, ever, say anything "off the record" if you don't want to see it in print. That phrase is no protection. Finally, if a journalist acts as if the "interview" portion of the conversation is over, and switches to a "just friends" mode, don't be lulled into saying something impolitic or catty. It, too, may be attributed to you.

- **You won't be sent a copy of the article or show.** People commonly ask journalists for copies or tapes of the final piece, but unless you're famous or the journalist owes you a favor, you'll likely find that both the journalist and the media outlet are too busy to provide it. Try to get as much information as you can about when the piece will be run, and then follow the news yourself, making your own copy or tape. Some larger television and radio stations allow you to buy copies of shows, which can be a reasonable alternative if the price is right. If your organization is one of the few that's regularly in the news, you might want to hire a clipping service to gather all mentions of your organization's name or issue.

- **You may be surprised at whose side the journalist was really on.** Especially if your organization does controversial work (either promotes or opposes the death penalty, for example), you can be sure that some of the reporters who call will be taking the other side. And if they do, they may try to bait you with innocent-sounding questions like, "Wouldn't you like to tell your side of the story," or "I'm very interested in why you believe such and such." In fact, they may have a different agenda altogether—perhaps an exposé on your organization, a sneering look at how muddle-headed people rally around a foolish cause, or something equally offensive. To protect against this, it helps to know who you are talking to. To find out, look up their past articles or shows (a Google search should get you quick results) before agreeing to any lengthy conversations.

- **You may get trapped into defending your organization.** If you've agreed to an interview but find that the journalist is on the attack, you'll want to practice some of the maneuvers honed by skilled politicians. The most important thing is to stay on message: Know what you want to convey, and then stick to it. Your message should center on the community need for the work you do, and your organization's commitment to serving a group of people or other creatures, or a particular cause. For example, if you know a liberal reporter wants to mock the pro–death penalty stance of your victims' rights group, you might want to repeat over and over again that your group is primarily interested in getting and keeping criminals off the street and that you only favor the death penalty for murderers of police officers, prison guards, and those killed by acts of terrorism. If the reporter seems to ignore this qualification while continuing to ask open-ended questions about the death penalty, you could even say "People for a Safe City only favors the death penalty in three limited situations, and we would appreciate it if your article makes that absolutely clear." Finally, no matter how tough, impertinent, or ridiculous a question, don't reply, "No comment." This sounds like Richard Nixon on a bad day, and will almost surely be featured in the article. Better to use humor to deflect an absurd line of questioning.

Enough negativity. With good planning, you should be able to develop relationships with a select list of media professionals who are accessible, interested in your work, and can be counted on not to misuse your time and trust. As a general rule, however, protecting your interests means limiting the number of people at your organization who have direct contact with the media. For smaller organizations, this may be no one beyond the E.D. and possibly the board president. At larger organizations, it might also include the development director, key program staff, select members of the board or advisory council, and, if you're lucky enough to have one, your media coordinator. Whoever you choose as spokespeople, make sure that everyone in the organization knows who they are.

Your spokespeople should obviously be articulate people of good judgment. It also helps greatly if they have enough experience with your organization and its issues to clearly explain its positions and policies. If the person can mix in colorful, short, and jargon-free anecdotes, so much the better. If they're going to be on-air, a good speaking voice and an ability to think on their feet helps, as well. According to C.S. Soong, host and producer of *Against the Grain*, a public affairs show on KPFA radio in Berkeley, "My ideal interviewee is someone who's articulate, has an efficient and forceful but not overbearing delivery, and can back up general statements with specific examples or illustrations." The host of a news-oriented show, however, would probably add a preference for people who can talk in sound bites. You should also make sure the interviewee is ready to repeat your organization's name, phone number, and website without checking notes—the host is likely to ask for it; even if the host forgets, your representative should try to work it in at least once.

Instruct nonspokesperson staff that if they happen to field a cold call from the media (a general question to the organization, not to a particular person), they should get some details on who is calling and what they're looking for, then say something like, "Let me get right back to you as soon as I've figured out who our best person to talk to you is." The best person may indeed be that very staffperson, but to make sure the organization stays on message, he or she should check in with the E.D. or another spokesperson before proceeding. Try to return all media phone calls quickly, however—if they don't get the information they're looking for almost immediately, they'll move on to another source or another story.

For television interviews, your spokesperson should dress up a bit, but avoid looking like a banker or big-firm lawyer. Just as it's usually best to avoid T-shirts, pierced eyebrows, and extreme hairstyles, you also want to avoid coming on as too affluent or establishment. Thus the male E.D. of a land trust organization will do better to appear in a corduroy jacket and slacks than in a three-piece pinstriped suit with a gold watch.

TIP

Script your own interview. If a journalist really wants to hear your story, he or she will probably be grateful, not annoyed, if you suggest the best questions to elicit information from you. Especially if you present your suggestions on one side of a sheet of paper and deferentially point out that they are just possible ideas, your help will almost always be welcome. I've given interviews that I scripted from start to finish in advance, including the bullet points flashed on the television screen.

Always Follow Up

A radio journalist told me, "Once someone has gotten a story on the air, they've overcome the biggest hurdle. At that point, if the person was articulate and knew their stuff, I'll be happy to hear from them again and consider their story ideas. But so many people drop the ball right here. In fact, many of them say to me, 'Can I let you know about other stories or our upcoming events?' and I say, 'Sure,' and then I never hear from them again."

TIP

Clip and save any favorable articles. Good media coverage is worth its weight in gold for establishing your credibility with funders and prospective donors. You can send these pieces out with mailings, reprint them in your newsletters (after getting permission of course, to avoid copyright violations), mention and link to them on your website, and attach copies to grant proposals.

Worksheet Number	Chapter in Book	Worksheet Title
Fundraising Worksheet 1	Chapter 3	Sample Cost Analysis
Fundraising Worksheet 2	Chapter 3	Fundraising Assets
Fundraising Worksheet 3	Chapter 3	Fundraising Strategy Chart
Fundraising Worksheet 4	Chapter 4	Mailing Evaluation
Fundraising Worksheet 5	Chapter 6	Meeting Checklist
Fundraising Worksheet 6	Chapter 8	Projected Special Event Expenses
Fundraising Worksheet 7	Chapter 8	Projected Special Event Income
Fundraising Worksheet 8	Chapter 10	Grantseeking Chart
Fundraising Worksheet 9	Chapter 10	Grants Worksheet
Fundraising Worksheet 10	Chapter 12	Check Your Website's Fundraising Effectiveness
Fundraising Worksheet 11	Chapter 13	Press Release Template

Fundraising Worksheet 1: Sample Cost Analysis

Item	Cost per year	Notes
Salaries and benefits	$	
Fees to independent contractors and consultants	$	
Travel (trainings, donor visits)	$	
Office supplies	$	
Graphic design/printing	$	
Dues and publications	$	
Staff trainings and networking events	$	
Web, database, and other technical support	$	
Telephone	$	
Postage	$	
Food (such as coffee or meals with donors)	$	
Special event costs	$	
Other special program costs	$	
Total	$	

Fundraising Worksheet 2: Fundraising Assets

Asset Type	Asset Description	Possible Fundraising Use
Organization's mission		
Organization's programs		
Organization's reputation or history among certain foundations or individuals		
Organization's access to certain members of community		
Organization's physical facilities or resources		
Physical facilities or resources owned or accessible by board, staff, or volunteers		
Executive director		
Development director		
Development assistant		
Other development staff		
Board members		
Board fundraising committee		
Particularly active individual volunteers		
Volunteer program generally		
Other friends of your organization		

Fundraising Worksheet 3: Fundraising Strategy Chart

Activity or Funding Source	Amount It Should Raise	New or Unusual Expenses	Total Amount (column 2 minus column 3)
	$		$
	$		$
	$		$
	$		$
	$		$
	$		$
	$		$
	$		**Grand Total:** $

Fundraising Worksheet 4: Mailing Evaluation

For mailing sent [*date*], consisting of:		
Describe appeal and any special enclosures:		
A. Number of letters sent out		
B. Total expenses of mailing		$
C. Number of new supporters		
D. Total amount of donations		$
E. Usual donation amount		$
F. Percentage of response	(C divided by A)	%
G. Net profit	(D minus B)	$
H. Cost of acquiring each new supporter	(B divided by C)	$
Comments		

Fundraising Worksheet 5: Meeting Checklist

Here's a summary of things to consider bringing to your donor meeting:

❏ Brochure

❏ Annual report

❏ Historical information

❏ Mission description

❏ Case statement

❏ Budget

❏ Plans for the future

❏ Publicity materials

❏ Copies of any recent newspaper articles

❏ Premiums and recognition opportunities

❏ Pledge card

❏ Receipt book

Fundraising Worksheet 6: Projected Special Event Expenses

Expense Category	Projected Cost	Description of Reasoning or Assumptions, Particularly for Discount or Donated Items
Physical Space		
Room, building, outdoor space	$	
Chairs, tables, performance platform	$	
Site manager and other staff fees	$	
Heating or air conditioning	$	
Sound system, projector, screen, other equipment	$	
Traffic/parking permits	$	
Subtotal:	$	
Decorations		
Banners	$	
Lighting	$	
Flowers	$	
Candles	$	
Balloons	$	
Party favors, gifts, award plaques, and certificates	$	
Other	$	
Subtotal:	$	
Food and Drink		
Snacks or appetizers (for participants and volunteers	$	
Main meal	$	
Extra catering or corkage fees	$	
Alcohol, other drinks, ice	$	
Plates, cups, napkins, cutlery	$	
Waiters and bar staff	$	
Subtotal:	$	

Performers/Speakers		
Performance fee or honorarium	$	
Transportation and parking (airfare, shuttle, rental car, cabs, or limousine)	$	
Hotel	$	
Meals	$	
Telephone and other extras	$	
Subtotal:	$	
Publicity		
Graphic designer and/or artist	$	
Printing (save-the-date postcards, invitations, posters, programs, ad books)	$	
Stationery, envelopes	$	
Postage (invitations, press releases)	$	
Professional mailing services	$	
Event photographer	$	
Subtotal:	$	
Miscellaneous		
Taxes on goods sold	$	
Photocopying	$	
Supplies for volunteer meetings and information packets	$	
Reimbursement of volunteers' expenses (i.e., gasoline, telephone)	$	
Unexpected or emergency expenses	$	
Subtotal:	$	
Total:	$	

Fundraising Worksheet 7: Projected Special Event Income

Income Category	Projected Amount	Description of Reasoning or Assumptions
Tickets	$	_____ of guests at $_____ per ticket
Ad books or ad space in program	$	_____ of advertisers at $_____ per _____
Exhibitors' or vendors' rental fees	$	_____ of exhibitors/vendors at $_____ per booth
Corporate sponsorships	$	
Sales of food or goods	$	
Silent auction or raffle proceeds	$	
Total:	$	

Fundraising Worksheet 8: Grantseeking Chart

Clients or issue to be served:	
Greater goal being pursued:	
Minimum useful grant amount:	$
Geographic area served or covered:	
Any unacceptable restrictions:	
Any unacceptable sources of funds:	

Fundraising Worksheet 9: Grants Worksheet

Basic Information	
Foundation/funder's name & address:	
Foundation's stated mission and purpose:	
Contact person:	
Contact person's telephone, email:	
Names and titles of other staff members:	
Names of board members and trustees:	
Total grants made annually:	$

Eligibility Information	
Grant subject matter:	
Grant eligibility requirements:	
Geographical limitations:	
Other limitations:	
Maximum grant amount:	$
Funding duration:	

"Good Fit" Indicators	
Other organizations that have received grants for similar work (name the organization(s), list how much received and for what work):	
Typical grant amount:	$
Limitations on overhead/administrative costs:	%
Prospects for grant renewal:	
Special considerations:	

Application Process	
First steps:	❑ query letter? ❑ full proposal?
Printed application form or guidelines:	❑ available? ❑ obtained?
Next application deadline(s) (if any):	
Board meeting dates:	
Likely to hear answer by:	
Research Trail	
Have checked	
❑ Website	
❑ Directories (name them):	
❑ Form 990	
❑ Annual report	

Fundraising Worksheet 10: Check Your Website's Fundraising Effectiveness

❏ **Basic Contact Information:** Does your website clearly state what your organization does, where it's located, and every possible way to get in touch with development and other staff?

❏ **Your Organization's Personality:** Does your website convey your organization's personality in a manner that's consistent with your fundraising and other marketing materials?

❏ **Freshness:** Does your website appear current and up to date?

❏ **Content:** Does your website present interesting content about your organization's cause?

❏ **Donation Information:** Does your website lead viewers easily to information on how to donate or get involved?

❏ **Information on Where the Money Goes:** Does your website tell donors how their money will be spent?

❏ **Funder and Donor Information:** Does your website find space to publicly thank funders and donors?

❏ **Tracking Users:** Does your website allow you to track where viewers go within the site and how successfully you're leading them to donation or involvement options?

Press Release Template

[Your organization's name; preferably with logo]

FOR IMMEDIATE RELEASE

Contact: *[Name of one or preferably two persons they can call]*

[Date]

[Phone number of contacts]

[Email address of contacts]

[Centered title of press release, in larger font]

[Your state, in capital letters, such as "OKLAHOMA"]

[Text of press release, in short paragraphs, ending with a brief description of your organization and references to where they can obtain more information, such as on your website.]

###
[traditional signal of end of text]

Index

Get the Latest in the Law

Nolo's Legal Updater

We'll send you an email whenever a new edition of your book is published!
Sign up at **www.nolo.com/legalupdater**.

Updates at Nolo.com

Check **www.nolo.com/update** to find recent changes in the law that
affect the current edition of your book.

Nolo Customer Service

To make sure that this edition of the book is the most recent one, call us at
800-728-3555 and ask one of our friendly customer service representatives
(7:00 am to 6:00 pm PST, weekdays only). Or find out at **www.nolo.com**.

Complete the Registration & Comment Card ...

... and we'll do the work for you! Just indicate your preferences below:

Registration & Comment Card

NAME _____   DATE _____

ADDRESS _____

CITY _____   STATE _____   ZIP _____

PHONE _____   EMAIL _____

COMMENTS _____

WAS THIS BOOK EASY TO USE?   (VERY EASY)   5   4   3   2   1   (VERY DIFFICULT)

☐ Yes, you can quote me in future Nolo promotional materials. *Please include phone number above.*

☐ Yes, send me **Nolo's Legal Updater** via email when a new edition of this book is available.

Yes, I want to sign up for the following email newsletters:

   ☐ **NoloBriefs** (monthly)
   ☐ **Nolo's Special Offer** (monthly)
   ☐ **Nolo's BizBriefs** (monthly)
   ☐ **Every Landlord's Quarterly** (four times a year)

☐ Yes, you can give my contact info to carefully selected
partners whose products may be of interest to me.

NOLO

EFFN2

Nolo
950 Parker Street
Berkeley, CA 94710-9867
www.nolo.com

YOUR LEGAL COMPANION